THE ALTERNATIVE INVESTMENT MARKET HANDBOOK

SECOND EDITION

Keith Hatchick, *Partner, Marshall Hatchick, Solicitors*

Keith Smith, *Director, Nabarro Wells & Co*

Paul Watts, *Partner, HLB Kidsons*

This edition is dedicated to the memory of David Vincent Collins
20 December 1946 – 21 December 1998

JORDANS

2002

Published by
Jordan Publishing Limited
21 St Thomas Street
Bristol BS1 6JS

British Library Cataloguing-in-Publication Data
A catalogue record for this book is available from the British Library.

ISBN 0 85308 588 9

Typeset by Mendip Communications Ltd, Frome, Somerset
Printed by MPG Books Ltd, Bodmin, Cornwall

FOREWORD

The second edition of *AIM Handbook* comes at a most interesting time for AIM and I welcome its publication very keenly.

Over the last year, at a time when most markets have been quiet, AIM has enjoyed around 90 initial public offerings and has grown to well over 600 companies. Increasingly, we are seeing interest from overseas too. Indeed, we are beginning to experience the transformation of a successful domestic market into an exciting international one targeted at good quality, smaller companies from Europe, Australia, North America and Asia.

AIM Handbook is an important and weighty source of reference on the development of AIM and its current practice for all those who wish to gain a better understanding of this dynamic, fast growing market.

The views expressed are, of course, those of the authors rather than necessarily those of the Stock Exchange but, as the wise man said, different views make a market. In any event, the informed, professional opinions expressed in this book can only assist AIM's further development.

The publication of this revised edition of *AIM Handbook* is evidence of the growing interest in AIM from around the world and I wish it every success.

SIMON BRICKLES
Head of AIM
January 2002

BIOGRAPHIES

After qualifying as a solicitor in 1981, **Keith Hatchick** worked for several years in the corporate commercial departments of two large City firms, where he specialised in all forms of corporate acquisition and disposal, corporate finance and stock exchange work before becoming a partner at Stoneham Langton Passmore. Keith subsequently co-founded the specialist business law firm of Marshall Hatchick. He has contributed to a number of books, journals and other publications and has spoken at and chaired seminars.

Keith Smith is a Director of Nabarro Wells & Co Limited, a corporate finance business specialising in smaller companies. He began his career as a stockbroker, becoming a Member of the Stock Exchange in 1962 and a partner in a stockbroking firm in 1968. He was senior partner of his firm at the time of '*Big Bang*' in 1986. He has been involved in corporate finance throughout his career. As the former head of corporate finance at Gerrard Vivian Gray, he was responsible for one of the first ten companies to be admitted to AIM on the first day of trading and has subsequently arranged many further admissions. Keith is a Fellow of the Institute of Management, a Member of the Securities Institute and formerly an Associate of the Institute of Investment Management and Research.

Paul Watts qualified as a chartered accountant in 1989 and is a partner in the London office of HLB Kidsons. He has acted as Reporting Accountant on a variety of AIM flotations and is a member of the HLB Kidsons' corporate finance team who have been involved in over 20 AIM admissions in recent years. HLB Kidsons also publish an annual survey, *Taking AIM*, which canvasses the views of potential entrants and existing AIM companies.

PREFACE TO THE FIRST EDITION

One of the most exciting new markets to emerge in the 1990s is the Alternative Investment Market (AIM) – created by the London Stock Exchange in 1995 after a detailed consultation process. The intention was to introduce a secondary market which would be open to smaller companies (which could be newly formed businesses) and which would act as a forum for the valuation and trading of shares and enable members to have easier direct access to outside funding.

One early worry was that the market might be under-regulated, but the Stock Exchange has made a determined effort with the creation of a regulatory role of the Nominated Adviser to achieve a balance so as to give confidence but keep costs in check and so increase its availability to potential applicants. AIM has attracted investment not just from individual investors, but also from fund managers and institutions.

This book is written to assist those interested in AIM, whether they are entrepreneurs, directors or managers, who might be considering admission to AIM, and also for the general investor wanting to know more about this market. It may also be useful as an aide-mémoire to professional advisers who will value its extensive Appendices. The form this handbook takes is to provide an introduction and selected commentary to the rules and general law with appendices containing the materials referred to in the text. The writers have, through their combined experience in business and as professional advisers in the law, accountancy and banking, tried where appropriate to give examples and illustrations. Each would welcome readers' comments and suggestions (through the publisher) as to how the content may be able to be improved in future editions.

In the preparation of the content of this book, help was generously provided by the London Stock Exchange (Vivienne Cassley of the AIM team), Martin West and his team at Jordans (who, in equal measure, provided encouragement and candour), and professional colleagues. I particularly want to thank Nicholas Marshall of Marshall Hatchick, and a colleague, Trevor Asserson. I am also grateful for assistance and time provided by Sue Best and Nigel Bell of the marketing team of Kidsons Impey. I especially want to pay tribute to my two collaborators, David V Collins and Keith R Smith who, in addition to providing first-rate material, also gave constructive criticism to my own efforts.

Finally, I should like to express each writer's thanks to the loyal and devoted team of assistants and secretaries who transcribed the notes and voices into clean typed script. I refer to Dianne Johnson and Hazel O'Neill and, in particular, to Carolyn Dawnay who typed over half the script with interest and wit, correcting my occasional lapse of grammar and assisting in overcoming my procrastination.

The authors and publishers are grateful to the following for giving their kind permission to reproduce materials set out in the Appendices of this book: the Stock Exchange for the material set out in Appendix 2; The Stationery Office for the statutory material set out in Appendix 1; Gee Publishing Limited for the material set out in Appendix 4.

KEITH HATCHICK
March 1997

PREFACE TO THE SECOND EDITION

The ink was hardly dry on the first edition of this book before discussions were beginning concerning when the second edition should be published. Unfortunately, being largely a labour of love for each of the busy contributors, it was only towards the end of 1998 that work commenced. In the intervening four or so years, there have been immense changes, not all of which have been beneficial to the market.

The performance of smaller companies in recent years has been a major surprise to the companies themselves, investors and the market as a whole. In 1999, the AIM index outperformed the FTSE all share by 130% – possibly this upturn has been due to a general undervaluation of smaller companies, but the result was largely driven by the IT sector and has attracted comment of being a two-tier affair. IT concerns, like ARM Holdings and QXL.com, had seen huge jumps in value, in the former case from a market value of £264m into the FTSE 100 and in the latter to FTSE 250. The Stock Exchange responded to this by the creation in October 1999 of the TechMart for companies in the full market. In the AIM market itself, there have been celebrated performances from such companies as BATM Advanced Communications (now on the main exchange) and Teather & Greenwood Holdings (a NOMAD which itself decided to become admitted to AIM with considerable success).

The running debate over the period occasionally voiced but, only an underlying presence, is how regulated the market should be. It was not envisaged to be a market which would be appropriate for widows and orphans, but should form an affordable forum to developing companies needing to find funding. In the early days, a market capital of £2m to £5m would have been sufficient and, indeed, there was a place for start-ups, but this has changed and the usual minimum required by NOMADs is £10m to £12m. Similarly, as the regulation has increased, so have disproportionately the costs of bringing a company to the market – what could have been done for little over £100k or less is now costing upwards of £180k. This clearly affects the number of companies able to seek a listing and pushes other companies to less regulated areas like VCTS, private placements (frequently allied to Enterprise Investment Schemes) and share clubs like OFEX. Start-up companies looking for seed finance now are left to these sources, or finding overdraft or short-term bank finance. The accusation that AIM is not far from the regulation needs and cost of the full listing is one well versed in corporate finance circles, and is sadly and unnecessarily too prevalent. Early in 2000 the Stock Exchange announced a merger with the German Stock Exchange (Deutsche Borse) in Frankfurt to form the IX. This produced a hostile bid from the Swedish OM Group: neither the proposed merger nor the hostile bid succeeded. In October 2000 the Stock Exchange also made an announcement about the proposed formation of a new market on a similar basis to those markets represented by the Euro NM. At the time of writing, no further details have been announced concerning this new market. There has been much discussion in the financial press concerning future potential alliances that the Stock Exchange may or may not develop. However, with the huge success that AIM has had, it is unlikely that this market will be changed in any substantial manner.

This edition has sought to maintain the structure of the previous edition but at the same time extend, develop and improve the 'recipe'. The contributors are grateful to Vivienne Cassley and Graham Spooner who have assisted in the revision of this book. I would also like to thank Jane Bulman for her secretarial assistance. Tragically, at an early stage of the reworking, David Collins unexpectedly passed away and this edition is dedicated to his memory as a friend and a colleague.

Finally, the authors and publishers are grateful to the following for giving their kind permission to reproduce materials set out in the Appendices to this book: the Stock Exchange for the material set out in Appendix 2; the Financial Services Authority for the Combined Code; and the Institute of Chartered Accountants in England and Wales for Internal Control: Guidance for Directors on the Combined Code, both set out in Appendix 4.

KEITH HATCHICK
Marshall Hatchick
December 2001

CONTENTS

TABLE OF CASES

References are to paragraph numbers.

TABLE OF STATUTES

References are to paragraph numbers and appendix numbers.

TABLE OF STATUTORY INSTRUMENTS

References are to paragraph numbers and appendix numbers.

TABLE OF EC MATERIALS

References are to paragraph numbers.

TABLE OF NON-STATUTORY MATERIALS AND FOREIGN LEGISLATION

References are to paragraph numbers and appendix numbers

GLOSSARY OF TERMS AND ABBREVIATIONS

ABI	Association of British Insurers
ACBE	Advisory Committee on Business and the Environment
the 1985 Act	Companies Act 1985
ADR	American Depository Receipts
AIM	the Alternative Investment Market regulated by the London Stock Exchange plc
AIM rules	the rules for AIM companies (formerly contained in Chapter 16 of Rules of the London Stock Exchange plc) and their nominated advisers as issued from time to time by the London Stock Exchange plc
AIM trading rules	Chapter 17 of the Rules of the London Stock Exchange plc
ASB	Accounting Standards Board
CAO	Companies Announcements Office of the Stock Exchange
CISCO	The City Group for Smaller Companies
Combined Code	Principles of Good Governance and Code of Best Practice (derived by the Committee on Corporate Governance from the Committee's Final Report and from the Cadbury and Greenbury Reports)
CREST	the computer-based system and procedures (operated through CRESTCo Ltd, a clearing house recognised under FSA 1986) for the holding and transfer of shares without the use of share certificates and stock transfer forms regulated pursuant to US Regulations 1995
CVS	Corporate Venturing Scheme
Daily Official List	the London Stock Exchange's register of securities and details of transactions executed with respect to both fully listed and AIM companies
DTI	Department of Trade and Industry

ECU	European Currency Unit (approximate currency value at 1 January 1997 is £1 = ECU 1.36)
EIS	Enterprise Investment Scheme
FRED	financial reporting exposure draft
FRS	Financial Reporting Standard
FSA	Financial Services Authority (previously known as SIB)
FSA 1986	Financial Services Act 1986
FSMA 2000	Financial Services and Markets Act 2000
IMRO	Investment Management Regulatory Organisation
IPC	Investment Protection Committee
Listed securities	those securities offered to the public admitted to the Official List of the UKLA or subject to an application for listing
Listing Rules	the rules imposed by FSA on companies on the Official List
Mandatory quote period	the period of time when all registered market-makers in a security must display their prices. For SEAQ and SEATS the period is from 8.00am to 4.30pm
Market-maker	a Stock Exchange member firm which is obliged actively to offer to buy and sell throughout the mandatory quote period the securities in which it is registered (formerly known as jobbers)
NAPF	National Association of Pension Funds
NASDAQ	National Association of Securities Dealers Automated Quotation System
NOMAD	nominated adviser
OFEX	an unregulated trading facility for dealing in unquoted companies which is operated by JP Jenkins Limited in association with Newstrack Limited, a sister company. OFEX is a registered trademark of SJ & S Holdings Ltd, the parent company to JP Jenkins Limited. The latter is a London Stock Exchange plc member firm and as such regulated by the SFA
Official List	the Official List of the UKLA

PIA	Personal Investment Authority
plc	public limited company
POS Regulations 1995	Public Offers of Securities Regulations 1995, SI 1995/1537 (as amended)
Principal	a Stock Exchange member firm which deals in securities on its own behalf
Prospectus	a document offering securities to the public
QCA	Quoted Company Alliance (formerly the City Group for Smaller Companies)
Quote vendor	a third-party agency responsible for collating and disseminating market price information to end users
Regulatory News Service (RNS)	the electronic information dissemination service operated by the Company Announcements Office of the Stock Exchange through which announcements required under The Listing Rules and AIM Rules are distributed to the public
Related party	has the same meaning as is relevant for listed companies and includes directors, shadow directors and their families and substantial shareholders and their associates
Reverse takeover	an acquisition or series of acquisitions in a 12-month period which exceed 100% in any of the percentage ratios relevant for the purposes of calculating if a transaction is a substantial transaction or which would result in a fundamental change in the business, or in a change in board or voting control of the issuer
SEAQ	Stock Exchange Automated Quotations system for UK securities. A continuously updated computer database containing price quotations, ie the market-makers' bids and offers volume information and trade reports in UK securities
SEATS PLUS	Stock Exchange Alternative Trading Service. A service supporting the trading of listed and AIM securities in which turnover is insufficient for the competing market-making system
SEC	Securities and Exchange Commission
SFA	Securities and Futures Authority
SIB	Securities and Investments Board (now known as the Financial Services Authority)

SIR	Statement of Investment Circular Reporting Standards
SORP	Statement of Recommended Practice
Sponsor	all applicants to the Official List must be represented by an approved sponsor which would typically be an investment or merchant bank, stockbroker, accountancy or law firm or other financial adviser, which has been approved by the Stock Exchange to undertake the role
SRI	socially responsible investment
SROs	Self-Regulating Organisations
Stock Exchange	the London Stock Exchange plc
Substantial shareholder	has the same meaning as is relevant for listed companies and includes any person (other than a bare trustee) who is, or was in the preceding 12 months, entitled to exercise or control the exercise of 10% or more of the votes able to be cast on all or substantially all matters at general meetings of the issuer. In January 1997, the rule was amended to 3% for the purposes of disclosure in the admission document
TSD Regulations 1994	Traded Securities (Disclosure) Regulations 1994, SI 1994/188
Touch price	the best bid or offer price in the market for a given security displayed on the SEAQ system
UITF	Urgent Issues Task Force
UKLA	United Kingdom Listing Authority, the FSA acting in its capacity as the competent authority for the purposes of the Financial Services Act 1986
US GAAP	United States Generally Accepted Accounting Principles
USM	Unlisted Securities Market
US Regulations 1995	Uncertificated Securities Regulations 1995, SI 1995/3272
Unlisted securities	those securities offered to the public not admitted to the Official List to which either Part II of POS Regulations 1995 or s 57 of FSA 1986 apply
VCT	venture capital trusts, as introduced in the Finance Act 1995

XSP service   a service operated by the Stock Exchange to facilitate the delivery of stock and the payment of money arising out of non-Talisman settled transactions between member firms

Chapter 1

THE ALTERNATIVE INVESTMENT MARKET

1.1 INTRODUCTION

1.1.1 The Stock Exchange Consultative Document

In September 1994, the Stock Exchange issued an exciting consultative document on the proposed Alternative Investment Market (AIM) for smaller and growing companies. The spirit of this document can be gauged by its opening sentence: 'The London Stock Exchange is determined to play a full role in stimulating economic growth by ensuring that its markets are accessible to a wide range of companies.' This was largely prompted by the popularity of the rule 4.2 facility which allowed a limited trading of non-listed companies in the manner of a matched bargain facility. Rule 4.2 of the Stock Exchange rules permitted member firms to deal in specific securities which were neither listed nor quoted on the Unlisted Securities Market (USM). This rule was first formulated to provide an occasional dealing facility in unquoted securities for member firms. This became an active and continual market and for the 12 months ended 30 June 1994, 264 companies had their securities traded under this rule with a total trading value of £482m. Particularly of note is the presence of smaller companies, since more than 50% of those traded had a market capitalisation of less than £15m. The consultative document proposed, amongst other things:

(i) applicants to AIM should not need to appoint a sponsor (optional);
(ii) responsibility for disclosure and compliance should be a matter for the directors of a company from time to time (the hope was that this would reduce the cost to the companies seeking admission and in this way make the market more attractive to smaller companies);
(iii) companies must publish price-sensitive information promptly;
(iv) no minimum nor maximum limits on capitalisation for entry;
(v) no minimum limits on shares in public hands;
(vi) no minimum trading record requirement;
(vii) market to be accessible to both institutional and private investors.

The key principles were:

(a) to provide a marketplace for smaller and growing companies, with lower access and continuing costs than the Official List;
(b) to be accessible to a wide range of companies;
(c) to be clearly differentiated from the Official List.

1.1.2   The nominated adviser

It is probably fair to say that the consultative document received only a cautious welcome and a number of important associations like the British Venture Capital Association expressed concern over the lack of regulation and raised worries as to investor protection. To allay this concern the Stock Exchange created the important role of the nominated adviser (NOMAD) (see Chapter 2). It is the NOMAD who is largely responsible for ensuring that his client respects the rules and legislation applicable to admittance to AIM.

1.1.3   The commencement of AIM

After considering responses and having carried out their normal consultancy process, the Stock Exchange unveiled AIM and it commenced business on 19 June 1995. It started business with only 10 companies, but by its first anniversary 164 companies had joined the market. Members of the market are a highly eclectic collection and include dentists, football clubs, cyber cafés and garden centres; the Stock Exchange has categorised these into more than 30 different sectors. Initially the financial press was fairly pessimistic and was concerned over a number of issues including:

(i)   lax joining rules which it was feared would attract unsuitable companies;
(ii)   liquidity problems which traditionally have beset other, failed, smaller company markets;
(iii) that the creation of the market followed several high profile corporate collapses and fund managers were hostile after incurring such losses;
(iv)   the policing mechanism – institutional critics were concerned that companies could come to AIM without having a minimum trading period nor with a minimum limit on the number of shares that they could issue to the public.

1.1.4   The experience of AIM

AIM's first year success was underpinned by three main factors:

(i)   with effect from 29 September 1995, the Stock Exchange abolished rule 4.2 which was being used by over 300 unlisted companies to trade their shares. Of these rule 4.2 companies, 82 transferred to AIM giving the new market a critical mass and a body of companies with the credibility of long trading records and stable revenues;
(ii)   the world market conditions over the first 12-month period spurred the majority of shares upwards, with 60% quoting a higher price than their admission price. It has been seen that rich private investors have made a steady demand for AIM shares which has improved the liquidity of the market; and
(iii) there was no significant corporate disaster which might have had the effect of undermining investor confidence.

From a survey carried out by the Stock Exchange on companies traded on AIM, it was reported that 89% of the 82 companies which responded confirmed that their business had grown and improved. More significant is that 30% of

AIM companies have acquired another company or business and it was estimated that almost 1,000 jobs had been created.

1.1.5 The AIM and the USM

The Unlisted Securities Market (USM) was originally introduced by the Stock Exchange in 1980 to trade shares in small companies not suitable for a full listing. The intention was that the cost of joining that market should be substantially less than that for a full listing and that the market should reflect the requirements of such smaller companies. Initially the USM was successful, but with the various changes in the Stock Exchange rules and with the modification of the qualification periods for a full listing it became less attractive. It was perceived in the market that the two markets had become very similar and with the cost of obtaining a quotation on the USM having become substantial, its days were clearly numbered. The USM ceased to exist at the end of December 1996 and the companies quoted (assuming they satisfied the eligibility criteria) could either join AIM or join the Official List.

AIM is regulated in a different manner to the USM since the regulatory responsibility has effectively been transferred to the NOMAD. It was hoped that this would provide greater investor confidence and also help control costs, making it attractive to the smaller company. In order for a company quoted on the USM to join AIM, an application form needed to be completed and confirmation needed to be given concerning the appointment of a nominated adviser and a nominated broker. From the 86 companies quoted on the USM in January 1996, 14 have joined AIM and 71 have taken a full listing.

The Stock Exchange provides regular updates of market statistics from which, on 31 January 2001, it shows the total number of companies on AIM as being 536, with a combined market capital of £15,649.5m. Since the launch of the market, £6,265.113m has been raised.

1.1.6 Advantages of an AIM quotation

With the introduction of AIM, the Stock Exchange introduced an exciting innovation to the established financial markets which will enable entrepreneurs to raise new capital and allow established businesses to unlock the value of their companies. It appeals particularly to the following:

(i) companies which would previously have traded under rule 4.2 and which do not want the cost and regulatory requirements which would be imposed for full listing;

(ii) young businesses without a particular track record and companies in fast-growing businesses (eg computer technology, telecommunications, dotcom and other similar sectors);

(iii) shareholders looking for an exit route who may otherwise be locked into a particular investment for a particular period of time or until a particular event occurs (eg Enterprise Investment Scheme companies, management buy-outs, venture capital investment trusts, etc). There have been a series of VCT 'promoted' companies in the dotcom and internet fields introduced to AIM;

(iv) family owned businesses that may be seeking external investment without losing control to a market competitor;

(v) former USM companies or companies with a full listing wishing to restructure into a less regulated market;

(vi) overseas companies wishing to establish a foothold in the UK – there are a number of companies based in the Middle East which have successfully established businesses within the UK through admission to AIM;

(vii) companies for which a full listing is attractive in the medium term but which require short-term access to funding or determining a market position.

There are a number of significant advantages to companies of admission to AIM, which may or may not be considered a first step on the road to a full listing. Having a quotation on AIM would allow companies and their shareholders to:

(a) create a status for their company raising its profile in the marketplace;

(b) establish a value for the shares of the company, which can frequently be very difficult where companies are not admitted – trading on AIM will establish a value for the shares quoted on the market;

(c) enable shareholders to establish an exit route with controlled share sales through the marketplace;

(d) assist in resolving the frequently different requirements of shareholders in an unlisted company – for example, some such shareholders may require retention of shares for investment purposes, whereas others may wish to realise their investments;

(e) facilitate expansion by takeovers and mergers.

1.2　TYPES OF COMPANY SEEKING ADMISSION TO AIM

Chapter 16 of the Stock Exchange rule book originally contained the AIM admission rules. This has been amended and they are now issued as the AIM rules produced by the Stock Exchange. Eligibility has been simplified. There is now only one form of company eligible, namely a company incorporated inside or outside the UK which has been validly established under the relevant laws of the jurisdiction in which it was established, and under the law of that jurisdiction it must be permitted to offer securities to the public.

This means that a public limited company would qualify as a company incorporated within the UK.

1.2.1　Eligibility

In order to qualify for admission, in addition to having the appropriate corporate vehicle (referred to above), rule 28 requires that the relevant securities be free from restrictions of transferability – there should also be no limit on size of holding or with respect to the class or identity of the holder.

Certain limited restrictions are permissible which may relate to:

(i)   where the law in the jurisdiction where a company operates places restrictions on transferability; or

(ii)   where the issuer itself imposes such restrictions concerning numbers of shareholders to avoid the application of restrictions by an overseas jurisdiction.

Other requirements include the following:

(i)   the issuer must appoint a NOMAD and a company broker (see Chapter 2);

(ii)   the company's published accounts must be prepared in accordance with national law, ie the law of the country in which the company was formed *and* in accordance with UK or US Accounting Standards or International Accounting Standards;

(iii)   arrangements concerning the transfer of securities must be appropriately made. The earlier edition of the AIM rules required securities to be registered within 14 days. This is still thought to be good practice;

(iv)   there must be no issued securities of the same class that are not admitted to trading on AIM;

(v)   the issuer must pay the fees required from time to time by the Stock Exchange.

The above key features are particularly interesting for what is *not* required, ie:

(a)   there is no requirement for a trading record, ie a company does not have to have several years of accounts in order to qualify. There is, however, a rule that if a company does not have a two-year record its directors and shareholders will have to undertake not to dispose of their shares for a minimum of one year after admission to AIM;

(b)   there is no requirement for a minimum market capitalisation;

(c)   there is no minimum number of shares which need to be in public hands; and

(d)   there is no particular rule concerning the manner in which shares are offered for sale to the public.

Although the looseness of the AIM rules in these respects is a welcomed aspect of a secondary market, in practice the market, since its very earliest days, has been manipulated and policed by the nominated advisers and company brokers to ensure that the issuer is of an appropriate size and nature for the market before ensuring its introduction. For this reason, there have been fewer start-ups or companies having an issued share capital of less than £10m.

1.3   FACTORS THAT SHOULD BE CONSIDERED BY A COMPANY SEEKING ADMISSION TO AIM

There are important factors that need to be considered and steps which need to be taken during the period leading up to admission to the AIM market (or any other market). A detailed consideration of these matters is outside the scope of this book but it might be helpful to list the principal points which need to be considered. The list is provided in approximately the order in which the steps are likely to be taken, although in any particular case, a different order, and indeed additional matters, might be necessary.

(1)	Consider whether there are features of the business which would be undesirable in a public company and, if so, take steps to eliminate them. Examples might include trading with related parties at uncommercial prices, assets which are partly used for private purposes such as yachts or villas, subsidiary companies that should properly be wound up since their purpose or financial viability is suspect.

(2)	Review the staff and management structure of the business, with a particular view to ensuring that there are no significant gaps in the skills available, and that succession is catered for. Appoint a solicitor specialising in company commercial work or corporate finance work to advise generally and to revise all director and senior manager service contracts to reflect recommendations of the Cadbury, Greenbury and Hampel Reports (now issued as the Combined Code).

(3)	Reflect whether the flotation will need to involve the raising of capital and, if so, consider the likely scale of funds required, how this might be achieved, and through whom the capital raising should be organised, ie considerations of the appointment of a suitable NOMAD and nominated broker and possibly other advisers.

(4)	In conjunction with the previous point, the preparation of business forecasts of profits, cash and net assets will be proceeding.

(5)	Consideration of the suitability of the present auditors, and whether new auditors should be appointed, and whether reporting accountants would be needed to produce an accountants' report. Appointment of the nominated adviser to deal with the flotation would probably take place at about this stage, together with confirmation of the company broker appointment, and completion of the flotation 'team'.

(6)	Work on a long form report on the business, for the information of the directors and the various advisers will, in most cases, be necessary, together with commencement of the other due diligence work. These efforts often give pointers to other steps which need to be taken to prepare the company for flotation.

(7)	Among the points that arise from preparation of a long form report, one often finds that the company has considerable trading reliance on small numbers of suppliers, customers or both, and it is often advisable to consider whether more formal trading relationships and long-term contracts can be put in place to protect the company in these relationships. Possibly the company's terms of business should also be revised. The contractual position concerning patents and other intellectual property matters may also need to be formally documented and use made of a specialist patent agent.

(8)	Consideration needs to be given as to whether a single company is to be floated or whether a group structure of parent and subsidiaries is more appropriate, and plans laid to put the appropriate structure in place. If a group reorganisation is required, tax clearances will not need to be applied for in most cases.

(9) If a company has insufficient non-executive directors, consideration needs to be given at a relatively early stage to finding and appointing suitable candidates.

(10) The memorandum and articles of association of the company to be floated will need to be drafted, or amended if the company is already in existence.

(11) The long form report will consider the company's accounting policies and accounting and internal control systems and, in most cases, some changes or improvements will need to be made in these areas.

(12) Consideration will need to be given to the remuneration policies for the management and other employees. Frequently, new bonus schemes, incentive schemes or share option schemes are introduced before flotation proceeds or old schemes are extended or modified as appropriate.

(13) The company will also need to select and appoint Registrars to deal with its share register following its flotation, and printers to deal with the admission document, and public relations consultants will also need to be appointed.

1.4   THE APPLICATION PROCEDURE

The Stock Exchange will make available an application form which needs to be signed by a director. This form (reproduced at Appendix 2) is mainly concerned with detailing the amounts and with descriptions of securities for which the application is made and requiring various contact names, addresses and phone numbers etc. The form more importantly contains a declaration and undertaking which:

(i)   confirms that the directors have received advice and guidance on the nature of responsibilities and obligations of AIM admission and have undertaken to be bound by the AIM rules as amended from time to time;

(ii)   the issuer has taken appropriate advice and has acted on that advice;

(iii) the admission document complies with the AIM rules and makes a full disclosure of such information as an investor would reasonably require or reasonably expect to find in the relevant admission document to enable the investor to make 'an informed assessment of the assets, liabilities, financial position, profits and losses and prospects of the issuer of the securities and the rights attaching to the securities';

(iv)   that having made due and careful enquiry the issuer is of the opinion that working capital available is sufficient for its present requirements;

(v)   that due and careful enquiry has been made by the issuer of any profit forecast, estimate or projection set out in the admission document; and

(vi)   proper procedures have been established to enable directors to make judgements as to the financial position and prospects of the issuer and its group.

The undertaking is in two parts:

(a)   that the issuer will comply with the rules of the Stock Exchange as amended from time to time; and

(b)   that the issuer will, where appropriate, seek advice and guidance from the nominated adviser and will act on such advice.

The following needs to accompany the application form (see guidance notes attached to the rules):

(a)   six copies of the admission document;

(b)   confirmation by the company broker of its appointment – there is no set format and a letter confirming appointment and accepting this role and responsibility is sufficient;

(c)   a declaration form completed and signed by the nominated adviser; and

(d)   the requisite fee (£5,000 per annum. For those members who are admitted after 1 September in any year, the fee of £5,000 applies until the end of the next calendar year). The amounts are net of VAT which will need to be added at the appropriate rate which is currently 17½%.

The Stock Exchange requires that an intending AIM company gives at least 10 business days' (this amounts to two weeks) prior notification of its admission to the market. A suggested format for an announcement is given below. In addition to the information stated there the Stock Exchange also requires details of the anticipated accounting reference date and the name and address of any person who is disclosed in the admission document (see further in Chapter 3). Any subsequent changes must be notified to the Stock Exchange immediately and the Stock Exchange has the discretion to delay the date of admission by a further 10 business days (rule 2). Schedule 1 to the AIM rules sets out the information needed with the application which includes the details set out in the announcement.

Announcement to be made by prospective AIM company at least 10 business days prior to admission	
Company name	*Aimco plc*
Country of incorporation	*England*
Company business	*Ownership and management of leisure centres*
Details of securities to be admitted (ie, where known, number of shares, nominal value and issue price)	*12,555,00 ordinary shares of 10p of which 4,000,000 have been placed at an issue price of 100p per share*
Capital to be raised on admission	*£4 million (before expenses)*
Full names and functions of directors, including proposed directors	*Allan Norman Other* *Chairman* *John Doe* *Chief Executive* *Joseph Henry Bloggs FCA* *Financial Director* *Nancy O'Hara* *Operations Director* *Jane Isabel Doe* *Non-Executive*
Person(s) interested in 3% or more of the issuer's capital, expressed as a percentage of the issued share capital	*Institutional Investor plc* *15.09%* *Venture Capital plc* *10.45%* *The Doe Children's Settlement* *9.55%*
Name and address of nominated adviser	*Nomad Limited*
Name and address of company broker	*Company Broker Limited*
Location of address at which admission document is available at time of admission containing full details of the company and of its securities	*Aimco plc*
Date of notification	2001
New/Update	*New*

1.5   AIM BY NUMBERS

The charts set out below show the development of AIM up to 29 December 2000. The charts are followed by data reproduced from AIM Market Statistics, February 2001, showing the size of the AIM broken down by business type and chronologically.

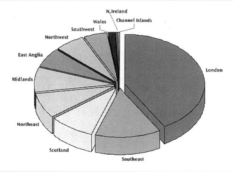

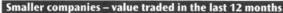

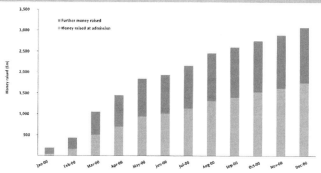

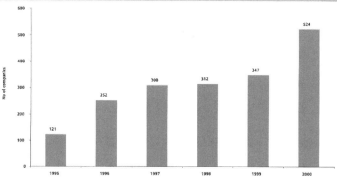

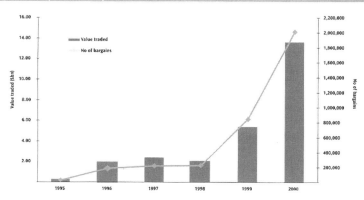

Equity trading by sector

February 2001

Business sector		Total turnover			No. of Companies	Market Capitalisation (£m)
		Value (£)	No. of Bargains	No. of Shares		
4	Mining	67,208,075	7,300	107,749,219	21	663.2
7	Oil & Gas	10,478,240	2,655	99,441,220	17	471.5
0	**Total Resource**	**77,686,315**	**9,955**	**207,190,439**	**38**	**1,134.7**
11	Chemicals	4,310,605	1,718	43,670,329	3	54.1
13	Construction & Building Materials	5,629,741	2,238	38,010,544	8	100.2
15	Forestry & Paper	0	0	0	0	0.0
18	Steel & Other Metals	849,745	220	323,189	1	40.5
10	**Total Basic Industries**	**10,790,091**	**4,176**	**82,004,062**	**12**	**194.8**
21	Aerospace & Defence	0	0	0	0	0.0
24	Diversified Industrials	688,568	133	3,494,839	3	60.2
25	Electronic & Electrical Equipment	4,453,324	1,595	17,490,940	8	62.8
26	Engineering & Machinery	21,454,730	1,668	42,650,348	11	512.7
20	**Total General Industrial**	**26,596,622**	**3,396**	**63,636,127**	**22**	**635.7**
31	Automobiles	28,628,634	478	3,396,771	5	303.5
34	Housing Goods & Textiles	3,533,395	1,680	112,680,302	17	212.5
30	**Total Cyclical Consumer Good**	**32,162,029**	**2,158**	**116,077,073**	**22**	**516.0**
41	Beverages	257,624	28	255,566	1	14.0
43	Food Producers & Processors	756,220	175	254,509	3	84.8
44	Health	23,761,424	3,764	42,218,139	10	364.0
46	Packaging	631,080	63	245,065	2	153.8
47	Personal Care & Household Products	590,002	279	2,939,504	2	37.5
48	Pharmaceuticals	28,981,465	4,225	34,803,968	9	583.6
49	Tobacco	0	0	0	0	0.0
40	**Total Non-Cyclical Consumer Good**	**54,977,815**	**8,534**	**80,716,751**	**27**	**1,237.7**
51	Distributors	2,855,137	771	6,180,436	11	86.6
52	General Retailers	7,259,770	1,216	37,448,896	16	288.8
53	Leisure, Entertainment & Hotels	39,085,423	6,318	83,885,290	65	1,369.8
54	Media & Photography	65,864,792	16,157	515,926,550	64	1,438.7
58	Support Services	55,661,091	7,419	148,144,399	55	1,621.7
59	Transport	7,479,609	1,039	3,431,850	9	462.4
50	**Total Cyclical Service**	**178,205,822**	**32,920**	**795,017,421**	**220**	**5,268.1**
63	Food & Drug Retailers	760,613	179	4,161,068	4	44.7
67	Telecommunication Services	2,552,563	533	18,432,089	5	74.8
60	**Total Non-Cyclical Service**	**3,313,176**	**712**	**22,593,157**	**9**	**119.5**
72	Electricity	0	0	0	0	0.0
73	Gas Distribution	0	0	0	0	0.0
78	Water	0	0	0	0	0.0
70	**Total Utilities**	**0**	**0**	**0**	**0**	**0.0**
81	Banks	0	0	0	0	0.0
83	Insurance	305,362	73	13,507,187	4	33.5
84	Life Assurance	0	0	0	0	0.0
85	Investment Companies	24,253,761	3,776	329,135,683	21	275.8
86	Real Estate	2,609,607	688	11,779,839	24	1,051.6
87	Speciality & Other Finance	60,913,885	9,085	669,752,373	68	1,830.3
89	Investment Companies Other	0	0	0	0	0.0
80	**Total Financial**	**88,082,615**	**13,622**	**1,024,175,082**	**117**	**3,191.2**
93	Information Technology Hardware	13,940,085	1,243	9,622,050	7	238.0
97	Software & Computer Services	58,058,159	10,182	149,625,787	68	1,952.4
90	**Total Information Technology**	**71,998,244**	**11,425**	**159,247,837**	**75**	**2,190.4**
	Grand Total Equities	**543,812,730**	**86,898**	**2,550,657,949**	**542**	**14,487.9**

TURNOVER

MONTH	No. Companies	Market Capital: £m	Money Raised: £m	Value (£)	No. BGNS.	No. Shares	FTSE AIM INDEX	Average Bargain Size
1995								
June	14	£82	£6.2	£922,132	194	4,276,131		4,753
July	23	£111	£6.9	£7,159,456	832	18,400,647		8,605
August	33	£248		£16,183,558	1,338	16,183,558		12,095
September	81	£1,479	£9.4	£40,000,873	4,734	60,028,376		8,450
October	105	£1,770	£25.7	£46,934,635	6,528	156,257,703		7,190
November	110	£2,028	£4.4	£79,317,050	8,734	143,167,552		9,081
December	121	£2,297	£42.1	£84,311,204	6,649	145,964,776		12,680
1996								
January	126	£2,589	£26.9	£123,501,651	14,558	475,744,636	1,048.88	8,483
February	128	£2,649	£52.7	£108,877,301	12,551	575,036,528	1,020.60	8,675
March	136	£2,658	£46.4	£133,387,703	15,547	434,191,818	989.90	8,580
April	147	£3,052	£56.2	£146,595,251	17,722	596,628,806	1,065.10	8,272
May	159	£3,435	£62.8	£177,013,721	16,804	737,519,818	1,140.40	10,534
June	173	£3,652	£77.2	£187,153,634	15,342	449,442,026	1,079.80	12,199
July	199	£4,007	£177.5	£154,454,071	15,298	399,463,237	1,049.40	10,096
August	207	£4,390	£52.5	£186,782,324	16,627	380,128,012	1,082.40	11,234
September	213	£4,301	£24.9	£1,611,933,903	17,031	353,730,544	1,030.10	94,647
October	226	£4,788	£130.2	£213,890,419	18,065	375,108,174	1,025.00	11,840
November	242	£5,161	£83.0	£186,475,126	15,866	440,706,823	1,038.00	11,753
December	252	£5,292	£26.3	£158,195,892	12,499	307,335,647	1,042.90	12,657
1997								
January	254	£5,751	£50.5	£279,920,517	21,413	508,258,850	1,119.50	13,072
February	262	£5,905	£33.0	£244,961,742	24,570	578,382,833	1,134.30	9,970
March	269	£5,862	£157.1	£360,317,843	20,763	798,625,171	1,109.30	17,354
April	277	£5,895	£91.2	£266,994,619	23,908	748,379,272	1,080.40	11,168
May	280	£5,867	£30.3	£180,838,610	17,959	345,429,671	1,073.50	10,070
June	286	£5,876	£37.0	£193,986,708	17,966	449,206,946	1,055.70	10,797
July	291	£5,574	£52.1	£160,750,182	17,318	409,102,031	1,014.90	9,282

TURNOVER

MONTH	No. Companies	Market Capital: £m	Money Raised: £m	Value (£)	No. BGNS.	No. Shares	FTSE AIM INDEX	Average Bargain Size
August	291	£5,543	£21.9	£123,960,261	12,786	389,141,847	1,022.32	9,695
September	294	£5,467	£35.7	£132,050,957	14,886	601,361,582	1,003.84	8,871
October	298	£5,354	£36.7	£188,729,849	19,323	688,129,135	986.60	9,767
November	301	£5,313	£35.2	£151,576,959	13,350	465,438,438	967.50	11,354
December	308	£5,655	£113.9	£131,188,842	13,184	461,559,402	992.00	9,951
1998								
January	308	£5,495	£3.7	£124,470,854	14,706	398,339,153	973.61	8,464
February	307	£5,799	£49.7	£178,879,131	19,149	577,790,002	1,006.45	9,341
March	310	£6,125	£46.6	£259,237,463	29,440	739,621,693	1,059.10	8,806
April	306	£6,608	£97.1	£207,420,340	22,387	718,348,549	1,080.10	9,265
May	306	£6,864	£36.3	£250,449,125	29,758	474,420,445	1,133.50	8,416
June	312	£6,541	£89.0	£240,602,243	25,433	510,225,401	1,095.70	9,460
July	312	£6,274	£68.8	£208,358,526	20,619	401,293,733	1,063.00	10,105
August	314	£5,266	£25.6	£115,564,599	14,076	433,855,445	898.60	8,717
September	314	£4,695	£31.0	£85,599,309	13,258	715,364,994	833.80	8,210
October	311	£4,293	£93.4	£89,187,560	11,889	819,213,759	789.30	7,502
November	313	£4,415	£13.5	£97,751,575	14,794	831,200,007	816.30	6,608
December	312	£4,438	£28.4	£76,593,524	9,237	297,075,347	801.60	8,292
1999								
January	310	£4,618	£12.2	£130,603,916	20,719	683,105,956	834.90	6,304
February	312	£4,441	£9.5	£121,213,708	17,032	676,454,686	823.47	7,117
March	311	£4,727	£35.6	£191,525,316	27,105	1,163,110,149	866.84	7,066
April	312	£4,959	£47.3	£191,184,430	27,491	780,282,623	955.70	6,541
May	315	£5,519	£24.0	£213,116,220	29,230	851,287,039	976.98	7,291
June	323	£6,174	£75.4	£223,665,450	26,378	918,829,954	1,017.60	8,479
July	326	£6,926	£70.3	£362,096,686	57,418	2,024,754,105	1,076.69	6,306
August	332	£6,734	£69.2	£266,612,440	41,605	945,194,442	1,114.60	6,408
September	332	£6,775	£31.6	£369,867,632	39,685	1,071,021,472	1,117.85	9,320

TURNOVER

MONTH	No. Companies	Market Capital: £m	Money Raised: £m	Value (£)	No. BGNS.	No. Shares	FTSE AIM INDEX	Average Bargain Size
October	333	£7,202	£154.4	£414,555,661	57,810	1,069,449,351	1,219.96	7,171
November	337	£10,023	£114.7	£1,330,875,466	241,264	6,182,107,006	1,638.54	5,516
December	347	£13,468	£287.8	£1,619,208,876	259,729	4,892,924,098	1,932.68	6,234
2000								
January	351	£16,019	£177.6	£2,151,476,561	378,781	6,650,042,648	2,238.49	5,680
February	362	£19,594	£252.0	£2,812,585,402	372,493	5,093,008,737	2,745.80	7,551
March	385	£18,036	£617.6	£2,675,203,052	380,952	4,909,257,205	2,256.92	7,022
April	396	£13,825	£397.9	£969,417,909	161,684	2,520,412,183	1,763.96	5,996
May	416	£13,508	£416.5	£557,230,680	90,908	2,154,182,799	1,645.21	6,130
June	429	£14,264	£90.3	£667,628,939	90,176	3,094,309,156	1,717.60	7,404
July	440	£14,847	£222.7	£648,659,189	85,035	1,906,046,222	1,693.42	7,628
August	460	£17,333	£301.0	£602,857,775	95,707	2,727,491,745	1,835.50	6,299
September	471	£17,038	£141.6	£839,012,684	113,265	3,348,500,069	1,776.50	7,408
October	488	£15,910	£149.8	£562,378,110	88,282	2,371,594,346	1,627.02	6,370
November	509	£14,766	£147.0	£597,480,121	100,694	2,773,429,912	1,461.20	5,934
December	524	£14,935	£178.5	£521,712,214	55,609	1,962,060,134	1,437.76	9,382
2001								
January	536	£15,649	£95.4	£622,089,788	88,190	2,861,482,840	1,449.58	7,054
February	543	£14,488	£70.0	£543,812,730	86,916	2,550,657,949	1,335.26	6,258
March	550	£12,990	£110.2	£414,607,197	73,144	2,640,291,933	1,171.86	5,668
April	554	£13,322	£125.1	£404,748,363	56,123	2,241,466,675	1,202.95	7,212
May	567	£13,764	£65.9	£504,376,918	66,243	2,359,068,687	1,221.85	7,614
June	576	£13,321	£112.2	£422,910,627	56,271	2,325,973,137	1,137.01	6,384
July	587	£12,409	£120.8	£409,353,909	49,518	2,213,146,078	1,041.22	8,267

Chapter 2

THE NOMINATED ADVISER AND THE COMPANY'S BROKER

2.1 INTRODUCTION

AIM was developed after considerable consultation between the Stock Exchange, practitioners and market users, and one result of this consultation was the creation of the specific roles of nominated adviser and company broker. This was an entirely new concept and not related to the role of sponsor on the Official List.

The AIM rules were, and are, less demanding than those of the Official List. This has resulted in AIM being a disclosure-driven market and one of the prime responsibilities of a nominated adviser is to ensure that the companies for which he acts make adequate and timely disclosure regarding their activities, trading and financial position.

In the six years since AIM commenced trading the rules governing nominated advisers and company brokers have been modified in the light of experience, and, as in all marketplaces, changes have come about through custom and use.

In 1995 the original AIM rules were contained in Chapters 16 and 17 of the Rules of the London Stock Exchange Limited. Chapter 16 related to companies and advisers, and Chapter 17 related to trading in shares on AIM. The London Stock Exchange plc (the Stock Exchange) ceased to be the competent listing authority in 2000, when this role was transferred to the Financial Services Authority (FSA) which set up the United Kingdom Listing Authority (UKLA).

On 12 February 2001 the Stock Exchange promulgated new rules in respect of AIM (the AIM rules). The AIM rules replace Chapter 16 and do not form part of the London Stock Exchange rules per se; trading is still covered by Chapter 17. At the same time, the concept of the nominated broker was abandoned, although every AIM company must retain a broker at all times (rule 31).

The AIM rules were formulated on experience of the market since inception and feedback from market participants including companies, accountants, lawyers, market makers, brokers and nominated advisers. The intention was to simplify Chapter 16 and make it easier to understand and give the market a more international flavour.

The AIM rules and Schedules thereto are contained in a booklet published by the Stock Exchange that also contains guidance notes that do not form part of the rules.

The following paragraphs describe the duties of both the nominated adviser and the company's broker, together with comment on such duties and the services that they may reasonably be expected to provide to their corporate clients.

Any company wishing to have its securities traded on AIM must appoint a nominated adviser (rule 1). It must also retain a broker (rule 31). The company's broker must be a member firm of the Stock Exchange. The nominated adviser and company's broker have different duties, although the same firm may perform these duties. The nominated adviser must confirm that the directors of an issuer have received advice and guidance in respect of their responsibilities and obligations to ensure compliance by the issuer with the AIM rules, and, in addition, he may provide corporate and financial advice to the company. It is the responsibility of the company's broker to ensure an orderly market in the shares once trading commences. This means that the company's broker should use his best efforts to promote liquidity in the shares of the company for which he is acting, particularly in the absence of a market-maker.

2.2   THE NOMINATED ADVISER

The nominated adviser (NOMAD) has a crucial role to play in AIM. He is de facto, if not de jure, the market regulator, since the Stock Exchange relies on his judgement as to the suitability or otherwise of a company that wishes to have its shares traded on AIM and it is his responsibility to ensure that the company continues to act in an appropriate manner after admission.

The Stock Exchange remains the ultimate regulator with power to discipline a company if it considers that the company has contravened the AIM rules. The Stock Exchange may do one or more of the following:

(a)   fine the company;
(b)   censure the company;
(c)   publish the fact that the company has been fined or censured; and/or
(d)   cancel the admission of the company's AIM securities (rule 37).

In practice, the Stock Exchange tends to exercise its regulatory powers through the NOMAD, and only becomes directly involved in the event of a serious breach of the rules.

The NOMAD must be independent of the issuer, and must be:

(a)   a member firm of the Stock Exchange; or
(b)   a person authorised in terms of the Financial Services and Markets Act 2000 (FSMA 2000).

A prospective NOMAD must satisfy the Stock Exchange that he is competent to discharge the duties of a nominated adviser.

The NOMAD must be entered on a register maintained by the Stock Exchange (rule 34).

2.2.1   *Application requirements*

Applicants to be registered as a NOMAD must follow the same procedures as those already authorised. They must apply formally to the Stock Exchange on

Form NA1, and their executives must apply separately on Form NA2. The qualifications required are open to some discretion by the Stock Exchange and there is provision for work experience to be taken into account instead of formal qualifications. Requirements for a NOMAD are broadly as follows.

(a)   Depth

This means the adviser must have at least four 'suitably' qualified and experienced staff.

(b)   Experience

The firm must have been acting in 'a principal corporate advisory role for at least three years'. At least four of the executive staff must have been involved in at least three transactions where the firm has acted in a principal corporate advisory role over this three-year period.

(c)   Qualifications

The firm's executive staff must either have passed the relevant examinations of the Financial Services Authority (FSA) or they must have been granted exemption as a result of experience gained under supervision. The Stock Exchange will generally waive the examination requirement where an individual has reasonably continuous relevant corporate finance experience in the securities industry since January 1986; has had three years' recent and reasonably continuous corporate finance advice and has qualifications as a barrister, advocate or solicitor; is qualified as an auditor, accountant or public company secretary in the UK; or is a member of the Securities Institute.

(d)   Regulation

The firm must be either a member firm of the Stock Exchange or a member of an SRO.

(e)   Supervision

The Stock Exchange must be satisfied that a NOMAD has satisfactory supervision and control procedures.

The Stock Exchange amended these requirements in 2001 in order to enable overseas firms to become NOMADs.

The minimum criteria for the approval of future NOMADs are:

–   the prospective NOMAD must be a firm or company;
–   have practised corporate finance for two years; have acted as the principal corporate finance adviser in three 'relevant transactions' during the two-year period; and
–   employ at least four 'qualified executives'.

The Stock Exchange has discretion to waive the requirement for a two-year track record where the prospective NOMAD has highly experienced 'qualified executives'. The Stock Exchange could exercise this discretion, for example, if substantially the entire team of 'qualified executives' transferred from an existing NOMAD. The Stock Exchange also has the absolute discretion to decline to register a potential NOMAD, notwithstanding that he meets the minimum criteria, if the Stock Exchange considers that the reputation and integrity of AIM may be put at risk.

A 'qualified executive' is a full-time employee of the potential NOMAD who is involved in giving corporate finance advice and who has acted in a corporate finance advisory role, which includes the regulation of corporate finance, for at least three years and in at least three relevant transactions.

The Stock Exchange will not regard an employee as a 'qualified executive' if he has been subject to disciplinary action by a regulator or law enforcement agency in the context of financial services or corporate finance or if, following any interview, the Stock Exchange considers that the employee has an inadequate understanding of corporate finance, market practice or the legal or regulatory framework of corporate finance.

'Relevant transactions' fall into two categories.

(1)   Generally qualifying transactions
      Transactions requiring listing particulars or a prospectus (under the European Directive No 80/390/EEC and No 89/298/EEC) in any Member State of the European Union. At least two of these transactions must be in respect of shares quoted on a regulated market (as defined by European Directive No 93/22/EEC).

(2)   Other major transactions
      The Stock Exchange will consider similar initial public offerings and other major corporate transactions for publicly quoted companies including mergers and acquisitions within the European Union or elsewhere in the world.

The Stock Exchange will decide whether a transaction is relevant, and only transactions on the major stock exchanges of the world will be included. The Stock Exchange will not accept a transaction as a 'relevant transaction' unless the prospective NOMAD has acted as the principal corporate finance adviser and was named 'prominently and unequivocally as such in public documentation pertaining to the transaction'.

The Stock Exchange will want to be satisfied that the firm is well established and reputable and that it will not 'endanger the reputation or integrity of AIM'. In considering whether a firm applying to be a NOMAD might endanger the reputation and integrity of AIM, the Stock Exchange will examine:

–   whether the applicant is properly regulated;
–   the applicant's standing with its regulators;
–   whether the applicant or any of its executives have been the subject of adverse disciplinary action by any legal, financial or regulatory authority;
–   whether the applicant is facing such disciplinary action; and
–   insofar as relevant the commercial and regulatory performance of its clients to whom it has given corporate advice.

Once registered, members of the AIM team are likely to visit NOMADs to discuss with them both the Stock Exchange requirements and the NOMAD's view of the AIM market. NOMADs who are not members of the Stock Exchange must also be prepared to have their corporate finance activities reviewed by the FSA as well as the Stock Exchange in the same way as member firms. A NOMAD must provide an annual confirmation to the Stock Exchange of its eligibility to act as a NOMAD, including details of all relevant changes to personnel during the past 12 months.

The Stock Exchange has considerable power over NOMADs. In the event that the Stock Exchange considers that a firm of NOMADs is in breach of its responsibilities or has not acted with due care or skill, or that the integrity and reputation of the market has been impaired as the result of the conduct or judgement of a NOMAD, the Stock Exchange may take sanctions against the firm. The Stock Exchange may:

– censure the NOMAD;
– remove it from the register; and/or
– publish the action it has taken and the reasons for that action (rule 38).

This latter action would prevent a firm acting as a NOMAD and any censure may also be attended by harmful publicity. The Stock Exchange may also take action against a NOMAD if the number of suitably qualified and experienced staff falls below four.

The Stock Exchange conducts regular reviews of NOMADs.

The Stock Exchange makes a charge to a NOMAD of an initial application fee (£10,000) and thereafter an annual subscription (presently £4,000) payable on 1 January. The initial application fee is non-refundable.

Initially, the Stock Exchange authorised 31 firms as NOMADs, not all of which were members of the Stock Exchange. The number of NOMADs has varied over the years, and in January 2001 there were 41 such firms.

Before a company can have its shares traded on AIM, the NOMAD must confirm to the Stock Exchange that:

(a) the directors of the AIM company have received advice and guidance (from the NOMAD or other appropriate professional adviser) as to the nature of their responsibilities and obligations to ensure compliance by the AIM company with the AIM rules;
(b) to the best of the knowledge and belief of the NOMAD, having made due and careful enquiry, all relevant requirements of the AIM rules (save for the admission document's compliance with reg 9 of the POS Regulations 1995) have been complied with; and
(c) in the NOMAD's opinion the applicant and the securities which are the subject of the application are appropriate to be admitted to AIM (Schedule 6).

The Stock Exchange also requires the NOMAD to give ongoing advice to the company after admission (rule 34).

It is a requirement that the NOMAD should be available at all times to give advice to its clients.

2.2.2 *Duties and responsibilities*

The primary duties of the NOMAD are to the Stock Exchange. Many documents bear the rubric:

> 'NOMAD Limited which is regulated by the Financial Services Authority, is the Company's nominated adviser for the purpose of the AIM Rules. Its responsibilities as the Company's nominated adviser under the AIM Rules are owed solely to the London Stock Exchange and are not owed to the Company, any director nor to any other person in respect of his decision to acquire New Ordinary Shares in reliance on any part of this document. No representation or

warranty, express or implied, is made by NOMAD Limited as to any of the contents of this document.'

This does not prevent a NOMAD agreeing with the issuer to provide advice and undertaking duties and responsibilities in addition to those required by the Stock Exchange.

A NOMAD must confirm to the Stock Exchange that the directors of an issuer that is producing an admission document have received advice and guidance on their responsibilities and obligations and have agreed to comply with the rules relating to AIM. The NOMAD must further confirm to the Stock Exchange that the issuer has complied with all the relevant requirements of the AIM rules 'to the best of [his] knowledge and belief' (Schedule 6).

The wording of the Schedule 'to the best of knowledge and belief' of the NOMAD means that the NOMAD need not necessarily himself take charge of the due diligence exercise as long as he ensures that the directors of the issuer have instituted satisfactory procedures. The NOMAD must, of course, be able to demonstrate that his view that satisfactory procedures have been instituted is reasonably held. Schedule 6 specifically excludes the NOMAD from having to take responsibility for the issuer's compliance with reg 9 of the POS Regulations 1995. Regulation 9 requires that a prospectus contains:

> 'All such information as investors would reasonably require ... [to make] ... an informed assessment of (a) the assets and liabilities, financial position, profits and losses and prospects of the issuer ... and (b) the rights attaching to these securities.'

The Stock Exchange requires the same information to be included in an AIM admission document. The negation of this specific responsibility may mean that a NOMAD does not have the duty to make the searching enquiry into other matters of which investors should be informed. The NOMAD, however, must still confirm that the issuer has met the specific reporting requirements of the Stock Exchange and, in practice, competent NOMADs will still demand full due diligence.

The Stock Exchange expects a NOMAD to satisy himself that an appropriate verification exercise has been carried out on the admission document. This means that a NOMAD may wish to conduct extra due diligence in respect of an issuer to satisfy himself in regard to its current position and future prospects, and that the issuer maintains appropriate internal financial reporting and compliance controls.

The level of investigatory work will depend upon the nature of the company. A company that has a long trading record, or which can demonstrate either stability or continuous growth in trading, and where the auditors have been constant for five years or more, may require less work than a 'start-up' or loss-making company trading in high-risk markets or one that has recently or repeatedly changed its auditors. Similarly, a company with a large number of subsidiaries engaged in different activities in different markets may require more due diligence than a single-product company.

The NOMAD must provide the Stock Exchange 'with such information as it may require' (rule 34). It is difficult to define what 'such information' may be, since it falls within the absolute discretion of the Stock Exchange. The Stock Exchange expects the NOMAD to be in regular contact with the company and to review its trading performance against any profit forecast or projection made in any admission document in order to determine whether any announcement may be necessary to maintain an orderly market. It is the NOMAD's duty to advise the company if any announcement regarding current trading is required under rule 15. The NOMAD must be prepared to provide information following unusual share price movements or suspicious or undisclosed transactions by directors, or late announcements of price-sensitive information. It is, of course, the responsibility of the NOMAD to try to ensure that none of these events occur, although in practical terms he cannot always guarantee to do so.

It is for these reasons that NOMAD agreements will normally contain clauses requiring both the company and individual directors to give notice to the NOMAD if either becomes aware of any breach of the AIM rules. In addition, the NOMAD may well wish each director to personally sign a letter giving a similar undertaking. Examples of such undertakings are contained in Appendix 3.

One important consequence of the changes to Chapter 16 is the fact that directors of AIM companies are no longer bound by the Securities Code (formerly the Model Code), although in practice a competent NOMAD is likely to insist that his clients still observe this discipline, and there are provisions in the rules (rule 19) to enforce the prevention of dealings in any 'close period' by directors and applicable employees.

2.2.3 Resignation or dismissal

The NOMAD also has considerable power in that if he resigns or is dismissed the Stock Exchange will suspend trading in the company's shares (rule 30) until a replacement NOMAD is appointed. The NOMAD must notify the Stock Exchange when it ceases to be the company's NOMAD, in advance of any such change where possible, so that it can co-ordinate the suspension of the company's securities with the announcement of the loss of the company's NOMAD in order to avoid a disorderly market.

The company then has one month in which to replace the NOMAD (assuming he is not replaced immediately), and if no replacement can be found within that time the admission of the company's AIM securities will be cancelled. In order for the company's securities to be readmitted, a new admission document must be produced and approved by the replacement NOMAD. The Stock Exchange advises that Nominated Adviser Agreements should include a notice period of at least one month, and although a NOMAD will invariably take the right to resign immediately in the event of any serious breach of the AIM rules, most Nominated Adviser Agreements will contain longer notice periods.

There are occasions when a company wishes to change its NOMAD and an amicable handover is arranged to another firm. An immediate announcement of such event is required and it is customary for both NOMADs to liaise and the appropriate notification to be made to the Stock Exchange simultaneously. The new NOMAD must submit a nominated adviser's declaration (rule 34).

NARRATIVE

2.2.4   *Nominated adviser as a 'responsible person'*

The AIM rules are drafted to provide maximum protection to the NOMAD from the legal liability for the contents of an AIM admission document. However, a NOMAD bringing a company to AIM may become a *'responsible person'* under the POS Regulations 1995, and in addition he may voluntarily take responsibility for the document in the role of sponsor. In all such cases the NOMAD will wish to satisfy himself fully that the admission document has been properly compiled.

The NOMAD may become a 'responsible person' by virtue of selling shares. This can occur when there are vendor shareholders at the time of flotation, who decline to take responsibility for the prospectus and admission document. The unwillingness to take responsiblity can arise when a venture capitalist is a vendor, since venture capitalists tend to argue that they are investors not actively involved in the management of the business, and therefore are unwilling to accept legal liability for the accuracy of the document on the same basis as the directors and the company. The NOMAD will also become a 'responsible person' if he decides to act as a principal and sells shares to investors rather than acting as agent for the vendors.

2.2.5   *Services to corporate clients*

A corporate client may reasonably expect a NOMAD to provide the following services:

(a)   advice on the AIM rules;
(b)   preparation of any admission document;
(c)   co-ordination of other advisers, including solicitors, accountants etc;
(d)   ongoing advice after admission;
(e)   advice, in conjunction with the company's broker, on the value of the business;
(f)   assistance in fund raising; and
(g)   assistance in the preparation of presentations to institutional and other investors.

A NOMAD must, of necessity, be able to advise on the AIM rules. He should have the ability to prepare an admission document in conjunction with the company's solicitors, the auditors, reporting accountants and his own lawyers. He will rely on the solicitors for the legal due diligence and the accountants for the financial due diligence; however, he will wish to test their findings and conduct certain due diligence himself. This due diligence will normally be into the company's business, its products, the markets in which it operates, its shareholders and specifically the history and experience of its management and directors. Each director of an AIM company is required to provide: details of all companies and partnerships of which he is currently a director or partner or has been a director or partner during the five years prior to admission; details of any unspent convictions in relation to indictable offences; details of any bankruptcies or individual voluntary arrangements; and details of any liquidations or receiverships (of whatever nature) of entities of which he was a director or partner in the 12 months prior to such event (rule 3 and Schedule 2). This is an area in which the NOMAD will take a close interest at an early stage, since the director's curriculum vitae will have a significant influence on his view of the company's suitability for AIM. Similarly, he will be interested in obtaining information regarding the company's major shareholders and the influence (if any) that they exert over the management.

The NOMAD will prepare the timetable in respect of a proposed admission and submit the '10-day' document (rule 2 and Schedule 1) to the Stock Exchange. A copy of the '10-day' notice is shown in Chapter 1 and a sample timetable is included at Appendix 3.

The NOMAD is obliged, under the AIM rules, to provide continuing advice after admission, and a good NOMAD will build a relationship with the company's directors that will ensure a full flow of information to enable him to provide appropriate advice. A competent NOMAD should have sufficient commercial experience to enable him to assess the value of a business and, in conjunction with the company's broker, its potential market capitalisation both before and after fund raising.

Fund raising is primarily the responsibility of the company's broker; however, a NOMAD, in the course of his business, will have established contact with certain professional investors specialising in the AIM market. He should be in a position to know which investor is interested in which sector of the market and assist the company's broker in fund raising; similarly, he should be willing and able to help the company in the preparation of presentations to professional investors before and after admission.

2.3 THE COMPANY'S BROKER

The company's broker must be a member of the Stock Exchange. He should provide dealing services to the public and possibly advice. He may also trade on his own account.

The company's broker is expected to use his best endeavours to find a matching buyer for a seller, or vice versa, if there is no market-maker in an AIM security. Matching bargains may take several days or even several weeks to execute, depending upon the size of the buy or sell order, and the company's broker may decide to satisfy all or part of the order by acting as a principal and trading for his own account.

In securities where there is no market-maker the 'instant' dealing which may be achieved through a market-maker will not be available; however, it must be remembered that even on the Official List, large buy and sell orders in smaller companies may effectively become matched bargains.

The company's broker is also required to input and regularly update information through the Stock Exchange Alternative Trading Services (SEATS PLUS). This information includes:

– the number of shares in issue;
– the free market capitalisation (that is the percentage of shares in public hands);
– the last reported turnover;
– the profit after tax;
– the indicated date of the announcement of the annual and interim results; and

–   details relating to any dividend payment.

The Stock Exchange may extend these requirements if it sees fit.

A company may reasonably expect its broker to provide the following services:

(a)   regular contact and advice on market-related matters;
(b)   advice on the potential market impact of any proposed announcement;
(c)   assistance in fund raising; and
(d)   placing of lines of stock on behalf of major shareholders or directors.

The broker should remain in close contact with both the company and the NOMAD. He should advise each of any major, or untoward, movement in the share price and assist in the preparation of any announcement that may need to be made as a result of such movement.

He should also be prepared to review and comment on any announcement that the company wishes to make in conjunction with the NOMAD. He should be prepared to express an opinion on the likely impact on market sentiment and the effect on the share price of any such announcement.

He should be prepared to raise fresh capital for the company, and in certain circumstances to either underwrite or procure underwriters for primary or secondary issues.

There will be occasions on which a major shareholder or a director wishes to dispose of, or reduce, his holding in the company. The company's broker should be in a position to facilitate such a transaction since he should be aware of all the potential buyers of the stock, and thus be in a position to place stock on behalf of the vendor. He should also be aware of potential sellers and so be able to find lines of stock for purchasers or holders wishing to increase their stake.

2.4   APPENDIX TO CHAPTER 2

Example 1

Undertaking in Nominated Adviser Agreement

The company and each of the directors hereby acknowledge that the NOMAD owes responsibilities to the Stock Exchange as nominated adviser, and that the Stock Exchange may review the NOMAD's registration as a nominated adviser and impose sanctions upon the NOMAD with regard to the conduct of the company and the directors in relation to the AIM rules and, accordingly:

–   the company and each of the directors hereby undertakes to comply (and insofar as he is able to do so, to procure such compliance by the company) forthwith with all proper and reasonable directions given by the NOMAD in relation to the AIM rules;
–   the company agrees to indemnify the NOMAD and each of its directors, officers, employees and agents against all losses, liabilities, demands, claims, costs, charges and expenses (including proper and reasonable legal fees and expenses) which any of them may suffer or incur as a result of or arising out of or in connection with any breach of the AIM rules by the company or any director and which does not arise as a result of the provision by the NOMAD of material or incorrect advice in relation to the AIM rules.
–   the company and each of the directors undertakes to inform the NOMAD forthwith upon becoming aware of any breach by the company and/or any director of the AIM rules and to request the advice and guidance of the NOMAD in relation to all matters relevant to the company's compliance with the AIM rules.

The company undertakes to the NOMAD to comply on a timely basis with all obligations upon AIM companies in the form from time to time specified by the Stock Exchange, the obligations at the date of this agreement being those referred to in the AIM rules and each director severally undertakes that for so long as he is a director of the company he will do everything reasonably within his power as such to procure that the company complies with such continuing obligations.

Example 2

Director's letter to a nominated adviser

Dear Sirs

I hereby confirm that, being a director of [...] plc (the company) I have had explained to me by [...][1] my responsibilities as a director of a company whose securities are traded on the Alternative Investment Market.

In consideration of your agreeing to be the nominated adviser to the company, I hereby undertake:

---

1   This may be the nominated adviser, the company's lawyer or the director's personal lawyer.

(a)   to comply forthwith with all proper and reasonable directions given by you in relation to compliance of the AIM rules;

(b)   to inform you forthwith upon becoming aware of any breach by the company and/or any director of the AIM rules and to request your advice and guidance in relation to all matters relevant to the company's compliance with the AIM rules;

(c)   to comply on a timely basis for so long as I am a director of the company and to do everything reasonably within my power as such to procure that the company complies with all obligations upon AIM companies in the form from time to time specified by the Stock Exchange, the obligations at the date of this letter being those referred to in the AIM rules.

Chapter 3

THE ADMISSION DOCUMENT

3.1   INTRODUCTION

The admission document is the single most important document which a company will need to produce in conjunction with its advisers in the submission for admission to AIM (if the securities are being offered to the public for the first time). In addition to the AIM admission rules, the company wishing to apply for admission will need also to be aware of and comply with the requirements of the FSA 1986, the Financial Services and Markets Act 2000 (FSMA 2000) and the provisions of the POS Regulations 1995 (as amended).

3.1.1   Regulatory background

The Wilson Committee, which reported in 1980, felt that the system of self-regulation which had been a well-respected procedure governing City institutions was generally working. However, whole new markets were developing and it was thought that the Prevention of Fraud (Investments) Act 1958 and the licensing activities carried out under it by the DTI were not adequate to cope with such developments. Statutory intervention was also being pressed by the EU and various directives and draft directives in financial services were issued. Then in October 1979 exchange controls were removed. The pressure caused major reforms to the Stock Exchange Rule Book which was the precursor to the 'Big Bang' in October 1986 which mainly resulted in the removal of minimum commissions and also the distinction between brokers and jobbers. Membership was also open to corporate bodies and, in particular, foreign banks. The response was that the Government felt the time was right to introduce a regulatory framework and it commissioned a detailed report from Professor Gower. The resulting legislation was the FSA 1986. The salient details (so far as this publication is concerned) of this Act and its recent successor, the FSMA 2000, are set out below, but the FSA 1986 did the following.

(1)   It endorsed the Prevention of Fraud (Investments) Act 1958 by preventing any person from being involved in investment business or advertisement or soliciting of investments unless expressly authorised. The relevant activities covered by the FSA 1986 were very wide, incorporating most forms of investment other than land, goods and banking deposits.

(2)   The main policing authority was initially to be the DTI and subsequently the Treasury. However, the principal body was a newly created Securities and Investment Board (SIB). The SIB was responsible for the founding of various self-regulating organisations (SROs) and also for recognised professional bodies (RPBs) who in turn enforced rules and regulations on their members. The SIB, although a private company and subject to control from the DTI, is effectively a government quango. The SIB originally founded five SRIs, but these have subsequently been reduced to three, namely (i) the Securities and Futures Authority (SFA), which regulates money market dealers, and those involved with domestic and international securities, futures, options and corporate finance advisers; (ii) the Investment Management Regulatory Organisation (IMRO) – concerned with portfolio management, for pension funds, collective investment schemes or private clients etc; and (iii) the Personal Investment Authority (PIA) – this is for those involved in the production and selling of life insurance, collective investment schemes and other investment services to private clients.

The Stock Exchange initially hoped itself to be an SRO in a similar manner to the New York Stock Exchange. However, it now forms a major part of the SFA.

Since the mid-1990s there has been a general relaxation of control by the SIB over SROs who have been deemed to become professional regulators and SROs have been recognised as being able to discipline their own individual employees and members. There is also an ability on each SRO now to control their relationship with their members and impose a disciplinary regime.

One of the first acts of the new Government in May 1997 was to overhaul the existing system. The Bank of England was under the control of the SIB (now somewhat confusingly renamed the Financial Services Authority (FSA)) who were to take direct responsibility for the authorisation and supervision of the SROs (thereby abandoning the two-tier system). This meant that the FSA had become the new 'super regulator'.

The background explained above is somewhat simplistic, but gives a flavour of the thinking behind both the FSA 1986 and the FSMA 2000 which are further considered in the regulatory context of statutory controls.

3.2   PUBLIC OFFERS OF SECURITIES REGULATIONS 1995 AND FINANCIAL SERVICES AND MARKETS ACT 2000

Sections 57 and 58 of FSA 1986 have been replaced by provisions of the FSMA 2000, the main provisions of which came into force on 1 December 2001. Like the FSA 1986, the new Act places an emphasis on the boundary between what is lawful and unlawful. Part I includes a general prohibition against carrying on or the promotion of any regulated activity in the UK unless the firm is authorised or is exempt (all communications concerning such activity must similarly be approved by such authorised firm).

Examples of exempt entities include the Stock Exchange, CREST and members of Lloyds (Lloyds itself is authorised). Other exempt persons are those qualifying under a DPB like lawyers and accountants who are authorised under their RPB.

Failure to comply with these provisions can amount to a criminal offence and could render any contract made in these circumstances unenforceable. If an authorised firm inadvertently strays outside its sphere of operations (perimeter) contracts etc do remain valid, but may lead the firm into civil liability or disciplinary measures from the FSA.

Part VI of the FSMA 2000 repeats much of Part IV of the FSA 1986 reconciling it with the POS Regulations 1995. It really only applies to securities which are seeking a listing, but there are provisions that can lend themselves to further regulation.

On 1 May 2000 the UK Listing Authority (UKLA) was taken over by the FSA from the Stock Exchange. It is now the FSA who can, as a result of the FSMA 2000, enforce the listing rules and indeed agree to admissions on the Official List. The FSA's authority is ultimately controlled by the Treasury.

The role of the UKLA is to ascertain which securities qualify to be admitted to the Official List and, after listing, satisfy the ongoing provisions. The UKLA has power to levy fees from issuers and sponsors for the admission and continuation of listing. Determining such amounts as may be required, the UKLA is not permitted to take into consideration any fines it may have levied, etc. In considering UK companies for listing, there is an underlying requirement which entitles the UKLA to refuse any application if 'granting it would be detrimental to the interests of investors' (FSMA 2000, s 75(5)). Other relevant provisions which should be noted are as follows.

(1)   The six-month rule – the FSA has up to six months to consider an application or has up to six months to make a decision from the last request for information. Where the FSA is unfavourable there are objection procedures which need to be followed and the applicant has a right to refer the matter to a tribunal. Where the time-limits are not complied with, it is deemed that there has been a refusal.

(2)   After securities have been listed, it cannot be challenged (in order to protect investors).

(3)   The FSA has wide discretion to waive or modify rules, but in practice is unlikely to do this. In any event, the listing documents require the FSA's approval and are also required to be filed in the normal way with the Registrar of Companies.

(4)   Detailed information needs to be given which 'must contain all such information as investors and their professional advisers would reasonably require, and reasonably expect to find there for the purposes of making an informed assessment of – (a) the assets and liabilities, financial position, profits and losses, and prospects of the issuer of the securities; and (b) the rights attaching to the securities' (FSMA 2000, s 80(1)).

(5)   The FSA can dispense with/modify the application of the Listing Rules if disclosure would be: (i) contrary to the public interest – this requires a ministerial certificate; (ii) would be seriously detrimental to the issuer and not essential for any likely acquirer to know in order to make an

informed assessment; or (iii) is unnecessary given those expected to deal in a particular type of security.

(6)   Supplemental listing particulars are needed when, prior to dealings commencing, there is either: (i) a significant change affecting matters required to be included in the listing particulars; or (ii) a significant new matter which would properly have been included in the original particulars. Where such supplemental listing particulars are needed, all those responsible are under an obligation to notify the issuer of any such change.

(7)   The FSA's prior approval is needed to any formal notification announcing the listing or any other advertisement giving summary particulars, etc.

(8)   Any new issues of the same class will require new listing particulars unless it relates to a capitalisation issue, conversion into shares of listed convertibles, exercise of listed warrants, shares or depository receipt for listed shares of no greater nominal value or, most importantly, relating to shares amounting to less than 10% of that class already in issue.

(9)   Overseas companies which had a prospectus or listing particulars approved by another competent authority within the European Economic Area (this is the EU plus Iceland, Liechtenstein and Norway) in the last three months can use the same document for the purposes of listing on the Stock Exchange. However, this must have details of tax, meeting notices and dividend payments relevant to UK residents and must also be translated into English. The FSA has a discretion to refuse a listing if it 'considers the issuer has failed to comply with any obligations to which he is subject as a result of that [other] listing' (FSMA 2000, s 75(6)).

The sanctions which the FSA now has are very similar to the general powers which the Stock Exchange had, ie a power to suspend a listing 'where the smooth operation of the market is, or may be, temporarily jeopardised or where the protection of investors so required'. Where such suspension lasts more than six months, it could lead to cancellations. The new powers under the FSA are more clearly delineated since the FSA has discretion to suspend or discontinue a listing 'if satisfied that there are special circumstances which preclude regular dealings in them'. Holders of securities are not permitted to challenge decisions in this respect even through judicial review (see further, FSMA 2000, ss 77 and 78). The Quotations Committee of the Stock Exchange has previously had power to rebuke the issuer and any director involved or suspend or cancel a listing where an issuer has failed to comply with its obligations. These rights have now been assumed by the FSA and the powers have been put on a statutory basis. Sections 89 and 91 of the FSMA 2000 govern the fining regime. Regard must be had to:

(a)   whether the person to be fined is an individual;
(b)   the extent to which any circumvention was deliberate or reckless; and
(c)   the seriousness of the abuse.

The nature of the sanction could be from two years' imprisonment and a fine where securities are offered for public issue in the UK before a prospectus is published, to just a fine where, for example, listing particulars or a prospectus is not filed with the Registrar of Companies on or before a particular date. Where an advertisement in connection with a listing has not been approved or authorised by the FSA, this is also punishable by up to two years in prison and a fine, but there is a defence where it can be shown that it was reasonable to believe that it had so been authorised or approved.

There are also various statutory defences set out in Part XXVII of the FSMA 2000. These largely reflect supplying or omitting to supply information which could produce a misleading statement or practice. Giving a misleading statement is a serious offence whereas being economic with the truth is a crime only where it is done with 'dishonesty'. No guidance is given by the FSMA 2000 as to what is meant by 'dishonesty' but established case-law (*R v Ghosh* [1982] 1 QB 1053) would seem to indicate that to be honest it must conform to standards of reasonable and honest people and the defendant must have realised that it was dishonest by that standard.

There are also crimes for market manipulation and insider dealing. Detailed consideration of these provisions and possible defences are outside the scope of this book, but advice should be sought at an early stage.

The persons to be responsible are almost identical to those under the FSA 1986 (see ss 152 and 154A(b)). The list includes the issuer of securities, directors (and the proposed directors) of the issuer, anyone named in the document as accepting responsibility for all or part of it, anyone else authorising all or part of the document and, in the case of a prospectus, anyone else offering securities as a principal.

The general EU requirements concerning the continuing obligations of those companies which are listed are significantly less than those which are required by the Stock Exchange (now under the FSA) and are largely restricted to three main heads:

(i)   the publication of accounts properly audited within six months of that company's year end;

(ii)   within four months of the first half of that company's financial year the publication of a financial report (of that first half);

(iii)   the general announcement rule – as in the rule presently set out in Listing Rules 9.1 *vis* properly published details of 'any major development' in its activity which are not public knowledge but could affect the development of assets and liabilities or the financial position or the general course of business thereby leading to 'a substantial movement' in the share price or (in the case of debt securities which are listed) 'significantly affect its ability to meet its commitments'.

3.2.1 Application

The POS Regulations 1995 were issued under the authority of the European Communities Act 1972 and came into force on 19 June 1995 to coincide with the creation of AIM. With effect from that same date the prospectus provisions set out in the Companies Act 1985 were repealed. These Regulations were amended in 1999. The general requirement is set out in reg 4 of the POS Regulations 1995 which states that when securities are offered to the public in the UK for the first time a prospectus should be published available to the

public free of charge at an address in the UK from the time the offer is first
made until the end of the period during which the offer remains open. A copy
of this prospectus must also be delivered to the Registrar of Companies for
copying onto the company's file retained at Companies House. The POS
Regulations 1995 do include certain well-defined exemptions (see reg 7), but a
company seeking admission to AIM would not qualify under these exemptions.

Part II of the POS Regulations 1995 applies to any investment not admitted to
the Official List (or subject to an application), namely:

(i)   shares and stock of a company (but not to deferred shares of building
        societies);
(ii)   debentures having a maturity of more than one year from their date of
        issue (if less, it falls outside the POS Regulations 1995); and
(iii)   warrants and other instruments entitling the holders to obtain any such
        security listed in (i) or (ii);

so long as such security is offered to the public in the UK. It is whether there can
be said to be an 'offer' which is the determining factor. (It should be noted that
there is no requirement that an offer be in writing.) Regulation 6 reinforces this
by stating that where a person offers securities to the public, to the extent it is to
persons in the UK, it is made to the public.

Regulation 4 requires publication (with a prospectus etc) and registration of
securities with the Registrar of Companies before such securities can be offered
to the public for the first time.

3.2.2   *Requirements*

Regulation 9 of the POS Regulations 1995 contains a general obligation
requiring disclosure in the prospectus of all such information as 'investors
would reasonably require and reasonably expect to find' in order to make an
informed assessment of:

(i)   the assets, liabilities, financial position, profits and losses and prospects of
        the issuer; and
(ii)   the rights attaching to those securities.

The obligation on the directors is such that they would need to include such
information as is known or may reasonably be known after having made
appropriate enquiries (reg 9(2)).

Under reg 13, there is a clear statement of responsibility for a prospectus and
this is dealt with at greater length in Chapter 4.

3.2.3   *The prospectus*

Schedule 1 to the POS Regulations 1995 sets out the form and content
requirements for the prospectus under ten headings, eight of which are
significant. These include the following.

(1)   General requirements

(i)   Name and address of persons offering the securities.
(ii)   Names and functions of the directors of the issuer.

(iii) Date of publication of prospectus.

(iv) Confirmation that it has been delivered to the Registrar of Companies.

(v) Confirmation that the prospectus has been drawn up in accordance with the POS Regulations 1995.

(vi) The prospectus must also contain a general warning to investors bearing the following or similar:

> 'If you are in any doubt about the contents of this document you should consult a person authorised under the Financial Services Act 1986 who specialises in advising on the acquisition of shares and other securities.'

(2) Responsible persons

(i) The prospectus should contain names, addresses (which may be home or business) and functions of those persons responsible for the prospectus or any particular part (and specifying such part).

(ii) There needs to be a declaration by the directors (being the responsible individuals) of the company issuing securities that:

> 'to the best of their knowledge the information contained in the prospectus is in accordance with the facts and that the prospectus makes no omission likely to affect the import of such information.'

(iii) A statement by any person who accepts responsibility for the prospectus or any part of it that he does accept.

(3) The securities section

(i) A description of the securities offered including the class to which they belong and the description of the rights attaching to them, for example voting, dividends, return of capital on winding up and redemption together with a summary of consents needed for variation of any such rights.

(ii) When the securities are debentures, details should be included regarding interest payable and repayment of the principal.

(iii) Where the securities are convertible, details will need to be inserted concerning the terms and dates upon which the holders can exercise the right of conversion and the procedures for doing this.

(iv) Dividend date or date upon which interest will arise.

(v) Particulars of tax on income from securities withheld at source including tax credits.

(vi) Details of any pre-emption rights attaching to the securities.

(vii) Details of any restrictions on the free transferability of the securities.

(viii) A statement as to whether such securities have been admitted to any recognised investment exchange. If no such application has been made or where an application has been made and refused, a statement needs to be included as to whether any other arrangements for dealing are to be made.

(ix) The purpose for which securities are being issued and the number being issued or offered.

(x) The total proceeds expected to be raised and the expected net proceeds after deduction of expenses.

(xi) Where a prospectus relates to the offer of shares for subscription there
      should be particulars as to:

    (a) the minimum amount which in the opinion of directors of the
        issuer must be raised to provide sums required for:

        – the purchase price of any property purchased or to be
           purchased which is to be defrayed in whole or part from the
           proceeds;

        – any preliminary expenses payable by the issuer and any
           commission payable to any person in consideration of that
           person agreeing to subscribe for or procuring the agreement
           for subscription to any of the shares of the issuer;

        – the repayment of any money borrowed by the issuer in respect
           of these matters;

        – working capital; and

    (b) where amounts are to be provided otherwise than out of proceeds of
        the issue, details of the sources out of which those amounts are to be
        provided should also be inserted.

(xii) The names of any persons underwriting or guaranteeing the offer.

(xiii) The estimated expenses of the offer and by whom they are payable and
      the commission payable by the issuer to any person agreeing to subscribe
      for the securities or procuring the subscription of those securities.

(xiv) The period during which the offer of securities is to remain open.

(xv) The price at which securities are offered or if this cannot be determined
      the procedure, method and timetable for fixing this price.

(xvi) The arrangements for payment for the securities being offered and the
      timetable for their delivery.

(xvii) When applications for securities are not accepted in whole or part, details
      relating to the timetable and return of this money.

(4) General information about the issuer and its capital

(i) Date and place of incorporation of the issuer – for a non-UK issuer, its
    principal office in the UK (if any) and for a UK issuer, its registered office
    and company registration number.

(ii) The title of the company or legal format of the issuer including the
    legislation under which it was formed and to which it is answerable.

(iii) A summary of the issuer's memorandum of association setting out its
    objects.

(iv) Details of limited liability of the issuer's members and the amount of its
    authorised share capital, and any limit for the duration of the
    authorisation to issue such share capital.

(v) Amount of the issued share capital.

(vi) Number of shares in each class making up the authorised and issued
    share capital, the nominal value of such shares and the amount paid up
    on the shares.

(vii) Details of the issuer's group structure, if any, including its position in that
    structure.

(5) Activities of the issuer

(i)   The principal activities of the issuer and any exceptional factors which have influenced its activities.
(ii) Whether the issuer is dependent on patents or other intellectual property rights, licences or particular contracts which are of fundamental importance to its business.
(iii) Where it may be significant, information regarding investments in progress.
(iv) Information on any active, pending or threatened legal or arbitration proceedings that are being brought or may be brought against the issuer or any member of its group which could have a significant effect on the issuer's financial position.

(6) Finance

The financial position of the issuer: where available, this should include the issuer's annual accounts for the last three years, and a report by the auditor stating that in its opinion the accounts give a true and fair view of the state of affairs and profit and loss of the issuer and its subsidiary undertakings (the Public Offer of Securities (Amendment) Regulations 1999, SI 1999/734 have offered, from 10 May 1999, some relief concerning subsidiary undertakings stating that there is no requirement to include in the prospectus their accounts or any other information relating thereto if such is not reasonably necessary in making an informed assessment of the issuer's assets and liabilities, financial position, profits/losses and prospects), or a full accountants' report (see Chapter 7 for a fuller description of financial accounting matters).

(7) Administration, management, supervision of issuer

(i)   Details of directors' existing and proposed service contracts unless such contracts can be determined without payment of compensation within one year.
(ii) Aggregate remuneration and benefits in kind granted to directors of the issuer during the last completed financial year together with an estimate of the aggregate amount payable and benefits in kind to be granted to directors and proposed directors for the current financial year at the date on which the offer is first made.
(iii) Statement as to whether any director of the issuer has any interest in the share capital whether on a beneficial basis or non-beneficial basis and distinguishing between the two, for example share options in a director's personal name and those held by a director as trustee for others.

(8) Recent business developments and prospects for issuer

Details should be included of any recent trends concerning the issuer's business, and information on the issuer's prospects for at least the current financial year.

3.2.4   *Other EU Member States*

Regulation 20 of the POS Regulations 1995 also allows for the mutual recognition of prospectuses and listing particulars with respect to other Member States of the EU. There are a number of conditions which are required to be satisfied. These are set out in Sch 4 to the Regulations. Its requirements include:

(i)   a prospectus which has been approved by a competent authority in another Member State;
(ii)   that the prospectus is translated into English by a certified translation;
(iii)   that the offer of securities is made simultaneously with the making of an offer in the Member State approving the prospectus (or within three months of that offer);
(iv)   that a summary of taxation treaties relevant to UK residents is included, and also the names and addresses of paying agents (for the payment of dividends etc to UK shareholders) and details of the mechanism for giving notice of meetings to UK residents.

3.3   STOCK EXCHANGE REQUIREMENTS

Requirements for the Stock Exchange are largely set out in the AIM rules which state that a document must be published in English containing the information required by the POS Regulations 1995 whether or not the issuer is making an offer of securities to the public which would need a prospectus published under those Regulations. Rule 3 requires that the admission document must be available publicly, free of charge, for at least one month after the admission to the market and that the document contains the information set out in Schedule 2 to the AIM rules which includes the following.

(i)   A statement made by its directors that, in their opinion, having made due and careful enquiry the consolidated working capital will be sufficient for its present requirements (that means for a minimum of 12 months from the date of admission of its securities).
(ii)   When profit forecasts, estimates or projects are made (which includes references made to any minimum or maximum profit levels or data from which similar calculations can be made even if no actual reference to the words 'profit' and 'loss' has been made) there should be:
   (a)   a statement by its directors that any such forecasts, estimate or projection has been made only after due and careful enquiry;
   (b)   the principle assumptions for each factor that could materially affect the achievement of forecast, estimate or projection that has been made. These assumptions should be readily understandable by investors and 'be specific and precise'; and
   (c)   confirmation needs to be given by the NOMAD to the company seeking admission that it has satisfied itself that the forecast, estimate or projections have only been made after due and careful enquiry by the directors of that company.

(iii)   There needs to be prominently displayed on the first page in bold print the name of the NOMAD with the health warning:

> 'The Alternative Investment Market (AIM) is a market designated primarily for emerging or smaller companies to which a higher investment risk tends to be attached than to larger or more established companies. AIM securities are not officially listed.
>
> A prospective investor should be aware of the risks of investing in such companies and should make a decision to invest only after careful consideration and if appropriate, consultation with an independent financial adviser. The London Stock Exchange plc has not itself examined or approved the contents of this document.'

(iv)   Where the issuer's main activity has not been earning revenue for at least two years or is a new business, it must ensure that all persons who, at the time of admission to trading on AIM, are a 'related party' or employees of the issuer (unless they hold less than 0.5% of the relevant class of share) agree not to dispose of any interest in their AIM securities for a period of one year from the date of admission to trading on AIM (unless there is an intervening court order, a takeover becomes or is declared unconditional or upon the death of the director or employee). The prospectus should contain a statement to this effect. The term 'related party' is widely defined in the definitions to the AIM rules and includes directors, family (spouse and child under 18), trustee (other than related to pensions), a company under the control of any such person and other categories.

(v)   With reference to directors and shadow directors, the following information should be included:

    (a)   the full names and any previous names of directors together with their ages;

    (b)   their directorships or partnerships held over the previous five years;

    (c)   any unspent convictions in relation to indictable offences;

    (d)   details of any bankruptcies (or individual voluntary arrangements) or any receiverships of companies or assets, administrations or liquidations of companies or partnerships where they were directors at the time of or within 12 months preceding such events; and

    (e)   any public criticism by statutory or regulatory authorities including recognised professional bodies and details of any disqualification as a director or firm acting in the management or conduct of the affairs of any company.

(vi)   Name of any person (unless a trade supplier or a professional adviser and disclosed in the prospectus) who received within the preceding 12 months prior to the relevant application by the issuer, or who has a contract (not otherwise disclosed) to receive on or after such admission fees, in aggregate in excess of £10,000 or securities of this value or any other benefits which could be valued at £10,000 or more. In this case, the full relationship with the issuer of any such persons needs to be disclosed along with details of the full benefits. Receipt also includes circumstances where it may have been received indirectly, for example through a third party or on a contingency basis.

(vii)   Names and addresses of both the NOMAD and the company's broker.

(viii) Names (so far as known to the directors) of all substantial shareholders and percentages each hold (being 3% or more, with effect from 2 January 1997).
(ix) If the issuer is an investing company (one which in the opinion of the Stock Exchange has a primary business in investing of its funds), details of its investment strategy.
(x) A 'catch all' provision – the prospectus may also contain any other information which the issuer reasonably considers necessary for investors to form a full understanding of the matters contained in it.

The disclosures required by items (d) and (e) of point (v) above can give rise to some unexpected difficulty. Under (d), there is no time-limit after which a receivership, for example, can be ignored, so a director who has at some stage in his career acted as a 'company doctor', perhaps 20 years before, may find that he has a long list of matters to disclose. Under (e), a director who is a solicitor or accountant, for example, would have to disclose any criticism levied by regulators on his firm, even though he personally was not involved.

The Stock Exchange requires that at least 10 days' prior notification be given to them of intending admissions.

No prospectus is needed by an issuer where securities of the same class are already admitted unless the POS Regulations 1995 otherwise require. If information may also be omitted under the POS Regulations 1995 the Stock Exchange may authorise the same omission.

If shares are to be offered on a pre-emptive basis to existing shareholders, as long as up-to-date information of equivalent import is given, it need not be repeated to satisfy the POS Regulations 1995 (under paras 41–47 of Sch 1).

A prospectus may not be required at all if the number, estimated value or nominal value, or where no nominal value the accounting par value, is less than 10% of the number or the corresponding value of the same class already admitted to AIM and up-to-date information otherwise required by the POS Regulations 1995 is available.

Under each situation set out in the previous two paragraphs, the NOMAD should confirm to the Stock Exchange in writing that the relevant up-to-date information is available. There is no definition of when information should become available and unless the information is part of something, for example, registered at Companies House or has been disclosed in an annual report or shareholder circular, it is best to assume that the information has not been made available.

3.3.1 Omissions from the admission documents

Where the POS Regulations 1995 would allow information to be omitted, the Stock Exchange can also authorise a similar omission. There are also technical rules in Sch 1, para 10 allowing omission shares to be offered on a pre-emptive basis to some or all of the existing holders of shares, provided up-to-date equivalent information is otherwise available or the estimated value, nominal value (or failing this the accounting par value) of the shares is less than 10% of the number or value already admitted and up-to-date information required by the POS Regulations 1995 is available.

Where an issuer wishes to omit information from its admission document, the Stock Exchange may authorise this where the NOMAD has confirmed that: (a) the information is of minor importance only and would not influence the issuer's assets, liabilities, financial position, profits and losses and prospects; or (b) such disclosure would be seriously detrimental to the issue and its omission is unlikely to mislead investors.

The NOMAD is also required to confirm to the Stock Exchange that the relevant up-to-date information referred to is available.

3.4   NEW BUSINESS

Brief reference has been made above to the admission of new businesses to AIM. In practice, the market discourages start-ups from going onto the market, but rule 7 states that where the applicant's principal activity has not been independent and earning revenue for at least two years, all related parties and applicable employees must agree not to dispose of securities for a minimum of one year following the admission of those securities to the market. There are exceptions to this rule to allow for an intervening court order and also in the event of the death of a party affected by this rule or in the case of an acceptance of a take-over or an offer for the company which is applicable to all shareholders.

3.5   THE STOCK EXCHANGE RESPONSE

The Stock Exchange can make other responses in addition to confirming that a listing should proceed. It may, for example, under rule 8 impose special conditions or refuse an admission where the applicant has not complied with any special condition which it is felt appropriate and of which it has informed the applicant and its NOMAD. The Stock Exchange can also delay an admission for up to two business days where matters have been brought to its attention which could affect the applicant's appropriateness. In this case, the Stock Exchange will inform the applicant and its NOMAD and will also notify the Company Announcements Office (CAO) at the Stock Exchange that it has asked the applicant and its NOMAD to undertake further due diligence.

3.6   GENERAL DISCLOSURE PRINCIPLES

There is a general rule of promptness that any information that needs to be notified should be delivered to the CAO no later than that information may be published elsewhere. There is a general duty on each AIM company to make certain that reasonable care is taken to ensure that any information notified is not 'misleading, false or deceptive' and does not omit any relevant piece of information (rule 9).

Admission becomes effective only when the Stock Exchange issues a dealing notice to that effect (rule 6). Rule 10 of the AIM rules requires compulsory notification to the CAO 'without delay' of:

(i)   any new development which is not available to the general public concerning a financial condition of the company;

(ii)   its sphere of activity;

(iii)   the performance of its business; or

(iv)   its expectation of its performance;

which were it to be made public, may lead to a 'substantial movement' in its share price.

In addition, there is a general requirement upon the company to make a disclosure to the CAO 'without delay' of events set out in rule 16. This includes:

(i)   deals by directors;

(ii)   changes to any significant shareholding (see below);

(iii)   resignation, dismissal or appointment of any director;

(iv)   any change in its accounting reference date;

(v)   any material change between the actual trading performance or financial condition or profit forecast, estimate or projection included in the admission document or otherwise made to the public on its behalf;

(vi)   where there is a decision to make any payment with respect to AIM securities (in this case details of net amount payable together with the payment date and 'record date' (this is defined in the rules as the last date upon which investors must appear on the shareholder register in order to receive a benefit from the company)));

(vii)   where AIM securities are issued or cancelled, the reason for this; and

(viii) the resignation, dismissal or appointment by the company of its NOMAD or company broker.

The type of information to be provided under rule 15 where it involves directors or significant shareholders is set out in Schedule 5 and includes the following:

(i)   identity of the director or significant shareholder concerned;

(ii)   the date upon which disclosure was made to it;

(iii)   the date on which the event was effected, together with the price, amount and class of security involved;

(iv)   nature and extent of the director/significant shareholder's interest in the transaction; and

(v)   If this happens in a closed period (see further para **5.3** below), the date upon which the CAO was notified and upon which the Stock Exchange granted permission to deal (this is usually only to mitigate severe personal hardship).

3.7   PUBLICATION

Rule 3 of the AIM rules requires that the admission document must be published by making copies available free of charge to the public at an address within the UK specified in the document from the date of admission to trading on AIM and for not less than one month after that date.

The admission document will also appear on the company's file maintained by the Registrar of Companies. It is therefore permanently available for inspection by members of the general public.

3.8   CASE-LAW

An interesting summary of the law is presented in the Chancery Division judgment of Lightman J in the case of *Possfund Custodian Trustee v Diamond* [1996] 2 All ER 774. The action arose out of a company which had issued a prospectus in connection with a flotation of shares on the USM in April 1992. The company subsequently went into receivership and damages for deceit and negligence in relation to material misrepresentations contained in the prospectus of the company's financial position was brought. In his judgment, Lightman J felt it was debatable that the persons responsible for the issue of the company's share prospectuses owed a duty of care to and could be liable in damages at the instance of subsequent purchasers of that company's shares on the USM. Only if it could be established at the date of preparation and circulation of the original share prospectus that the defendants had intended to inform and encourage after-market purchasers could it be said that a duty of care existed. This case raises interesting implications, and judgment does seem persuasive. It is, however, only a High Court decision and therefore should be treated with some caution.

Chapter 4

RESPONSIBILITIES OF DIRECTORS AND OTHER PERSONS INVOLVED IN AN ADMISSION TO AIM

4.1 RESPONSIBILITIES UNDER THE POS REGULATIONS 1995

The POS Regulations 1995 contain a number of important provisions affecting the legal responsibilities which need to be noted and carefully respected in the preparation of a prospectus. Most, but not all, of the obligations in this respect are centred on the duties of directors.

Regulation 13 of the POS Regulations 1995 states that the persons responsible for a prospectus are:

(i)   the issuer of the securities to which the prospectus relates;

(ii)   for companies issuing securities, each person who is a director at the time when the prospectus is published;

(iii)   any other person who has allowed himself to be named and is named in the prospectus, who either becomes a director at the time of admission or at a future time;

(iv)   each person who has accepted responsibility for all or part of the prospectus;

(v)   the offeror of the securities where he is not the issuer and each director of that concern;

(vi)   any other person not set out above but who has authorised the contents or any part of the prospectus.

Where a director can show that a prospectus has been published without his knowledge or consent (and/or on becoming aware of its publication he gives reasonable public notice that it was not published with his knowledge or consent) he can avoid responsibility (reg 13(2)).

There is a limited exclusion introduced by the Public Offers of Securities (Amendment) Regulations 1999, SI 1999/734. From 10 May 1999, a person is deemed not responsible as an offeror of securities where the issuer is responsible and it was drawn up primarily by the issuer, and it is made clear that the offeror is only acting 'in association' with the issuer.

Where a person suffers loss as a result of an untrue or misleading statement in a prospectus or an omission from it of a matter which should have been included, the person or persons responsible for the prospectus are liable to pay compensation to make good such loss (reg 14).

There are certain exceptions to liability and these are set out in reg 15 of the POS Regulations 1995 so that, for example, a responsible person would not normally be liable if he can establish that, having made all reasonable enquiries, at the date of registration he reasonably believed the statement to be true and not misleading or that the matter omitted was properly omitted.

In certain limited circumstances, the NOMAD may be responsible for failure to register the prospectus with the Registrar of Companies or failure to properly publish the prospectus in accordance with reg 4 of the POS Regulations 1995 or failure to comply with the advertisement requirements set out in reg 12.

4.2   RESPONSIBILITIES UNDER THE AIM RULES

The AIM rules clearly vest full responsibility both collectively and individually on the directors of the issuing company for a strict compliance with the AIM rules. Rule 37 sets out sanctions which are available to the Stock Exchange against the issuer, its directors and nominated advisers for failure to comply with their respective obligations under the AIM admission rules.

4.2.1   *Directors' responsibilities*

Rule 27 requires the issuer to ensure that each of its directors accept full responsibility both as individuals and collectively for compliance with all Stock Exchange requirements. Each director must also make a full disclosure of information needed under rule 15 (directors' interests). The standard on each director is that compliance must be 'so far as that information is known to the director or could with reasonable diligence have been ascertained by that director'. Disclosure must be made within five business days following the day on which the relevant information becomes known to that director.

With reference to the model code, this should be adopted by a board resolution and the issuer is required to ensure compliance by the directors and relevant other employees with a code of dealing being required which is 'no less exacting' as that set out in the model code. The issuer is also obliged to ensure its directors obtain advice and guidance from the NOMAD concerning compliance and that all such advice and guidance is taken into account.

4.2.2   *Disclosure obligations on the issuer*

Since the replacement of Chapter 16 by the AIM rules there has been a slight but noticeable change of emphasis on the disclosure requirements. The fundamental base is now set out in rule 9 which requires notification of the company to be made to the CAO 'no later than it is published elsewhere'. All such information needs to be clearly stated and comprehensive. Other provisions, like in rule 10 (price sensitive information) and rule 15 (all other disclosures), refer to the need to disclose to the CAO 'without delay'.

The typical things which require disclosure include changes in financial conditions (this could be for the better or worse), activity, performance or expectations where if it made public is 'likely to lead to a substantial movement' in the price of its securities (rule 10), transactions of the substantial nature (rule 11), related party transactions (rule 11), reverse takeovers (rule 13) and miscellaneous items (directors' dealing, changes in significant shareholders, appointment or retirement of directors, material changes from financial data in admission document or which may otherwise have been made public, changes to quoted securities, a change to the NOMAD or broker (rule 15).

It is interesting to note what apparently does not need to be notified to the CAO. Negotiations being made by the company in itself does require disclosure. It is also clear that information of a confidential basis may be disclosed to the issuer's professional advisers and other third parties who need to know, for example, employees, government departments, Bank of England, Monopolies and Mergers Commission etc. Such disclosure can only be on the basis that the information cannot be used ('published elsewhere' – rule 9) until it has been made public.

4.2.3   Action against issuer

If the Stock Exchange considers that the issuer has contravened the AIM rules, it may do any of the following (rule 37):

(i)   fine the issuer;
(ii)   censure the issuer;
(iii)   publish the fact that the issuer has been fined or censured for failure to comply with the AIM rules; or
(iv)   discontinue the admission of the issued securities to trading.

The Stock Exchange may at any time require the issuer to provide it with such information in such form and within such time-limits (as the Stock Exchange may specify) and publish this information (rule 20). The Stock Exchange is entitled to disclose any information in its possession to cooperate with the regulation of financial services or law enforcement (this also extends to jurisdictions outside England) or where the Stock Exchange needs to discharge its proper duties and when it otherwise has the consent from whom it was obtained and the person to whom it relates (rule 21).

The issuer is required at all times to have a NOMAD and a company broker and where either ceases to act the Stock Exchange will suspend trading for the relevant security. If this failure is not remedied within one month, trading will be discontinued (rule 30). One of the overriding matters which is addressed by the AIM rules relates to the need for the maintenance of an orderly market. With this in mind, the Stock Exchange had wide powers of suspension (rule 35) of any AIM security where trading is not conducted in an orderly manner or if the Stock Exchange considers an AIM company may be in breach of the AIM rules. There are also grounds to protect the 'integrity and reputation of the market' or where it considers the investors require protection. If a suspension is not revoked within six months the admission is deemed cancelled. These very broad and somewhat general powers provide the Stock Exchange with considerable muscle.

If the issuer is fined, this must be disclosed in its audited accounts relating to the period in which the fine is imposed.

4.2.4   Appeals

Any decision taken by the Stock Exchange relating to the AIM rules can be appealed against to the Appeals Committee appointed by the Stock Exchange, which is composed of persons not employed by the Stock Exchange (rule 40).

4.3   GENERAL RESPONSIBILITIES OF DIRECTORS

The above summary of duties of a director deals only with those duties laid down expressly by the POS Regulations 1995 and the AIM rules. There are significant other obligations which, at common law and under the companies legislation, directors will need to respect. The scope of these duties is extensive and consideration is outside the ambit of this book. For a detailed summary, see the excellent book by Peter Loose, Michael Griffiths and David Impey, *The Company Director – Powers, Duties and Responsibilities* 8th edn (Jordans, 2000).

4.3.1   Misrepresentation

Under common law, if a person suffers loss through the reliance on a statement which is untrue or misleading, the law of contract or tort may provide an appropriate remedy.

It was really the case of *Hedley Byrne v Heller* [1964] AC 465 which established the duty of care principle from which the rules of misrepresentation are derived. So long as a person making a statement owes a duty of care to the person suffering loss in reliance on it, there would be a remedy for negligent misstatement. To establish such a duty of care there would need to be shown a special relationship whereby the person making the statement could be said to owe a duty of care to the person relying upon it. There have been a number of cases involving professional advisers and, in particular, the case of *Caparo Industries plc v Dickman* [1990] 2 AC 605 considered in depth the general duty of care owed by auditors.

In the early decision of *Peek v Gurney* (1873) LR 6 HL 377, the House of Lords considered the question of a fraudulent prospectus. Whilst clearly a remedy would lie where reliance was placed by purchasers for the relevant shares referred to in the prospectus, it could not apply to shares already on the market – the purchasers could not be said to have been induced to buy the new shares. The case of *Al-Nakib Investments (Jersey) Ltd v Longcroft* [1990] 1 WLR 1390 held that the persons putting their names into a prospectus owed such a duty to persons who would subscribe or purchase the shares in reliance on the information in that prospectus. In that case the duty was expressed to be owed to only those persons who had accepted the rights issue offer, but did not extend to purchasers of shares in the market since the court felt that they were too remote. This case should be compared with *Possfund Custodian Trustee Ltd v Diamond* [1996] 2 All ER 774.

An action will lie under the laws of contract for damages only where there is privity of contract (this legal concept in its most simplistic form, means that a contract can only be enforced by a party who is signatory to it). There have been a number of exceptions to this rule of contract law and most recently a new Act has been passed called the Contracts (Rights of Third Parties) Act 1999 which allows third parties, when they are expressly identified in a contract by name or as a member of a class or as answering to a particular description and the relevant contract confers a benefit on that person, to have the right to enforce the relevant term. (The effect of this new Act, which received Royal Assent and came into force on 11 November 1999, is difficult to predict, but it is suggested that the restricted nature of the need to confer benefit may limit its application in the case of a prospectus.) In the case of a prospectus this would not be sufficient to give rise to a cause of action for breach of contract unless an underlying contract letter or agreement could be shown referring to the prospectus. The courts' normal approach is to look upon statements in a prospectus as not being terms of a formal contract. However, under the Misrepresentation Act 1967 (for Scotland, the Law Reform (Miscellaneous Provisions) (Scotland) Act 1985, s 10) where there is an untrue or misleading statement or where there is a statement or omission which makes a prospectus misleading or untrue, there may be a right of action.

The remedies mentioned by the Misrepresentation Act 1967 are rescission of the contract and/or damages. The former will be lost where the subscriber or purchaser accepts the contract, for example through failing to act within a reasonable time of discovery of the position. This right would extend to only the original purchaser or subscriber and not anyone purchasing from that subscriber. A claim under the Misrepresentation Act 1967 would lie only against the issuer in an offer for subscription or against a vendor in an offer for sale due to the rules of privity of contract. There is a defence under the Act where the respondent can prove that he believed on reasonable grounds up to the time when the contract was made that the statement complained of was true.

4.3.2   *Who are directors?*

Since the obligations upon a director are so extensive, not just in general law but also, for the purposes of this book, for an admission to AIM, it is important to look at what may constitute directorship. It has a number of meanings as follows.

(i)   A person who has consented to be a director (either when the company was formed on Companies House Form 10 or subsequently on Form 288a) and has been appropriately appointed in accordance with the articles and has not at the relevant date been disqualified or resigned from that office. (A company will not be formed until Form 10 has been completed and filed with the Registrar of Companies. Form 288a should be filed within 14 days of the appointment.)

(ii)   Where there has been a defect in the appointment as director, s 285 of the Companies Act 1985 validates all acts 'of a director or manager' irrespective that a defect may afterwards be discovered in his appointment or qualification (s 292 of the Act sets out a procedure for the appointment of directors at a general meeting of a public limited company making a resolution void if carried out in contravention of this general principle; this will not, however, affect the validation already referred to under s 285).

(iii)   Shadow directors: s 741 of the Companies Act 1985 contains a definition of a director being 'any person occupying the position of a director by whatever name called' and goes on to define a 'shadow director' as being 'a person in accordance with whose directions or instructions the directors of a company are accustomed to act'. The section also expressly excludes a person from being a shadow director when the directors 'act on advice given by him in a professional capacity'.

The statutory definition of a shadow director would include any person with whom the board of directors is in regular consultation and upon whom they rely. For example, this might include a senior manager or consultant advising the board regularly or possibly a person assuming the role of a 'company doctor', who may be appointed by a company undergoing problems. What is clear is that directorship is not dependent upon whether a person may have signed a Form 288a consenting to be a director, but whether he assumes the role of a director de facto. With respect to the role of a NOMAD, it would ostensibly seem that the NOMAD is acting in his professional capacity. Each particular case would need to be scrutinised given its own particular characteristics, but a number of NOMAD agreements give rise to suspicion that the relationship could sometimes become too close. For example, should the NOMAD be entitled to attend all board meetings and receive notice of meetings as if he was a director and indeed obtain copies of minutes after that meeting? There would probably be no difficulty in the event that such attendance was limited to those meetings where matters being discussed may have material implications on the share price or the admission to AIM. Assuming that the NOMAD's representative limited his input at such meetings, accordingly it is suggested that it is unlikely that shadow directorship would be deemed to exist. The relationship between the NOMAD and the issuer is more extensively considered with respect to the agreement entered into between the two referred to in Chapter 6 at **6.10**. It is suggested that with respect to such an agreement there is some limitation set out in the agreement restricting the nominated adviser's role with regard to the day-to-day business of the company and expressly excluding areas outside his sphere of expertise.

4.4   THE COMPANY SECRETARY

Every company needs a company secretary. In smaller companies, frequently one of the directors will also assume this role, but for public companies it is usual to appoint a separate officer. Under s 286 of the Companies Act 1985, a public limited company needs a person with suitable knowledge and experience and the Act requires a person with a particular qualification (the class includes chartered and certified accountants, chartered secretaries and lawyers). The company secretary is usually considered to be an employee of a company and, although an officer, is not one bearing responsibility to the outside world for the acts or omissions of a company. There are no particular obligations on the company secretary under the AIM rules or the POS Regulations 1995, but under general company law being an officer of the company will make the company secretary potentially liable with the directors in particular circumstances, for example fines for the late filing of returns to the Registrar of Companies.

Chapter 5

CONTINUING STOCK EXCHANGE REQUIREMENTS

5.1 DISCLOSURE

The Stock Exchange has attempted to reduce the extensive disclosure and other continuing obligations imposed upon those companies with a full listing for those companies that are traded on AIM. The rules largely repeat requirements set out in the Traded Securities (Disclosure) Regulations 1994, SI 1994/188 which require the issuer to inform the public as soon as possible of any major new development in the issuer's sphere of activity which is not public knowledge and which may by virtue of its effect on the issuer's assets and liabilities or financial position or on the general course of its business, lead to a substantial movement in the price of that security. For example, a prospecting company which discovers unknown mineral reserves would be required to make an appropriate disclosure.

The Stock Exchange has the ability, however, to exempt the issuer from making a public disclosure if it is satisfied that such a disclosure would prejudice the legitimate interests of that issuer.

Where notification is required the issuer (normally this will be through the NOMAD) will, without delay (not being later than such information is published elsewhere – rule 9), need to give written notification to the CAO. Where notification relates to a substantial transaction (rule 11), the following details should be included (Schedule 4 to the AIM rules):

(i)   details of the transaction including the name of any company or business involved;

(ii)   description of the nature of the business concerned in the transaction or using net assets of the issuer, for example details of what the target does, its products, markets and location etc;

(iii)   the consideration which requires to be paid and how it may be satisfied. For example, if there is an acquisition it will clearly need to be stated how much has to be paid in cash for the business and whether there may be an earn-out or other form of deferred consideration;

(iv)   the value of the net assets affected by the transaction and the profits attributable to those net assets;

(v)   the benefits and other effects which the issuer may expect from the transaction;

(vi)   details of service contracts of new directors to be appointed as a result of the transaction;

(vii) if the transaction involves disposals how much will be derived and how will the sale proceeds be dealt with, is there any paper consideration such as shares or other securities as part of the consideration and how such paper will be dealt with;

(viii) a 'catch-all' provision requiring disclosure of any other information 'necessary' to investors in order that they can consider the effect of the transaction on the issuer.

The general rules of notification do not impinge upon an issuer which has only non-equity securities admitted to trading on AIM.

5.1.1 Substantial transactions

Whether or not a transaction constitutes a 'substantial transaction' is determined through the use of various ratio tests. There are six main tests (Schedule 3 to the AIM rules):

(i) The gross assets tests – the formula for this is:

$$\frac{\text{gross assets of the subject of the transaction}}{\text{gross assets of the AIM company}} \times 100\%$$

A detailed reading of the complexity of this rule is essential when such acquisitions or disposals are contemplated. In simplified shorthand, it is the ratio of gross assets of the subject of the transaction: the gross assets of the AIM company.

(ii) The profits test – the formula provided for this is:

$$\frac{\text{profits attributable to the assets of the subject of a transaction}}{\text{profits of the AIM company}} \times 100\%$$

Simplistically, this is the ratio of profits attributable to the assets of a transaction: the profits of the AIM company.

(iii) The turnover test – the formula for this is given as:

$$\frac{\text{turnover attributable to assets of the subject of the transaction}}{\text{turnover of the AIM company}} \times 100\%$$

This is the ratio of turnover attributable to the assets of a transaction to turnover of the AIM company.

(iv) The consideration test – the formula for this is:

$$\frac{\text{consideration}}{\text{the aggregate market value of all ordinary shares}} \times 100\%$$
$$\text{of the AIM company}$$

This is the ratio of the consideration: the aggregate market value of all ordinary shares of the AIM company.

(v) The gross capital test – the formula for this is:

$$\frac{\text{the gross capital of a company or business being acquired}}{\text{the gross capital of the AIM company}} \times 100\%$$

The ratio for this is gross capital of a company or business being acquired:

the gross capital of the issuer. In this respect the gross capital of the AIM company is ascertained by adding the aggregate market value of the AIM company's securities, all other liabilities other than current liabilities, but including minority interests and deferred taxation and any excess of current liabilities over current assets. The figures need to be ascertained from market values on the day prior to the announcement of the transaction.

(vi) The substitute test – if the above tests produce an anomalous result or a result which is inappropriate to the sphere of activity of the AIM company concerned, the Stock Exchange may (unless the transaction is concerned with a related part) ignore the calculation and substitute any other relevant indicator it chooses.

If any of the ratios show the company with a percentage ratio of 10% or more then there is a substantial transaction, details of which must be notified to the Stock Exchange under rule 11 of the AIM rules. Expressly excluded from this rule as being a substantial transaction would be one of a pure revenue nature done by the issuer in the ordinary course of its business, for example the buying and selling of property for a property development company, or where the transaction raises finance which does not involve the acquisition or disposal of any fixed asset of the issuer (or any subsidiary). Also excluded is a transaction where the issuer does not have any equity securities admitted on to AIM. There is, however, no additional requirement for the company to publish a circular to shareholders or require shareholders to give prior approval, unless the transaction amounts to a reverse takeover.

5.1.2 *Related party transactions*

A 'related party transaction' is determined by the same ratio tests as with respect to a substantial transaction above and affects an AIM company when it enters into a transaction with a related party. This is defined in the same way as for a fully listed company and includes substantial shareholders, directors, shadow directors and their associates. When the result is a percentage ratio of 5% or more then, again, an announcement is required containing, in addition to the information that would be required to be given for substantial transactions, details regarding the nature and extent of the interest of the related party. There is no requirement for shareholders' approval but notification must include a statement from the directors of the issuer (but not any involved as a related party) that in their opinion, having consulted the issuer's NOMAD, the terms of the proposed transaction are fair and reasonable for the shareholders of the issuer. If the percentage ratio is greater than 0.25% and there is a related party aspect this must be disclosed in the next annual report even if notification to the CAO is not needed.

5.1.3 *Aggregation*

Directors of AIM companies should also be aware of creeping aggregation of transactions (rule 14) which may make it necessary over a 12-month period to make a substantial transaction or related party announcement. This would be the case where the transactions:

(i)   are with the same or connected parties; or
(ii)   relate to the same assets of the company; or
(iii) together result in a change ('principal involvement') of the business activities of the issuer.

5.1.4 *Reverse takeovers*

A 'reverse takeover' (rule 13) occurs where an acquisition or series of acquisitions in a 12-month period exceeds 100% in any of the percentage ratios referred to above, or where the takeover would result in a fundamental change in the business, or in a change in board or voting control of the issuer. A 'reverse takeover' may also occur in the case of an investing company departing 'substantially' (not defined) from the investment strategy stated in its admission document. Where a proposed acquisition could involve a reverse takeover, the Stock Exchange will suspend the company's quotation on AIM (unless the target is another AIM company and an explanatory circular is available when notice is given to the CAO) and the company must:

(i)   send an explanatory circular to shareholders; and
(ii)   obtain prior approval in general meeting. Any agreement seeking to effect the transaction must be conditional upon such approval being obtained.

If shareholder approval is not forthcoming or the acquisition aborts, trading can recommence on AIM (unless other grounds exist to prevent this). If, however, the approval is given and the acquisition is completed, admission to AIM will be discontinued. In this case, if the company wishes to be re-admitted to AIM it will need to reapply in due course, under all the normal procedures which apply for a fresh application for admission.

5.2 PUBLICATION OF ACCOUNTS

All companies traded on AIM must publish audited accounts within six months of the year end and also publish a half yearly report within three months of the end of that relevant period. This subject is referred to in more detail in Chapter 8. Accounts must be notified to the CAO promptly. Any other document which is circulated by the AIM company to its members must also be available for public inspection and notified to the CAO.

5.3 RESTRICTIONS ON DEALS

Until recently, the Stock Exchange published a Model Code which applied to all companies admitted to AIM. If a company wished to adopt its own code it could do this so long as it was not less exacting than that published by the Stock Exchange. The intention of the Model Code was to prevent abuse of secrets and other insider information not otherwise known to the general public by the use of price-sensitive information for private gain. Although the Code did not impose criminal sanctions, it was quite likely that, where abuse occurred, there would be a potential for criminal sanctions which could be brought under the general law for insider dealing (see further, Part V of the Criminal Justice Act 1993).

The new provisions, which are very similar to the old Model Code, are incorporated principally in rule 19. The AIM company must ensure that its directors or applicable employees (these are largely employees who together with their family members have a holding or interest in 0.5% or more of securities issued by the AIM company) comply with the requirements. The principal provision is that such people may not deal in any of those securities during a closed period. This is defined as being the two months preceding the publication of the AIM company's annual results and the two months immediately preceding notification of a half-yearly report. If the company reports on a quarterly basis, the closed period also means one month immediately preceding notification of quarterly results. Other closed periods include any period when the company is in possession of 'unpublished price sensitive information' or at any time it becomes reasonably probable that the information will require to be formally notified to the CAO .

There is a specific exception where individuals have entered into a binding commitment prior to the AIM company entering into a closed period in circumstances where it was not thought reasonably foreseeable at the time that a closed period was likely to be relevant and that the commitment was notified to the CAO at the time it was made. If, therefore, the directors of the company, for example, think that they may need to sell shares as a result of a contract, they should prudently notify the CAO at the time the contract is entered into as a precaution against violation of this provision.

The Stock Exchange has discretion to allow a director or employee who is affected by the restrictions to sell their securities during a closed period in order to alleviate 'severe personal hardship'. These words should be interpreted literally, but the Stock Exchange is sympathetic in genuine cases.

There is a general duty upon AIM companies to provide the Stock Exchange with such information within such time as the Stock Exchange requires and this information can be published by the Stock Exchange if it so chooses (rule 20).

There is also a general right upon the Stock Exchange to disclose information for law enforcement or regulatory supervision of financial services or as part of its legal or regulatory functions (rule 21). In any other situation, it needs the consent of the person from whom the information was obtained and (where the person is different) the person to whom it relates (rule 21).

The recommendations of the Cadbury, Greenbury and Hampel Reports have been issued in the form of a combined code. There is no requirement for AIM companies to follow the code and indeed even less reason for a company in a foreign jurisdiction to do so, but it is frequently considered by advisers to be good practice.

5.4 THE COMBINED CODE

Against the background of corporate failures during the 1980s, it was felt that more needed to be done to support investors' confidence and, indeed, the stabilisation and promotion of UK companies generally. The first move in this direction was a committee formed under Sir Adrian Cadbury which was set up in May 1991 by the Stock Exchange, Financial Reporting Council and the accountancy profession to examine the financial aspects of corporate governance. The committee produced a draft report in May 1992 which was published in a definitive form at the end of 1992 having taken into account responses from various interest parties.

A second committee specifically devoted to directors' remuneration was established by the CBI in January 1995 under the chairmanship of Sir Richard Greenbury. This reported in July 1995 (The Greenbury Report). A third committee under the chairmanship of Sir Ronald Hampel was set up in November 1995 to review the implementation of the Cadbury and Greenbury Committees and also to look at the role of shareholders, auditors and directors generally. Its terms of reference were fairly broad and included an obligation to 'seek and promote' high standards of corporate governance in the interests of investor protection and in order to preserve and enhance the standing of companies listed on the Stock Exchange. The Hampel Committee reported on 28 January 1998 and largely endorsed the findings of the previous two committees and recommended that a single code be produced – now called The Combined Code of Practice which was issued in June 1998.

In September 1999, a further report was published called The Turnbull Report (which was produced by the Stock Exchange and the Institute of Chartered Accountants for England and Wales) for the purpose of providing guidance for internal control of listed companies to facilitate the implementation of the requirements of The Combined Code.

The Combined Code consists of a preamble, with two parts, the first part concentrates on principles of good governance which deals with: the role of directors, directors' remuneration, the company's relationship with shareholders and accountability and audit. There is a separate section dealing with institutional shareholders. The second part of the Code consists of The Code of Best Practice with very similar parts. A full account of the Code can be read in Appendix 4, but in particular the following should be noted.

–   The Combined Code is more than just a regurgitation of the three reports. It also includes a number of changes made by agreement following consultation.

–   The Stock Exchange is to introduce a requirement of listed companies to make a disclosure statement in two specific parts (how it applies the principles of the Combined Code – companies have a free hand to explain their governance policies and any special circumstances which have persuaded them to use a particular approach). The other part is a requirement for the company to confirm that it complies with the Combined Code's provisions or, if it does not, provide an explanation to its shareholders.

5.4.1   Principles of good governance

–   There should be an effective board in day-to-day control of the company which should be run by two key positions, namely the chairman and the chief executive officer (CEO). Each company should have a clear division

of responsibility between these two roles and no one individual should have an unfettered power to make decisions.
– Non-executive directors (including independent non-executive) are an important ingredient in maintaining a balance and no one director or small group of individuals should be able to dominate decision making.
– There should be a transparent and formal procedure for the appointment of new directors and for their re-election (which should at least be once every three years). The board should be supplied with such information of a form and quality appropriate to enable it to properly discharge its responsibilities.
– Directors' remuneration – this should be sufficient, but should avoid paying more than is necessary. The Combined Code suggests that a proportion of an executive director's remuneration should be linked to rewards for corporate/individual performance. The policy on executive remuneration and the fixing of such remuneration should be dealt with in a formal and transparent procedure with no director being involved in deciding his or her own remuneration. The remuneration policy should be set out in a company's annual return together with details of each director's remuneration.
– Dialogue with shareholders – when practical, there should be dialogue between companies and institutional directors, the board should also use the AGM as a method to communicate with private investors and encourage participation.
– Accountability and audit – there needs to be a balanced and understandable assessment of the company's position and prospects presented by the board which should also maintain a proper system of control to safeguard shareholder investment and company assets. Formal and transparent arrangements for financial reporting and internal control principles should be maintained with an appropriation relationship with the company's external auditors.
– Institutional shareholders – they have three main responsibilities, namely to make a responsible decision as to how to use their votes, be prepared where practical to enter into dialogue with companies and give due weight to all relevant factors drawn by the company to their attention when considering the company's governance arrangements and especially those relating to the board structure and composition.

5.4.2 Code of Best Practice

Unlike the rest of the Combined Code, the Code of Best Practice is set out through the use of 17 points of principle, each of which has an explanatory commentary. A number of the principles have been cited earlier in the Combined Code and in many instances it is a type of good practice which any well-established company might wish to adopt.

The board. The Code of Best Practice further examines how a board should be composed and what qualities directors should possess. It considers the role of the Chairman and CEO and how duties should be split between two senior officers. The non-executive directors should be people of calibre so that their views can carry 'significant weight' in the decision making. Non-executive directors should comprise not less than one-third of the board and the majority of non-executives should be independent of the management and free from any business or other relationship which could materially interfere with the exercise of their independent judgment.

For the appointment of new directors there should normally be a nomination committee to make recommendations to the board on all new appointments. The majority of this committee should be comprised of non-executive directors and the chairman should be either the chairman of the board or a non-executive director. The annual report would need to identify members of a nomination committee and its chairman.

Directors' remuneration should vest with a remuneration committee who should use comparable companies to assess the quantum of remuneration and directors' performance. Service agreements with directors should be for a maximum period of three years and a normal termination period but notice should not be longer than 12 months (these periods should be used as an objective by the board even if it cannot be instantly achieved). The remuneration committee should consist exclusively of non-executive directors who are independent of the management and free from business or other relationships which could materially interfere with the exercise of their independent judgment. Their names should be listed each year in the board's remuneration report to shareholders and it should form part of or be an annex to the company's annual report and accounts. The report should set out the company's policy on executive directors' pay and shareholders should be invited to approve any long-term incentive schemes.

The audit committee. In order for formal and transparent arrangements to be made for the publication of financial reporting and internal controls, an audit committee should be established consisting of at least three directors and all the non-executive directors, a majority of whom should be independent non-executive directors and be named in the report and accounts. The committee's duties are to review the scope and results of the audit and examine the cost-effectiveness, independence and objectivity of the auditors and also to examine the non-audit services which may be supplied by the auditors. These should be reviewed and represent value for money.

5.4.3   *The Turnbull Report*

The Turnbull Report emphasised the importance of internal control and risk management. The Report has been welcomed by a number of commentators who have noted that its compliance procedures are similar to those adopted in the US and elsewhere. There are four main parts to the Report:

(a)   maintenance of an appropriate system of internal control;
(a)   how best to retain an effective control;
(c)   a statement in the company's annual report on internal control;
(d)   an ongoing review of the need for an internal audit function.

The responsibility for these duties vests with the board of directors. It is a board which must establish guidelines for risk and control and ensure these guidelines effectively evolve. The Report did, however, acknowledge that control could only be 'reasonable, but not absolute' and in particular it would not be possible to provide protection with certainly against a company, for example, by failing to meet business objectives or failing to keep a check upon acts of negligence or fraud, breaches of law, etc.

Turnbull emphasises the evolving nature of internal control. The Report does identify that, at a minimum, the board should disclose that there is some ongoing process for 'identifying, evaluating and managing the significant risks faced by a company'.

The annual report and accounts should make some reference to internal control. Indeed, the Listing Rules require the board to disclose when it has failed to conduct a review of the effectiveness of the company's system of internal control. With respect to the internal audit function, Turnbull recommends that it be reviewed annually. The type of issues which should be examined by the board relate to specific issues, with such considerations including scale, diversity and complexity of activities carried out, the number of employees and cost-benefit considerations. Such considerations should also look at external trends like the markets and other external factors.

5.5 THE LISTING RULES

The Listing Rules now require listed companies in the UK to include in their annual report and accounts a statement regarding the extent or otherwise of their compliance with the Combined Code. A remuneration committee report to the shareholders is required to be included in the accounts, containing quite extensive disclosure of directors' compensation packages. Whilst these rules do not formally apply to an AIM company, it would seem sensible for such companies to include this information in their annual accounts.

5.6 ABI GUIDELINES AND GUIDANCE NOTES

In addition to the Combined Code, AIM companies should also bear in mind the guidelines and guidance notes produced by the ABI (a list of which is set out in Appendix 5).

A detailed discussion of the various guidelines is outside the ambit of this book, but guidelines have been issued on such diverse topics as share option schemes, shareholder resolutions on new share issues and pre-emption rights under ss 80 and 95 of the Companies Act 1985, the purchase by a company of its own shares, scrip dividends, the role and duties of directors, the responsibility of institutional shareholders and long-term remuneration for senior executives. There are also publications by the Pre-Emption Group concerning shareholders' pre-emptive rights setting out various pre-emption guidelines. Copies of all relevant guidelines are readily available from the ABI's office in London.

AIM companies should observe the rules set out in:

(a)   The City Code on Takeovers and Mergers; and
(b)   the Rules governing Substantial Acquisition of Shares.

A detailed review of these is not relevant to this book, but those involved with AIM companies need to be aware of the broad range of matters which they cover. The City Code sets out detailed procedural rules and restrictions governing all aspects of takeovers and mergers where the target company is publicly quoted.

The rules governing Substantial Acquisition of Shares apply whenever one company obtains control (with its associates if any) of 30% of the shares of another publicly quoted company – in these cases a bid for all the remaining shares at the same price will normally be required.

If transactions are contemplated which might involve these situations, or could lead to them, the directors of an AIM company should seek advice of their nominated adviser and broker immediately.

The ABI have not yet issued any releases dealing with the Pensions Act 1998 and SRI implications, but it is expected that guidelines will be issued in due course.

Chapter 6

COMPANY LAW COMPLIANCE, ANCILLARY AGREEMENTS AND DOCUMENTATION

6.1   INTRODUCTION

In the bringing of securities to the market through the Stock Exchange, whether AIM or full listing, a significant involvement by the solicitors acting for the company and for the nominated adviser will be necessary. The summary set out below is only an introduction but can be used as a checklist to the more substantial matters which will need to be addressed in any application for admission to AIM.

Paragraphs **6.2** to **6.8** inclusive are restricted to company law requirements for UK companies. A company incorporated outside the UK will need to conform with the requirements of the relevant jurisdiction in which it is established and local legal advice will be required to ensure that all necessary legal formalities have been complied with.

6.2   PUBLIC LIMITED COMPANY

The Companies Act 1985, s 1 defines a public company as being one which has a share capital and:

(i)   whose memorandum states that the company is a public company; and

(ii)   is one which was registered or re-registered as a public company under the 1985 Act or former Companies Acts. The main distinction is between a public company and a private one and consists of three major differences:

    (a)   the company's name must end with the words 'public limited company' (or its abbreviation plc) or if it is a Welsh company the Welsh equivalent 'cwmni cyfyngedig cyhoeddus' (or ccc);

    (b)   the company's memorandum needs to be in the required format as stated by the Companies (Tables A to F) Regulations 1985 or as near to it as the situation permits (Companies Act 1985, s 3(1)). The main distinction between the memorandum for a private and that for a public company is that there needs to be an additional clause for a public company stating that the company is a public company;

    (c)   the nominal value of the company's issued and allotted share capital must not be less than the authorised minimum (which can be varied by the Secretary of State under s 11 of the Companies Act 1985), but is presently £50,000. Under s 101 of the Companies Act 1985, a share may not be allotted unless at least one-quarter of nominal value and the whole of any premium on it has been paid.

A public limited company may either be formed for the purpose or more usually will be a private company first which has followed the procedures for re-registration as a public limited company.

6.2.1   *Formation of a public limited company*

The proper form of memorandum of association in the format set out by the Companies (Tables A to F) Regulations 1985 must be filed with the Registrar of Companies together with:

(i)   a set of articles of association. Whereas the Companies Act 1985 will for private companies apply Table A (which may or may not be amended by the company concerned) this will not be the case for a public company. Frequently, however, a public limited company will use a similar format to Table A, making amendments appropriate for the company's status;

(ii)   a statement of first directors and secretary with their signature consenting to act, and the situation of the registered office (Form 10);

(iii) a statutory declaration of compliance with the required formalities which will need either to be signed by a director or secretary of the relevant company or the solicitor engaged; and

(iv)   the statutory fee, which as at 1 January 2001 is £20.

No trade should be commenced before the relevant certificate confirming incorporation as a public limited company has been given by the Registrar of Companies. If the company fails to honour this, the company and its officers may be liable to a fine and, more importantly, if the company fails to comply with any obligation to third parties, the directors are jointly and severally liable to that third party.

In order to form a public company, it is also necessary to satisfy the Registrar of Companies that all the special plc requirements have been met. This is normally done by filing with the Registrar a duly completed Form 117 completed by the director or the secretary of the company stating that the nominal value of the company's allotted share capital is not less than the authorised minimum (see above) and giving the following information:

(a)   the amount paid up at the time of the application on the allotted share capital (which as stated above must be at least one-quarter of the nominal value and the whole premium);

(b)   the amount or estimated amount of preliminary expenses and the persons by whom these expenses have been paid or are payable; and

(c)   any amount or benefit paid or given or intended to be paid or given to the promoters of the company.

6.2.2   *Re-registration of a private company as a public limited company*

Re-registration requires in addition to the compliance with the minimum capital requirements for plc status, the passing of a special resolution (or written resolution signed by all shareholders) which should be sent to the

Registrar of Companies within 15 days of the date of the meeting proposing the resolution (or the date the last member signed by written resolution). A Form 43(3) also needs to be completed which is accompanied by:

(i)   a printed copy of the up-to-date articles and memorandum;

(ii)   a statement signed by the auditors that in their opinion the balance sheet shows net assets not less than the aggregate of called-up share capital and undistributable reserves; and

(iii)   a copy of the balance sheet (not more than seven months old) with an unqualified auditors' report. If there is a qualification the auditors would need to state that the qualification is not material for purposes of determining whether (at the balance sheet date) the net assets exceeded the aggregate of its called-up share capital and undistributable reserves.

The Form contains a statutory declaration confirming that all required procedures have been complied with and the share capital requirements have been satisfied.

6.3   CHANGE TO SHARE CAPITAL

Frequently, a company will need to carry out various changes to its share capital structure. For example, a company with 100 ordinary shares of £1 each may wish to subdivide those into 1,000 shares of 10p each or possibly 10,000 of 1p each. The advantage to the company in doing this is that, without increasing its authorised share capital, it creates a greater number of units which it can offer to investors.

The other common requirement for a company is that of increasing its authorised share capital. For example, the £100 company already referred to may wish to increase its share capital to £200,000 and it will do this by the creation of an additional 199,900 ordinary shares of £1 each. These shares would be expressed to rank pari passu in all respects with the existing ordinary shares of £1 each in the capital of the company to avoid the creation of any additional class of share.

The Companies Act 1985 requires that any subdivision of shares or increase in authorised share capital be approved by an ordinary resolution of the company (see **6.8**). When a company subdivides its share capital or increases its nominal capital it must under ss 122 and 123 respectively of the 1985 Act give notice of such subdivision or increase to the Registrar of Companies on the prescribed form (for a subdivision, this is Form G122 and for an increase of authorised share capital, Form G123). Form G122 must be sent to the Registrar so as to arrive within one month of the relevant resolution. Form G123 should be received by the Registrar within 15 days after the passing of the resolution. Sections 122(2) and 123(4) of the 1985 Act enable the Registrar to fine the company and every officer for contravention (including a daily default fine).

6.4 AUTHORITY TO ALLOT SHARES

Sections 80 and 80A of the Companies Act 1985 state that directors are not entitled to allot shares in the company or rights to subscribe for or convert into shares of a company unless they have been authorised by the company in general meeting in the form of an ordinary resolution, or by the company's articles of association. The relevant articles or resolution will need to state the maximum number of securities which can be issued under it and the date such authority will expire. This date should not be later than five years from the date of the relevant resolution or relevant change to the articles (in the case of those articles being in the form of the original articles it would date from the date of incorporation). This power to allot shares can be renewed by ordinary resolution for such period (up to five years).

It should be remembered that under s 88(2) of the 1985 Act, when a company makes an allotment of shares, it must within one month of that allotment deliver to the Registrar of Companies the prescribed form (Form 88(2)) stating the number and nominal amount of the shares comprised in the allotment, the names and addresses of the recipients and the full amount paid (if any) for each share. Section 88(5) of the 1985 Act states that where there is default in filing particulars with the Registrar every officer is liable to a fine and for continual contravention a daily default fine; but an application can be made to the court for relief under s 88(6), and relief may be given if default is accidental or it is just and equitable to do so.

6.5 PRE-EMPTIVE RIGHTS

The companies legislation incorporates principles to assist shareholders in the preservation of the proportion of the total equity that a shareholder may hold in a particular company. Such rights are normally referred to as pre-emptive rights. The Stock Exchange also lends weight to this principle (the Listing Rules, paras 9.18 to 9.20).

The basic rule is set out in s 89 of the Companies Act 1985, which provides that a company should not allot equity securities to anyone unless they are first offered on the same or more favourable terms to each person who already holds the relevant shares, as nearly as may be possible, in the same proportion as their existing holding (frequently referred to as pro rata). Section 90 sets out the procedure under which a pre-emptive offer is to be communicated, requiring that it must be made in writing and be open for acceptance for at least 21 days.

The statutory pre-emptive provisions referred to above are frequently disapplied by a company using the statutory exemptions set out in s 95 of the 1985 Act. This requires a special resolution (see further below).

The Listing Rules emphasise the need to respect the rights of existing shareholders stating they should be treated with equality. Rule 9.18 includes a pre-emption right allowing the company to disapply the requirements of s 89(1) under s 95 of the 1985 Act only for a fixed period of time which needs to be less than 15 months after the passing of the relevant special resolution.

If the relevant company is a subsidiary and it is its parent which has notified it of its wish to participate, any such authority to disapply the pre-emption rules must be limited to within 12 months of the relevant general meeting authorising this but this can be renewed by shareholders. In the voting the holding company needs to abstain.

In addition to the Listing Rules, note should be taken of the guidelines produced by the Investment Protection Committees of the ABI and the NAPF. The guidelines limit the amount of share capital a company can issue on a non-pre-emptive basis. The limits as at 30 September 2001 based on the most recent annual accounts are:

(i) 5% per annum of the issued ordinary share capital of a company; and
(ii) over a rolling three-year period, a cumulative limit of 7.5% of the issued ordinary share capital of a company.

The guidelines should be considered in detail before any disapplication of pre-emption to ensure compliance and, in particular, consideration will need to be given to the guidelines detailing discounts, the cumulative limits and monitoring provisions.

To clarify the position, the Stock Exchange in conjunction with the Investor Protection Committees in October 1987 made available a summary of their combined views.

For a public company wishing to issue shares on AIM, it becomes important to ensure that the statutory rights are appropriately excluded. This would normally be done by special resolution, the typical wording of which is:

> 'That the directors be and are hereby empowered in accordance with section 95 of the Companies Act 1985 ("the Act") to allot equity securities (as defined in section 94 of the Act) for cash pursuant to the authority conferred on them by [this should refer to the s 80 authority, see above] as if section 89(1) of the Act did not apply to such allotment provided that the power conferred by this resolution shall be limited to:
>
> (a) the allotment of equity securities by way of a rights issue or other pre-emptive offer in favour of the holder's ordinary shares in the capital of the Company where the equity securities respectively attributable to the interests of such holders are proportionate (as nearly as may be) to the respective number of ordinary shares in the capital of the company held by them on the record date for such allotment, subject only to such exclusions or other arrangements as the directors may consider necessary or expedient to deal with the fractional entitlements or legal or practical difficulties under the laws of or requirements of any recognised regulatory body in any territory or otherwise; and
>
> (b) the allotment (other than set out in (a) above) of equity securities up to an aggregate nominal value not exceeding £[   ];
>
> and so that this power, unless renewed or revoked, shall expire on the date falling 15 months after the date of the passing of this resolution or at the end of the next annual general meeting of the Company (whichever shall be the earlier) and so that all previous authorities of the directors pursuant to this said section 89 be and are hereby revoked.'

6.6   SHARE PREMIUM ACCOUNT

Section 130 of the Companies Act 1985 requires that an amount equal to the aggregate sum or value of premiums (ie the amount above the nominal value of shares paid to the company upon issue) shall be transferred to a 'share premium account' which effectively will be dealt with as if it was part of paid-up share capital. In respect of both the company and its annual accounts and reports, it is necessary to distinguish between share capital and share premium account.

The main use of the amount held by the share premium account would be to use it to write off the company's preliminary expenses and commissions on any issue of company shares. It can also be used for providing premiums that may be payable on redemption of debentures of the company, or in a capitalisation issue. This is the payment of a bonus by the issue of shares to existing shareholders of the company in proportion to each such shareholder's holding of shares (referred to frequently as a pro rata distribution).

6.7   PURCHASE BY A COMPANY OF ITS OWN SHARES

Sometimes a company making an application for admission to AIM will also want to take power to enable it in future to purchase its own shares. To make such a purchase it must be approved by shareholders (s 165) by a special resolution (s 164). For a public limited company the resolution needs to state the date the authority to purchase expires (within 18 months of the passing of that special resolution). A typical such resolution would take the following form:

> 'That the Company be and is hereby generally and unconditionally authorised, in accordance with Article [   ] of its Articles of Association and Chapter VII of the Companies Act 1985, to make market purchases (within the meaning of section 163 of the Companies Act 1985) on the Alternative Investment Market of the London Stock Exchange Limited ("SE") of [   ] ordinary shares in the capital of the company, provided that:
>
> (i)   no more than [   ] ordinary shares then in issue may be so acquired pursuant to such authority;
> (ii)   the minimum price which may be paid for ordinary shares is [par value] (exclusive of expenses);
> (iii)   the maximum price which may be paid for an ordinary share is an amount equal to 105% of the average of the middle market quotations for the ordinary share derived from the daily Official List of the SE during the period of 10 business days immediately preceding the day on which the relevant ordinary shares are contracted to be purchased (exclusive of expenses);
> (iv)   the authority hereby conferred shall expire at the conclusion of the next annual general meeting of the company; and
> (v)   the company may under the authority hereby conferred and prior to the expiry of that authority make a contract to purchase its own shares which will or may be executed wholly or partly after the expiry of that authority and may make a purchase of its own shares impursuant to any such contract.'

6.8 GENERAL MEETINGS AND RESOLUTIONS

In addition to the requirement for a company to hold an AGM within the first 18 months after incorporation and then at intervals not greater than 15 months, there is also a duty to convene extraordinary general meetings (more commonly referred to as general meetings) when the company requires to pass resolutions. There are also provisions in the Companies Act 1985 enabling minority shareholders to require meetings to be convened (see, generally, ss 170 and 368).

6.8.1 Notice

Where a special resolution is to be proposed at a general meeting (or AGM), at least 21 clear days' notice in writing must be given to each member. If only an ordinary resolution is to be proposed, 14 days' notice is sufficient. The notice must be given to a member personally or be sent to him at his registered address. Non-UK residents need to give a company a UK address for this purpose. Frequently, a company's articles of association will contain provisions excusing accidental omissions. However, for the prudent company secretary a notice should be sent out at least three days prior to the required minimum notice date.

The contents of the notice will specify the date, time and venue of the meeting and give full details of both the ordinary and special resolutions to be proposed (normally this will take the form of sending a copy of the relevant resolutions to be considered).

The notice will attach a form for the appointment of a proxy which will be in a two-way format: it will enable a member to appoint someone to act in his absence and vote for or against a resolution. In a public limited company, a proxy will usually have a right to attend the meeting and join in a demand for a poll. A proxy may only vote on a poll (unless the articles of association of the company specify otherwise).

6.8.2 Voting

The main purpose of a company's general meeting is the putting and passing of resolutions. For the purposes of the company administration required for an admission to AIM only two types of resolution are relevant – ordinary and special.

An ordinary resolution is one passed by simple majority of those voting and is always the resolution required unless another type is expressly required under the articles of the company or by the 1985 Act.

A special resolution is one passed by a three-quarters majority of those voting. Generally the 1985 Act requires a special resolution to be passed before any important constitutional change or measure likely to materially affect shareholders can be taken.

Voting at meetings will either be in person or by proxy (referred to above). Voting will usually be conducted on a show of hands with each person present having one vote. A poll is required for important decisions. The articles will often refer to what is required for holding a poll but (s 373) cannot exclude the right to demand a poll: nor can it make ineffective a demand by five or more members having a right to vote or by a member holding 10% of the total voting rights. If the articles are quiet as to the requirements for a poll, any member may demand a poll (*R v Wimbledon Local Board* (1882) 8 QBD 459). If there is a possibility that on the show of hands vote a misrepresentation of the feeling of the meeting can occur, it is the duty of the chairman of the meeting to exercise his right to demand a poll so as to reverse any such likelihood (see *Second Consolidated Trust v Ceylon Amalgamated Tea and Rubber Estates* [1943] 2 All ER 567). In practice, the nature of the resolutions to be put to the meeting to approve an application for admission to AIM are such as a chairman would automatically require a poll.

Copies signed by the chairman of the meeting of all special resolutions and certain ordinary resolutions (eg to increase the capital, or vary directors' authority to issue shares under s 80 of the Companies Act 1985) need to be forwarded to the Registrar of Companies within 15 days after they are passed for copying onto the company's file at Companies House (which is available for inspection by members of the public).

6.9   CORPORATE RESPONSIBILITY AND VERIFICATION NOTES

There is a high level of responsibility placed on the company and, in particular, on its board of directors who in law are collectively responsible for the day-to-day running of the company. The Stock Exchange has no practical involvement in the preparation and settling of prospectuses for AIM companies, or in the form applications take. It is for this reason that the nominated adviser and the company's officers will be most concerned to ensure that due diligence is at all times exercised and that the prospectus and all other submissions made to the Stock Exchange are accurate and unambiguous and contain no omissions and provide a true representation of the particulars that are required to be disclosed or which should be disclosed to give a full rounded picture. There is no one means of achieving this end, but one method which is commonly used is the preparation of verification notes.

The purpose of verification notes is to record formally the steps taken to ensure that the accuracy of all statements of fact and opinion set out in the admission document has been properly checked and that the admission document complies with the appropriate standards and contains the information required (eg by the POS Regulations 1995, the AIM rules etc). In particular, such notes should be designed to ensure that:

(i)   no statement is misleading in the form and context in which it is included;
(ii)   no material facts are omitted which make any statement of fact or opinion misleading; and
(iii) any implication which a reader may reasonably draw from any statement is true.

Verification notes will form the basis of direct responsibility and it is normal for the directors to be required by the nominated adviser to sign the notes acknowledging this responsibility.

The typical format of verification notes is a series of statements, each of which is required to be confirmed by the directors. The following are typical examples:

(a) that each director has read a proof of the document and is satisfied as to the accuracy of the information given and that there are no material facts or omissions which would make any statement misleading;

(b) that the NOMAD has been appointed to act for the company but that his duties and responsibilities are limited in the manner set out in a letter of engagement;

(c) confirmation that each director's details, experience and responsibilities are accurately stated in the document, for example 'please confirm and provide evidence that between August 1980 and April 1988 you were employed by [X Ltd] as sales director';

(d) details particular to the business concerned including its customers and trade connections etc, for example 'please confirm and provide evidence that [Y Ltd] is your company's largest single customer and has accounted for more than 25% of your sales in each of the last three financial years, and during the present year to date'.

In addition to the verification notes, there will usually be a responsibility statement signed by each of the directors addressed to the issuer and also the NOMAD. This will set out the ambit of a director's responsibility and authorise the release of the various documents and acknowledge:

(i) that it is the directors who are responsible for the information contained in the various documentation and that to the best knowledge and belief of the directors such information is true and does not omit anything likely to affect the import of that information. Such responsibility will be accepted by the directors on a joint and several basis;

(ii) that details of the directors' interests in any of the securities are correct and complete. A director will normally also undertake in the event of any changes to immediately notify the issuer and the NOMAD;

(iii) that the director will authorise that a copy of the letter be delivered to all appropriate bodies, for example the Stock Exchange, Panel on Takeovers and Mergers etc.

6.10 NOMAD AGREEMENT

The NOMAD agreement will normally be prepared by the solicitor acting for the NOMAD. Its purpose is to set out the terms under which a NOMAD (and broker if the same) are to act with respect to the admission of the issuer to AIM and also setting out its relationship after that admission. The provisions one would expect to see in an agreement of this nature include the following.

(1) *Appointment*

A provision concerning the appointment will cover such matters as the commencement date and what period of notice may be required to terminate the arrangement (normally this would be at least one month). Typically, it will also entitle the NOMAD to resign forthwith if in its opinion there is a material breach by either the company or its directors of the obligations in the agreement, the AIM rules or any warranties given.

(2)   *The fee structure and payment dates*

These would be set out in detail.

(3)   *General duties of the NOMAD*

Duties of the NOMAD include, for example, preparing the AIM application, providing such advice and guidance to the directors on an ad hoc basis concerning their responsibilities and obligations to ensure compliance by the company of the AIM rules, and releasing to the Stock Exchange on behalf of the company all information required to be announced under the AIM rules.

(4)   *Warranties*

Warranties are written promises which will frequently be required to be given by the company to the NOMAD. In the event that they are discovered to be wrong, a breach of such provisions would entitle the NOMAD to damages for breach of contract. Normally, a 'loss' would need to be proved by the NOMAD arising from the default, but if an indemnity exists this would effectively advance the NOMAD's ability to obtain payment. Detailed consideration of warranties and their scope and enforcement is outside the ambit of this book, but the following are examples of warranties a legal adviser would expect to see:

(i)   that the information contained in the admission document is true;
(ii)   that the directors' responsibilities for financial reporting procedures have been adhered to;
(iii)   that details of working capital requirements, and the financial information set out in the accounts (and possibly also the management accounts) are true and omit nothing of material importance;
(iv)   that the trading position as set out in the accounts and management accounts can be relied upon by the NOMAD and the directors have no knowledge of a circumstance which will or may make such a trading position inaccurate;
(v)   that the premises and plant and machinery etc of the company are insured for normal risk (or possibly more if circumstances so dictate);
(vi)   that the directors are not aware of any undisclosed bad or doubtful debts;
(vii)   that full, accurate and honest replies have been given to the statements set out in the verification notes;
(viii) that there is no litigation pending or expected.

Where exceptions exist to the numerous warranties, these are normally set out in a formal letter known as a 'disclosure letter'.

The level of liability for warranties will usually be limited by one or all of the following:

(a)   a minimum aggregate liability before a claim can be brought by the nominated adviser, for example £10,000;
(b)   a maximum aggregate liability after which those giving warranties are no longer liable, for example £1,000,000;
(c)   a date after which no action may be brought, ie the warranties would have to be deemed to have expired, for example 36 months.

For example, if a claim is brought within the warranty period, say in month 15 after the commencement of the warranty period for a claim amounting to £2.5m, and the company had to accept liability it would only be liable for £1m (its maximum limit) and no further actions for the balance or indeed any new liability under the warranties would be able to be made.

Liability to warranties is usually made jointly and severally on the company and each director (but possibly not on non-executive directors). This means that any one or more of that group can be held liable at law for the full amount of the liability to the NOMAD, and the NOMAD would be in a position to choose who it may wish to make a claim against. (However, this would not stop that person or persons from making a claim for contribution from the other persons providing a warranty.)

(5) *Indemnity clause*

An indemnity clause would include indemnifying the NOMAD and each of its directors, officers, employees and agents in the event that they suffer loss, liability, costs, claims, charges etc (including all legal expenses etc) for such things as a breach of the warranties or any other provision of the agreement or the admission document being found to be misleading or inaccurate etc.

(6) *Directors to comply with AIM rules*

There will be a requirement placed on directors to comply with the AIM rules by the NOMAD and the compliance with all proper and reasonable directions given by the NOMAD in compliance with the AIM rules. There will also be an obligation upon the company and its directors to inform the NOMAD when it becomes aware that the company may be in breach of the AIM rules. The NOMAD will sometimes require to be entitled to attend all board meetings of the issuing company and be reimbursed for its expenses in so doing. A provision of this nature is not probably in the NOMAD's best interests due to the possibility that this could amount to a shadow directorship of the company. It is suggested that the NOMAD's interests are best served by a provision requiring prior notice if the meeting is likely to consider matters of interest to the NOMAD and in this case give the NOMAD the right to attend and receive minutes etc.

(7) *Directors to obtain legal advice*

The NOMAD will frequently require the directors to obtain legal advice from the company's solicitor concerning their responsibility as a director of the company whose shares are to be traded on AIM.

(8) *General duties of the company*

The company will be expected to:

(i) comply promptly with proper and reasonable directions given by the NOMAD in respect of the AIM rules;

(ii) inform the NOMAD upon becoming aware of any breach by the company or any director of the AIM rules and to request the NOMAD's advice and guidance in all matters relevant to the company's compliance with the AIM rules;

(iii)   ensure that the company complies with the obligations imposed by the Stock Exchange in respect of a company admitted to AIM;

(iv)   give to the NOMAD one month's notice of all board meetings at the same time as it is given to the directors, together with details of the business to be considered at that meeting;

(v)   if requested, provide complete and accurate copies of papers and other information set before board meetings and of all board minutes;

(vi)   supply in compliance with the AIM rules audited consolidated annual accounts within six months of the end of the financial year to which they relate, and supply half year results within four months;

(vii) give confirmation that the working capital of the company and any subsidiary is sufficient for its present requirements.

(9)   *Announcements*

The NOMAD will frequently require that all announcements are to be agreed by it with the company in advance of release. The NOMAD may also require, subject to the requirements of the general law and the AIM rules, that the company should not make any public announcement or a circular etc which may be expected to have an effect on the attitude of investors or potential investors without consulting the adviser first. Similarly, the company may be required to give advance notice and discuss with the NOMAD any announcements of profits or losses or dividends or any other information which is likely to affect the character or value of the company and lead to substantial movements in the market price. Where matters require disclosure under the AIM rules the company will normally be expected to notify and consult with the NOMAD before making any announcement (and allow the NOMAD to comment upon all proofs of documents before being despatched).

(10)   *Share dealing provisions*

The model code contains restrictions as to dealings of shares by directors and these will frequently be repeated (or made more extensive) (see Chapter 5).

(11)   *Restrictive covenants*

Since the value of a share will be dependent upon the quality of management, the NOMAD will frequently require a restrictive covenant to be entered into by the existing management to discourage directors from leaving the company or, if they should so choose, to seek to minimise the likely damage which may be done to the company. The effect of a clause of this nature would depend upon how carefully the clause has been drafted. In particular, courts are unwilling to uphold clauses which they consider may act as an unreasonable restriction. The court would, however, take into account the added value that that director may have received by being party to the agreement, for example through admission to AIM. It may be that the NOMAD would seek for the board of directors and senior staff to enter into new service contracts dealing with these matters and complying with the recommendations of the Combined Code.

6.11 OTHER DOCUMENTS

The various advisers retained by the issuing company will be required to sign letters consenting to have their names incorporated in the admission document and accepting responsibility, for example where accounts have been prepared in previous years which are relied upon as part of the admission document, the accountant preparing those reports would be expected to take responsibility for them. Similarly, the solicitor acting for the issuer would need to confirm to the NOMAD that the admission document contains all information required by the AIM rules and complies with the relevant sections of the POS Regulations 1995.

6.12 REVISION OF DOCUMENTS

Obtaining admission to AIM is a major step in the life of any company and frequently it will be used as an opportunity (sometimes required by the nominated adviser) for a revision and updating of important administrative matters and legal documentation. For example:

(a)   new service contracts for senior personnel (as referred to above). Such a contract would normally re-examine the salary, notice provisions, share options and other benefits in kind;

(b)   review and updating of key man insurance or other insurances covering the management and possibly product liability, consequential loss cover and similar policies;

(c)   formalising and review of contracts with customers and suppliers;

(d)   review of, and taking steps to determine or settle disputes and litigation.

Chapter 7

COMPANY ACCOUNTS: REGULATIONS ON ADMISSION TO AIM

7.1 INTRODUCTION

The Stock Exchange launched AIM in 1995 with the objective of making it a market in which the participating companies were lightly regulated, with much responsibility for compliance with the rules, and investor protection generally, being devolved from the Stock Exchange to other parties; these include the nominated adviser (NOMAD) and a broker (or company broker, previously referred to as a nominated broker), who is directly responsible to the Stock Exchange under the AIM rules. Unlike the procedure for the Official List, there is no pre-vetting of AIM admissions; this is the responsibility of the NOMAD.

The method adopted by the Stock Exchange relies partly upon the fact that the company law, together with accounting and auditing standards, are in the most part applicable to all sizes and types of company (with a few exceptions which will be noted later), and these requirements should be sufficient to ensure that accounts are complete and reliable. It is also reasonable to believe that the NOMAD and broker will insist that a member of AIM also complies with their specific requests, when considered appropriate, to provide additional information in the accounts and to the market.

Whether the NOMAD or broker will in any particular case require such additional information or disclosure will, presumably, be determined by them in the light of the circumstances of the individual company concerned, and this introduces a degree of flexibility. For example, requests by the NOMAD and broker for additional disclosure may be more extensive or frequent for an AIM company with a large shareholder list and which has raised capital on the market, and less onerous for a smaller company, perhaps with only a short shareholder list of mainly family members, and which has not raised capital on the market. This concept of flexibility is in marked contrast to the very detailed regulations applied by the UK Listing Authority for full listings, particularly at the prospectus stage. Admission to AIM is based more upon disclosure rather than the detailed suitability criteria required for a full listing.

In the first years of AIM there were several high profile cases where, arguably, a lack of diligence by the appointed NOMAD resulted in a lack of disclosure by companies. However, at the time of writing, six years after the launch of AIM, NOMADs have adopted a more robust approach to AIM companies. This approach has removed much of the flexibility that was originally envisaged by the Stock Exchange, but gives comfort to investors and professional advisers alike over the quality of information provided on AIM quoted companies.

7.2   ACCOUNTING REQUIREMENTS PRIOR TO ADMISSION

The principal regulations concerning accounts, accounting matters and accountants are to be found in the POS Regulations 1995 (as amended by the POS (Amendment) Regulations 1999, which came into force on 10 May 1999), where the detail is principally in Sch 1, para 45, to which detailed reference should be made by anyone concerned to prepare the information correctly.

An AIM company must be 'duly incorporated or otherwise validly established according to the relevant laws of its place of incorporation or establishment'. Thus, an AIM company could be established anywhere in the world, but the rules go on to state that the company must publish accounts which are prepared 'in accordance with the issuer's national law and with United Kingdom Accounting Standards, International Accounting Standards or United States Accounting Standards'.

This flexibility has been utilised, with the AIM market as at August 2001 containing 597 companies of which 37 are registered overseas. It is conceivable that even a combination of UK, US or International Accounting Standards with the company legislation of the issuer's country of incorporation may not provide adequate disclosure or reliability of information, in the eyes of the NOMAD or broker. Those parties will have a responsibility, particularly at the stage of preparation of a prospectus, to satisfy themselves that enough reliable information is being made available to enable investors to judge the financial position and performance of the company. A NOMAD or broker whose advice on this (or indeed any other) significant matter is ignored appears to have no sanction against the company, except to resign. However, every AIM company has to retain a NOMAD and broker, and in practice if either resigns for reasons connected with inadequate or inaccurate disclosure of information, the company may find it difficult to replace them. Hence the tension that would arise between company and NOMAD or broker in these circumstances may well be in itself sufficient to ensure that an AIM company which wishes to retain its status on the market will take heed of the advice which they receive from these parties.

The POS Regulations 1995 even contemplate the possibility (in Sch 1, para 45(8)) that an issuer may not have been required to prepare accounts at all in the period up to its admission to the market. However, if such a case arises, the POS Regulations 1995 require that the prospectus includes an accountants' report which would include details of the 'profit or loss ... in respect of the period beginning with the date of its formation and ending on the latest practicable date before ... the offer ... and of its state of affairs at that date ...' and the reporting accountant must give a 'true and fair' opinion in that report. Although this appears to permit a single profit figure to be reported, for however long that period from incorporation to admission might be, it seems likely that in practice those responsible for the prospectus would require much more detail to be given of the timing of such profits over the period. Indeed, such information would probably fall to be required under the POS Regulations 1995 as being 'all such information as investors would reasonably require, and reasonably expect to find' (reg 9).

7.3 ACCOUNTING REQUIREMENTS ON ADMISSION

Broadly, the POS Regulations 1995 allow a company to include in its admission document either accounts for its last three years, precisely as previously provided to its shareholders, or an accountants' report covering those three years, by a person qualified to be an auditor, also known as a short form report. The provision allowing a candidate for admission simply to reproduce its accounts in the admission document is a significant relaxation in comparison with the requirements of the Listing Rules for fully listed companies, which require either a full accountants' report, or a comparative table of results, assets and liabilities to be prepared. It is likely to be useful for those candidates whose history over the three-year period has been straightforward, which have had no prior year adjustments or changes of accounting policy in that period, and which have not undergone a group reorganisation or restructuring in the period leading up to admission. Where any of those events have occurred, it is likely that a full accountants' report will be required.

If it is proposed to include in the admission document three years' audited accounts, the auditors have to be named, and have to accept responsibility for the accounts. This might be difficult, for example, if there has been a change of auditor, or if the audit firm is no longer practising, or for some other reason is unable or unwilling to provide the confirmation required; in these circumstances an accountants' report may be the only practical route to take.

The POS Regulations 1995 contain rules which differ in detail, but not in principle, depending on whether the candidate is a company incorporated in Great Britain, or not. The former case is dealt with first.

7.3.1 *British-incorporated company*

If a company incorporated in Great Britain chooses for its admission document the option of simply reproducing its annual accounts covering at least the last three years, then all that is needed in addition is:

(i) a statement by the directors that the accounts comply with the Companies Act 1985, and that they accept responsibility for them (or a statement why they are unable to say that, which seems a highly unlikely state of affairs in practice);

(ii) the name and address of the auditors, and copies of the auditors' reports, although presumably these will have already been included with the accounts;

(iii) a statement by the auditors that they consent to the inclusion of their reports in the document and accept responsibility for them, and a statement that they have not become aware since they originally made their audit reports of matters which affect the validity of those reports. This is significant in that it effectively extends the auditors' responsibility to considering the possible disclosure of post-balance-sheet events up to the date of the admission document itself, even though they might have signed off the original audit report some time previously. If the alternative route of preparing an accountants' report is chosen, which is likely to be so in all but the simplest of admission cases, then that report will be based upon the published annual accounts of the candidate covering at least the last three years. This report must be provided by a person qualified to act as an auditor (but need not be the actual auditor appointed by the company, but in this case the auditor must be named) and the reporting accountant would need to state that in his opinion the report gives a true and fair view of the state of affairs, profit and loss, cash flows and recognised gains and losses of the undertakings concerned. He will also need to state that he consents to the inclusion of the report in the document and accepts responsibility for it (or state why he is unable to make that confirmation, which in practice appears most unlikely to happen).

7.3.2 Non-British company

A company incorporated outside Great Britain also has the option of simply reproducing the last three years' annual accounts, or of providing an accountants' report. If the option of reproducing its annual accounts is chosen, then the POS Regulations 1995, Sch 1, para 45(2) requirements apply, which may be summarised as follows:

(i)   the company accounts for the last three years (and if it is a parent undertaking, its subsidiary undertakings' accounts as well) are to be reproduced;

(ii)   the document must state the name and address of the person responsible for the accounts. The term is not defined in the POS Regulations 1995, so presumably those responsible for the document will need to decide from the facts of the particular case who is the most appropriate person to accept this responsibility;

(iii)   a statement must be included by the person responsible for the accounts that the accounts have been properly prepared in accordance with the applicable law and that the person responsible accepts responsibility for them (or the unlikely statement as to why he is unable to make that statement);

(iv)   the document must give the names and addresses of the auditors of the accounts, and copies of their reports;

(v)   there must be included a statement of responsibility by the auditors in similar terms to that for a British company, as described above. However, para 45(5) acknowledges that the law applicable to an overseas company may not require its accounts to be audited, and therefore requires a prospectus to state whether or not the accounts have, in fact, been audited, if those circumstances apply.

If the non-British company adopts the alternative route of preparing an accountants' report, then the requirements are similar to those for a British company (see above) and are set out in full in para 45(2)(b).

7.3.3 Matters applicable to both British and overseas companies

There are at least three fairly common situations where an issuer may not have been required to produce audited accounts for the three-year period leading up to admission:

(i) it may be incorporated in a country where there is no requirement for audit of small, or any, company accounts, or indeed there may be no requirement to produce accounts in any format recognisable to a British investor; or

(ii) it may be a new start-up company seeking initial funds, or a company started within the three-year period; or

(iii) it may be a new parent company, which has just acquired or is about to acquire as subsidiary companies those trading operations which are the subject of the new group's business activity. It is quite common for the flotation vehicle to be a new public limited company, formed for the purpose with the most appropriate capital structure and nature, and without a past history. The businesses which are to become subsidiaries may have been private companies or may have been unincorporated businesses or divisions of larger companies, and thus unsuitable themselves as the listing vehicle.

In each of these cases, the provision of the POS Regulations 1995, Sch 1, para 45, and especially sub-paras (8), (9) and (9A), will need to be considered carefully to determine what historical accounting information will need to be included in the admission document, and in what form. It is likely that in every case an accountants' report will be required, covering the results and financial positions of all the businesses of the issuer's group for the three-year period up to a date within nine months before the issue date (or since those businesses commenced, if less than three years of trading have occurred). This may be on a consolidated basis, or may be provided in the form of separate information for each company; the precise form of the information and sources for it will need to be considered carefully by the reporting accountant, together with the directors and other advisers, at an early stage. In doing so, they will need to bear in mind the general prospectus rules that the information therein must be, in colloquial terms, complete, not misleading, and readily understandable.

The reporting accountant will have to report whether a true and fair view is given by the report of the state of affairs, profit and loss, cash-flows and recognised gains and losses of the undertakings concerned, and take responsibility for the report.

There are provisions which allow an issuer to omit from the admission document the excessive detail that might result if it were otherwise required to include both its consolidated group accounts and the separate accounts of itself and all its subsidiaries. These provisions are set out in para 45(3) and (4). There is no requirement to include in the prospectus accounts for financial years ended less than three months before the prospectus date (unless those accounts have already been prepared) (para 45(7)), but conversely where more than nine months have elapsed at the prospectus date since the end of the last financial year, then interim accounts are required (para 45(10)) that cover at least the first six months of the current financial period. There are also provisions in para 45(8) which deal with the unusual situation of an overseas issuer which has never been required to prepare accounts in its own jurisdiction, and in para 45(11) there is a requirement to include in the prospectus details of any interim accounts which an issuer may have published since its last financial year end.

There may be occasions when the information required by para 45(1) and (2) of Sch 1 would not by itself cover every subsidiary company in a group for the three-year period; for example, a subsidiary acquired 18 months before admission would only feature for the latter part of the three years. Originally, para 45(9) remedied this by requiring full information to be provided for *every* present subsidiary for *all* of the three-year period. However, this has been amended by the Public Offer of Securities (Amendments) Regulations 1999, SI 1999/734. This states that the information in respect of each present subsidiary is not required where 'the information is not reasonably necessary for the purpose of making an informed assessment of the issuer's assets and liabilities, financial position, profits and losses and prospects, or of the securities being offered'. This brings the POS Regulations 1995 into line with the requirements of the Listing Rules.

Conversely, there is no explicit requirement to include financial details or accounts for a company which is to become a subsidiary after the date of the prospectus, for example using funds raised at the admission for the purpose. However, if the proposed acquisition is of significant size or importance, details would be required to be disclosed under the general rule in the POS Regulations 1995, reg 9 'all such information as investors would reasonably require ... for the purpose of making an informed assessment of the ... financial position ... and prospects of the issuer'.

7.4   REPORTING ACCOUNTANTS' RESPONSIBILITIES

7.4.1   *Accountants' report (short form report)*

Whilst the POS Regulations 1995, Sch 1, para 45 contain the legal requirements to prepare and publish in the admission document an accountants' report, the law does not give significant detail about the content or format of such a report, nor how it should be prepared and presented. However, accountants have been preparing such reports for public company flotations for many years and the general structure, format and contents are well established by custom and precedent.

In preparing such a report, reference should be made to:

(i)   the 'Statement of Investment Circular (SIR) Reporting Standards 100 and 200' issued by the Auditing Practices Board in December 1997;
(ii)   the Listing Rules, especially Chapter 12, which, although not applicable to an AIM company, reflects accepted practice in this area; and
(iii)   previously published prospectuses for companies in similar circumstances.

Curiously, the POS Regulations 1995 do not refer to the possibility of 'adjustments' being necessary in preparing the figures to be published in the accountants' report, from the original accounting information on which the report is to be based. Such adjustments are commonly required in order for the accountants' report to give a true and fair view, for example to ensure consistency of accounting policies across the group and throughout the period, or to place transactions which were originally accounted for in the 'wrong' period into the correct period, with the benefit of hindsight. The Listing Rules contains detailed provisions for a 'Statement of Adjustments' to be prepared for every accountants' report (or a statement that no adjustments are required), for it to be approved by the UK Listing Authority and for it to be made available for public inspection. SIR 200 (Accountants' Reports on Historical Financial Information in Investment Circulars) confirms that adjustments of this type are permitted by the POS Regulations 1995, and recommends that reporting accountants make the adjustments necessary to provide a true and fair view, and goes on to say that 'it may be appropriate for a statement of adjustments to be made available for public inspection'. SIR 200 includes in its appendices useful examples of reports and letters typically required of reporting accountants.

The Auditing Practices Board intends to publish further SIRs covering topics such as profit forecasts and projections, working capital reports and comfort letters.

7.4.2 Long form report

The reporting accountants will also be instructed by the NOMAD to prepare a long form report which is an independent due diligence report on the company that covers all aspects of the company's activities. This is not published in the prospectus but is a private document addressed to the NOMAD, the directors of the company and the broker. In addition to detailed commentary on the historical financial results, it also contains information on financial controls, management and the company's products or services.

7.4.3 Financial reporting requirements

A UK Listing Authority requirement that is becoming best practice for AIM flotations relates to financial reporting requirements (rule 2.11 of the Listing Rules). The sponsor (or in the case of AIM, the NOMAD) must write to the UK Listing Authority (or, in the case of AIM, the Stock Exchange) to confirm that they are satisfied that the company has established procedures to provide 'a reasonable basis for the company to make proper judgements as to its financial position'. The reporting accountant will be required to produce a comfort letter on accounting systems and controls. The board of directors is also required to provide a written confirmation of financial reporting requirements.

7.5 OTHER REQUIREMENTS FOR THE ADMISSION DOCUMENT

7.5.1 The 'working capital statement'

In addition to the requirements outlined above which derive from the POS Regulations 1995, the AIM rules require (Schedule 2(b)) that the admission document must contain a statement by the company that, in their opinion, having made due and careful enquiry, the working capital available to the company and its group will be sufficient for their present requirements, that is for at least 12 months from the date of admission of its securities. This is more commonly referred to as the 'working capital statement' and is a most important part of any prospectus.

Before making the statement, the directors of the candidate company will need to prepare or obtain detailed profit and cash flow projections (which are not themselves published) at the least 12 months and more commonly 18 months or two years forward, and review this critically in conjunction with available funds and borrowing facilities, the assumptions underlying the forecast, its sensitivity to variations in those assumptions, and so on. The directors would also need to take into account the certainty or otherwise of resources available to the group, from the projected share issue if any, from bank and other borrowing facilities, and other sources. The company's NOMAD and broker would also normally enquire into the work done to support the working capital forecast, and the reporting accountants would be asked to review and comment upon the forecasts underlying the working capital statement, and discuss the results of their enquiries with the NOMAD, broker and directors.

7.5.2   *Information accompanying profit forecast*

The AIM rules also contain (Schedule 2(c)) requirements to publish within the admission document certain information if the document contains any profit forecast, estimate or projection. It should be stressed that there is no *requirement* involved for an admission document to contain such a forecast and, indeed, because the requirements attaching to the forecast are onerous, it is sometimes preferable on the grounds of simplicity and cost to avoid making public any such forecast of future results. If a forecast is to be included in the document, very careful consideration needs to be given by the directors and all their advisers to the nature of the forecast, the amounts to be quoted, and the period of time to which the forecast will relate. The rules require that any forecast must be accompanied by a statement of the principal assumptions upon which it is based, a statement by the issuer that the forecast has been made after due and careful enquiry by him, and a report by the auditors or reporting accountants on the forecast. This latter report within the admission document is limited to a statement that the forecast has been 'properly compiled on the basis stated and . . . is presented on a basis consistent with the accounting policies of the issuer'.

Whilst this statement for inclusion in the admission document appears somewhat limited in its scope, it should be stressed that the work involved on the part of the auditors or reporting accountants, in conjunction with the other advisers, in satisfying themselves that a profit forecast can properly be included in an admission document, is very extensive.

7.5.3   *Pro-forma financial information*

In certain circumstances, it may be appropriate to include pro-forma financial information in a form similar to that provided for in rules 12.28 to 12.35 of the Listing Rules. Such information is not an AIM requirement but if such information is included in a prospectus it is considered best practice for the reporting accountant to report publicly in the form required by the Listing Rules. The pro-forma financial information must provide investors with information about the impact of the transaction on the subject of the document by illustrating how that transaction might have affected the financial information presented in the document, had the transaction been undertaken at the commencement of the period being reported on or, in the case of a pro-forma balance sheet or net asset statement, at the date reported. The pro-forma financial information must not be misleading, must assist investors in analysing the future prospects of the issuer and must include all appropriate accounting adjustments (as permitted by rule 12.34 of the Listing Rules) of which the issuer is aware.

7.5.4   Statement of indebtedness

Although not required by the AIM rules or, since January 2000 in most cases by the Listing Rules, it is still considered best practice to include a statement of indebtedness. This gives details of the company's total debts, including term loans, overdrafts and hire purchase as at a date no more than 42 days prior to the date of publication of the prospectus. The reporting accountant will be required to confirm the indebtedness figure by obtaining written confirmation from third party lenders.

7.5.5   Other responsibilities of the reporting accountant

The reporting accountant is also required to provide the following letters addressed to the company directors, NOMAD and broker.

(i) Letter of consent

This confirms that the reporting accountants consent to the short form report being included in the prospectus and they accept responsibility for the report.

(ii) Confirmation of taxation information

This letter confirms that the information in the prospectus relating to taxation, the Enterprise Investment Scheme (EIS), Venture Capital Trusts and other information has been reviewed by the reporting accountants and is, in their opinion, correct.

(iii) Confirmation of financial information in the prospectus

The reporting accountant is required to review the financial information in each part of the prospectus and ensure that it is consistent with that disclosed in the accountants' report.

7.5.6   Information to be complete and comprehensible

It should be mentioned that reg 8(2) of the POS Regulations 1995 states that if any particular information is required by the regulations to be included in the prospectus but is inappropriate to that particular issuer, then the requirement is replaced by a requirement to include equivalent information, or if there is no equivalent information then the requirement shall not apply. The following paragraph requires information (of all types) in the prospectus to be presented in 'as easily analysable and comprehensible a form as possible'.

There is a general requirement in reg 9(1) of the POS Regulations 1995 to the effect that a prospectus shall 'contain all such information as investors would reasonably require, and reasonably expect to find there, for the purpose of making an informed assessment of ... the assets and liabilities, financial position, profits and losses, and prospects of the issuer'. This general and overriding requirement, which carries the force of law, is one which should be carefully considered, by all those involved in preparing an admission document, towards the end of the process of preparation. In colloquial terms, those responsible should stand back from the detail, consider all they know about the issuer and ask themselves generally whether a potential investor who reads the prospectus and nothing else, will by so doing find all the information that he would reasonably expect, and find it both comprehensible and easily analysable. They should also pose for themselves the rather difficult question as to whether there is information which *should* be in the draft prospectus but is at present missing.

7.5.7   Exceptions

The previous paragraphs have considered factors which must be included in an admission document. On the other hand, reg 11 of the POS Regulations 1995 contains certain exceptions from what would otherwise be required to be included in a prospectus of this type. The Treasury or Secretary of State may authorise omission of information which it would be contrary to the public interest to disclose, and, under reg 11(3), the Stock Exchange may authorise omission of information which is of minor importance, or where disclosure would be seriously detrimental to the issuer, if its omission would not be likely to mislead investors. In practice, it is likely that obtaining the benefit of these exceptions would be difficult to achieve, and therefore if an issuer contemplates taking advantage of these exceptions, it would be wise to make an early approach to the appropriate authority for permission.

Chapter 8

COMPANY ACCOUNTS: CONTINUING REQUIREMENTS FOLLOWING ADMISSION

8.1 INTRODUCTION

Following admission to AIM, the company will be required to produce full annual accounts and a half-yearly report in the normal way, in compliance with its own constitution, national law and one of the three alternative accounting standards regimes.

Under UK company law, private companies which fall within the criteria defining 'small' and 'medium-sized' companies are permitted to file with the Registrar of Companies abbreviated accounts, which do not include all the information demanded by company law and accounting standards for the 'full' accounts. Some companies, which meet the criteria for, particularly, medium-sized status, are in fact large enough for the AIM market, and indeed some companies of that size are on the market already. They have, however, converted to plc status, and from that point onwards are no longer permitted to file abbreviated accounts. Such a company will have to include within its prospectus, or base the accountants' report in its prospectus on, its full unabbreviated annual accounts for previous years, in the form that they were supplied to its shareholders, rather than the abbreviated accounts which may have been filed with the Registrar of Companies.

8.2 SOURCES OF REGULATION AND RECOMMENDED PRACTICE

In relation to periodic accounts to be prepared by an AIM company, these requirements are to be found by reference to:

(i) the 'national law' of the company's country of incorporation;
(ii) UK Accounting Standards or International Accounting Standards or US Accounting Standards;
(iii) Urgent Issues Task Force (UITF) Pronouncements;
(iv) AIM admission rules (essentially the only requirements here are to publish annual audited accounts within six months of the year end and a half-yearly unaudited report within three months of that period end); and
(v) the company's own regulations, for example its articles of association if a UK company, or similar constitution document in other cases.

In addition, there may well be encouragement from advisers, auditors or others for AIM companies to comply with the Principles of Good Governance and

Code of Best Practice published by the Committee on Corporate Governance, appended to the Listing Rules (the Combined Code).

All these regulatory requirements and recommendations are examined more fully in the following paragraphs.

8.3 NATIONAL LAW

As mentioned earlier, a company admitted to AIM may be incorporated anywhere in the world and its accounts will need to be prepared in accordance with the law of that country relevant to the company. In the UK, this means of course the Companies Acts and regulations made by statutory instrument relating to them, and in any other case detailed reference would need to be made to the law of that country. It is well known that accounting requirements set by national laws around the world vary considerably, from the extreme prescriptive regime in some countries to almost no rules at all in other countries.

The variety of accounting methods and disclosures which might result from the variety in accounting requirements is, however, greatly reduced by the requirement of the Stock Exchange that every AIM company must prepare its accounts for publication in accordance with acceptable accounting standards. These may be either UK Accounting Standards issued by the Accounting Standards Board, International Accounting Standards issued by the International Accounting Standards Committee, or US Accounting Standards. A company incorporated either in the UK or the USA must presumably follow UK or US standards respectively, but companies incorporated in other countries would appear to have a choice between one of these three regimes.

In preparing a company for admission to AIM, and during the process of preparing the admission document which will incorporate either three years' accounts or an accountant's report, it is clear that a decision would be reached as to which of the three alternative sets of standards would be complied with at that stage, and it would be expected that the company would continue to comply with that set of standards in respect of its annual and half-yearly interim accounts.

A detailed comparison of these three sets of accounting standards is beyond the scope of this book; it would perhaps be fair to say in general terms that the International Accounting Standards are the most flexible, and give the most scope for interpretation. Compliance with UK Accounting Standards is somewhat more onerous and, in almost all respects, a company which complied with UK Accounting Standards would also find that it fell within International Accounting Standards.

US Accounting Standards are considerably more prescriptive and, in several respects, differ significantly from UK Accounting Standards. For example, US GAAP (Generally Accepted Accounting Principles) permit the use of last-in, first-out methods for arriving at the cost of stock, whereas this method is not permitted under UK Accounting Standards.

Whichever set of standards is adopted at the outset as the regime for a particular AIM company, it will of course be necessary for the company to adopt any new standards as they are brought into effect by the appropriate body. In choosing the appropriate set of standards to adopt and follow (where a choice exists), a company's directors should have some regard to the expectations of the majority of its shareholders; for example, a 'high-tech' company with significant numbers of US-based investors might well choose to follow US Accounting Standards, even if it were incorporated in a non-US dollar territory.

Finally, whilst there appears to be nothing in the regulations to prevent a company switching from one set of accounting standards to another, this would presumably be unusual, would require explanation, and probably a prior year adjustment in the accounts of the year of change to reflect the adoption of different standards. It is likely that this course of action would follow only a very significant change in the nature of the company's operations, or perhaps a change in the domicile of its main base.

8.4 ANNUAL AND INTERIM REPORTS

The AIM rules require an AIM company to publish its annual audited accounts within six months of the end of the financial period, to notify the CAO of the publication of those accounts and to include in them the name and address of the nominated adviser and the nominated broker. The rules also require an AIM company to prepare a half-yearly report within three months of the end of the relevant period and send a copy to the CAO. If the company changes its accounting reference date, the effect of which is to extend its accounting period to more than 14 months, further interim reports must be prepared for each subsequent six-month period expiring prior to the new accounting reference date. There are no specific requirements as to the contents of the half-yearly report and no requirement to send the interim report to the shareholders or place it as an advertisement in a national newspaper, which are the requirements applicable to a fully listed company. It would seem sensible, in the interests of good shareholder relationships, for an AIM company to adopt one of those methods of communicating the results to its shareholders, even in the absence of a requirement so to do. As to the contents of the half-yearly report, this is left to the discretion of the directors of the company. It is suggested that the very basic requirements of the Listing Rules applicable to a listed company should be the bare minimum for an AIM company, ie a summarised profit and loss account for the period and an explanatory statement from the directors.

Current practice in relation to fully listed companies has moved significantly in recent years following the issue in September 1997 of the Accounting Standards Board's non-mandatory statement 'Interim Reports'. It is now common for such companies to include interim balance sheets and cash flow statements in summary form, with comparative figures for all financial information, together with rather more explanatory text than was the case a few years ago. The experience of the authors is that AIM companies are coming under increasing pressure from shareholders to follow this trend.

As with a fully listed company, there is no requirement for the interim report to be audited, although there has been considerable informal pressure to that end. The Cadbury Report on corporate governance recommended both the expansion of information within interim reports and that interim reports should be 'reviewed' by the auditors, and in November 1993 the Auditing Practices Board issued a bulletin on the subject of the review of interim financial information. This was followed by the issue of a supplementary bulletin in June 1998, although both were superseded by a new bulletin issued in July 1999. Many listed companies have adopted the recommendations and instruct their auditors to review their interim reports before publication and, in many of those cases, a review report provided by the auditors is published with the interim figures. It would clearly not be inappropriate for AIM companies to also follow these trends.

The Accounting Standards Board (ASB) issued a non-mandatory statement on preliminary announcements of results in July 1998. The statement encourages companies to issue their preliminary announcements of annual results within 60 days of the year end and the full report and accounts as soon as practicable thereafter. Fully listed companies are required to issue a preliminary statement of results by the Listing Rules, but there is no such requirement for an AIM company. Many AIM companies do, however, follow this procedure as a matter of practice, although it is likely that the ASB's 60-day target will prove ambitious for some companies. An AIM company is required by rule 15 to notify the CAO without delay of any decision to pay a dividend or make a distribution which, in the case of final dividends for financial years, is likely to coincide with the approval by the board of the results for the year as a whole.

8.5   ACCOUNTING AND REPORTING 'RECOMMENDATIONS'

There have in recent years been a multitude of pronouncements and exhortations relating to accounting matters and accounts disclosures, made by a number of bodies in the UK. These carry varying degrees of authority, from those which it would be most unwise for any public company to ignore, to those which even some listed companies do not feel it is necessary to follow. The following paragraphs describe the principal groups of these pronouncements.

8.5.1   *Urgent Issues Task Force Abstracts*

The Urgent Issues Task Force (UITF) is a committee of the ASB which was established with the aim of avoiding the development of unsatisfactory or conflicting interpretations of law or accounting standards. As the name implies, it is charged with responding rapidly when matters of concern are referred to it, or observed by it, in the development of accounting and reporting practice amongst public interest companies. Whilst its pronouncements, published in the form of 'abstracts', do not have the authority of Accounting Standards, the degree of difference appears marginal. This is achieved by putting the onus on individual members of the accountancy bodies if they are involved in either the preparation or publication of company accounts, or auditing or reporting on them, to ensure that the relevance of a UITF pronouncement to a particular set of accounts is well understood by those responsible for the accounts. They must use their best endeavours to ensure that UITF pronouncements are followed or, if not, that the accounts adequately disclose any significant departures, and those individual members could, it appears, be subject to disciplinary procedures by their professional bodies if they are unable to justify their action or lack of action in relation to a failure to comply with a UITF abstract by a company with which they are associated. Thus, it seems to the authors that UITF pronouncements carry virtually the same authority as Accounting Standards for practical purposes.

By June 2001, 30 UITF abstracts had been issued, of which 11 have subsequently been withdrawn and two revised. Because they are intended to deal quickly with developing matters, it is expected that in some cases the recommendations of UITF abstracts will be incorporated within the relevant Accounting Standards in due course. For example, UITF abstract 16, 'Income and expenses subject to non-standard rates of tax', has now been superseded by Financial Reporting Standard 16 'Current tax'. Some UITF abstracts are on specialised subjects, such as 'The Acquisition of a Lloyd's Business', but others are of much wider interest, for example website development costs and the manner of presentation of long-term debtors in balance sheets.

In summary, it is believed that an AIM company which prepares its accounts under UK Accounting Standards should regard UITF abstracts as carrying virtually the same authority as those Standards and should comply with them in all normal circumstances.

8.5.2   *Exposure drafts of Accounting Standards*

It is normal practice for proposed Accounting Standards to be introduced first as exposure drafts for public discussion and comment. Some exposure drafts are relatively uncontroversial, represent a codification of currently accepted best practice and are likely to proceed to the status of a full Standard without major change. However, such cases are becoming more rare as most of the easier subjects for incorporation into Accounting Standards have been covered.

At the time of writing, there is only one financial reporting exposure draft in issue, FRED 22, which deals with proposed revisions to FRS 3, 'Reporting Financial Performance'. This may be expected to result in an amended accounting standard in due course. Discussion papers have been issued on a number of topics, such as leases, and FREDs on these topics may be expected to follow.

Those responsible for the accounts of companies whose shares are publicly traded, on AIM or any other market, should consider the likely impact of exposure drafts as they are issued, and consider whether or not they should adopt recommendations made by exposure drafts on accounting matters before they become full Standards. Even if it is decided not to adopt proposals made in exposure drafts at that stage, early consideration can be useful in pointing the way in which regulation is likely to lead and the company can make appropriate changes to its way of doing business or internal procedures in good time. For example, the proposals relating to provisions which were contained in FRED 14, issued in June 1997, are likely to have led to some modification of companies' attitudes towards provisions before Financial Reporting Standard (FRS) 12 took effect in March 1999.

Thus, in summary, exposure drafts carry no formal weight, but they do give warning to the directors of AIM companies of the likely direction of Accounting Standards development and they also give an opportunity for public comment and debate before the matter in question is settled.

8.5.3   Statements of Recommended Practice

Statements of Recommended Practice (SORPs) may be developed and issued by the ASB, or developed and issued, after the ASB's approval, by representative groups from industry or commerce. They generally deal with subjects which are too specialised to necessitate the issue of an Accounting Standard on the subject and they are only issued if their recommendations take account of the principles laid down in Accounting Standards.

At the time of writing, the only SORPs which are likely to be relevant to AIM companies are those relating to the banking and insurance industries and oil and gas exploration development and production businesses. An AIM company operating in these sectors, or any sector for which a SORP might be issued in the future, would be expected to be aware of and to follow the recommendations applicable to it.

8.5.4   The Combined Code

The Combined Code was published in June 1998, following the report of the Hampel Committee on Corporate Governance. The Code is derived both from that report and from the earlier Cadbury Report on the Financial Aspects of Corporate Governance (December 1992) and Greenbury Report on directors' remuneration (July 1995). The Combined Code is now appended to the Listing Rules.

An AIM company is not required in a strict sense to comply with the recommendations of the Combined Code. However, the AIM market has attracted, and no doubt will continue to attract, a wide range of types and sizes of companies, whose boards of directors will also have a wide range of different aspirations for their companies. There will be some, perhaps a sizeable proportion, who will be anxious to project themselves and their companies as good examples of corporate responsibility and, as part of that process, they will seek to model their companies and their actions on those examples of best practice as are to be found in large and well-managed companies listed on the main market of the Stock Exchange. It is imagined that this would be particularly so for those AIM companies which have raised fresh capital on joining the AIM market, or who have ambitions to raise further capital through share issues or rights issues on the market, those which might have ambitions to use their own shares as consideration for the acquisition of other companies and those which have ambitions towards a full listing on the main Stock Exchange market in due course.

In all those cases, it would be eminently sensible for the company and its directors to adopt and follow from an early stage all those recommendations concerning corporate governance which are widely accepted by fully listed companies, and no doubt they will be under some pressure from their NOMADs and brokers to follow this route.

The subjects covered in the Combined Code include the composition, duties, responsibilities and remuneration of the board of directors of a public company, including the duties and responsibilities of non-executive directors. It recommends that companies should set up a remuneration committee, made up wholly of non-executive directors independent of management, to determine executive directors' pay and an audit committee of non-executive directors to keep under review the relationship between the auditors and the company and to deal with issues of concern to the auditors. There are recommendations which state that the board should meet regularly and exercise direction and control over the company without any one individual having unfettered powers of decision. There are also recommendations concerning the board's duty to present the company's position in the accounts in a balanced and understandable fashion and to specifically include in the accounts a statement of their own responsibilities concerning accounting matters.

On directors' remuneration, the Combined Code's principle is that 'levels of remuneration should be sufficient to attract and retain the directors needed to run the company successfully, but companies should avoid paying more than is necessary for this purpose. A proportion of executive directors' remuneration should be structured so as to link rewards to corporate and individual performance'. It is suggested that the performance-related elements of remuneration should form a significant proportion of the total remuneration package of executive directors, both to align their interests with those of shareholders and to encourage the directors to perform at the highest levels. Guidance is also given on notice periods, which the Combined Code states should generally not be greater than one year, and compensation payments in cases of early termination of contracts.

The Combined Code also recommends that the board should report to the shareholders each year on remuneration, including a full analysis of each director's emoluments which specifies salary, benefits in kind, bonuses, long-term incentives (including share options) and pension entitlements. The company's remuneration policy should also be stated.

The effect of the Combined Code's proposals on directors' remuneration (and the earlier Greenbury Committee proposals on which they are based) has been to extend considerably the disclosure in listed company accounts, which had previously only provided the brief summary of directors' remuneration required by company law.

One of the provisions of the Combined Code which generated considerable discussion at the time of its issue was its recommendation that the directors should, at least annually, conduct a review of the company's system of internal control and report to the shareholders that they have done so. The review should cover all controls, including financial, operational and compliance controls and risk management. This extended the recommendations in the Cadbury Report, which asked only for a review of internal financial control.

To provide guidance for directors of listed companies in implementing the new requirements relating to internal control, the Institute of Chartered Accountants in England and Wales established a working party (the Turnbull Committee), who published their recommendations in *Internal Control: Guidance for Directors on the Combined Code* in September 1999. Their guidance calls on companies to ensure that their system of internal control is embedded in the operations of the company, is capable of responding to the changing risks it faces and includes procedures for reporting major weaknesses immediately to appropriate levels of management. It requires companies to identify, evaluate and manage their key risks and assess how they are controlled, consider whether weaknesses are being remedied promptly, ensure that all aspects of internal control are regularly reviewed on an appropriate cyclical basis and have regular board level reviews of reports on internal control.

The Combined Code and the Internal Control: Guidance for Directors on the Combined Code (Turnbull Guidance) are reproduced in Appendix 4.

The Listing Rules now require listed companies to include in their annual report and accounts, for UK companies, a statement regarding the extent or otherwise of their compliance with the Combined Code, including the Turnbull proposals. Whilst these rules do not formally apply to an AIM company, it would seem sensible for such companies to include this information in their annual accounts.

8.5.5   *Environmental reporting*

In June 1996, the Advisory Committee on Business and the Environment (ACBE) issued a draft guideline on good practice which suggested that a public company should include in the operating and financial review part of its directors' report, in its annual report and accounts, a summary of the environmental risks facing the business, the environmental costs incurred and initiative taken. There were further suggestions for comments to be included on the existence and operation of the company's environmental management system and how this fits into its corporate plan and business operations, and that the annual report should quantify the financial implications of its measured performance on environmental matters. Some AIM companies operate in environmentally sensitive businesses, such as oil and gas, mining or power generation and distribution, and would be well advised to consider this guideline and its implications for their reporting procedures in annual accounts. Guidance on good practice may also be found in the annual reports of fully listed companies operating in environmentally sensitive areas, some of which are now including extensive environmental and health and safety information in their annual reports, in certain cases in the form of separate sections dealing specifically with this topic.

8.6   AUDIT RELATIVE TO AN AIM COMPANY

In line with the lightly regulated nature of the AIM market generally, there are virtually no requirements relative to audit and auditors which are specific to an AIM company.

The only reference in the AIM rules to such requirements appears in rule 17 which requires an AIM company to 'publish annual *audited* accounts' within six months of the end of the financial period. There are no rules concerning the identity or qualifications of the auditors because an AIM company may be incorporated anywhere in the world and must, therefore, comply with the audit requirements in its own country, as a first stage. As mentioned elsewhere, an AIM company must publish accounts prepared in accordance with the issuer's national law and with one of the three alternative sets of accounting standards.

Thus, in preparing a company for admission to AIM, and considering the appropriateness or otherwise of its national law and in choosing the accounting standards which it will adopt, the question of the identity and qualifications of the auditors, and the audit regime under which they operate, should also be considered.

The expectations of the general body of shareholders of the AIM company should also be borne in mind at this point. If the shareholders are likely to be mainly British, then they would expect a British-style audit report from a British-based auditor; in other circumstances, the expectation might be different and in each case the shareholders' expectations should be considered in the interests of maintaining good relationships between the company and its owners.

Whilst the primary duty of the auditors is, of course, to examine and produce a written report on the financial accounts, their role has been extended significantly in recent years in relation to fully listed companies on the Stock Exchange. Whilst it is stressed that the requirements do not strictly apply to an AIM company, they could perhaps be considered as best practice and may well be appropriate for most AIM companies to follow in practice.

These additional auditors' responsibilities include the following.

(i)   When a listed company announces its preliminary statement of annual results, they must have first been agreed with the company's auditors and, if the auditors' report is likely to be qualified, details of the nature of the qualification should be given.

(ii) As described in para **8.5.4**, the Combined Code on corporate governance and directors' remuneration matters entails considerable additional disclosures within the annual report and accounts of listed companies. Again, it may well be appropriate for many AIM companies to give similar disclosures relating to corporate governance and directors' remuneration in their annual report and accounts. However, if they do so, it is not appropriate for the auditors to report on such information, since this is outside the auditors' responsibilities.

The Listing Rules now require fully listed companies to make a statement as to whether or not they have complied throughout the accounting period with the detailed 'Code Provisions' set out in section 1 of the Code and, in respect of certain of the Code Provisions, for the statement to be reviewed before publication by the auditors. As a result of this requirement, the Auditing Practices Board has recommended that the auditors of listed companies should explain in their audit reports their responsibilities for the various parts of the annual report, specifically those aspects which they have audited, reviewed for accuracy or merely read to consider consistency with the body of the accounts. The practice which had developed of a separate published report by the auditors on the directors' statement on corporate governance compliance is now considered inappropriate in view of the narrow scope of the review required by the auditors and the introduction of a statement of auditors' responsibilities.

(iii) Listed companies are required to publish a half-yearly report on their activities and profit or loss for the first six months of each financial year.

The auditors may then report their findings privately to the directors, or may provide a report on their review (emphasising that it is *not* an audit) for publication in the interim statement itself. Once again, it is stressed that there is no formal obligation on an AIM company to involve its auditors in the preparation or publication of its half-yearly report, but it may well be considered good practice for an AIM company to follow similar procedures to those for a listed company in this matter.

Chapter 9

TAXATION AND THE AIM COMPANY

9.1 INTRODUCTION

It is important, if unexciting, to note that a UK-resident company traded on AIM would be taxed on its profits and chargeable gains in exactly the same way, at exactly the same rates, as if it were not traded on that market. An AIM listing makes no difference to the internal taxation position. Similarly, the taxation treatment of dividends which it might pay to its shareholders is subject to the same tax regime as any other UK-resident company.

As for the taxation treatment of profits earned by, and dividends paid by, companies resident outside the UK that will, of course, depend upon the tax regime of the country of residence. Since an AIM company may be resident anywhere in the world, it would clearly be beyond the scope of this book to provide details in each case; it would be a matter which would need to be explained in full in the admission document of the AIM company in question, so that the shareholder or potential shareholder would be well aware of the position.

However, there are a number of potentially significant tax advantages attaching to an investment in the shares of an AIM company, for a shareholder who is liable to UK tax, and these are briefly described in the following paragraphs. Again, it is not practical to deal with the position of non-UK taxpaying shareholders in this book. Indeed, what follows can be only a brief and necessarily incomplete guide to the position and any shareholder who may be affected by these provisions should seek specific advice rather than rely on the descriptions which follow.

These taxation reliefs and allowances all stem from an announcement in the spring of 1995 by the Financial Secretary to the Treasury to the effect that AIM securities would not be treated as quoted or listed for tax purposes. Thus, in spite of AIM providing a market under the Stock Exchange rules for the buying and selling of securities, the Inland Revenue will treat those securities as unquoted and, therefore, qualifying for a number of tax reliefs which are otherwise available principally to private companies. These reliefs are not generally available to companies with a full Stock Exchange listing.

The principal effects of unquoted status are explained in paras **9.2** to **9.8** below.

9.2   INHERITANCE TAX: BUSINESS PROPERTY RELIEF

Inheritance tax is the successor to capital transfer tax and estate duty and is chargeable upon the value of assets passing following a death, or on certain lifetime gifts. The maximum rate is currently 40%, and the first £242,000 of chargeable transfers are free of tax. There is at present a business property relief of 100% for any size of shareholding in an unquoted trading company. In most cases, therefore, an AIM shareholder could be eligible for the relief on the value of those shares, provided a number of conditions are satisfied. The conditions in this context relate to the activities of the AIM company, for example, they exclude companies mainly dealing or investing in land and securities. In addition, the shares need to be owned for two years before they qualify for the relief.

9.3   CAPITAL GAINS TAX: HOLD-OVER RELIEF ON GIFTS

Capital gains tax, currently at rates similar to income tax rates, is chargeable on disposals of chargeable assets, which include company shareholdings. A gift of such shares is treated for tax purposes as a disposal, with the disposal proceeds being deemed to be the open market value of the shares. However, it is possible, if both donor and recipient agree, for an election to be made to hold over the gain which would otherwise arise on a gift, so that the tax becomes chargeable only if the recipient later disposes of the shares in question. This relief is restricted to certain classes of assets which include shares in unquoted trading companies, or holding companies of trading groups; AIM shares fall within this category if the company's activity is classified as 'trading' and, therefore, provided certain other conditions are met, the relief can be claimed and the gain held over. The relief is available only to individual or trustee shareholders. Under anti-avoidance provisions introduced in 2000, the relief is no longer available when the gift of shares is made to a company.

9.4   RELIEF FOR LOSSES ON UNQUOTED SHARES IN TRADING COMPANIES

Whilst one would presumably not invest in an AIM company, or anything else, with a view to incurring a loss on the investment, there is a potentially valuable relief to soften the blow if losses do occur. An individual who subscribes for AIM shares in a qualifying trading company, and incurs a loss on disposal of those shares, may claim to set off that loss against his other income, for income tax purposes, instead of claiming a capital loss. Similar provisions apply to investment companies which may set off losses against other income chargeable to corporation tax. It should be noted that these reliefs are available only for the original subscriber to the shares, not to an investor who has purchased the shares on the market.

9.5   ENTERPRISE INVESTMENT SCHEME

The Enterprise Investment Scheme (EIS) was introduced in 1994 to replace the former Business Expansion Scheme. Since 1994, the EIS legislation has been extensively modified, and there are now four reliefs potentially available for individual shareholders who subscribe for EIS qualifying shares.

(a)   *Income tax relief*

An individual who subscribes for EIS qualifying shares is entitled to income tax relief, reducing his income tax liability by up to 20% of the amount subscribed. There is a minimum subscription of £500, and a maximum subscription (for all EIS shares in total) of £150,000 per annum. If a subscription is made in the first half of a tax year, half the amount subscribed, up to a maximum of £25,000, may be treated as having been expended in the previous tax year.

The relief may be withdrawn in various circumstances, including sale of the shares within three years, or the company ceasing to meet the EIS qualifying conditions within three years of subscription.

(b)   *Capital gains tax exemption*

If income tax relief is available, and is not withdrawn, any gain on sale of EIS shares will be wholly exempt from capital gains tax. A sale within three years of subscription, or if income tax relief has been withdrawn for other reasons, will be liable in full to capital gains tax – there is no partial tax exemption.

(c)   *Loss relief on disposal of shares*

If EIS shares are disposed of at a loss, the investor has the choice of taking a capital loss, or setting off the loss against income chargeable to income tax. This operates on a similar basis to that described at **9.4**, save that the loss is restricted to the loss net of any EIS income tax relief.

(d)   *Capital gains tax deferral on EIS investment*

An individual or trustee, who realises a capital gain on disposal of any asset, may defer taxation on that gain if it is invested in EIS qualifying shares. The capital gain in question must be realised within a period of three years before, or one year after, the EIS investment is made. Any amount of capital gain can be deferred in this way, ie the £150,000 limit on the EIS subscription qualifying for income tax relief does not apply for this purpose. On disposing of the EIS shares, the original gain will become taxable, irrespective of whether or not any gain on the EIS shares is tax exempt.

There are numerous restrictions upon the type of companies which qualify for EIS relief, and upon individuals who may be entitled to it. If it appears likely that a company will qualify, the Inland Revenue will normally be prepared to grant advance assurances as to its qualifying status, and it is often desirable to make reference to this in documents issued to potential shareholders. However, because certain bona fide business transactions can result in denial of relief, including clawback of income tax relief already given, it may be necessary to state that the confirmed availability of tax relief cannot be guaranteed.

9.6   VENTURE CAPITAL TRUSTS

Venture capital trusts (VCTs) were introduced in 1995, and are companies quoted on the Stock Exchange, each of which is required to own and manage a portfolio of investments in unquoted trading companies in order to retain its VCT qualifying status. Because AIM shares are treated as unquoted for this purpose, VCTs commonly include qualifying AIM companies in their portfolios and have become an important source of venture capital. An individual subscriber who buys new shares in a VCT can obtain income tax relief at up to 20% of the amount subscribed, for subscriptions up to £100,000 per annum, can utilise the same investment cost for capital gains tax deferral relief similar to that described at part (d) of **9.5**, and also benefits from receiving tax-free dividends from the VCT and tax-free capital profits on disposal of those shares. The income tax relief will be withdrawn if the shares are held for less than three years, but the other reliefs are available without that time period applying.

There are, of course, restrictions on the types of companies in which a VCT may hold shares, but it is likely that those AIM companies which have a structure and a trading pattern which brings them within the definition of qualifying for EIS purposes may be attractive to those who manage VCTs. Again, the Inland Revenue are normally prepared to consider granting advance assurances as to VCT qualifying status, and VCT managers will frequently require such assurances before committing funds.

9.7   CORPORATE VENTURING SCHEME

The Corporate Venturing Scheme (CVS) was introduced in 2000 and provides a package of three reliefs to a corporate investor which are similar to those available to individuals under the EIS.

(a)   *Corporation tax relief*

A company that subscribes for CVS qualifying shares is entitled to corporation tax relief on its investment at a rate of 20%. There is no maximum monetary limit on investment, however the investing company may not own more than 30% of the issuing company. As with EIS, the relief may be withdrawn if qualifying conditions cease to be met, or if shares are sold within three years.

(b)   *Deferral relief*

If gains arise on disposal of CVS qualifying shares, the investing company may defer the gains by reinvestment into new CVS shares.

(c)   *Loss relief on disposal of shares*

Losses, net of CVS relief, may be set off against income chargeable to corporation tax.

As with EIS, there are numerous restrictions. In particular, the investing company must be a non-financial trading company, and at least 20% of the issuing company's shares must be owned by individuals other than its directors or employees. There is a formal clearance mechanism under which the Inland

Revenue can be requested to confirm that an issuing company will meet the relevant CVS requirements. Subject to the 20% individual requirement, most EIS qualifying companies will also qualify under CVS.

9.8 CAPITAL GAINS TAX TAPER RELIEF

Until 1998, individuals, trustees and companies were subject to broadly similar capital gains tax rules. Subject to an indexation allowance, to exclude purely inflationary gains, any profit on sale of shares was potentially liable to tax. Various reliefs, such as an annual exemption for individuals, might reduce the tax actually due.

In April 1998 the rules changed radically for individuals and trustees but remained unchanged for corporate shareholders. Individuals and trustees became entitled to taper relief, under which the taxable gain is reduced according to the period of ownership of the asset in question. Taper relief was significantly extended in April 2000, and the principles set out below apply to AIM shares acquired since that date. Shares acquired before that date may be subject to the earlier, less favourable, legislation and detailed advice should be sought as to the tax consequences of disposal. Nonetheless, many shareholders who held shares in April 1998 will be able to benefit from a tax rate as low as 10% upon disposals on or after 6 April 2002.

If an AIM company is a trading company, or the holding company of a trading group, any individual or trustee shareholder qualifies for maximum taper relief. For an individual shareholder, liable to tax at the higher rate of 40%, effective tax rates on gains are:

Period of share ownership	Effective tax rate
Under one year	40%
One to two years	35%
Two to three years	30%
Three to four years	20%
Over four years	10%

From April 2001, the same rates will apply to an employee of a non-trading company, provided that he or she holds no more than 10% of its share capital.

In June 2001, shortly after the General Election, the Chancellor of the Exchequer announced an extension to taper relief. The necessary period of ownership to achieve the minimum 10% effective tax rate is to be reduced from four years to two years. Gains realised in the first year of ownership will be taxed at the full 40% tax rate, and an effective 20% rate will apply to gains realised in the second year of ownership. It is anticipated that legislation will be introduced by the 2002 Finance Act and, at the time of writing, it is not known how the new legislation will affect existing shareholders.

9.9   TAX RELIEF GENERALLY

The above paragraphs represent only a very brief description of the main aspects of the tax reliefs potentially available to investors in AIM shares and VCTs; in all cases the legislation surrounding these reliefs is complex, and designed with a view to allowing the relief only in those cases intended by the legislators. In particular, there are many restrictions on the activities of the companies in which investments may be contemplated, for example, companies which hold or deal in property or investments are often excluded, companies with overseas trades, interest or subsidiary companies are restricted, and there are strict time-limits imposed in various ways.

In short, any investor who may be interested in claiming these reliefs will need to take advice on the specific regulations which may restrict their availability. It must also be said that the comments above are based on the law at the time of writing and a number of these reliefs have been introduced in recent years and have already been subject to significant amendment; they may, therefore, be further amended at Budget time, or indeed at any other time. It should also be said that many of the factors which could operate to prevent a relief being available, or remaining available, are not actually within the control of the investor at all; a company, which appears at the time of investment suitable for the obtaining of a particular form of relief by the investor, may subsequently take some action which disqualifies it from that relief. Unless the directors of the AIM company have made some form of commitment to conducting their business in a way which will continue to qualify, there would be little that the investor could do to remedy his position in those circumstances. It may be that directors of AIM companies will be unwilling to commit themselves to accept the constraints of continuing to qualify, although there may well be cases where directors would accept some constraint in that direction in order to make the shares in their company attractive to new investors. It would be wise, therefore, for a potential investor in an AIM company, or in a VCT, who has an interest in obtaining one or more of these tax reliefs, to read very carefully the prospectus and other information concerning the company, in order to determine both the present status of the company in relation to the particular tax reliefs and to form a view as to whether the company is likely to continue to qualify for the reliefs.

9.10   SUMMARY

There are three main points to note.

(1)   The tax reliefs which may be available to AIM or VCT investors are complex and have been subject to frequent legislative changes; they may change in the future.
(2)   Any potential investor should seek professional advice concerning the tax aspects of the proposal.

(3)   It would be unusual to make an investment in anything just to obtain a tax relief – it is the underlying value of the investment which should be the primary consideration, with any tax benefit regarded as an additional bonus.

Chapter 10

TRADING AND SETTLEMENT ON AIM

10.1   INTRODUCTION

Trading in shares on AIM is governed by Chapter 17 of the rules of the Stock Exchange.

Shares traded on the Official List are primarily traded on a screen-based system, SEAQ/SETS, and transactions are settled through CREST. There is nothing to stop shareholders agreeing to deal themselves without going through the Stock Exchange, and the Tradepoint system is a computerised dealing service designed to allow institutional shareholders to trade between themselves and that is also used by certain Stock Exchange member firms.

Under the AIM rules, member firms of the Stock Exchange must trade AIM securities with each other through the Stock Exchange. This does not prevent off-market transactions between non-members.

10.2   'QUOTE-DRIVEN SYSTEM'

A key element of the way in which trading on the Stock Exchange operates is the use of market-makers and what is called a 'quote-driven system'. One or more member firms of the Stock Exchange will make a market in a particular security by offering to buy at the 'bid price' or to sell at the 'offer price'. These prices will be publicised through the computer system of the Stock Exchange and both the bid and offer prices, together with a number of shares that may be traded at either price, are guaranteed. Thus, if the price quoted by a market-maker for the shares in company 'Alpha' is 100p to 105p, in a size of 5,000 shares, then any broker can ring up and deal in up to that number of shares at that price. The broker does not have to specify whether he is a buyer or seller in order to establish the price. A market-maker is, of course, entitled to change his price at any time, either as a result of business that he has transacted, or business that may have been indicated to him. The market-maker may also make a different price in a larger number of shares, but this price will not be displayed on the screen; a market-maker may also choose to deal 'inside' his displayed price, without being obliged to change the screen price. This means that on being challenged by a broker in the examples given above, he may decide to pay 101p for 5,000 shares rather than the 100p displayed on the screen ('inside' the price) or to sell, say, 10,000 shares at 107p (a larger market).

10.3   SEATS

There are certain securities which have no market-maker and these, together with less liquid securities which only have one market-maker, can be traded through the Stock Exchange Alternative Trading System (SEATS). This provides for a mixture of market-making and order-driven trading. Under order-driven trading, someone who wants to buy shares in company Alpha at a price will input this price through a member firm into the system where it will be displayed awaiting a seller at the same price.

This system was improved to become SEATS PLUS on the introduction of AIM in June 1995. SEATS PLUS allows more than one market-maker's quote to be displayed and can show indicative and mid-market prices as well as firm quotes, and provides additional details relating to the company.

An example of a SEATS PLUS display is given at the end of this chapter.

10.4   THE MARKET-MAKER

The key element to trading is the market-maker. There are a number of market-makers in AIM securities, the best known probably being Winterflood Securities, which has made a commitment to trade in all AIM companies. At the end of January 2001 there were 22 firms market-making in AIM securities. This represents a dramatic increase on the three companies that started the market in 1995.

Chapter 17 of the Stock Exchange rules sets out the duties of both the broker and the market-maker.

Each AIM security must have a broker, and it is the broker's duty to input into SEATS PLUS such information about the issuer for display on SEATS PLUS as the Stock Exchange may specify from time to time. In addition, the broker during the mandatory quote period shall, upon request, use its best endeavours to find matching business in those securities in which there is no registered market-maker.

Rules 17.5, 17.11 and 17.15 set out the principal obligations of market-makers. These include the fact that only a member firm registered as a market-maker in the AIM security in question may display prices for that security on SEATS PLUS (rule 17.5).

Rule 17.11 imposes certain requirements on market-makers. For example, during the mandatory quote period (normally 8.00am to 4.30pm) a registered market-maker in an AIM security must display on SEATS PLUS:

(i)   firm continuous two-way prices;
(ii) indicative continuous two-way prices; or
(iii) indicative continuous mid prices.

The prices display must be in not less than the minimum quote size in each AIM security in which the market-maker is registered. In addition, if at least one market-maker is displaying firm continuous two-way prices in a security, all market-makers in that security must make firm, continuous, two-way prices.

A market-maker displaying firm prices must deal with an enquiring member firm at the price in up to the size displayed.

A market-maker must obtain the consent of the Stock Exchange before withdrawing or re-entering its quotation of a particular security. There are special provisions (rule 17.12) if, because of a computer failure, a market-maker has had to withdraw or re-enter its quotation in an AIM security.

A market-maker who wishes to change from displaying indicative prices to displaying firm prices in an AIM security, must give three days' notice of its intention to the Stock Exchange and display firm prices in that security for at least three months thereafter. Less notice is required where a market-maker wishes to change from displaying firm prices to displaying indicative prices in an AIM security, and the requirement is to notify the Stock Exchange by 13.00 hours the day before the proposed change (rule 17.11).

The normal requirements regarding 'best execution'[1] apply to transactions effected in AIM securities.

Transactions sometimes take place outside the mandatory quote period for securities on the Official List, but such transactions are not necessarily protected by the 'best execution' requirements, and the same applies to AIM securities.

Market-makers have obligations after the end of the mandatory quote period (rule 17.15) and in respect of limit orders (rule 17.26). The purpose of these rules is to protect the interests of investors.

10.5   SETTLEMENT

Rule 32 of the AIM rules states: 'An AIM company must ensure that appropriate settlement arrangements are in place. In particular, save where the Exchange otherwise agrees, AIM securities must be eligible for electronic settlement.' This means that virtually all AIM securities are settled through CREST.

10.5.1   The CREST system

The CREST system enables shares to be held and transferred without use of share certificates and stock transfer forms. This has been facilitated by the Uncertificated Securities Regulations 1995, SI 1995/3272 which came into force on 19 December 1995. It enables title to units of securities to be evidenced and transferred without a written instrument through use of a computer-based system and procedures. A person who wishes to operate such a relevant system has to be approved by the FSA. The securities covered by the regulations are very broadly drawn. Where a company's articles of association are inconsistent with the relevant system, a directors' board resolution under reg 16 is sufficient

---

1   Best execution is a duty incumbent upon a firm which deals with or for a private customer, and also where it fulfils an order for a non-private customer unless the non-private customer has waived the requirement. Best execution obliges the firm to take reasonable care to ascertain that the price at which a transaction is made is the best available for the customer in the relevant market at the time for transactions of the kind and size concerned. Thus, if any order is executed with a market-maker on his quoted price in his quoted size this may be regarded as best execution; similarly, dealing 'inside' the quoted price or outside the price in a larger market, as described above, should also qualify as 'best execution'.

to disapply such articles, but notice must be given to each shareholder of the intention to pass this resolution or that such resolution has been passed (and this notice must be within 60 days of the passing of the resolution). This would seem to be an alternative to a formal amendment of the articles of association by special resolution since the Regulations do not prevent a company from amending its articles in the normal way. (In practice, most new entrants to AIM adopt new articles prior to admission.)

Where shares can be transferred through a relevant system, it must be so distinguished on the register of members, which should point out those shareholdings which are certificated as opposed to those conducted under the relevant system which are uncertificated (reg 19). Irrespective of being uncertificated, the issuer still needs to maintain a register in respect of all such holdings. The register constitutes evidence as to the title to the uncertificated securities and this is of fundamental importance when considering transfers and registrations. The transferee of securities under the CREST system has by virtue of reg 25 an equitable interest in securities being transferred from the time the instruction to the company is made. Usually such transfer needs to be registered within two hours of receipt of instruction. Regulation 23 requires the company to transfer title to accord with any such transfer instruction unless there are specific reasons for preventing this, for example where the transfer is void and the company has notice of this, or where there is a court order which prohibits the transfer of that security. When the central system receives notification from a CREST member concerning the transfer, it will check that the transferor is able to transfer a relevant number of securities and that the transferee has the funds to enable payment of a transfer. It is only then that the instruction will be confirmed.

The background of the Regulations is to ensure that all instructions are properly authenticated and there are detailed specifications to safeguard an instruction through the system and prevent tampering with this.

The system is operated by what is termed as a sponsor and it is this sponsor who is responsible for sending and receiving messages. Both CRESTCo Limited (which is responsible for the system) and the sponsor fall within the FSA, but the operator through an exemption order (Financial Services Act 1986 (Exemption) Order 1996, SI 1996/1587) has been deemed to be an exempted person (as are various persons who provide networks for carrying properly authenticated dematerialised instructions).

Example of SEATS PLUS system

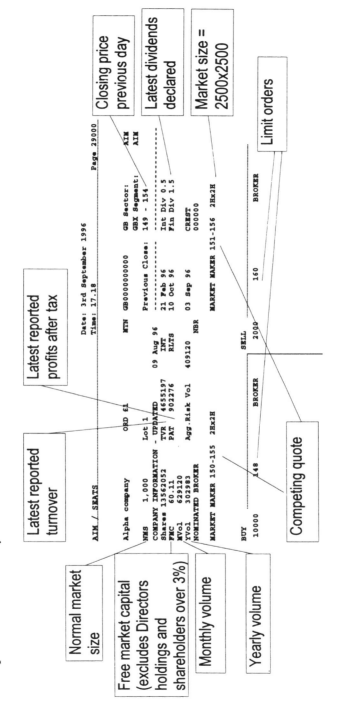

Chapter 11

THE ALTERNATIVES

11.1 INTRODUCTION

The last few years have seen dramatic changes in the markets or share clubs giving opportunities to both insurers and investors. All of the options referred to below have rule books and admission requirements, but the degree of regulation varies considerably from the strictly regulated ambit of NASDAQ and NASDAQ Europe to the more informal arrangements contained, for example, in the OFEX rulebook. This book does not intend to consider any of these markets in great detail but summarises some of the more relevant aspects of each.

11.2 NASDAQ EUROPE

NASDAQ Europe is derived from the takeover in 2001 of EASDAQ by NASDAQ.

The objective of EASDAQ was to establish and operate a pan-European regulated stock market targeted towards young and fast-growing companies which wish to raise capital from international investors. Trading commenced on 27 November 1996 and by 16 January 1997 five companies were quoted. The intention was that it would mirror the NASDAQ market established in the US by being a screen-based stock market acting independently from existing European exchanges. It was not competitive to NASDAQ and, indeed, NASDAQ had provided both technical and practical support and assistance in the setting up of EASDAQ. A number of US companies which were already listed on NASDAQ and which either had a European element to their operations or had aspirations in this direction would have been listed on EASDAQ.

NASDAQ Europe is based in Brussels and has a high standard of regulation. It is authorised by the Belgian Banking and Finance Commission. The EASDAQ rule book had been closely modelled on NASDAQ's rules and allowed for companies to comply with information requirements of the Securities and Exchange Commission (SEC) of the USA.

A rule book is available together with details of issuers' admission and ongoing requirements. From these a number of characteristics can be noted:

(i)   the companies making an application need to be properly established and incorporated under domestic law in the country in which they were formed and they must be permitted to offer securities to the public market;

(ii)   there is a minimum total assets requirement of ECU 3.5m on admission and the issuer must have capital and reserves of at least ECU 2m;

(iii) each company seeking to issue securities will need to appoint a lead manager and be supported by two market makers;

(iv)   where the security is in the form of convertible debt there must be outstanding at least ECU 9m on admission (which as a continuing obligation is reduced to at least ECU 4.5m);

(v)   there is a prohibition on directors' disposal of shares for a minimum of 18 months from the date of admission for an issuer whose shares have not been previously traded on the public market;

(vi)   there is a requirement for the publishing of financial data which is required to accord with the US Accounting Standards and the International Accounting Standards or in accordance with domestic principles reconciled with this standard. There is also an obligation to provide quarterly reports (which may be unaudited);

(vii) company boards must have a minimum of two independent directors;

(viii) remuneration and audit committees must be established. For the former, all the members must be independent directors but, for the audit committee, it is sufficient that they be in the majority;

(ix)   there should be an adequate free float of shares (being 20% of the total value) and there should be an adequate spread of shareholder (probably at least 100);

(x)   in addition to the director prohibition referred to above, for an issuer whose shares have not been traded on the public market, it will need to procure that the shareholders will not dispose of more than 20% of their shares for a specified period of time and this must be disclosed in the prospectus;

(xi)   a prospectus will need to be issued setting out specific data concerning the issuing company. Companies which are already listed on a regulated market and wish to take out a secondary listing on NASDAQ Europe will not be required to issue a prospectus provided they do not raise additional capital at the time of the listing.

Trading on NASDAQ Europe is 'driven'. It is currently screen and telephone based, and makes use of an ISMA trade reporting system known as TRAX. It is intended that a new trading system will be launched which will further automate the process. Cross-border settlement is through Euroclear or Cedel. For more information, reference should be made to the market itself. Its website contains a serious amount of information including the rules and can be accessed on www.nasdaqeurope.com.

11.3   NASDAQ

The NASDAQ market began life in 1971 as an electronic system which collected and disseminated quotes from competing dealers trading in unlisted equities over the counter. By 1994, it was the second largest stock market in dollar terms after the New York Stock Exchange. NASDAQ offers two tiers for listing, namely the NASDAQ National Market and the NASDAQ SmallCap Market (which has less demanding listing requirements). Both markets work within a regulatory framework determined by the SEC (established under the Securities Exchange Act of 1934 which implements the US legislation designed to protect investors against malpractice in the securities market). Since NASDAQ computerised, there is no Stock Exchange floor but, instead, there are in excess of 200,000 vendor terminals throughout the world. Trading is done through NASD firms in the US (through a multiple market-maker system). NASDAQ has become a major international player with overseas offices in London and Sao Paulo and representative links worldwide. Recent developments have seen the establishment of NASDAQ Japan and NASDAQ Europe which offer Japanese and European investors an opportunity to invest in growth stocks and provide a new market for IPSs to encourage Japanese and European companies. NASDAQ has also signed regulatory agreements with the Stock Exchange in Hong Kong which is a pilot scheme that will enable NASDAQ listed companies to trade in SEHK. NASDAQ has also announced plans to open an office in Shanghai, China. NASDAQ lists more than 4,900 companies.

For a company wishing to obtain a listing at NASDAQ, there are a number of choices which can be made. A US company may wish to list existing shares before floating new stock to enable the company to familiarise itself with the workings of NASDAQ and the regulations of the SEC. For non-US shares, frequently, American Depository Receipts (ADRs) will be listed. An ADR is evidence of ownership underlying non-US shares which have been deposited in a specific recognised custodian bank in the company's country of domicile. The ADRs are then freely traded without need for delivery of the non-US shares represented. Ordinary shares are also frequently listed by non-US companies directly on NASDAQ's stock market. There are now more than 260 non-US ordinary share listings on this market of which Canadian companies are more particularly prominent. Since 1995, NASDAQ has helped companies receive in excess of $125 billion through IPOS.

The listing requirements are more intensive for the National Market than for the SmallCap Market but, as has already been indicated, the regulatory framework imposed by the SEC is the same. However, the SEC does allow some tolerance for non-US companies by excluding them from complying with requirements which are contrary to generally accepted business regulations in the issuer's home country.

Companies seeking a listing on NASDAQ will be expected to have in place a team of professional advisers including an experienced investment bank/ underwriter, a US attorney with knowledge of the industry and market, and an accountant with similar experience. Where ADRs are involved, the authorised depository will normally be part of a large US banking institutional trust company and it is this which will take ownership of the non-US security and offer ADRs backed by the security to US investors.

Before a company can be listed, it will need first to be registered with the SEC (completion of a Form 20-F registration statement, which is a comprehensive report of the company's business activities and financial results). A compliance report of the company's business activities and financial results will be reviewed by the SEC before registration is deemed to be effected. The financial statements will need to be in line with the US AGAPE and, frequently, the disclosure requirements will require non-US companies to publish segmental reports for the first time (in which figures are broken down across both operational and geographical divisions). Following registration, companies will need to continue to file a Form 20-F with the SEC every year within six months of a year end. Quarterly reports are not required from non-US companies but are required from US companies. The SEC and NASDAQ will review the registration documents of a company making an offer for sale to the public.

It is most likely that in the process of bringing a company to the market a prospectus will need to be issued. Under US law, a prospectus is the sole form of information that issuers can distribute concerning the offer. Under US law, the company, its officers and members of the board of directors are wholly liable for any misstatement or omission of information even if there was no intent to deceive. It is therefore important that the narrative and the accounting sections are clear, accurate and complete. Since it is the only document that can be distributed, it needs to serve both as a disclosure document and a selling document. It is therefore vital that an appropriate balance is brought to the document. It is for this reason that lawyers take the prime responsibility for drafting the narrative with accountants preparing the financial statements and investment bankers providing the underwriting details. The prospectus needs to contain a detailed description of the business, its management and financial statements, as analysis of operations, risks and financial conditions. There also needs to be reference made to the intended use for proceeds of sale and what effect the issue will have on the dilution of existing shares. Details of dividend policy and capitalisation will also need to be referred to. So far as underwriting is concerned, full details of the syndicate or underwriting agreement will need to be disclosed and there will need to be some form of statement as to whether the underwriting is a 'firm commitment' or merely a 'best efforts' undertaking.

Market makers are independent dealers who compete with others for investors' orders in each NASDAQ listed stock. Under the NASDAQ trading system, each market maker has equal access through quotation broadcasts and can use their own capital to buy or sell stock. There are presently more than 500 dealers registered as market makers for NASDAQ. There are additional means of bringing customer orders to NASDAQ, namely through Electronic Communications Networks. These must be registered and approved with the SEC and display actual orders and can assist institutions and market makers through an anonymous route to become involved in the market. The main advantage to this is that it does not rely upon market makers committing capital and this enhances market liquidity. Towards the end of 1999, a new highly advanced electronic trading system was introduced to NASDAQ called the Optmark Trading System which matches large order anonymously.

NASDAQ operates a vast network which is accessible on the internet (NASDAQ.com). This averages 9 million page views per day and is a major source of financial information on the internet. The site covers information such as stock reports, SEC filings and key information on all publicly traded companies.

There is also an obligation to file at least one Form 6-K annually providing updates on operation and significant corporate developments. If there is a change over the course of a year, such change may need to be reported on a more frequent basis. The general obligation is that, if any report or press release is distributed to a non-US company's own jurisdiction, it should also be reported to the SEC.

The registration requirements and regulatory requirements are keenly policed. The company, its corporate offices and members of the board of directors are liable for a misstatement or omission of information in the registration documents even if there is no intent to deceive. This places an obligation to ensure that the narrative and accounting sections are full, accurate and unambiguous. Lawyers and accountants have appropriate responsibilities for ensuring scrupulous honesty in the assessment and drafting of details. The prospectus needs to contain detailed information about the business, its management structure, audited financial statements and analysis of operations, financial conditions and potential risk. It would also need to give details of the intended use of proceeds of sale and the effect of any dilution on existing shares. There should be provided details of dividend policy and capitalisation and any underwriting syndicate.

In particular, it is required to be stated whether the underwriting is of a firm commitment or a best efforts basis (is underwriting in place or is it still to be found by the underwriters concerned using their best endeavours). The estimated costs of seeking a list are considerable and are estimated to be in the region of 10% of the offer value.

11.4   EURO.NM

This is a pan-European group of regulated markets aimed at frequently young, innovative companies with high growth potential. It is open to companies regardless of their sector of activity or home country. The members of EURO.NM and their respective growth markets currently including Nouveau Marché (which is part of the Paris Borse), the Neuer Markt (which is part of the Deutsche Borse in Frankfurt), the AEX-EURO.NM (which is part of the Amsterdam Stock Exchange), the BXS-EURO.NM Belgium (which is part of the Brussels Stock Exchange) and the Nuovo Mercato (which is part of the Italian Exchange in Milan). It is likely that this union will grow further since the stock exchanges located in Stockholm, Copenhagen, Zurich, Oslo and Helsinki are all looking to become involved in this grouping.

The main philosophy behind EURO.NM is the belief that, in maximising accessibility and opportunity for all market participants, it can be best accomplished by joining the experience, resources and networks of existing national markets. Such a decentralised approach provides significant advantages by building on well-established domestic foundations across the many European financial centres. This is the theoretical position but, in practice, the market is heavily geared towards the 273 companies which were listed in May 2000 on the Neuer Markt. Only Paris approaches this number with 132 companies listed, Amsterdam has 15, Belgium 15 and Milan 13 respectively.

Each member adopts a convergent, regulatory and operational standard in compliance with harmonisation agreements between the basic exchanges. This requires common standards in areas of listing requirements, membership criteria, trading procedures and disclosure requires and also includes a requirement for quarterly reporting.

This is a dual trading system with a central order book regulating the fixings between the continuous trading and market making. Since 4 January 1999, all shares are quoted in Euros.

Trading can easily occur electronically through cross access links between the various members since all EURO.NM stocks are listed throughout the networks.

By the end of March 2000, the total amount of new capital raised on EURO.NM was in excess of 18.4 billion Euros, with a total market capitalisation standing at 244.5 billion Euros. There is a total of 394 listed companies from 13 countries, 27 of which were dual listed with NASDAQ and 7 with other markets. The daily average turnover exceeded 1.3 billion Euros and the All Share Index has risen 561% since the start of 1998.

In October 2000 the Stock Exchange announced that it was to form a new market modelled on Euro.NM. Since then there has been little indication as to how this may proceed and, indeed, the most active part of Euro.NM is now part of Euronext.

11.5 OFEX

It must be emphasised that this is not a formal institution or formally recognised market, but is effectively a trading facility operated by J P Jenkins Limited in association with Newstrack Limited. It is an off exchange share matching and trading facility which allows dealing in unlisted and unquoted companies. Companies who are quoted by OFEX are not quoted or dealt with on the Stock Exchange and are not subject to the rules. OFEX was officially launched on 2 October 1995 and, at that stage, was looked upon as being an option for the 45 companies which previously traded under rule 4.2 of the Stock Exchange which was terminated in September 1995 (under this rule, trading for certain unquoted companies was allowed by member firms of the Stock Exchange).

The attraction of OFEX is that companies with a comparably small market capitalisation (perhaps as little as £100,000) could become involved. OFEX companies cover a broad range of activities including engineering, exploration, sporting clubs, regional brewers, property and other sectors. OFEX does not see itself as a competitor to AIM or other recognised secondary markets, but a facility for trading off the market.

OFEX does have a rule book, but it is clearly less regulated than almost all the other markets referred to in this chapter or indeed to AIM. The following points may usefully be noted:

(i) companies do not need to be PLCs to qualify but, if one is raising money from the public, it would need to have a PLC status and publish a prospectus under the POS Regulations 1995. Where a prospectus is not needed, the company would need to comply with Investment Advertisement regulations as set out in the Financial Services Act 1986;

(ii)   companies are required under the OFEX Code to publish price-sensitive information through the Newstrack announcement service;

(iii)   all documents produced by the company are the responsibility of the company directors and once submitted must comply with the ongoing obligations stipulated in the OFEX Code;

(iv)   although there is no maximum or minimum limit on capitalisation, it is likely that a corporate adviser would demand a basic minimum. Any company applying to join OFEX needs to appoint a corporate adviser who effectively acts as a facilitator.

The types of companies that go to OFEX are similar (but smaller) in nature to those which may be attracted to AIM or to EURO.NM, but a company may decide that either it does not, for some reason, qualify for this regulated market or, alternatively, the costs of doing so outweigh the benefits. OFEX typically would appeal to the following categories:

–   companies with only a few shareholders;
–   those seeking EIS relief;
–   young growing companies;
–   family owned companies – these can benefit from high rates of inheritance tax relief which are available for unlisted securities;
–   companies raising capital but which are concerned about keeping costs as low as possible;
–   companies who have investors looking for an exit route, etc.

Trade on OFEX is done strictly through stockbrokers regulated by the SFA. The normal procedure adopted for companies applying to join OFEX is as follows.

(i)   A company appoints a Corporate Adviser who needs to be regulated in the conduct of investment business by the SFA, the Association of Chartered Certified Accountants, the Institute of Chartered Accountants in England, Wales, Scotland and Ireland or the Law Society of England, Scotland or Northern Ireland. Normally, it would be a stockbroker who is appointed in this role since companies frequently would be interested in due course in taking their stock to a more senior market.

(ii)   A company would either seek membership to OFEX by a mere introduction, ie where the company has no funding requirement, but nomally it will be through a fund raising by way of a public offer or a private placing of shares.

(iii)   All companies are required to provide audited report and accounts for the last three years – the most recent year must be free from audit qualification. Where companies cannot provide three years, a business plan must also be provided, the memorandum and articles of association of the company (these will need to be free of restrictions relating to share transfers or pre-emption rights), details of each director's business activity, completion of the OFEX company information questionnaire and the OFEX and Newstrack agreements, payment of a non-refundable application fee and disclosure of details of any agreements which are important to the business of the company. Where a company is also raising capital, it will need to provide a prospectus to comply with the POS

Regulations 1995. If these regulations do not apply, the company will need to consider the implications of the Investment Advertisement Regulations of the Financial Services Act 1986.

Trading in OFEX is done electronically and settlement is through the use of CREST which matches buyers with sellers. CREST can either be used through a wholly paperless system or one which uses a residual means of providing stock transfer forms, share certificates and the like.

OFEX has attracted both praise and criticism but, recently, it has been seen as a useful adjunct to the more regulated market places providing a useful alternative means for smaller companies to find finance. In its early days the amounts which could be raised were small and rarely exceed £500,000, but more recently much larger sums have been negotiated. It has been suggested that the more regulated a market becomes the more costly it is to raise money and the more likely it is that other sources like OFEX will be used.

COMPARISON OF ADMISSION AND MEMBERSHIP RULES FOR EASDAQ, THE NOUVEAU MARCHÉ AND AIM

	*EASDAQ	Nouveau Marché	AIM
Balance sheet totals on admission	Total assets must be at least ECU 3.5 million	Balance sheet totals must be a minimum of FF20 million	No restrictions
Shareholders' funds	Capital and reserves must be at least ECU 2.0 million	Shareholders' equity must amount to at least FF8 million	No restrictions
Minimum amount to be subscribed for by the public	Must be at least 100 holders of the security	FF10 million	No minimum percentage of shares required to be in public hands
Track record	Directors, original shareholders and employees must not dispose of any of their shares for at least two years if there is a trading record of less than one year except through a public offering	No track record is needed although for companies that have been in business for under two years, the initial listing must take the form of a capital increase	Prohibited sales of shares by directors and employees for 12 months following admission if the company has a trading record of two years or less
Extra restrictions on founders and managers	None other than those for track record	Founders and managers must agree to retain 80% of their investment at the time of listing for at least three years. Further restrictions apply if the company has been in operation for less than two years	None, other than those for track record

	*EASDAQ	Nouveau Marché	AIM
Disclosure of information	Must publish annual audited accounts and unaudited quarterly reports	Must publish yearly and half yearly audited financial statements	Must publish annual audited accounts and unaudited six month results
Advisers	Must appoint and retain EASDAQ approved sponsor	In all cases must have a listing adviser and market maker although they do not have to be of the same firm	Must appoint and retain a London Stock Exchange approved 'nominated adviser'
Brokers	Must maintain a minimum of two registered and active market makers	In all cases must have a listing adviser and market maker although they do not have to be of the same firm	Must appoint and retain a 'broker' who must be a member of the Stock Exchange
Published accounts	Must be in accordance with either US or International Accounting Standards. If in accordance with standards of home country, must quantify differences	Must be in accordance with the schedule and conditions set down by the Société de Nouveau Marché	Must be in accordance with UK, US or International Accounting Standards
Need to isuse prospectus/ admission document	Yes	Yes	Yes
Need to comply with ongoing obligations	Yes	Yes	Yes

* Note: EASDAQ has now been taken over by NASDAQ and is now known as NASDAQ Europe. The rules relating to the market are still in draft format and are open to review

From a booklet originally published by Coopers & Lybrand, 'EASDAQ Aim, the Nouveau Marché: an Update'.

APPENDICES

Appendix 1

STATUTORY MATERIALS

COMPANIES ACT 1985

88 Return as to allotments, etc

(1) This section applies to a company limited by shares and to a company limited by guarantee and having a share capital.

(2) When such a company makes an allotment of its shares, the company shall within one month thereafter deliver to the registrar of companies for registration—

   (a) a return of the allotments (in the prescribed form) stating the number and nominal amount of the shares comprised in the allotment, the names and addresses of the allottees, and the amount (if any) paid or due and payable on each share, whether on account of the nominal value of the shares or by way of premium; and

   (b) in the case of shares allotted as fully or partly paid up otherwise than in cash—

   (i) a contract in writing constituting the title of the allottee to the allotment together with any contract of sale, or for services or other consideration in respect of which that allotment was made (such contracts being duly stamped), and

   (ii) a return stating the number and nominal amount of shares so allotted, the extent to which they are to be treated as paid up, and the consideration for which they have been allotted.

(3) Where such a contract as above mentioned is not reduced to writing, the company shall within one month after the allotment deliver to the registrar of companies for registration the prescribed particulars of the contract stamped with the same stamp duty as would have been payable if the contract had been reduced to writing.

(4) Those particulars are deemed an instrument within the meaning of the Stamp Act 1891; and the registrar may, as a condition of filing the particulars, require that the duty payable on them be adjudicated under section 12 of that Act.

(5) If default is made in complying with this section, every officer of the company who is in default is liable to a fine and, for continued contravention, to a daily default fine, but subject as follows.

(6) In the case of default in delivering to the registrar within one month after the allotment any document required by this section to be delivered, the company, or any officer liable for the default, may apply to the court for relief; and the court, if satisfied that the omission to deliver the document was accidental or due to inadvertence, or that it is just and equitable to grant relief, may make an order extending the time for the delivery of the document for such period as the court thinks proper.

Pre-emption rights

89 Offers to shareholders to be on pre-emptive basis

(1) Subject to the provisions of this section and the seven sections next following, a company proposing to allot equity securities (defined in section 94)—

    (a) shall not allot any of them on any terms to a person unless it has made an offer to each person who holds relevant shares or relevant employee shares to allot to him on the same or more favourable terms a proportion of those securities which is as nearly as practicable equal to the proportion in nominal value held by him of the aggregate of relevant shares and relevant employee shares, and

    (b) shall not allot any of those securities to a person unless the period during which any such offer may be accepted has expired or the company has received notice of the acceptance or refusal of every offer so made.

(2) Subsection (3) below applies to any provision of a company's memorandum or articles which requires the company, when proposing to allot equity securities consisting of relevant shares of any particular class, not to allot those securities on any terms unless it has complied with the condition that it makes such an offer as is described in subsection (1) to each person who holds relevant shares or relevant employee shares of that class.

(3) If in accordance with a provision to which this subsection applies—

    (a) a company makes an offer to allot securities to such a holder, and

    (b) he or anyone in whose favour he has renounced his right to their allotment accepts the offer,

subsection (1) does not apply to the allotment of those securities, and the company may allot them accordingly; but this is without prejudice to the application of subsection (1) in any other case.

(4) Subsection (1) does not apply to a particular allotment of equity securities if these are, or are to be, wholly or partly paid up otherwise than in cash; and securities which a company has offered to allot to a holder of relevant shares or relevant employee shares may be allotted to him, or anyone in whose favour he has renounced his right to their allotment, without contravening subsection (1)(b).

(5) Subsection (1) does not apply to the allotment of securities which would, apart from a renunciation or assignment of the right to their allotment, be held under an employees' share scheme.

90 Communication of pre-emption offers to shareholders

(1) This section has effect as to the manner in which offers required by section 89(1), or by a provision to which section 89(3) applies, are to be made to holders of a company's shares.

(2) Subject to the following subsections, an offer shall be in writing and shall be made to a holder of shares either personally or by sending it by post (that is to say, prepaying and posting a letter containing the offer) to him or to his registered address or, if he has no registered address in the United Kingdom, to the address in the United Kingdom supplied by him to the company for the giving of notice to him.

    If sent by post, the offer is deemed to be made at the time at which the letter would be delivered in the ordinary course of post.

(3) Where shares are held by two or more persons jointly, the offer may be made to the joint holder first named in the register of members in respect of the shares.

(4) In the case of a holder's death or bankruptcy, the offer may be made—

    (a) by sending it by post in a prepaid letter addressed to the persons claiming to be entitled to the shares in consequence of the death or bankruptcy by name, or by the title of representatives of the deceased, or trustee of the bankrupt, or by any like description, at the address in the United Kingdom supplied for the purpose by those so claiming, or

    (b) (until such an address has been so supplied) by giving the notice in any manner in which it might have been given if the death or bankruptcy had not occurred.

(5) If the holder—

    (a) has no registered address in the United Kingdom and has not given to the company an address in the United Kingdom for the service of notices on him, or

    (b) is the holder of a share warrant,

the offer may be made by causing it, or a notice specifying where a copy of it can be obtained or inspected, to be published in the Gazette.

(6) The offer must state a period of not less than 21 days during which it may be accepted; and the offer shall not be withdrawn before the end of that period.

(7) This section does not invalidate a provision to which section 89(3) applies by reason that that provision requires or authorises an offer under it to be made in contravention of any of subsections (1) to (6) above; but, to the extent that the provision requires or authorises such an offer to be so made, it is of no effect.

91 Exclusion of ss 89, 90 by private company

(1) Section 89(1), section 90(1) to (5) or section 90(6) may, as applying to allotments by a private company of equity securities or to such allotments of a particular description, be excluded by a provision contained in the memorandum or articles of that company.

(2) A requirement or authority contained in the memorandum or articles of a private company, if it is inconsistent with any of those subsections, has effect as a provision excluding that subsection; but a provision to which section 89(3) applies is not to be treated as inconsistent with section 89(1).

92 Consequences of contravening ss 89, 90

(1) If there is a contravention of section 89(1), or of section 90(1) to (5) or section 90(6), or of a provision to which section 89(3) applies, the company, and every officer of it who knowingly authorised or permitted the contravention, are jointly and severally liable to compensate any person to whom an offer should have been made under the subsection or provision contravened for any loss, damage, costs or expenses which the person has sustained or incurred by reason of the contravention.

(2) However, no proceedings to recover any such loss, damage, costs or expenses shall be commenced after the expiration of 2 years from the delivery to the registrar of companies of the return of allotments in question or, where equity securities other than shares are granted, from the date of the grant.

93 Saving for other restrictions as to offers

(1) Sections 89 to 92 are without prejudice to any enactment by virtue of which a company is prohibited (whether generally or in specified circumstances) from offering or allotting equity securities to any person.

(2) Where a company cannot by virtue of such an enactment offer or allot equity securities to a holder of relevant shares or relevant employee shares, those sections have effect as if the shares held by that holder were not relevant shares or relevant employee shares.

94 Definitions for ss 89–96

(1) The following subsections apply for the interpretation of sections 89 to 96.
(2) 'Equity security' in relation to a company, means a relevant share in the company (other than a share shown in the memorandum to have been taken by a subscriber to the memorandum or a bonus share), or a right to subscribe for, or to convert securities into, relevant shares in the company.

(3) A reference to the allotment of equity securities or of equity securities consisting of relevant shares of a particular class includes the grant of a right to subscribe for, or to convert any securities into, relevant shares in the company or (as the case may be) relevant shares of a particular class; but such a reference does not include the allotment of any relevant shares pursuant to such a right.

(4) 'Relevant employee shares', in relation to a company, means shares of the company which would be relevant shares in it but for the fact that they are held by a person who acquired them in pursuance of an employees' share scheme.

(5) 'Relevant shares', in relation to a company, means shares in the company other than—

  (a) shares which as respects dividends and capital carry a right to participate only up to a specified amount in a distribution, and
  (b) shares which are held by a person who acquired them in pursuance of an employees' share scheme or, in the case of shares which have not been allotted, are to be allotted in pursuance of such a scheme.

(6) A reference to a class of shares is to shares to which the same rights are attached as to voting and as to participation, both as respects dividends and as respects capital, in a distribution.

(7) In relation to an offer to allot securities required by section 89(1) or by any provision to which section 89(3) applies, a reference in sections 89 to 94 (however expressed) to the holder of shares of any description is to whoever was at the close of business on a date, to be specified in the offer and to fall in the period of 28 days immediately before the date of the offer, the holder of shares of that description.

95 Disapplication of pre-emption rights

(1) Where the directors of a company are generally authorised for purposes of section 80, they may be given power by the articles, or by a special resolution of the company, to allot equity securities pursuant to that authority as if—

  (a) section 89(1) did not apply to the allotment, or
  (b) that subsection applied to the allotment with such modifications as the directors may determine;

and where the directors make an allotment under this subsection, sections 89 to 94 have effect accordingly.

(2) Where the directors of a company are authorised for purposes of section 80 (whether generally or otherwise), the company may by special resolution resolve either—

  (a) that section 89(1) shall not apply to a specified allotment of equity securities to be made pursuant to that authority, or
  (b) that that subsection shall apply to the allotment with such modifications as may be specified in the resolution;

and where such a resolution is passed, sections 89 to 94 have effect accordingly.

(3) The power conferred by subsection (1) or a special resolution under subsection (2) ceases to have effect when the authority to which it relates is revoked or would (if not renewed) expire; but if the authority is renewed, the power or (as the case may be) the resolution may also be renewed, for a period not longer than that for which the authority is renewed, by a special resolution of the company.

(4) Notwithstanding that any such power or resolution has expired, the directors may allot equity securities in pursuance of an offer or agreement previously made by the company, if the power or resolution enabled the company to make an offer or agreement which would or might require equity securities to be allotted after it expired.

(5) A special resolution under subsection (2), or a special resolution to renew such a resolution, shall not be proposed unless it is recommended by the directors and there has been circulated, with the notice of the meeting at which the resolution is proposed, to the members entitled to have that notice a written statement by the directors setting out—

  (a) their reasons for making the recommendation,
  (b) the amount to be paid to the company in respect of the equity securities to be allotted, and
  (c) the directors' justification of that amount.

(6) A person who knowingly or recklessly authorises or permits the inclusion in a statement circulated under subsection (5) of any matter which is misleading, false or deceptive in a material particular is liable to imprisonment or a fine, or both.

96 Saving for company's pre-emption procedure operative before 1982

(1) Where a company which is re-registered or registered as a public company is or, but for the provisions of the Companies Act 1980 and the enactments replacing it, would be subject at the time of re-registration or (as the case may be) registration to a pre-1982 pre-emption requirement, sections 89 to 95 do not apply to an allotment of the equity securities which are subject to that requirement.

(2) A 'pre-1982 pre-emption requirement' is a requirement imposed (whether by the company's memorandum or articles, or otherwise) before the relevant date in 1982 by virtue of which the company must, when making an allotment of equity securities, make an offer to allot those securities or some of them in a manner which (otherwise than because involving a contravention of section 90(1) to (5) or 90(6)) is inconsistent with sections 89 to 94; and 'the relevant date in 1982' is—

  (a) except in a case falling within the following paragraph, 22nd June in that year, and

(b) in the case of a company which was re-registered or registered as a public company on an application made before that date, the date on which the application was made.

(3) A requirement which—

(a) is imposed on a private company (having been so imposed before the relevant date in 1982) otherwise than by the company's memorandum or articles, and
(b) if contained in the company's memorandum or articles, would have effect under section 91 to the exclusion of any provisions of sections 89 to 94,

has effect, so long as the company remains a private company, as if it were contained in the memorandum or articles.

(4) If on the relevant date in 1982 a company, other than a public company registered as such on its original incorporation, was subject to such a requirement as is mentioned in section 89(2) imposed otherwise than by the memorandum or articles, the requirement is to be treated for purposes of sections 89 to 94 as if it were contained in the memorandum or articles.

*   *   *

163 Definitions of 'off-market' and 'market' purchase

(1) A purchase by a company of its own shares is 'off-market' if the shares either—

(a) are purchased otherwise than on a recognised investment exchange, or
(b) are purchased on a recognised investment exchange but are not subject to a marketing arrangement on that investment exchange.

(2) For this purpose, a company's shares are subject to a marketing arrangement on a recognised investment exchange if either—

(a) they are listed under Part IV of the Financial Services Act 1986; or
(b) the company has been afforded facilities for dealings in those shares to take place on that investment exchange without prior permission for individual transactions from the authority governing that stock exchange and without limit as to the time during which those facilities are to be available.

(3) A purchase by a company of its own shares is a 'market purchase' if it is a purchase made on a recognised investment exchange, other than a purchase which is an off-market purchase by virtue of subsection (1)(b).

(4) In this section 'recognised investment exchange' means a recognised investment exchange other than an overseas investment exchange within the meaning of the Financial Services Act 1986.

164 Authority for off-market purchase

(1) A company may only make an off-market purchase of its own shares in pursuance of a contract approved in advance in accordance with this section or under section 165 below.

(2) The terms of the proposed contract must be authorised by a special resolution of the company before the contract is entered into; and the following subsections apply with respect to that authority and to resolutions conferring it.

(3) Subject to the next subsection, the authority may be varied, revoked or from time to time renewed by special resolution of the company.

(4) In the case of a public company, the authority conferred by the resolution must specify a date on which the authority is to expire; and in a resolution conferring or renewing authority that date must not be later than 18 months after that on which the resolution is passed.

(5) A special resolution to confer, vary, revoke or renew authority is not effective if any member of the company holding shares to which the resolution relates exercises the voting rights carried by any of those shares in voting on the resolution and the resolution would not have been passed if he had not done so.

For this purpose—

    (a) a member who holds shares to which the resolution relates is regarded as exercising the voting rights carried by those shares not only if he votes in respect of them on a poll on the question whether the resolution shall be passed, but also if he votes on the resolution otherwise than on a poll;

    (b) notwithstanding anything in the company's articles, any member of the company may demand a poll on that question; and

    (c) a vote and a demand for a poll by a person as proxy for a member are the same respectively as a vote and a demand by the member.

(6) Such a resolution is not effective for the purposes of this section unless (if the proposed contract is in writing) a copy of the contract or (if not) a written memorandum of its terms is available for inspection by members of the company both—

    (a) at the company's registered office for not less than 15 days ending with the date of the meeting at which the resolution is passed, and

    (b) at the meeting itself.

A memorandum of contract terms so made available must include the names of any members holding shares to which the contract relates; and a copy of the contract so made available must have annexed to it a written memorandum specifying any such names which do not appear in the contract itself.

(7) A company may agree to a variation of an existing contract so approved, but only if the variation is authorised by a special resolution of the company before it is agreed to; and subsections (3) to (6) above apply to the authority for a proposed variation as they apply to the authority for a proposed contract, save that a copy of the original contract or (as the case may require) a memorandum of its terms, together with any variations previously made, must also be available for inspection in accordance with subsection (6).

165 Authority for contingent purchase contract

(1) A contingent purchase contract is a contract entered into by a company and relating to any of its shares—

    (a) which does not amount to a contract to purchase those shares, but

    (b) under which the company may (subject to any conditions) become entitled or obliged to purchase those shares.

(2) A company may only make a purchase of its own shares in pursuance of a contingent purchase contract if the contract is approved in advance by a special resolution of the company before the contract is entered into; and subsections (3) to (7) of section 164 apply to the contract and its terms.

166 Authority for market purchase

(1) A company shall not make a market purchase of its own shares unless the purchase has first been authorised by the company in general meeting.

(2) That authority—

 (a) may be general for that purpose, or limited to the purchase of shares of any particular class or description, and
 (b) may be unconditional or subject to conditions.

(3) The authority must—

 (a) specify the maximum number of shares authorised to be acquired,
 (b) determine both the maximum and the minimum prices which may be paid for the shares, and
 (c) specify a date on which it is to expire.

(4) The authority may be varied, revoked or from time to time renewed by the company in general meeting, but this is subject to subsection (3) above; and in a resolution to confer or renew authority, the date on which the authority is to expire must not be later than 18 months after that on which the resolution is passed.

(5) A company may under this section make a purchase of its own shares after the expiry of the time limit imposed to comply with subsection (3)(c), if the contract of purchase was concluded before the authority expired and the terms of the authority permitted the company to make a contract of purchase which would or might be executed wholly or partly after its expiration.

(6) A resolution to confer or vary authority under this section may determine either or both the maximum and minimum prices for purchase by—

 (a) specifying a particular sum, or
 (b) providing a basis or formula for calculating the amount of the price in question without reference to any person's discretion or opinion.

(7) A resolution of a company conferring, varying, revoking or renewing authority under this section is subject to section 380 (resolution to be sent to a registrar of companies within 15 days).

167 Assignment or release of company's right to purchase own shares

(1) The rights of a company under a contract approved under section 164 or 165, or under a contract for a purchase authorised under section 166, are not capable of being assigned.

(2) An agreement by a company to release its rights under a contract approved under section 164 or 165 is void unless the terms of the release agreement are approved in advance by a special resolution of the company before the agreement is entered into; and subsections (3) to (7) of section 164 apply to approval for a proposed release agreement as to authority for a proposed variation of an existing contract.

168 Payments apart from purchase price to be made out of distributable profits

(1) A payment made by a company in consideration of—

 (a) acquiring any right with respect to the purchase of its own shares in pursuance of a contract approved under section 165, or

(b) the variation of a contract approved under section 164 or 165, or

(c) the release of any of the company's obligations with respect to the purchase of any of its shares under a contract approved under section 164 or 165 or under a contract for a purchase authorised under section 166,

must be made out of the company's distributable profits.

(2) If the requirements of subsection (1) are not satisfied in relation to a contract—

(a) in a case within paragraph (a) of the subsection, no purchase by the company of its own shares in pursuance of that contract is lawful under this Chapter,

(b) in a case within paragraph (b), no such purchase following the variation is lawful under this Chapter, and

(c) in a case within paragraph (c), the purported release is void.

169 Disclosure by company of purchase of own shares

(1) Within the period of 28 days beginning with the date on which any shares purchased by a company under this Chapter are delivered to it, the company shall deliver to the registrar of companies for registration a return in the prescribed form stating with respect to shares of each class purchased the number and nominal value of those shares and the date on which they were delivered to the company.

(2) In the case of a public company, the return shall also state—

(a) the aggregate amount paid by the company for the shares; and

(b) the maximum and minimum prices paid in respect of shares of each class purchased.

(3) Particulars of shares delivered to the company on different dates and under different contracts may be included in a single return to the registrar; and in such a case the amount required to be stated under subsection (2)(a) is the aggregate amount paid by the company for all the shares to which the return relates.

(4) Where a company enters into a contract approved under section 164 or 165, or a contract for a purchase authorised under section 166, the company shall keep at its registered office—

(a) if the contract is in writing, a copy of it; and

(b) if not, a memorandum of its terms,

from the conclusion of the contract until the end of the period of 10 years beginning with the date on which the purchase of all the shares in pursuance of the contract is completed or (as the case may be) the date on which the contract otherwise determines.

(5) Every copy and memorandum so required to be kept shall, during business hours (subject to such reasonable restrictions as the company may in general meeting impose, provided that not less than 2 hours in each day are allowed for inspection) be open to inspection without charge—

(a) by any member of the company, and

(b) if it is a public company, by any other person.

(6) If default is made in delivering to the registrar any return required by this section, every officer of the company who is in default is liable to a fine and, for continued contravention, to a daily default fine.

(7) If default is made in complying with subsection (4), or if an inspection required under subsection (5) is refused, the company and every officer of it who is in default is liable to a fine and, for continued contravention, to a daily default fine.

(8) In the case of a refusal of an inspection required under subsection (5) of a copy or memorandum, the court may by order compel an immediate inspection of it.

(9) The obligation of a company under subsection (4) to keep a copy of any contract or (as the case may be) a memorandum of its terms applies to any variation of the contract so long as it applies to the contract.

170 The capital redemption reserve

(1) Where under this Chapter shares of a company are redeemed or purchased wholly out of the company's profits, the amount by which the company's issued share capital is diminished in accordance with section 160(4) on cancellation of the shares redeemed or purchased shall be transferred to a reserve, called 'the capital redemption reserve'.

(2) If the shares are redeemed or purchased wholly or partly out of the proceeds of a fresh issue and the aggregate amount of those proceeds is less than the aggregate nominal value of the shares redeemed or purchased, the amount of the difference shall be transferred to the capital redemption reserve.

(3) But subsection (2) does not apply if the proceeds of the fresh issue are applied by the company in making a redemption or purchase of its own shares in addition to a payment out of capital under section 171.

(4) The provisions of this Act relating to the reduction of a company's share capital apply as if the capital redemption reserve were paid-up share capital of the company, except that the reserve may be applied by the company in paying up its unissued shares to be allotted to members of the company as fully paid bonus shares.

*   *   *

346 'Connected persons', etc

(1) This section has effect with respect to references in this Part to a person being 'connected' with a director of a company, and to a director being 'associated with' or 'controlling' a body corporate.

(2) A person is connected with a director of a company if, but only if, he (not being himself a director of it) is—

(a)   that director's spouse, child or step-child; or
(b)   except where the context otherwise requires, a body corporate with which the director is associated; or
(c)   a person acting in his capacity as trustee of any trust the beneficiaries of which include—
    (i)   the director, his spouse or any children or step-children of his, or
    (ii)   a body corporate with which he is associated,
    or of a trust whose terms confer a power on the trustees that may be exercised for the benefit of the director, his spouse, or any children or step-children of his, or any such body corporate; or
(d)   a person acting in his capacity as partner of that director or of any person who, by virtue of paragraph (a), (b) or (c) of this subsection, is connected with that director; or
(e)   a Scottish firm in which—

(i)   that director is a partner,

(ii)   a partner is a person who, by virtue of paragraph (a), (b) or (c) above, is connected with that director, or

(iii)   a partner is a Scottish firm in which that director is a partner or in which there is a partner who, by virtue of paragraph (a), (b) or (c) above, is connected with that director.

(3) In subsection (2)—

(a)   a reference to the child or step-child of any person includes an illegitimate child of his, but does not include any person who has attained the age of 18; and

(b)   paragraph (c) does not apply to a person acting in his capacity as trustee under an employees' share scheme or a pension scheme.

(4) A director of a company is associated with a body corporate if, but only if, he and the persons connected with him, together—

(a)   are interested in shares comprised in the equity share capital of that body corporate of a nominal value equal to at least one-fifth of that share capital; or

(b)   are entitled to exercise or control the exercise of more than one-fifth of the voting power at any general meeting of that body.

(5) A director of a company is deemed to control a body corporate if, but only if—

(a)   he or any person connected with him is interested in any part of the equity share capital of that body or is entitled to exercise or control the exercise of any part of the voting power at any general meeting of that body; and

(b)   that director, the persons connected with him and the other directors of that company, together, are interested in more than one-half of that share capital or are entitled to exercise or control the exercise of more than one-half of that voting power.

(6) For purposes of subsections (4) and (5)—

(a)   a body corporate with which a director is associated is not to be treated as connected with that director unless it is also connected with him by virtue of subsection (2)(c) or (d); and

(b)   a trustee of a trust the beneficiaries of which include (or may include) a body corporate with which a director is associated is not to be treated as connected with a director by reason only of that fact.

(7) The rules set out in Part I of Schedule 13 apply for the purposes of subsections (4) and (5).

(8) References in those subsections to voting power the exercise of which is controlled by a director include voting power whose exercise is controlled by a body corporate controlled by him; but this is without prejudice to other provisions of subsections (4) and (5).

CRIMINAL JUSTICE ACT 1993

58 Information 'made public'

(1) For the purposes of section 56, 'made public', in relation to information, shall be construed in accordance with the following provisions of this section; but those provisions are not exhaustive as to the meaning of that expression.

(2) Information is made public if—

   (a) it is published in accordance with the rules of a regulated market for the purpose of informing investors and their professional advisers;
   (b) it is contained in records which by virtue of any enactment are open to inspection by the public;
   (c) it can be readily acquired by those likely to deal in any securities—
       (i) to which the information relates, or
       (ii) of an issuer to which the information relates; or
   (d) it is derived from information which has been made public.

(3) Information may be treated as made public even though—

   (a) it can be acquired only by persons exercising diligence or expertise;
   (b) it is communicated to a section of the public and not to the public at large;
   (c) it can be acquired only by observation;
   (d) it is communicated only on payment of a fee; or
   (e) it is published only outside the United Kingdom.

FINANCIAL SERVICES ACT 1986

57 Restrictions on advertising

(1) Subject to section 58 below, no person other than an authorised person shall issue or cause to be issued an investment advertisement in the United Kingdom unless its contents have been approved by an authorised person.

(2) In this Act 'an investment advertisement' means any advertisement inviting persons to enter or offer to enter into an investment agreement or to exercise any rights conferred by an investment to acquire, dispose of, underwrite or convert an investment or containing information calculated to lead directly or indirectly to persons doing so.

(3) Subject to subsection (4) below, any person who contravenes this section shall be guilty of an offence and liable—

  (a) on conviction on indictment, to imprisonment for a term not exceeding two years or to a fine or to both;
  (b) on summary conviction, to imprisonment for a term not exceeding six months or to a fine not exceeding the statutory maximum or to both.

(4) A person who in the ordinary course of a business other than investment business issues an advertisement to the order of another person shall not be guilty of an offence under this section if he proves that he believed on reasonable grounds that the person to whose order the advertisement was issued was an authorised person, that the contents of the advertisement were approved by an authorised person or that the advertisement was permitted by or under section 58 below.

(5) If in contravention of this section a person issues or causes to be issued an advertisement inviting persons to enter or offer to enter into an investment agreement or containing information calculated to lead directly or indirectly to persons doing so, then, subject to subsection (8) below—

  (a) he shall not be entitled to enforce any agreement to which the advertisement related and which was entered into after the issue of the advertisement; and
  (b) the other party shall be entitled to recover any money or other property paid or transferred by him under the agreement, together with compensation for any loss sustained by him as a result of having parted with it.

(6) If in contravention of this section a person issues or causes to be issued an advertisement inviting persons to exercise any rights conferred by an investment or containing information calculated to lead directly or indirectly to persons doing so, then, subject to subsection (8) below—

  (a) he shall not be entitled to enforce any obligation to which a person is subject as a result of any exercise by him after the issue of the advertisement of any rights to which the advertisement related; and

(b) that person shall be entitled to recover any money or other property paid or transferred by him under any such obligation, together with compensation for any loss sustained by him as a result of having parted with it.

(7) The compensation recoverable under subsection (5) or (6) above shall be such as the parties may agree or as a court may, on the application of either party, determine.

(8) A court may allow any such agreement or obligation as is mentioned in subsection (5) or (6) above to be enforced or money or property paid or transferred under it to be retained if it is satisfied—

(a) that the person against whom enforcement is sought or who is seeking to recover the money or property was not influenced, or not influenced to any material extent, by the advertisement in making his decision to enter into the agreement or as to the exercise of the rights in question; or

(b) that the advertisement was not misleading as to the nature of the investment, the terms of the agreement or, as the case may be, the consequences of exercising the rights in question and fairly stated any risks involved in those matters.

(9) Where a person elects not to perform an agreement or an obligation which by virtue of subsection (5) or (6) above is unenforceable against him or by virtue of either of those subsections recovers money paid or other property transferred by him under an agreement or obligation he shall repay any money and return any other property received by him under the agreement or, as the case may be, as a result of exercising the rights in question.

(10) Where any property transferred under an agreement or obligation to which subsection (5) or (6) above applies has passed to a third party the references to that property in this section shall be construed as references to its value at the time of its transfer under the agreement or obligation.

58 Exceptions from restrictions on advertising

(1) Section 57 above does not apply to—

(a) any advertisement issued or caused to be issued by, and relating only to investments issued by—
   (i) the government of the United Kingdom, of Northern Ireland or of any country or territory outside the United Kingdom;
   (ii) a local authority in the United Kingdom or elsewhere;
   (iii) the Bank of England or the central bank of any country or territory outside the United Kingdom; or
   (iv) any international organisation the members of which include the United Kingdom or another member State;

(b) any advertisement issued or caused to be issued by a person who is exempt under section 36, 38, 42, 43, 44 or 45 above, or by virtue of an order under section 46 above, if the advertisement relates to a matter in respect of which he is exempt;

(c) any advertisement which is issued or caused to be issued by a national of a member State other than the United Kingdom in the course of investment business lawfully carried on by him in such a State and which conforms with any rules made under section 48(2)(e) above;

(d) any advertisement which—
   (i) is subject to section 154 below; or
   (ii) consists of or any part of listing particulars, supplementary listing particulars, a prospectus approved in accordance with listing rules made under section 144(2) or 156A(1) below, a supplementary prospectus approved in

accordance with listing rules made for the purposes or any other document required or permitted to be published by listing rules under Part IV of this Act.

(2) [Repealed]

(3) Section 57 above does not apply to an advertisement issued in such circumstances as may be specified in an order made by the Secretary of State for the purpose of exempting from that section—

(a) advertisements appearing to him to have a private character, whether by reason of a connection between the person issuing them and those to whom they are issued or otherwise;

(b) advertisements appearing to him to deal with investment only incidentally;

(c) advertisements issued to persons appearing to him to be sufficiently expert to understand any risks involved; or

(d) such other classes of advertisement as he thinks fit.

(4) An order under subsection (3) above may require any person who by virtue of the order is authorised to issue an advertisement to comply with such requirements as are specified in the order.

(5) An order made by virtue of paragraph (a), (b) or (c) of subsection (3) above shall be subject to annulment in pursuance of a resolution of either House of Parliament; and no order shall be made by virtue of paragraph (d) of that subsection unless a draft of it has been laid before and approved by a resolution of each House of Parliament.

(6) Subsection (1)(c) above does not apply to any advertisement relating to an investment falling within paragraph 5 of Schedule 1 to this Act.

FINANCIAL SERVICES AND MARKETS ACT 2000

PART VI

OFFICIAL LISTING

The competent authority

72 The competent authority

(1) On the coming into force of this section, the functions conferred on the competent authority by this Part are to be exercised by the Authority.

(2) Schedule 7 modifies this Act in its application to the Authority when it acts as the competent authority.

(3) But provision is made by Schedule 8 allowing some or all of those functions to be transferred by the Treasury so as to be exercisable by another person.

73 General duty of the competent authority

(1) In discharging its general functions the competent authority must have regard to—

  (a) the need to use its resources in the most efficient and economic way;
  (b) the principle that a burden or restriction which is imposed on a person should be proportionate to the benefits, considered in general terms, which are expected to arise from the imposition of that burden or restriction;
  (c) the desirability of facilitating innovation in respect of listed securities;
  (d) the international character of capital markets and the desirability of maintaining the competitive position of the United Kingdom;
  (e) the need to minimise the adverse effects on competition of anything done in the discharge of those functions;
  (f) the desirability of facilitating competition in relation to listed securities.

(2) The competent authority's general functions are—

  (a) its function of making rules under this Part (considered as a whole);
  (b) its functions in relation to the giving of general guidance in relation to this Part (considered as a whole);
  (c) its function of determining the general policy and principles by reference to which it performs particular functions under this Part.

The official list

74   The official list

(1) The competent authority must maintain the official list.

(2) The competent authority may admit to the official list such securities and other things as it considers appropriate.

(3) But—

    (a)   nothing may be admitted to the official list except in accordance with this Part; and

    (b)   the Treasury may by order provide that anything which falls within a description or category specified in the order may not be admitted to the official list.

(4) The competent authority may make rules ('listing rules') for the purposes of this Part.

(5) In the following provisions of this Part—

'security' means anything which has been, or may be, admitted to the official list; and 'listing' means being included in the official list in accordance with this Part.

Listing

75   Applications for listing

(1) Admission to the official list may be granted only on an application made to the competent authority in such manner as may be required by listing rules.

(2) No application for listing may be entertained by the competent authority unless it is made by, or with the consent of, the issuer of the securities concerned.

(3) No application for listing may be entertained by the competent authority in respect of securities which are to be issued by a body of a prescribed kind.

(4) The competent authority may not grant an application for listing unless it is satisfied that—

    (a)   the requirements of listing rules (so far as they apply to the application), and

    (b)   any other requirements imposed by the authority in relation to the application,

are complied with.

(5) An application for listing may be refused if, for a reason relating to the issuer, the competent authority considers that granting it would be detrimental to the interests of investors.

(6) An application for listing securities which are already officially listed in another EEA State may be refused if the issuer has failed to comply with any obligations to which he is subject as a result of that listing.

76   Decision on application

(1) The competent authority must notify the applicant of its decision on an application for listing—

    (a)   before the end of the period of six months beginning with the date on which the application is received; or

(b)   if within that period the authority has required the applicant to provide further information in connection with the application, before the end of the period of six months beginning with the date on which that information is provided.

(2) If the competent authority fails to comply with subsection (1), it is to be taken to have decided to refuse the application.

(3) If the competent authority decides to grant an application for listing, it must give the applicant written notice.

(4) If the competent authority proposes to refuse an application for listing, it must give the applicant a warning notice.

(5) If the competent authority decides to refuse an application for listing, it must give the applicant a decision notice.

(6) If the competent authority decides to refuse an application for listing, the applicant may refer the matter to the Tribunal.

(7) If securities are admitted to the official list, their admission may not be called in question on the ground that any requirement or condition for their admission has not been complied with.

77   Discontinuance and suspension of listing

(1) The competent authority may, in accordance with listing rules, discontinue the listing of any securities if satisfied that there are special circumstances which preclude normal regular dealings in them.

(2) The competent authority may, in accordance with listing rules, suspend the listing of any securities.

(3) If securities are suspended under subsection (2) they are to be treated, for the purposes of sections 96 and 99, as still being listed.

(4) This section applies to securities whenever they were admitted to the official list.

(5) If the competent authority discontinues or suspends the listing of any securities, the issuer may refer the matter to the Tribunal.

78   Discontinuance or suspension: procedure

(1) A discontinuance or suspension takes effect—

(a)   immediately, if the notice under subsection (2) states that that is the case;
(b)   in any other case, on such date as may be specified in that notice.

(2) If the competent authority—

(a)   proposes to discontinue or suspend the listing of securities, or
(b)   discontinues or suspends the listing of securities with immediate effect,

it must give the issuer of the securities written notice.

(3) The notice must—

(a)   give details of the discontinuance or suspension;
(b)   state the competent authority's reasons for the discontinuance or suspension and for choosing the date on which it took effect or takes effect;

(c) inform the issuer of the securities that he may make representations to the competent authority within such period as may be specified in the notice (whether or not he has referred the matter to the Tribunal);

(d) inform him of the date on which the discontinuance or suspension took effect or will take effect; and

(e) inform him of his right to refer the matter to the Tribunal.

(4) The competent authority may extend the period within which representations may be made to it.

(5) If, having considered any representations made by the issuer of the securities, the competent authority decides—

(a) to discontinue or suspend the listing of the securities, or

(b) if the discontinuance or suspension has taken effect, not to cancel it,

the competent authority must give the issuer of the securities written notice.

(6) A notice given under subsection (5) must inform the issuer of the securities of his right to refer the matter to the Tribunal.

(7) If a notice informs a person of his right to refer a matter to the Tribunal, it must give an indication of the procedure on such a reference.

(8) If the competent authority decides—

(a) not to discontinue or suspend the listing of the securities, or

(b) if the discontinuance or suspension has taken effect, to cancel it,

the competent authority must give the issuer of the securities written notice.

(9) The effect of cancelling a discontinuance is that the securities concerned are to be readmitted, without more, to the official list.

(10) If the competent authority has suspended the listing of securities and proposes to refuse an application by the issuer of the securities for the cancellation of the suspension, it must give him a warning notice.

(11) The competent authority must, having considered any representations made in response to the warning notice—

(a) if it decides to refuse the application, give the issuer of the securities a decision notice;

(b) if it grants the application, give him written notice of its decision.

(12) If the competent authority decides to refuse an application for the cancellation of the suspension of listed securities, the applicant may refer the matter to the Tribunal.

(13) 'Discontinuance' means a discontinuance of listing under section 77(1).

(14) 'Suspension' means a suspension of listing under section 77(2).

Listing particulars

79   Listing particulars and other documents

(1) Listing rules may provide that securities (other than new securities) of a kind specified in the rules may not be admitted to the official list unless—

(a) listing particulars have been submitted to, and approved by, the competent authority and published; or

(b) in such cases as may be specified by listing rules, such document (other than listing particulars or a prospectus of a kind required by listing rules) as may be so specified has been published.

(2) 'Listing particulars' means a document in such form and containing such information as may be specified in listing rules.

(3) For the purposes of this Part, the persons responsible for listing particulars are to be determined in accordance with regulations made by the Treasury.

(4) Nothing in this section affects the competent authority's general power to make listing rules.

80 General duty of disclosure in listing particulars

(1) Listing particulars submitted to the competent authority under section 79 must contain all such information as investors and their professional advisers would reasonably require, and reasonably expect to find there, for the purpose of making an informed assessment of—

(a) the assets and liabilities, financial position, profits and losses, and prospects of the issuer of the securities; and

(b) the rights attaching to the securities.

(2) That information is required in addition to any information required by—

(a) listing rules, or

(b) the competent authority,

as a condition of the admission of the securities to the official list.

(3) Subsection (1) applies only to information—

(a) within the knowledge of any person responsible for the listing particulars; or

(b) which it would be reasonable for him to obtain by making enquiries.

(4) In determining what information subsection (1) requires to be included in listing particulars, regard must be had (in particular) to—

(a) the nature of the securities and their issuer;

(b) the nature of the persons likely to consider acquiring them;

(c) the fact that certain matters may reasonably be expected to be within the knowledge of professional advisers of a kind which persons likely to acquire the securities may reasonably be expected to consult; and

(d) any information available to investors or their professional advisers as a result of requirements imposed on the issuer of the securities by a recognised investment exchange, by listing rules or by or under any other enactment.

81 Supplementary listing particulars

(1) If at any time after the preparation of listing particulars which have been submitted to the competent authority under section 79 and before the commencement of dealings in the securities concerned following their admission to the official list—

(a) there is a significant change affecting any matter contained in those particulars the inclusion of which was required by—

      (i)   section 80,

      (ii) listing rules, or

      (iii) the competent authority, or

  (b)   a significant new matter arises, the inclusion of information in respect of which would have been so required if it had arisen when the particulars were prepared,

the issuer must, in accordance with listing rules, submit supplementary listing particulars of the change or new matter to the competent authority, for its approval and, if they are approved, publish them.

(2) 'Significant' means significant for the purpose of making an informed assessment of the kind mentioned in section 80(1).

(3) If the issuer of the securities is not aware of the change or new matter in question, he is not under a duty to comply with subsection (1) unless he is notified of the change or new matter by a person responsible for the listing particulars.

(4) But it is the duty of any person responsible for those particulars who is aware of such a change or new matter to give notice of it to the issuer.

(5) Subsection (1) applies also as respects matters contained in any supplementary listing particulars previously published under this section in respect of the securities in question.

82   Exemptions from disclosure

(1) The competent authority may authorise the omission from listing particulars of any information, the inclusion of which would otherwise be required by section 80 or 81, on the ground—

  (a)   that its disclosure would be contrary to the public interest;

  (b)   that its disclosure would be seriously detrimental to the issuer; or

  (c)   in the case of securities of a kind specified in listing rules, that its disclosure is unnecessary for persons of the kind who may be expected normally to buy or deal in securities of that kind.

(2) But—

  (a)   no authority may be granted under subsection (1)(b) in respect of essential information; and

  (b)   no authority granted under subsection (1)(b) extends to any such information.

(3) The Secretary of State or the Treasury may issue a certificate to the effect that the disclosure of any information (including information that would otherwise have to be included in listing particulars for which they are themselves responsible) would be contrary to the public interest.

(4) The competent authority is entitled to act on any such certificate in exercising its powers under subsection (1)(a).

(5) This section does not affect any powers of the competent authority under listing rules made as a result of section 101(2).

(6) 'Essential information' means information which a person considering acquiring securities of the kind in question would be likely to need in order not to be misled about any facts which it is essential for him to know in order to make an informed assessment.

(7) 'Listing particulars' includes supplementary listing particulars.

83   Registration of listing particulars

(1) On or before the date on which listing particulars are published as required by listing rules, a copy of the particulars must be delivered for registration to the registrar of companies.

(2) A statement that a copy has been delivered to the registrar must be included in the listing particulars when they are published.

(3) If there has been a failure to comply with subsection (1) in relation to listing particulars which have been published—

(a)   the issuer of the securities in question, and
(b)   any person who is a party to the publication and aware of the failure,

is guilty of an offence.

(4) A person guilty of an offence under subsection (3) is liable—

(a)   on summary conviction, to a fine not exceeding the statutory maximum;
(b)   on conviction on indictment, to a fine.

(5) 'Listing particulars' includes supplementary listing particulars.

(6) 'The registrar of companies' means—

(a)   if the securities are, or are to be, issued by a company incorporated in Great Britain whose registered office is in England and Wales, the registrar of companies in England and Wales;
(b)   if the securities are, or are to be, issued by a company incorporated in Great Britain whose registered office is in Scotland, the registrar of companies in Scotland;
(c)   if the securities are, or are to be, issued by a company incorporated in Northern Ireland, the registrar of companies for Northern Ireland; and
(d)   in any other case, any of those registrars.

Prospectuses

84   Prospectuses

(1) Listing rules must provide that no new securities for which an application for listing has been made may be admitted to the official list unless a prospectus has been submitted to, and approved by, the competent authority and published.

(2) 'New securities' means securities which are to be offered to the public in the United Kingdom for the first time before admission to official list.

(3) 'Prospectus' means a prospectus in such form and containing such information as may be specified in listing rules.

(4) Nothing in this section affects the competent authority's general power to make listing rules.

85   Publication of prospectus

(1) If listing rules made under section 84 require a prospectus to be published before particular new securities are admitted to the official list, it is unlawful for any of those securities to be offered to the public in the United Kingdom before the required prospectus is published.

(2) A person who contravenes subsection (1) is guilty of an offence and liable—

- (a) on summary conviction, to imprisonment for a term not exceeding three months or a fine not exceeding level 5 on the standard scale;
- (b) on conviction on indictment, to imprisonment for a term not exceeding two years or a fine, or both.

(3) A person is not to be regarded as contravening subsection (1) merely because a prospectus does not fully comply with the requirements of listing rules as to its form or content.

(4) But subsection (3) does not affect the question whether any person is liable to pay compensation under section 90.

(5) Any contravention of subsection (1) is actionable, at the suit of a person who suffers loss as a result of the contravention, subject to the defences and other incidents applying to actions for breach of statutory duty.

86 Application of this Part to prospectuses

(1) The provisions of this Part apply in relation to a prospectus required by listing rules as they apply in relation to listing particulars.

(2) In this Part—

- (a) any reference to listing particulars is to be read as including a reference to a prospectus; and
- (b) any reference to supplementary listing particulars is to be read as including a reference to a supplementary prospectus.

87 Approval of prospectus where no application for listing

(1) Listing rules may provide for a prospectus to be submitted to and approved by the competent authority if—

- (a) securities are to be offered to the public in the United Kingdom for the first time;
- (b) no application for listing of the securities has been made under this Part; and
- (c) the prospectus is submitted by, or with the consent of, the issuer of the securities.

(2) 'Non-listing prospectus' means a prospectus submitted to the competent authority as a result of any listing rules made under subsection (1).

(3) Listing rules made under subsection (1) may make provision—

- (a) as to the information to be contained in, and the form of, a non-listing prospectus; and
- (b) as to the timing and manner of publication of a non-listing prospectus.

(4) The power conferred by subsection (3)(b) is subject to such provision made by or under any other enactment as the Treasury may by order specify.

(5) Schedule 9 modifies provisions of this Part as they apply in relation to non-listing prospectuses.

Sponsors

88   Sponsors

(1) Listing rules may require a person to make arrangements with a sponsor for the performance by the sponsor of such services in relation to him as may be specified in the rules.

(2) 'Sponsor' means a person approved by the competent authority for the purposes of the rules.

(3) Listing rules made by virtue of subsection (1) may—

    (a)   provide for the competent authority to maintain a list of sponsors;
    (b)   specify services which must be performed by a sponsor;
    (c)   impose requirements on a sponsor in relation to the provision of services or specified services;
    (d)   specify the circumstances in which a person is qualified for being approved as a sponsor.

(4) If the competent authority proposes—

    (a)   to refuse a person's application for approval as a sponsor, or
    (b)   to cancel a person's approval as a sponsor,

it must give him a warning notice.

(5) If, after considering any representations made in response to the warning notice, the competent authority decides—

    (a)   to grant the application for approval, or
    (b)   not to cancel the approval,

it must give the person concerned, and any person to whom a copy of the warning notice was given, written notice of its decision.

(6) If, after considering any representations made in response to the warning notice, the competent authority decides—

    (a)   to refuse to grant the application for approval, or
    (b)   to cancel the approval,

it must give the person concerned a decision notice.

(7) A person to whom a decision notice is given under this section may refer the matter to the Tribunal.

89   Public censure of sponsor

(1) Listing rules may make provision for the competent authority, if it considers that a sponsor has contravened a requirement imposed on him by rules made as a result of section 88(3)(c), to publish a statement to that effect.

(2) If the competent authority proposes to publish a statement it must give the sponsor a warning notice setting out the terms of the proposed statement.

(3) If, after considering any representations made in response to the warning notice, the competent authority decides to make the proposed statement, it must give the sponsor a decision notice setting out the terms of the statement.

Appendix 1
STATUTORY MATERIALS

(4) A sponsor to whom a decision notice is given under this section may refer the matter to the Tribunal.

Compensation

90 Compensation for false or misleading particulars

(1) Any person responsible for listing particulars is liable to pay compensation to a person who has—

    (a)   acquired securities to which the particulars apply; and

    (b)   suffered loss in respect of them as a result of—

        (i)   any untrue or misleading statement in the particulars; or

        (ii)   the omission from the particulars of any matter required to be included by section 80 or 81.

(2) Subsection (1) is subject to exemptions provided by Schedule 10.

(3) If listing particulars are required to include information about the absence of a particular matter, the omission from the particulars of that information is to be treated as a statement in the listing particulars that there is no such matter.

(4) Any person who fails to comply with section 81 is liable to pay compensation to any person who has—

    (a)   acquired securities of the kind in question; and

    (b)   suffered loss in respect of them as a result of the failure.

(5) Subsection (4) is subject to exemptions provided by Schedule 10.

(6) This section does not affect any liability which may be incurred apart from this section.

(7) References in this section to the acquisition by a person of securities include references to his contracting to acquire them or any interest in them.

(8) No person shall, by reason of being a promoter of a company or otherwise, incur any liability for failing to disclose information which he would not be required to disclose in listing particulars in respect of a company's securities—

    (a)   if he were responsible for those particulars; or

    (b)   if he is responsible for them, which he is entitled to omit by virtue of section 82.

(9) The reference in subsection (8) to a person incurring liability includes a reference to any other person being entitled as against that person to be granted any civil remedy or to rescind or repudiate an agreement.

(10) 'Listing particulars', in subsection (1) and Schedule 10, includes supplementary listing particulars.

Penalties

91 Penalties for breach of listing rules

(1) If the competent authority considers that—

    (a)   an issuer of listed securities, or

    (b)   an applicant for listing,

has contravened any provision of listing rules, it may impose on him a penalty of such amount as it considers appropriate.

(2) If, in such a case, the competent authority considers that a person who was at the material time a director of the issuer or applicant was knowingly concerned in the contravention, it may impose on him a penalty of such amount as it considers appropriate.

(3) If the competent authority is entitled to impose a penalty on a person under this section in respect of a particular matter it may, instead of imposing a penalty on him in respect of that matter, publish a statement censuring him.

(4) Nothing in this section prevents the competent authority from taking any other steps which it has power to take under this Part.

(5) A penalty under this section is payable to the competent authority.

(6) The competent authority may not take action against a person under this section after the end of the period of two years beginning with the first day on which it knew of the contravention unless proceedings against that person, in respect of the contravention, were begun before the end of that period.

(7) For the purposes of subsection (6)—

   (a)   the competent authority is to be treated as knowing of a contravention if it has information from which the contravention can reasonably be inferred; and
   (b)   proceedings against a person in respect of a contravention are to be treated as begun when a warning notice is given to him under section 92.

92   Procedure

(1) If the competent authority proposes to take action against a person under section 91, it must give him a warning notice.

(2) A warning notice about a proposal to impose a penalty must state the amount of the proposed penalty.

(3) A warning notice about a proposal to publish a statement must set out the terms of the proposed statement.

(4) If the competent authority decides to take action against a person under section 91, it must give him a decision notice.

(5) A decision notice about the imposition of a penalty must state the amount of the penalty.

(6) A decision notice about the publication of a statement must set out the terms of the statement.

(7) If the competent authority decides to take action against a person under section 91, he may refer the matter to the Tribunal.

93   Statement of policy

(1) The competent authority must prepare and issue a statement ('its policy statement') of its policy with respect to—

   (a)   the imposition of penalties under section 91; and
   (b)   the amount of penalties under that section.

(2) The competent authority's policy in determining what the amount of a penalty should be must include having regard to—

   (a)   the seriousness of the contravention in question in relation to the nature of the requirement contravened;

   (b)   the extent to which that contravention was deliberate or reckless; and

   (c)   whether the person on whom the penalty is to be imposed is an individual.

(3) The competent authority may at any time alter or replace its policy statement.

(4) If its policy statement is altered or replaced, the competent authority must issue the altered or replacement statement.

(5) In exercising, or deciding whether to exercise, its power under section 91 in the case of any particular contravention, the competent authority must have regard to any policy statement published under this section and in force at the time when the contravention in question occurred.

(6) The competent authority must publish a statement issued under this section in the way appearing to the competent authority to be best calculated to bring it to the attention of the public.

(7) The competent authority may charge a reasonable fee for providing a person with a copy of the statement.

(8) The competent authority must, without delay, give the Treasury a copy of any policy statement which it publishes under this section.

94   Statements of policy: procedure

(1) Before issuing a statement under section 93, the competent authority must publish a draft of the proposed statement in the way appearing to the competent authority to be best calculated to bring it to the attention of the public.

(2) The draft must be accompanied by notice that representations about the proposal may be made to the competent authority within a specified time.

(3) Before issuing the proposed statement, the competent authority must have regard to any representations made to it in accordance with subsection (2).

(4) If the competent authority issues the proposed statement it must publish an account, in general terms, of—

   (a)   the representations made to it in accordance with subsection (2); and

   (b)   its response to them.

(5) If the statement differs from the draft published under subsection (1) in a way which is, in the opinion of the competent authority, significant, the competent authority must (in addition to complying with subsection (4)) publish details of the difference.

(6) The competent authority may charge a reasonable fee for providing a person with a copy of a draft published under subsection (1).

(7) This section also applies to a proposal to alter or replace a statement.

Appendix 1

STATUTORY MATERIALS

Competition

95   Competition scrutiny

(1) The Treasury may by order provide for—

  (a)   regulating provisions, and
  (b)   the practices of the competent authority in exercising its functions under this Part ('practices'),

to be kept under review.

(2) Provision made as a result of subsection (1) must require the person responsible for keeping regulating provisions and practices under review to consider—

  (a)   whether any regulating provision or practice has a significantly adverse effect on competition; or
  (b)   whether two or more regulating provisions or practices taken together have, or a particular combination of regulating provisions and practices has, such an effect.

(3) An order under this section may include provision corresponding to that made by any provision of Chapter III of Part X.

(4) Subsection (3) is not to be read as in any way restricting the power conferred by subsection (1).

(5) Subsections (6) to (8) apply for the purposes of provision made by or under this section.

(6) Regulating provisions or practices have a significantly adverse effect on competition if—

  (a)   they have, or are intended or likely to have, that effect; or
  (b)   the effect that they have, or are intended or likely to have, is to require or encourage behaviour which has, or is intended or likely to have, a significantly adverse effect on competition.

(7) If regulating provisions or practices have, or are intended or likely to have, the effect of requiring or encouraging exploitation of the strength of a market position they are to be taken to have, or be intended or be likely to have, an adverse effect on competition.

(8) In determining whether any of the regulating provisions or practices have, or are intended or likely to have, a particular effect, it may be assumed that the persons to whom the provisions concerned are addressed will act in accordance with them.

(9) 'Regulating provisions' means—

  (a)   listing rules,
  (b)   general guidance given by the competent authority in connection with its functions under this Part.

Miscellaneous

96   Obligations of issuers of listed securities

(1) Listing rules may—

  (a)   specify requirements to be complied with by issuers of listed securities; and

(b)   make provision with respect to the action that may be taken by the competent authority in the event of non-compliance.

(2) If the rules require an issuer to publish information, they may include provision authorising the competent authority to publish it in the event of his failure to do so.

(3) This section applies whenever the listed securities were admitted to the official list.

97   Appointment by competent authority of persons to carry out investigations

(1) Subsection (2) applies if it appears to the competent authority that there are circumstances suggesting that—

(a)   there may have been a breach of listing rules;
(b)   a person who was at the material time a director of an issuer of listed securities has been knowingly concerned in a breach of listing rules by that issuer;
(c)   a person who was at the material time a director of a person applying for the admission of securities to the official list has been knowingly concerned in a breach of listing rules by that applicant;
(d)   there may have been a contravention of section 83, 85 or 98.

(2) The competent authority may appoint one or more competent persons to conduct an investigation on its behalf.

(3) Part XI applies to an investigation under subsection (2) as if—

(a)   the investigator were appointed under section 167(1);
(b)   references to the investigating authority in relation to him were to the competent authority;
(c)   references to the offences mentioned in section 168 were to those mentioned in subsection (1)(d);
(d)   references to an authorised person were references to the person under investigation.

98   Advertisements etc. in connection with listing applications

(1) If listing particulars are, or are to be, published in connection with an application for listing, no advertisement or other information of a kind specified by listing rules may be issued in the United Kingdom unless the contents of the advertisement or other information have been submitted to the competent authority and that authority has—

(a)   approved those contents; or
(b)   authorised the issue of the advertisement or information without such approval.

(2) A person who contravenes subsection (1) is guilty of an offence and liable—

(a)   on summary conviction, to a fine not exceeding the statutory maximum;
(b)   on conviction on indictment, to imprisonment for a term not exceeding two years or a fine, or both.

(3) A person who issues an advertisement or other information to the order of another person is not guilty of an offence under subsection (2) if he shows that he believed on reasonable grounds that the advertisement or information had been approved, or its issue authorised, by the competent authority.

(4) If information has been approved, or its issue has been authorised, under this section, neither the person issuing it nor any person responsible for, or for any part of,

the listing particulars incurs any civil liability by reason of any statement in or omission from the information if that information and the listing particulars, taken together, would not be likely to mislead persons of the kind likely to consider acquiring the securities in question.

(5) The reference in subsection (4) to a person incurring civil liability includes a reference to any other person being entitled as against that person to be granted any civil remedy or to rescind or repudiate an agreement.

99   Fees

(1) Listing rules may require the payment of fees to the competent authority in respect of—

    (a)   applications for listing;
    (b)   the continued inclusion of securities in the official list;
    (c)   applications under section 88 for approval as a sponsor; and
    (d)   continued inclusion of sponsors in the list of sponsors.

(2) In exercising its powers under subsection (1), the competent authority may set such fees as it considers will (taking account of the income it expects as the competent authority) enable it—

    (a)   to meet expenses incurred in carrying out its functions under this Part or for any incidental purpose;
    (b)   to maintain adequate reserves; and
    (c)   in the case of the Authority, to repay the principal of, and pay any interest on, any money which it has borrowed and which has been used for the purpose of meeting expenses incurred in relation to—
        (i)   its assumption of functions from the London Stock Exchange Limited in relation to the official list; and
        (ii) its assumption of functions under this Part.

(3) In fixing the amount of any fee which is to be payable to the competent authority, no account is to be taken of any sums which it receives, or expects to receive, by way of penalties imposed by it under this Part.

(4) Subsection (2)(c) applies whether expenses were incurred before or after the coming into force of this Part.

(5) Any fee which is owed to the competent authority under any provision made by or under this Part may be recovered as a debt due to it.

100   Penalties

(1) In determining its policy with respect to the amount of penalties to be imposed by it under this Part, the competent authority must take no account of the expenses which it incurs, or expects to incur, in discharging its functions under this Part.

(2) The competent authority must prepare and operate a scheme for ensuring that the amounts paid to it by way of penalties imposed under this Part are applied for the benefit of issuers of securities admitted to the official list.

(3) The scheme may, in particular, make different provision with respect to different classes of issuer.

(4) Up to date details of the scheme must be set out in a document ('the scheme details').

(5) The scheme details must be published by the competent authority in the way appearing to it to be best calculated to bring them to the attention of the public.

(6) Before making the scheme, the competent authority must publish a draft of the proposed scheme in the way appearing to it to be best calculated to bring it to the attention of the public.

(7) The draft must be accompanied by notice that representations about the proposals may be made to the competent authority within a specified time.

(8) Before making the scheme, the competent authority must have regard to any representations made to it under subsection (7).

(9) If the competent authority makes the proposed scheme, it must publish an account, in general terms, of—

    (a)   the representations made to it in accordance with subsection (7); and
    (b)   its response to them.

(10) If the scheme differs from the draft published under subsection (6) in a way which is, in the opinion of the competent authority, significant the competent authority must (in addition to complying with subsection (9)) publish details of the difference.

(11) The competent authority must, without delay, give the Treasury a copy of any scheme details published by it.

(12) The competent authority may charge a reasonable fee for providing a person with a copy of—

    (a)   a draft published under subsection (6);
    (b)   scheme details.

(13) Subsections (6) to (10) and (12) apply also to a proposal to alter or replace the scheme.

101   Listing rules: general provisions

(1) Listing rules may make different provision for different cases.

(2) Listing rules may authorise the competent authority to dispense with or modify the application of the rules in particular cases and by reference to any circumstances.

(3) Listing rules must be made by an instrument in writing.

(4) Immediately after an instrument containing listing rules is made, it must be printed and made available to the public with or without payment.

(5) A person is not to be taken to have contravened any listing rule if he shows that at the time of the alleged contravention the instrument containing the rule had not been made available as required by subsection (4).

(6) The production of a printed copy of an instrument purporting to be made by the competent authority on which is endorsed a certificate signed by an officer of the authority authorised by it for that purpose and stating—

    (a)   that the instrument was made by the authority,
    (b)   that the copy is a true copy of the instrument, and
    (c)   that on a specified date the instrument was made available to the public as required by subsection (4),

is evidence (or in Scotland sufficient evidence) of the facts stated in the certificate.

(7) A certificate purporting to be signed as mentioned in subsection (6) is to be treated as having been properly signed unless the contrary is shown.

(8) A person who wishes in any legal proceedings to rely on a rule-making instrument may require the Authority to endorse a copy of the instrument with a certificate of the kind mentioned in subsection (6).

102   Exemption from liability in damages

(1) Neither the competent authority nor any person who is, or is acting as, a member, officer or member of staff of the competent authority is to be liable in damages for anything done or omitted in the discharge, or purported discharge, of the authority's functions.

(2) Subsection (1) does not apply—

    (a)   if the act or omission is shown to have been in bad faith; or

    (b)   so as to prevent an award of damages made in respect of an act or omission on the ground that the act or omission was unlawful as a result of section 6(1) of the Human Rights Act 1998.

103   Interpretation of this Part

(1) In this Part—

    'application' means an application made under section 75;

    'issuer', in relation to anything which is or may be admitted to the official list, has such meaning as may be prescribed by the Treasury;

    'listing' has the meaning given in section 74(5);

    'listing particulars' has the meaning given in section 79(2);

    'listing rules' has the meaning given in section 74(4);

    'new securities' has the meaning given in section 84(2);

    'the official list' means the list maintained as the official list by the Authority immediately before the coming into force of section 74, as that list has effect for the time being;

    'security' (except in section 74(2)) has the meaning given in section 74(5).

(2) In relation to any function conferred on the competent authority by this Part, any reference in this Part to the competent authority is to be read as a reference to the person by whom that function is for the time being exercisable.

(3) If, as a result of an order under Schedule 8, different functions conferred on the competent authority by this Part are exercisable by different persons, the powers conferred by section 91 are exercisable by such person as may be determined in accordance with the provisions of the order.

(4) For the purposes of this Part, a person offers securities if, and only if, as principal—

    (a)   he makes an offer which, if accepted, would give rise to a contract for their issue or sale by him or by another person with whom he has made arrangements for their issue or sale; or

    (b)   he invites a person to make such an offer.

(5) 'Offer' and 'offeror' are to be read accordingly.

(6) For the purposes of this Part, the question whether a person offers securities to the public in the United Kingdom is to be determined in accordance with Schedule 11.

(7) For the purpsoes of subsection (4) 'sale' includes any disposal for valuable consideration.

*　*　*

PART XXVII

OFFENCES

Miscellaneous offences

397　Misleading statements and practices

(1) This subsection applies to a person who—

   (a)　makes a statement, promise or forecast which he knows to be misleading, false or deceptive in a material particular;

   (b)　dishonestly conceals any material facts whether in connection with a statement, promise or forecast made by him or otherwise; or

   (c)　recklessly makes (dishonestly or otherwise) a statement, promise or forecast which is misleading, false or deceptive in a material particular.

(2) A person to whom subsection (1) applies is guilty of an offence if he makes the statement, promise or forecast or conceals the facts for the purpose of inducing, or is reckless as to whether it may induce, another person (whether or not the person to whom the statement, promise or forecast is made)—

   (a)　to enter or offer to enter into, or to refrain from entering or offering to enter into, a relevant agreement; or

   (b)　to exercise, or refrain from exercising, any rights conferred by a relevant investment.

(3) Any person who does any act or engages in any course of conduct which creates a false or misleading impression as to the market in or the price or value of any relevant investments is guilty of an offence if he does so for the purpose of creating that impression and of thereby inducing another person to acquire, dispose of, subscribe for or underwrite those investments or to refrain from doing so or to exercise, or refrain from exercising, any rights conferred by those investments.

(4) In proceedings for an offence under subsection (2) brought against a person to whom subsection (1) applies as a result of paragraph (a) of that subsection, it is a defence for him to show that the statement, promise or forecast was made in conformity with price stabilising rules or control of information rules.

(5) In proceedings brought against any person for an offence under subsection (3) it is a defence for him to show—

   (a)　that he reasonably believed that his act or conduct would not create an impression that was false or misleading as to the matters mentioned in that subsection;

   (b)　that he acted or engaged in the conduct—

      (i)　for the purpose of stabilising the price of investments; and

      (ii)　in conformity with price stabilising rules; or

   (c)　that he acted or engaged in the conduct in conformity with control of information rules.

(6) Subsections (1) or (2) do not apply unless—

(a) the statement, promise or forecast is made in or from, or the facts are concealed in or from, the United Kingdom or arrangements are made in or from the United Kingdom for the statement, promise or forecast to be made or the facts to be concealed;

(b) the person on whom the inducement is intended to or may have effect is in the United Kingdom; or

(c) the agreement is or would be entered into or the rights are or would be exercised in the United Kingdom.

(7) Subsection (3) does not apply unless—

(a) the act is done, or the course of conduct is engaged in, in the United Kingdom; or

(b) the false or misleading impression is created there.

(8) A person guilty of an offence under this section is liable—

(a) on summary conviction, to imprisonment for a term not exceeding six months or a fine not exceeding the statutory maximum, or both;

(b) on conviction on indictment, to imprisonment for a term not exceeding seven years or a fine, or both.

(9) 'Relevant agreement' means an agreement—

(a) the entering into or performance of which by either party constitutes an activity of a specified kind or one which falls within a specified class of activity; and

(b) which relates to a relevant investment.

(10) 'Relevant investment' means an investment of a specified kind or one which falls within a prescribed class of investment.

(11) Schedule 2 (except paragraphs 25 and 26) applies for the purposes of subsections (9) and (10) with references to section 22 being read as references to each of those subsections.

(12) Nothing in Schedule 2, as applied by subsection (11), limits the power conferred by subsection (9) or (10).

(13) 'Investment' includes any asset, right or interest.

(14) 'Specified' means specified in an order made by the Treasury.

398   Misleading the Authority: residual cases

(1) A person who, in purported compliance with any requirement imposed by or under this Act, knowingly or recklessly gives the Authority information which is false or misleading in a material particular is guilty of an offence.

(2) Subsection (1) applies only to a requirement in relation to which no other provision of this Act creates an offence in connection with the giving of information.

(3) A person guilty of an offence under this section is liable—

(a) on summary conviction, to a fine not exceeding the statutory maximum;

(b) on conviction on indictment, to a fine.

399   Misleading the Director General of Fair Trading

Section 44 of the Competition Act 1998 (offences connected with the provision of false or misleading information) applies in relation to any function of the Director General of Fair Trading under this Act as if it were a function under Part I of that Act.

Bodies corporate and partnerships

400   Offences by bodies corporate etc.

(1) If an offence under this Act committed by a body corporate is shown—

    (a)   to have been committed with the consent or connivance of an officer, or
    (b)   to be attributable to any neglect on his part,

the officer as well as the body corporate is guilty of the offence and liable to be proceeded against and punished accordingly.

(2) If the affairs of a body corporate are managed by its members, subsection (1) applies in relation to the acts and defaults of a member in connection with his functions of management as if he were a director of the body.

(3) If an offence under this Act committed by a partnership is shown—

    (a)   to have been committed with the consent or connivance of a partner, or
    (b)   to be attributable to any neglect on his part,

the partner as well as the partnership is guilty of the offence and liable to be proceeded against and punished accordingly.

(4) In subsection (3) 'partner' includes a person purporting to act as a partner.

(5) 'Officer', in relation to a body corporate, means—

    (a)   a director, member of the committee of management, chief executive, manager, secretary or other similar officer of the body, or a person purporting to act in any such capacity; and
    (b)   an individual who is a controller of the body.

(6) If an offence under this Act committed by an unincorporated association (other than a partnership) is shown—

    (a)   to have been committed with the consent or connivance of an officer of the association or a member of its governing body, or
    (b)   to be attributable to any neglect on the part of such an officer or member,

that officer or member as well as the association is guilty of the offence and liable to be proceeded against and punished accordingly.

(7) Regulations may provide for the application of any provision of this section, with such modifications as the Treasury consider appropriate, to a body corporate or unincorporated association formed or recognised under the law of a territory outside the United Kingdom.

Institution of proceedings

401 Proceedings for offences

(1) In this section 'offence' means an offence under this Act or subordinate legislation made under this Act.

(2) Proceedings for an offence may be instituted in England and Wales only—

(a) by the Authority or the Secretary of State; or
(b) by or with the consent of the Director of Public Prosecutions.

(3) Proceedings for an offence may be instituted in Northern Ireland only—

(a) by the Authority or the Secretary of State; or
(b) by or with the consent of the Director of Public Prosecutions for Northern Ireland.

(4) Except in Scotland, proceedings for an offence under section 203 may also be instituted by the Director General of Fair Trading.

(5) In exercising its power to institute proceedings for an offence, the Authority must comply with any conditions or restrictions imposed in writing by the Treasury.

(6) Conditions or restrictions may be imposed under subsection (5) in relation to—

(a) proceedings generally; or
(b) such proceedings, or categories of proceedings, as the Treasury may direct.

402 Power of the Authority to institute proceedings for certain other offences

(1) Except in Scotland, the Authority may institute proceedings for an offence under—

(a) Part V of the Criminal Justice Act 1993 (insider dealing); or
(b) prescribed regulations relating to money laundering.

(2) In exercising its power to institute proceedings for any such offence, the Authority must comply with any conditions or restrictions imposed in writing by the Treasury.

(3) Conditions or restrictions may be imposed under subsection (2) in relation to—

(a) proceedings generally; or
(b) such proceedings, or categories of proceedings, as the Treasury may direct.

403 Jurisdiction and procedure in respect of offences

(1) A fine imposed on an unincorporated association on its conviction of an offence is to be paid out of the funds of the association.

(2) Proceedings for an offence alleged to have been committed by an unincorporated association must be brought in the name of the association (and not in that of any of its members).

(3) Rules of court relating to the service of documents are to have effect as if the association were a body corporate.

(4) In proceedings for an offence brought against an unincorporated association—

(a) section 33 of the Criminal Justice Act 1925 and Schedule 3 to the Magistrates' Courts Act 1980 (procedure) apply as they do in relation to a body corporate;

  (b) section 70 of the Criminal Procedure (Scotland) Act 1995 (procedure) applies
       as if the association were a body corporate;
  (c) section 18 of the Criminal Justice (Northern Ireland) Act 1945 and Schedule 4
       to the Magistrates' Courts (Northern Ireland) Order 1981 (procedure) apply as
       they do in relation to a body corporate.

(5) Summary proceedings for an offence may be taken—

  (a) against a body corporate or unincorporated association at any place at which it
       has a place of business;
  (b) against an individual at any place where he is for the time being.

(6) Subsection (5) does not affect any jurisdiction exercisable apart from this section.

(7) 'Offence' means an offence under this Act.

PUBLIC OFFERS OF SECURITIES REGULATIONS 1995

(SI 1995/1537)

ARRANGEMENT OF REGULATIONS

PART I

General

PART II

Public Offers of Unlisted Securities

PART III

Amendments to Part IV of the Act etc.

PART IV

Miscellaneous

SCHEDULES

PART I

GENERAL

1 Citation, commencement and extent

(1) These Regulations may be cited as the Public Offers of Securities Regulations 1995 and shall come into force on 19th June 1995.

(2) These Regulations extend to Northern Ireland.

2 Interpretation

(1) In these Regulations, except where the context otherwise requires—

'the Act' means the Financial Services Act 1986;
'approved exchange' means, in relation to dealings in securities, a recognised investment exchange approved by the Treasury for the purposes of these Regulations either generally or in relation to such dealings, and the Treasury shall give notice in such manner as they think appropriate of the exchanges which are for the time being approved;
'body corporate' shall be construed in accordance with section 207(1) of the Act;
'convertible securities' means—

   (i) securities falling within paragraph 2 of Schedule 1 to the Act which can be converted into or exchanged for, or which confer rights to acquire, securities; or
   (ii) securities falling within paragraph 4 or 5 of that Schedule;

and 'conversion' in relation to convertible securities means their conversion into or exchange for, or the exercise of rights conferred by them to acquire, other securities ('underlying securities');
'credit institution' has the same meaning as it has for the purposes of paragraph 3 of Schedule 11A to the Act;
'director' shall be construed in accordance with section 207(1) of the Act;
'ecu' has the same meaning as it has for the purposes of paragraph 3 of Schedule 11A to the Act;
'European institution' has the same meaning as in the Banking Coordination (Second Council Directive) Regulations 1992;
'Euro-securities' has the same meaning as it has for the purposes of paragraph 3 of Schedule 11A to the Act;
'financial institution' has the same meaning as it has for the purposes of paragraph 3 of Schedule 11A to the Act;
'group' has the meaning given in section 207(1) of the Act;
'home-regulated investment business' has the same meaning as in the Banking Coordination (Second Council Directive) Regulations 1992;
'issuer', in relation to any securities, means the person by whom they have been or are to be issued;
'member State' means a State which is a Contracting Party to the Agreement on the European Economic Area signed at Oporto on 2nd May 1992 as adjusted by the Protocol signed at Brussels on 17th March 1993;
'private company' has the meaning given in section 1(3) of the Companies Act 1985;
'the registrar of companies', in relation to a prospectus relating to any securities, means—

   (a) if the securities are or are to be issued by a company incorporated in Great Britain, the registrar of companies in England and Wales or the registrar of companies in Scotland according to whether the company's registered office is in England and Wales or in Scotland;
   (b) if the securities are or are to be issued by a company incorporated in Northern Ireland, the registrar of companies for Northern Ireland;
   (c) in any other case, any of those registrars;

'recognised investment exchange' has the meaning given in section 207(1) of the Act;
'securities' means investments to which Part II of these Regulations applies; and
'sale' includes any disposal for valuable consideration.

(2) In the application of these Regulations to Scotland, references to a matter being actionable at the suit of a person shall be construed as references to the matter being actionable at the instance of that person.

(3) References to the Companies Act 1985 include references to the corresponding Northern Ireland provision.

PART II

PUBLIC OFFERS OF UNLISTED SECURITIES

3 Investments to which this Part applies

(1) This Part of these Regulations applies to any investment which—

  (a) is not admitted to official listing, nor the subject of an application for listing, in accordance with Part IV of the Act; and
  (b) falls within paragraph 1, 2, 4 or 5 of Schedule 1 to the Act.

(2) In the application of those paragraphs for the purposes of these Regulations—

  (a) debentures having a maturity of less than one year from their date of issue shall be deemed to be excluded from paragraph 2;
  (b) the note to paragraph 1 shall have effect with the omission of the words ', except in relation to any shares of a class defined as deferred shares for the purposes of section 119 of the Building Societies Act 1986,';
  (c) paragraphs 4 and 5 shall have effect with the omission of references to investments falling within paragraph 3; and
  (d) paragraph 4 shall have effect as though after the words 'subscribe for' there were inserted 'or acquire'.

4 Registration and publication of prospectus

(1) When securities are offered to the public in the United Kingdom for the first time the offeror shall publish a prospectus by making it available to the public, free of charge, at an address in the United Kingdom, from the time he first offers the securities until the end of the period during which the offer remains open.

(2) The offeror shall, before the time of publication of the prospectus, deliver a copy of it to the registrar of companies for registration.

(3) Paragraph (2) and regulations 5, 6 and 8 to 15 shall not apply to a prospectus submitted for approval in accordance with listing rules made under section 156A of the Act.

5 Offers of securities

A person is to be regarded as offering securities if, as principal—

  (a) he makes an offer which, if accepted, would give rise to a contract for the issue or sale of the securities by him or by another person with whom he has made arrangements for the issue or sale of the securities; or
  (b) he invites a person to make such an offer;

but not otherwise; and, except where the context otherwise requires, in this Part of these Regulations 'offer' and 'offeror' shall be construed accordingly.

6 Offers to the public in the United Kingdom

A person offers securities to the public in the United Kingdom if, to the extent that the offer is made to persons in the United Kingdom, it is made to the public; and, for this purpose, an offer which is made to any section of the public, whether selected as members or debenture holders of a body corporate, or as clients of the person making the offer, or in any other manner, is to be regarded as made to the public.

7 Exemptions

(1) For the purposes of these Regulations, an offer of securities shall be deemed not to be an offer to the public in the United Kingdom if, to the extent that the offer is made to persons in the United Kingdom—

(a) the condition specified in any one of the sub-paragraphs of paragraph (2) is satisfied in relation to the offer; or
(b) paragraph (3) applies in relation to the offer.

(2) The following are the conditions specified in this paragraph—

(a) the securities are offered to persons—
　(i) whose ordinary activities involve them in acquiring, holding, managing or disposing of investments (as principal or agent) for the purposes of their businesses; or
　(ii) who it is reasonable to expect will acquire, hold, manage or dispose of investments (as principal or agent) for the purposes of their businesses;
　or are otherwise offered to persons in the context of their trades, professions or occupations;
(b) the securities are offered to no more than fifty persons;
(c) the securities are offered to the members of a club or association (whether or not incorporated) and the members can reasonably be regarded as having a common interest with each other and with the club or association in the affairs of the club or association and in what is to be done with the proceeds of the offer;
(d) the securities are offered to a restricted circle of persons whom the offeror reasonably believes to be sufficiently knowledgeable to understand the risks involved in accepting the offer;
(e) the securities are offered in connection with a bona fide invitation to enter into an underwriting agreement with respect to them;
(f) the securities are the securities of a private company and are offered by that company to—
　(i) members or employees of the company;
　(ii) members of the families of any such members or employees; or
　(iii) holders of securities issued by the company which fall within paragraph 2 of Schedule 1 to the Act;
(g) the securities are offered to a government, local authority or public authority, as defined in paragraph 3 of Schedule 1 to the Act;
(h) the total consideration payable for the securities cannot exceed ecu 40,000 (or an equivalent amount);
(i) the minimum consideration which may be paid for securities acquired pursuant to the offer is at least ecu 40,000 (or an equivalent amount);
(j) the securities are denominated in amounts of at least ecu 40,000 (or an equivalent amount);
(k) the securities are offered in connection with a takeover offer;
(l) the securities are offered in connection with a merger within the meaning of Council Directive No. 78/855/EEC;

(m) the securities are shares and are offered free of charge to any or all of the holders of shares in the issuer;

(n) the securities are shares, or investments falling within paragraph 4 or 5 of Schedule 1 to the Act relating to shares, in a body corporate and are offered in exchange for shares in the same body corporate, and the offer cannot result in any increase in the issued share capital of the body corporate;

(o) the securities are issued by a body corporate and offered—
  (i) by the issuer;
  (ii) only to qualifying persons; and
  (iii) on terms that a contract to acquire any such securities may be entered into only by the qualifying person to whom they were offered or, if the terms of the offer so permit, any qualifying person;

(p) the securities result from the conversion of convertible securities and listing particulars or a prospectus relating to the convertible securities were or was published in the United Kingdom under or by virtue of Part IV of the Act, Part III of the Companies Act 1985 or these Regulations;

(q) the securities are issued by—
  (i) a charity within the meaning of section 96(1) of the Charities Act 1993;
  (ii) a housing association within the meaning of section 5(1) of the Housing Act 1985;
  (iii) an industrial or provident society registered in accordance with section 1(2)(b) of the Industrial and Provident Societies Act 1965; or
  (iv) a non-profit making association or body, recognised by the country or territory in which it is established, with objectives similar to those of a body falling within any of paragraphs (i) to (iii);
  and the proceeds of the offer will be used for the purposes of the issuer's objectives;

(r) the securities offered are shares and ownership of the securities entitles the holder—
  (i) to obtain the benefit of services provided by a building society within the meaning of section 119(1) of the Building Societies Act, an industrial or provident society registered in accordance with section 1(2) of the Industrial and Provident Societies Act 1965 or a body of a like nature established in a member State; or
  (ii) to membership of such a body;

(s) the securities offered are Euro-securities and are not the subject of advertising likely to come to the attention of persons who are not professionally experienced in matters relating to investment;

(t) the securities are of the same class, and were issued at the same time, as securities in respect of which a prospectus has been published under or by virtue of Part IV of the Act, Part III of the Companies Act 1985 or these Regulations;

(u) the securities are not transferable.

(3) This paragraph applies in relation to an offer where the condition specified in one relevant sub-paragraph is satisfied in relation to part, but not the whole, of the offer and, in relation to each other part of the offer, the condition specified in a different relevant sub-paragraph is satisfied.

(4) For the purposes of paragraph (3), 'relevant sub-paragraph' means any of sub-paragraphs (a) to (g), (k) to (n), (p), (q) and (t) of paragraph (2).

(5) For the purposes of this regulation, 'shares', except in relation to a takeover offer, means investments falling within paragraph 1 of Schedule 1 to the Act.

(6) For the purposes of determining whether the condition specified in sub-paragraph (b) or (h) of paragraph (2) is satisfied in relation to an offer, the offer shall be taken together with any other offer of securities of the same class which was—

(a) made by the same person;
(b) open at any time within the period of 12 months ending with the date on which the offer is first made; and
(c) deemed not to be an offer to the public in the United Kingdom by virtue of that condition being satisfied.

(7) In determining for the purposes of paragraph (2)(d) whether a person is sufficiently knowledgeable to understand the risks involved in accepting an offer of securities, any information supplied by the offeror shall be disregarded, apart from information about—

(a) the issuer of the securities, or
(b) if the securities confer the right to acquire other securities, the issuer of those other securities.

(8) For the purposes of paragraph (2)(f)—

(a) the members of a person's family are the person's husband or wife, widow or widower and children (including stepchildren) and their descendants, and any trustee (acting in his capacity as such) of a trust the principal beneficiary of which is the person himself or herself, or any of those relatives; and
(b) regulation 3(2)(a) shall not apply.

(9) For the purposes of determining whether the condition mentioned in sub-paragraph (h), (i) or (j) of paragraph (2) is satisfied in relation to an offer, an amount, in relation to an amount denominated in ecu, is an 'equivalent amount' if it is an amount of equal value, calculated at the latest practicable date before (but in any event not more than 3 days before) the date on which the offer is first made, denominated wholly or partly in another currency or unit of account.

(10) For the purposes of paragraph (2)(k), 'takeover offer' means—

(a) an offer which is a takeover offer within the meaning of Part XIIIA of the Companies Act 1985 (or would be such an offer if that Part of that Act applied in relation to any body corporate); or
(b) an offer made to all the holders of shares, or of shares of a particular class, in a body corporate to acquire a specified proportion of those shares ('holders' and 'shares' being construed in accordance with that Part);

but in determining for the purposes of sub-paragraph (b) whether an offer is made to all the holders of shares, or of shares of any class, the offeror, any associate of his (within the meaning of section 430E of that Act) and any person whose shares the offeror or any such associate has contracted to acquire shall not be regarded as holders of the shares.

(11) For the purposes of paragraph (2)(m), 'holders of shares' means the persons who, at the close of business on a date specified in the offer and falling within the period of 28 days ending with the date on which the offer is first made, were holders of such shares.

(12) For the purposes of paragraph (2)(o), a person is a 'qualifying person', in relation to an issuer, if he is a bona fide employee or former employee of the issuer or of another body corporate in the same group or the wife, husband, widow, widower or child or stepchild under the age of eighteen of such an employee or former employee.

Appendix 1
STATUTORY MATERIALS

8 Form and content of prospectus

(1) Subject to regulation 11 and to paragraphs (2), (4), (5) and (6), a prospectus shall contain the information specified in Parts II to X of Schedule 1 to these Regulations (which shall be construed in accordance with Part I of that Schedule).

(2) Where the requirement to include in a prospectus any information (the 'required information') is inappropriate to the issuer's sphere of activity or to its legal form or to the securities to which the prospectus relates, the requirement—

(a) shall have effect as a requirement that the prospectus contain information equivalent to the required information; but

(b) if there is no such equivalent information, shall not apply.

(3) The information in a prospectus shall be presented in as easily analysable and comprehensible a form as possible.

(4) Where, on the occasion of their admission to dealings on an approved exchange, securities falling within paragraph 1 of Schedule 1 to the Act are offered on a pre-emptive basis to some or all of the existing holders of such securities, a body or person designated for the purposes of this paragraph by the Treasury shall have power to authorise the omission from a prospectus subject to this regulation of specified information provided that up-to-date information equivalent to that which would otherwise be required by this regulation is available as a result of the requirements of that approved exchange.

In this paragraph, 'specified information' means information specified in paragraphs 41 to 47 of Schedule 1 to these Regulations.

(5) Where a class of securities falling within paragraph 1 of Schedule 1 to the Act has been admitted to dealings on an approved exchange, a body or person designated for the purposes of this paragraph by the Treasury shall have power to authorise the making of an offer without a prospectus, provided that—

(a) the number or estimated market value or the nominal value or, in the absence of a nominal value, the accounting par value of the securities offered amounts to less than ten per cent of the number or of the corresponding value of securities of the same class already admitted to dealings; and

(b) up-to-date information equivalent to that required by this regulation is available as a result of the requirements of that approved exchange.

(6) Where a person—

(a) makes an offer to the public in the United Kingdom of securities which he proposes to issue; and

(b) has, within the 12 months preceding the date on which the offer is first made, published a full prospectus relating to a different class of securities which he has issued, or to an earlier issue of the same class of securities,

he may publish, instead of a full prospectus, a prospectus which contains only the differences which have arisen since the publication of the full prospectus mentioned in sub-paragraph (b) and any supplementary prospectus and which are likely to influence the value of the securities, provided that the prospectus is accompanied by that full prospectus and any supplementary prospectus or contains a reference to it or them; and, for this purpose, a full prospectus is one which contains the information specified in Parts II to X of Schedule 1 (other than any information whose omission is authorised by or under paragraph (2) or (4) or regulation 11).

9 General duty of disclosure in prospectus

(1) In addition to the information required to be included in a prospectus by virtue of regulation 8 a prospectus shall (subject to these Regulations) contain all such information as investors would reasonably require, and reasonably expect to find there, for the purpose of making an informed assessment of—

(a) the assets and liabilities, financial position, profits and losses, and prospects of the issuer of the securities; and

(b) the rights attaching to those securities.

(2) The information to be included by virtue of this regulation shall be such information as is mentioned in paragraph (1) which is within the knowledge of any person responsible for the prospectus or which it would be reasonable for him to obtain by making enquiries.

(3) In determining what information is required to be included in a prospectus by virtue of this regulation regard shall be had to the nature of the securities and of the issuer of the securities.

(4) For the purposes of this regulation 'issuer', in relation to a certificate or other instrument falling within paragraph 5 of Schedule 1 to the Act, means the person who issued or is to issue the securities to which the certificate or instrument relates.

10 Supplementary prospectus

(1) Where a prospectus has been registered under this Part of these Regulations in respect of an offer of securities and at any time while an agreement in respect of those securities can be entered into in pursuance of that offer—

(a) there is a significant change affecting any matter contained in the prospectus whose inclusion was required by regulation 8 or 9; or

(b) a significant new matter arises the inclusion of information in respect of which would have been so required if it had arisen when the prospectus was prepared; or

(c) there is a significant inaccuracy in the prospectus,

the offeror shall deliver to the registrar of companies for registration, and publish in accordance with paragraph (3), a supplementary prospectus containing particulars of the change or new matter or, in the case of an inaccuracy, correcting it.

(2) In paragraph (1) 'significant' means significant for the purpose of making an informed assessment of the matters mentioned in regulation 9(1)(a) and (b).

(3) Regulation 4(1) shall apply to a supplementary prospectus delivered for registration to the registrar of companies in the same way as it applies to a prospectus except that the obligation to publish the supplementary prospectus shall begin with the time it is delivered for registration to the registrar of companies.

(4) Where the offeror is not aware of the change, new matter or inaccuracy in question he shall not be under any duty to comply with paragraphs (1) and (3) unless he is notified of it by a person responsible for the prospectus; but any person responsible for the prospectus who is aware of such a matter shall be under a duty to give him notice of it.

(5) Where a supplementary prospectus has been registered under this regulation in respect of an offer, the preceding paragraphs of this regulation have effect as if any

reference to a prospectus were a reference to the prospectus originally registered and that supplementary prospectus, taken together.

11 Exceptions

(1) The Treasury or the Secretary of State may authorise the omission from a prospectus or supplementary prospectus of information whose inclusion would otherwise be required by these Regulations if they or he consider that disclosure of that information would be contrary to the public interest.

(2) An offeror may omit from a prospectus or supplementary prospectus information with respect to an issuer whose inclusion would otherwise be required by these Regulations if—

    (a) he is not that issuer, nor acting in pursuance of an agreement with that issuer;

    (b) the information is not available to him because he is not that issuer; and

    (c) he has been unable, despite making such efforts (if any) as are reasonable, to obtain the information.

(3) The competent authority for the purposes of Part IV of the Act ('the competent authority') may authorise the omission from a prospectus or supplementary prospectus of information whose inclusion would otherwise be required by these Regulations, if—

    (a) the information is of minor importance only, and is not likely to influence assessment of the issuer's assets and liabilities, financial position, profits and losses and prospects; or

    (b) disclosure of that information would be seriously detrimental to the issuer and its omission would not be likely to mislead investors with regard to facts and circumstances necessary for an informed assessment of the securities.

(4) Paragraph (4) of regulation 9 applies for the purposes of paragraph (3) as it applies for the purposes of that regulation.

(5) The competent authority may make rules providing for the payment of fees to it for the discharge of its functions under paragraph (3).

(6) Section 156 of the Act shall apply to rules made under paragraph (5) as it applies to listing rules.

12 Advertisements etc. in connection with offer of securities

An advertisement, notice, poster or document (other than a prospectus) announcing a public offer of securities for which a prospectus is or will be required under this Part of these Regulations shall not be issued to or caused to be issued to the public in the United Kingdom by the person proposing to make the offer unless it states that a prospectus is or will be published, as the case may be, and gives an address in the United Kingdom from which it can be obtained or will be obtainable.

13 Persons responsible for prospectus

(1) For the purpose of this Part of these Regulations the persons responsible for a prospectus or supplementary prospectus are—

    (a) the issuer of the securities to which the prospectus or supplementary prospectus relates;

    (b) where the issuer is a body corporate, each person who is a director of that body corporate at the time when the prospectus or supplementary prospectus is published;

(c) where the issuer is a body corporate, each person who has authorised himself to be named, and is named, in the prospectus or supplementary prospectus as a director or as having agreed to become a director of that body either immediately or at a future time;

(d) each person who accepts, and is stated in the prospectus or supplementary prospectus as accepting, responsibility for, or for any part of, the prospectus or supplementary prospectus;

(e) the offeror of the securities, where he is not the issuer;

(f) where the offeror is a body corporate, but is not the issuer and is not making the offer in association with the issuer, each person who is a director of that body corporate at the time when the prospectus or supplementary prospectus is published; and

(g) each person not falling within any of the foregoing paragraphs who has authorised the contents of, or of any part of, the prospectus or supplementary prospectus.

(2) A person is not responsible under paragraph (1)(a), (b) or (c) unless the issuer has made or authorised the offer in relation to which the prospectus or supplementary prospectus was published, and a person is not responsible for a prospectus or supplementary prospectus by virtue of paragraph (1)(b) if it is published without his knowledge or consent and on becoming aware of its publication he forthwith gives reasonable public notice that it was published without his knowledge or consent.

(3) Where a person has accepted responsibility for, or authorised, only part of the contents of any prospectus or supplementary prospectus, he is responsible under paragraph (1)(d) or (g) only for that part and only if it is included in (or substantially in) the form and context to which he has agreed.

(4) Nothing in this regulation shall be construed as making a person responsible for any prospectus or supplementary prospectus by reason only of giving advice as to its contents in a professional capacity.

(5) Where by virtue of this regulation the issuer of any shares pays or is liable to pay compensation under regulation 14 for loss suffered in respect of shares for which a person has subscribed no account shall be taken of that liability or payment in determining any question as to the amount paid on subscription for those shares or as to the amount paid up or deemed to be paid up on them.

14 Compensation for false or misleading prospectus

(1) Subject to regulation 15 the person or persons responsible for a prospectus or supplementary prospectus shall be liable to pay compensation to any person who has acquired the securities to which the prospectus relates and suffered loss in respect of them as a result of any untrue or misleading statement in the prospectus or supplementary prospectus or the omission from it of any matter required to be included by regulation 9 or 10.

(2) Where regulation 8 requires a prospectus to include information as to any particular matter on the basis that the prospectus must include a statement either as to that matter or, if such is the case, that there is no such matter, the omission from the prospectus of the information shall be treated for the purposes of paragraph (1) as a statement that there is no such matter.

(3) Subject to regulation 15, a person who fails to comply with regulation 10 shall be liable to pay compensation to any person who has acquired any of the securities in question and suffered loss in respect of them as a result of the failure.

(4) This regulation does not affect any liability which any person may incur apart from this regulation.

(5) References in this regulation to the acquisition by any person of securities include references to his contracting to acquire them or an interest in them.

15 Exemption from liability to pay compensation

(1) A person shall not incur any liability under regulation 14(1) for any loss in respect of securities caused by any such statement or omission as is there mentioned if he satisfies the court that at the time when the prospectus or supplementary prospectus was delivered for registration he reasonably believed, having made such enquiries (if any) as were reasonable, that the statement was true and not misleading or that the matter whose omission caused the loss was properly omitted and—

   (a) that he continued in that belief until the time when the securities were acquired; or
   (b) that they were acquired before it was reasonably practicable to bring a correction to the attention of persons likely to acquire the securities in question; or
   (c) that before the securities were acquired he had taken all such steps as it was reasonable for him to have taken to secure that a correction was forthwith brought to the attention of those persons; or
   (d) that the securities were acquired after such a lapse of time that he ought in the circumstances to be reasonably excused, and, if the securities are dealt in on an approved exchange, that he continued in that belief until after the commencement of dealings in the securities on that exchange.

(2) A person shall not incur any liability under regulation 14(1) for any loss in respect of securities caused by a statement purporting to be made by or on the authority of another person as an expert which is, and is stated to be, included in the prospectus or supplementary prospectus with that other person's consent if he satisfies the court that at the time when the prospectus or supplementary prospectus was delivered for registration he believed on reasonable grounds that the other person was competent to make or authorise the statement and had consented to its inclusion in the form and context in which it was included and—

   (a) that he continued in that belief until the time when the securities were acquired; or
   (b) that they were acquired before it was reasonably practicable to bring the fact that the expert was not competent or had not consented to the attention of persons likely to acquire the securities in question; or
   (c) that before the securities were acquired he had taken all such steps as it was reasonable for him to have taken to secure that that fact was forthwith brought to the attention of those persons; or
   (d) that the securities were acquired after such a lapse of time that he ought in the circumstances to be reasonably excused and, if the securities are dealt in on an approved exchange, that he continued in that belief until after the commencement of dealings in the securities on that exchange.

(3) Without prejudice to paragraphs (1) and (2), a person shall not incur any liability under regulation 14(1) for any loss in respect of any securities caused by any such statement or omission as is there mentioned if he satisfies the court—

(a) that before the securities were acquired a correction or, where the statement was such as is mentioned in paragraph (2), the fact that the expert was not competent or had not consented had been published in a manner calculated to bring it to the attention of persons likely to acquire the securities in question; or

(b) that he took all such steps as it was reasonable for him to take to secure such publication and reasonably believed that it had taken place before the securities were acquired.

(4) A person shall not incur any liability under regulation 14(1) for any loss resulting from a statement made by an official person or contained in a public official document which is included in the prospectus or supplementary prospectus if he satisfies the court that the statement is accurately and fairly reproduced.

(5) A person shall not incur any liability under regulation 14(1) or (3) if he satisfies the court that the person suffering the loss acquired the securities in question with knowledge that the statement was false or misleading, of the omitted matter or of the change, new matter or inaccuracy, as the case may be.

(6) A person shall not incur any liability under regulation 14(3) if he satisfies the court that he reasonably believed that the change, new matter or inaccuracy in question was not such as to call for a supplementary prospectus.

(7) In this regulation 'expert' includes any engineer, valuer, accountant or other person whose profession, qualifications or experience give authority to a statement made by him; and references to the acquisition of securities include references to contracting to acquire them or an interest in them.

16 Contraventions

(1) An authorised person who contravenes regulation 4(1) or, where it applies, regulation 4(2), or who contravenes regulation 12, or who assists another person to contravene any of those provisions, shall be treated as having contravened rules made under Chapter V of Part I of the Act or, in the case of a person who is an authorised person by virtue of his membership of a recognised self-regulating organisation or certification by a recognised professional body, the rules of that organisation or body.

(2) A person other than an authorised person who contravenes regulation 4(1) or, where it applies, regulation 4(2), or who contravenes regulation 12, or who assists another person to contravene any of those provisions, shall be guilty of an offence and liable—

(a) on conviction on indictment, to imprisonment for a term not exceeding two years or to a fine or to both;

(b) on summary conviction, to imprisonment for a term not exceeding three months or to a fine not exceeding level 5 on the standard scale.

(3) Without prejudice to any liability under regulation 14, a person shall not be regarded as having contravened regulation 4 by reason only of a prospectus not having fully complied with the requirements of these Regulations as to its form or content.

(4) Any contravention to which this regulation applies shall be actionable at the suit of a person who suffers loss as a result of the contravention subject to the defences and other incidents applying to actions for breach of statutory duty.

(5) In this regulation 'authorised person' means a person authorised under Chapter III of Part I of the Act and 'recognised professional body' and 'recognised self-regulating organisation' have the meanings given in section 207(1) of the Act.

(6) A European institution carrying on home-regulated investment business in the United Kingdom which contravenes regulation 4(1) or, where it applies, 4(2) or which contravenes regulation 12, or which assists another person to contravene any of those provisions, shall be treated for all purposes—

(a) if it is not a member of a recognised self-regulating organisation, as having contravened rules made under Chapter V of Part I of the Act; or
(b) if it is a member of a recognised self-regulating organisation, as having contravened the rules of that organisation;

and the reference in paragraph (2) to a person other than an authorised person shall be treated as not including a reference to such an institution.

PART III

AMENDMENTS TO PART IV OF THE ACT ETC.

17 Amendments to the Act and other minor and consequential amendments

Schedule 2 to these Regulations shall have effect.

18 Penalties

Where these Regulations amend, extend the application of, or modify the effect of, a provision contained in Part IV of the Act and thereby create a new criminal offence which, but for this regulation, would be punishable to a greater extent than is permitted under paragraph 1(1)(d) of Schedule 2 to the European Communities Act 1972, the maximum punishment for the offence shall be the maximum permitted under that paragraph at the time the offence was committed, on conviction on indictment or on summary conviction, as the case may be.

PART IV

MISCELLANEOUS

19 Designations

For the purposes of Articles 11, 12, 13, 14, 18, 19, 20, 21 and 22 of Council Directive No. 89/298/EEC the Treasury may designate such bodies as they think fit and they shall give notice in such manner as they think appropriate of the designations they have made.

20 Mutual recognition

Schedule 4 to these Regulations shall have effect to make provision for the recognition of prospectuses and listing particulars approved in other member States.

21 Revocation

The Companies Act 1985 (Mutual Recognition of Prospectuses) Regulations 1991 and the Companies (Northern Ireland) Order 1986 (Mutual Recognition of Prospectuses) Regulations (Northern Ireland) 1991 are hereby revoked.

Appendix 1
STATUTORY MATERIALS

22 Registration of documents by the registrar of companies

For the purposes of the provisions mentioned in section 735B of the Companies Act 1985, regulations 4(2) and 10(1) shall be regarded as provisions of the Companies Acts.

23 Application of Part X of the Act

(1) Section 187(4) of the Act shall apply to the competent authority in the discharge or purported discharge of its functions under these Regulations as it applies to it in the discharge or purported discharge of its functions under Part IV of the Act.

(2) Section 188 of the Act shall apply to proceedings arising out of any act or omission (or proposed act or omission) of the competent authority in the discharge or purported discharge of any function under regulation 11 as it applies to the proceedings mentioned in that section.

(3) Section 192 of the Act shall apply to a person designated under regulation 19 in respect of any action which he proposes to take or has power to take by virtue of being so designated.

(4) Section 199 of the Act shall apply in relation to an offence under these Regulations as it applies in relation to the offences mentioned in that section.

(5) Subsections (1) and (5) of section 200 of the Act shall apply to applications under these Regulations as they apply to applications under the Act, and to requirements imposed on a person by or under these Regulations as they apply to requirements imposed on a person by or under the Act.

(6) Sections 201(1), 202 and 203 of the Act shall apply to offences under these Regulations as they apply to offences under the Act.

24 Amendments to regulations made under the Banking Act 1987

Schedule 5 to these Regulations shall have effect to amend regulations made under the Banking Act 1987.

SCHEDULE 1 Regulation 8

FORM AND CONTENT OF PROSPECTUS

PART I

INTERPRETATION

1. In this Schedule, except where the context otherwise requires—
'annual accounts' has the same meaning as in Part VII of the Companies Act 1985;
'control' means the ability, in practice, to determine the actions of the issuer; and 'joint control' means control exercised by two or more persons who have an agreement or understanding (whether formal or informal) which may lead to their adopting a common policy in respect of the issuer;
'debentures' means securities falling within paragraph 2 of Schedule 1 to the Act;
'financial year' has the same meaning as in Part VII of the Companies Act 1985;
'group accounts' has the same meaning as in Part VII of the Companies Act 1985;
'the last three years', in relation to an undertaking whose accounts are required to be dealt with in a prospectus, means three completed financial years which immediately precede the date on which the offer is first made and which cover a continuous period of at least 35 months, disregarding a financial year which ends less than three months before the date on which the offer is first made and for which accounts have not been prepared by that date;
'parent undertaking' and 'subsidiary undertaking' have the same meaning as in Part VII of the Companies Act 1985;
'state of affairs' means the state of affairs of an undertaking, in relation to its balance sheet, at the end of a financial year;
'subsidiary' and 'holding company' have the same meanings as in sections 736 and 736A of the Companies Act 1985; and
'undertaking' has the same meaning as in Part VII of the Companies Act 1985.

PART II

GENERAL REQUIREMENTS

2. The name of the issuer and the address of its registered office.

3. If different, the name and address of the person offering the securities.

4. The names and functions of the directors of the issuer.

5. The date of publication of the prospectus.

6. A statement that a copy of the prospectus has been delivered for registration to the registrar of companies in accordance with regulation 4(2), indicating to which registrar of companies it has been delivered.

7. A statement that the prospectus has been drawn up in accordance with these Regulations.

8. The following words, 'If you are in any doubt about the contents of this document you should consult a person authorised under the Financial Services Act 1986 who specialises in advising on the acquisition of shares and other securities', or words to the like effect.

PART III

THE PERSONS RESPONSIBLE FOR THE PROSPECTUS AND ADVISERS

9. The names, addresses (home or business) and functions of those persons responsible (which in this Part of this Schedule has the same meaning as in regulation 13) for the prospectus or any part of the prospectus, specifying such part.

10. (1) A declaration by the directors of the issuer (or, if the offeror is not the issuer, by the directors of the offeror) that to the best of their knowledge the information contained in the prospectus is in accordance with the facts and that the prospectus makes no omission likely to affect the import of such information.

(2) Without prejudice to paragraph 45 of this Schedule, a statement by any person who accepts responsibility for the prospectus, or any part of it, that he does so.

PART IV

THE SECURITIES TO WHICH THE PROSPECTUS RELATES AND THE OFFER

11. A description of the securities being offered, including the class to which they belong and a description of the rights attaching to them including (where applicable)—

   (a) if the securities are shares, rights as regards—
       (i) voting;
       (ii) dividends;
       (iii) return of capital on the winding up of the issuer;
       (iv) redemption;
       and a summary of the consents necessary for the variation of any of those rights;
   (b) if the securities are debentures, rights as regards—
       (i) interest payable;
       (ii) repayment of principal;
   (c) if the securities are convertible securities—
       (i) the terms and dates on which the holder of the convertible securities is entitled to acquire the related underlying securities;
       (ii) the procedures for exercising the entitlement to the underlying securities; and
       (iii) such information relating to the underlying securities as would have been required under paragraphs (a) or (b) if the securities being offered had been the underlying securities.

12. The date(s) (if any) on which entitlement to dividends or interest arises.

13. Particulars of tax on income from the securities withheld at source, including tax credits.

14. The procedure for the exercise of any right of preemption attaching to the securities.

15. Any restrictions on the free transferability of the securities being offered.

16. (1) A statement as to whether—

   (a) the securities being offered have been admitted to dealings on a recognised investment exchange; or
   (b) an application for such admission has been made.

(2) Where no such application for dealings has been made, or such an application has been made and refused, a statement as to whether or not there are, or are intended to be, any other arrangements for there to be dealings in the securities and, if there are, a brief description of such arrangements.

17. The purpose for which the securities are being issued.

18. The number of securities being issued.

19. The number of securities being offered.

20. The total proceeds which it is expected will be raised by the offer and the expected net proceeds, after deduction of the expenses, of the offer.

21. Where the prospectus relates to shares which are offered for subscription, particulars as to—

    (a) the minimum amount which, in the opinion of the directors of the issuer, must be raised by the issue of those shares in order to provide the sums (or, if any part of them is to be defrayed in any other manner, the balance of the sums) required to be provided in respect of each of the following—
        (i) the purchase price of any property purchased, or to be purchased, which is to be defrayed in whole or in part out of the proceeds of the issue;
        (ii) any preliminary expenses payable by the issuer and any commission so payable to any person in consideration of his agreeing to subscribe for, or of his procuring or agreeing to procure subscriptions for, any shares in the issuer;
        (iii) the repayment of any money borrowed by the issuer in respect of any of the foregoing matters;
        (iv) working capital; and
    (b) the amounts to be provided in respect of the matters mentioned otherwise than out of the proceeds of the issue and the sources out of which those amounts are to be provided.

22. The names of any persons underwriting or guaranteeing the offer.

23. The amount or the estimated amount of the expenses of the offer and by whom they are payable, including (except in so far as information is required to be included in the prospectus by section 97(3) of the Companies Act 1985) a statement as to any commission payable by the issuer to any person in consideration of his agreeing to subscribe for securities to which the prospectus relates or of his procuring or agreeing to procure subscriptions for such securities.

24. The names and addresses of the paying agents (if any).

25. The period during which the offer of the securities is open.

26. The price at which the securities are offered or, if appropriate, the procedure, method and timetable for fixing the price.

27. The arrangements for payment for the securities being offered and the arrangements and timetable for their delivery.

28. The arrangements during the period prior to the delivery of the securities being offered relating to the moneys received from applicants including the arrangements for the return of moneys to applicants where their applications are not accepted in whole or in part and the timetable for the return of such moneys.

PART V

GENERAL INFORMATION ABOUT THE ISSUER AND ITS CAPITAL

29. The date and place of incorporation of the issuer. In the case of an issuer not incorporated in the United Kingdom, the address of its principal place of business in the United Kingdom (if any).

30. The place of registration of the issuer and the number with which it is registered.

31. The legal form of the issuer, the legislation under which it was formed and (if different) the legislation now applicable to it.

32. A summary of the provisions in the issuer's memorandum of association determining its objects.

33. If the liability of the members of the issuer is limited, a statement of that fact.

34. The amount of the issuer's authorised share capital and any limit on the duration of the authorisation to issue such share capital.

35. The amount of the issuer's issued share capital.

36. The number and particulars of any listed and unlisted securities issued by the issuer not representing share capital.

37. The number of shares of each class making up each of the authorised and issued share capital, the nominal value of such shares and, in the case of the issued share capital, the amount paid up on the shares.

38. The amount of any outstanding listed and unlisted convertible securities issued by the issuer, the conditions and procedures for their conversion and the number of shares which would be issued as a result of their conversion.

39. If the issuer is a member of a group, a brief description of the group and of the issuer's position in it, stating, where the issuer is a subsidiary, the name of its holding company.

40. Insofar the offeror has the information, an indication of the persons, who, directly or indirectly, jointly or severally, exercise or could exercise control over the issuer and particulars of the proportion of the issuer's voting capital held by such persons.

PART VI

THE ISSUER'S PRINCIPAL ACTIVITIES

41. A description of the issuer's principal activities and of any exceptional factors which have influenced its activities.

42. A statement of any dependence of the issuer on patents or other intellectual property rights, licences or particular contracts, where any of these are of fundamental importance to the issuer's business.

43. Information regarding investments in progress where they are significant.

44. Information on any legal or arbitration proceedings, active, pending or threatened against, or being brought by, the issuer or any member of its group which are having or may have a significant effect on the issuer's financial position.

PART VII

THE ISSUER'S ASSETS AND LIABILITIES, FINANCIAL POSITION AND PROFITS
AND LOSSES

45. (1) If the issuer is a company to which Part VII of the Companies Act 1985 applies
otherwise than by virtue of section 700 of that Act—

(a) the issuer's annual accounts for the last three years together with—
  (i) a statement by the directors of the issuer that the accounts have been
  prepared in accordance with the law, and that they accept responsibility for
  them, or a statement why they are unable to make such a statement;
  (ii) the names and addresses of the auditors of the accounts;
  (iii) a copy of the auditors' reports on the accounts, within the meaning of
  section 235 of the Companies Act 1985; and
  (iv) a statement by the auditors that they consent to the inclusion of their
  reports in the prospectus and accept responsibility for them, and have not
  become aware, since the date of any report, of any matter affecting the
  validity of that report at that date; or a statement why they are unable to
  make such a statement; or
(b) a report by a person qualified to act as an auditor with respect to the state of
affairs and profit or loss shown by the issuer' s annual accounts for the last three
years together with—
  (i) the name and address of the person responsible for the report;
  (ii) if different, the name and address of the person who audited the accounts
  on which the report is based; and
  (iii) a statement by the person responsible for the report that in his opinion the
  report gives a true and fair view of the state of affairs and profit or loss of the
  issuer and its subsidiary undertakings, and that he consents to the inclusion
  of his report in the prospectus and accepts responsibility for it; or a
  statement why he is unable to make such a statement.

(2) If the issuer is not a company to which Part VII of the Companies Act 1985 applies (or
is a company to which that Part of that Act applies by virtue of section 700 of that Act)—

(a) the issuer's accounts (and, if it is a parent undertaking, its subsidiary undertakings' accounts) for the last three years, prepared in accordance with the
applicable law, together with—
  (i) the name and address of the person responsible for the accounts;
  (ii) a statement by the person responsible for the accounts that they have been
  properly prepared in accordance with the applicable law, and that he
  accepts responsibility for them, or statement why he is unable to make such
  a statement;
  (iii) the names and addresses of the auditors of the accounts and their reports;
  and
  (iv) a statement by the auditors that they consent to the inclusion of their
  reports in the prospectus and accept responsibility for them, and have not
  become aware, since the date of any report, of any matter affecting the
  validity of that report at that date; or a statement why they are unable to
  make such a statement; or
(b) a report by a person qualified to act as an auditor with respect to the state of
affairs and profit or loss shown by the issuer's accounts (and, if the issuer is a
parent undertaking, by its subsidiary undertakings' accounts) for the last three
years, such report to be drawn up in accordance with the applicable law, or as if

the provisions of the Companies Act 1985 relating to annual accounts applied to
the issuer, together with—

   (i) the name and address of the person responsible for the report;

   (ii) if different, the name and address of the person who audited the accounts
on which the report is based; and

   (iii) a statement by the person responsible for the report that in his opinion the
report gives a true and fair view of the state of affairs and profit or loss of the
issuer and its subsidiary undertakings and that he consents to the inclusion
of his report in the prospectus and accepts responsibility for it; or a
statement why he is unable to make such a statement.

(3) If, in accordance with the law applicable to it, the accounts of an issuer falling within
sub-paragraph (2) consist only of consolidated accounts with respect to itself and its
subsidiary undertakings, the prospectus is not required by virtue of sub-paragraph (2) to
include separate accounts for each undertaking, or to include a report which deals with
the accounts of each undertaking separately.

(4) If, in the case of an issuer falling within sub-paragraph (1) or (2), the prospectus
would, but for this sub-paragraph, include both separate accounts for the issuer and its
subsidiary undertakings and consolidated accounts, either the separate accounts or the
consolidated accounts may be omitted from the prospectus if their inclusion would not
provide any significant additional information.

(5) If an issuer falling within sub-paragraph (2) is not required by the law applicable to it
to have its accounts audited—

  (a) if the accounts have not been audited—

    (i) the prospectus shall contain a statement to that effect; and

    (ii) paragraph (a)(iii) and (iv) or, as the case may be, paragraph (b)(ii) of
sub-paragraph (2) shall not apply to the issuer; and

  (b) if the accounts have nonetheless been audited, the prospectus shall contain a
statement to that effect.

(6) Sub-paragraphs (7) and (8) shall apply in so far as the issuer has not been in
existence for the whole of the last three years.

(7) Subject to sub-paragraph (8)—

  (a) the requirement in sub-paragraphs (1)(a) and (2)(a) that the prospectus
contain accounts for the last three years shall be construed as a requirement that
the prospectus contain the accounts which the undertaking concerned was
required (by its constitution or by the law under which it is established) to
prepare for financial years during its existence, disregarding a financial year
which ends less than three months before the date on which the offer is first made
and for which accounts have not been prepared by that date; and

  (b) the requirement in sub-paragraphs (1)(b) and (2)(b) that the prospectus
contain a report with respect to the state of affairs and profit or loss for the last
three years shall be construed as a requirement that the prospectus contain a
report with respect to the accounts which the undertaking concerned was
required (by its constitution or by the law under which it is established) to
prepare for financial years during its existence, disregarding a financial year
which ends less than three months before the date on which the offer is first made
and for which accounts have not been prepared by that date.

(8) If an undertaking has not been required (by its constitution or by the law under
which it is established) to prepare any accounts for financial years, the requirement in
sub-paragraphs (1) and (2) that the prospectus contain accounts for, or a report with

respect to, the last three years shall be construed as a requirement that the prospectus contain a report by a person qualified to act as an auditor which includes—

   (a) details of the profit or loss of the undertaking in respect of the period beginning with the date of its formation and ending on the latest practicable date before (but not in any event more than three months before) the date on which the offer is first made, and of its state of affairs at that latest practicable date; and

   (b) a statement by the person responsible for the report that in his opinion it gives a true and fair view of the state of affairs and profit or loss of the undertaking and that he consents to the inclusion of his report in the prospectus and accepts responsibility for it; or a statement why he is unable to make such a statement.

(9) If the issuer is a parent undertaking, the requirements of sub-paragraph (1) or, as the case may be, sub-paragraph (2), shall apply to each subsidiary undertaking in respect of any part of the last three years for which information is not otherwise required by those sub-paragraphs.

(10) Where more than nine months have elapsed at the date on which the offer is first made since the end of the last financial year in respect of which accounts or a report are required to be included in the prospectus by this paragraph, there shall also be included in the prospectus—

   (a) interim accounts of the undertaking concerned (which need not be audited but which must otherwise be prepared to the standard applicable to accounts required for each financial year) covering the period beginning at the end of the last financial year in respect of which accounts or a report are required to be included in the prospectus by this paragraph, and ending on the latest practicable date before (but not in any event more than three months before) the date on which the offer is first made, together with the name and address of the person responsible for the interim accounts and a statement by him that the interim accounts have been properly prepared in accordance with the law applicable to the undertaking, and that he consents to the inclusion of the accounts and statement in the prospectus and accepts responsibility for them; or a statement why he is unable to make such a statement; or

   (b) a report by a person qualified to act as an auditor covering the same period with respect to the state of affairs and profit or loss of the undertaking concerned, prepared in accordance with the law applicable to the undertaking, together with the name and address of the person responsible for preparing the report, and a statement by him that he consents to the inclusion of the report in the prospectus and accepts responsibility for it; or a statement why he is unable to make such a statement.

(11) If any interim accounts of the issuer have been published since the end of the last financial year of the issuer in respect of which accounts or a report are required to be included in the prospectus by this paragraph, other than interim accounts included in a prospectus in accordance with sub-paragraph (10), they shall be included in the prospectus, together with—

   (a) an explanation of the purpose for which the accounts were prepared;

   (b) a reference to the legislation in accordance with which they were prepared; and

   (c) the name and address of the person responsible for them, and a statement from him that he consents to the inclusion of the accounts in the prospectus and accepts responsibility for them.

Appendix 1
STATUTORY MATERIALS

PART VIII

THE ISSUER'S ADMINISTRATION, MANAGEMENT AND SUPERVISION

46. A concise description of the directors' existing or proposed service contracts with the issuer or any subsidiary of the issuer, excluding contracts expiring, or determinable by the employing company without payment of compensation within one year, or an appropriate negative statement.

47. (1) The aggregate remuneration paid and benefits in kind granted to the directors of the issuer during the last completed financial year of the issuer, together with an estimate of the aggregate amount payable and benefits in kind to be granted to the directors, and proposed directors, for the current financial year under the arrangements in force at the date on which the offer is first made.

(2) The interests of each director of the issuer in the share capital of the issuer, distinguishing between beneficial and non-beneficial interests, or an appropriate negative statement.

PART IX

RECENT DEVELOPMENTS IN THE ISSUER'S BUSINESS AND PROSPECTS

48. The significant recent trends concerning the development of the issuer's business since the end of the last completed financial year of the issuer.

49. Information on the issuer's prospects for at least the current financial year of the issuer.

PART X

CONVERTIBLE SECURITIES AND GUARANTEED DEBENTURES

50. Where the prospectus relates to convertible securities, and the issuer of the related underlying securities is not the same as the issuer of the convertible securities, the information specified in this Schedule must be given in respect of the issuer of the convertible securities, and the information specified in paragraph 2 and Parts V, VI, VII, VIII and IX of this Schedule must be given in respect of the issuer of the underlying securities.

51. Where the prospectus relates to debentures which are guaranteed by one or more persons, the name and address and the information specified in Parts V, VI, VII, VIII and IX of this Schedule must also be given in respect of any guarantor who is not an individual.

SCHEDULE 2 Regulation 17

AMENDMENTS TO THE FINANCIAL SERVICES ACT 1986 AND MINOR AND CONSEQUENTIAL AMENDMENTS AND REPEALS

PART I

AMENDMENTS TO PART IV OF THE FINANCIAL SERVICES ACT 1986

1. (1) Section 142 of the Act shall be amended as follows.

(2) In subsection (7), immediately before the definition of 'issuer' there shall be inserted—

' "approved exchange" means, in relation to dealings in securities, a recognised investment exchange approved by the Treasury for the purposes of the Public Offers of Securities Regulations 1995 either generally or in relation to such dealings;'.

(3) After that subsection, there shall be inserted—

'(7A) For the purposes of this Part of this Act—

    (a) a person offers securities if, as principal—
        (i) he makes an offer which, if accepted, would give rise to a contract for their issue or sale (which for this purpose includes any disposal for valuable consideration) by him or by another person with whom he has made arrangements for their issue or sale; or
        (ii) he invites a person to make such an offer,
    but not otherwise; and, except where the context otherwise requires, "offer" and "offeror" shall be construed accordingly; and
    (b) whether a person offers securities to the public in the United Kingdom shall be determined in accordance with Schedule 11A to this Act.'.

2. (1) In section 144 of the Act, for subsection (2) there shall be substituted—

'(2) Listing rules shall require as a condition of the admission to the Official List of any securities for which application for admission has been made and which are to be offered to the public in the United Kingdom for the first time before admission—

    (a) the submission to, and approval by, the authority of a prospectus in such form and containing such information as may be specified in the rules; and
    (b) the publication of that prospectus.

(2A) Listing rules may require as a condition of the admission to the Official List of any other securities—

    (a) the submission to, and approval by, the authority of a document (in this Act referred to as "listing particulars") in such form and containing such information as may be specified in the rules; and
    (b) the publication of that document;

or, in such cases as may be specified by the rules, the publication of a document other than listing particulars or a prospectus.

(2B) Subsections (2) and (2A) have effect without prejudice to the generality of the power of the competent authority to make listing rules for the purposes of this section.'

(2) Schedule 3 to these Regulations shall have effect to insert Schedule 11A into the Act.

(3) After section 154 of the Act there shall be inserted—

'154A   Application of Part IV to prospectuses

Sections 146 to 152 and 154 above shall apply in relation to a prospectus required by listing rules in accordance with section 144(2) above as they apply in relation to listing particulars, but as if—

(a)   any reference to listing particulars were a reference to a prospectus and any reference to supplementary listing particulars were a reference to a supplementary prospectus; and

(b)   notwithstanding section 142(7) above, any reference in section 152 above (other than in subsection (1)(b) of that section) to the issuer of securities included a reference to the person offering or proposing to offer them.'.

(4) After section 156 of the Act there shall be inserted—

'156A   Approval of prospectus where no application for listing

(1) Listing rules may also provide for a prospectus to be submitted to and approved by the competent authority where—

(a)   securities are to be offered to the public in the United Kingdom for the first time;

(b)   no application for listing of the securities has been made under this Part of this Act; and

(c)   the prospectus is submitted by or with the consent of the issuer of the securities.

(2) Listing rules made under subsection (1) above may make provision—

(a)   as to the information to be contained in, and the form of, a prospectus submitted under any such rules; and

(b)   subject to the provisions of the Public Offers of Securities Regulations 1995, as to the timing and manner of publication of such a prospectus.

(3) Sections 146 to 152 above shall apply in relation to such a prospectus as they apply in relation to listing particulars but as if—

(a)   any reference to listing particulars were a reference to a prospectus and any reference to supplementary listing particulars were a reference to a supplementary prospectus;

(b)   in section 146(1) above—

(i)   the words "as a condition of the admission of any securities to the Official List" were omitted; and

(ii)   for the words "section 144 above" there were substituted "section 156A(1) below",

(c)   in section 147(1) above, for the words "under section 144 above and before the commencement of dealings in the securities following their admission to the Official List" there were substituted "under section 156A(1) below and before the end of the period during which the offer to which the prospectus relates remains open",

(d)   in subsections (1)(d) and (2)(d) of section 151 above—

(i)   the words "that he continued in that belief until after the commencement of dealings in the securities following their admission to the Official List and" were omitted; and

(ii) the words "and, if the securities are dealt in on an approved exchange, that he continued in that belief until after the commencement of dealings in the securities on that exchange" were added at the end;

(e) notwithstanding section 142(7) above, any reference in section 152 above (other than in subsection (1)(b) of that section) to the issuer of securities included a reference to the person offering or proposing to offer them; and

(f) in section 154(1) above, for the words "Where listing particulars are or are to be published in connection with an application for the listing of any securities" there were substituted "Where a prospectus is or is to be published in connection with an application for approval, then, until the end of the period during which the offer to which the prospectus relates remains open,".

(4) Listing rules made under this section may require the payment of fees to the competent authority in respect of a prospectus submitted for approval under the rules.

156B Publication of prospectus

(1) Where listing rules made under section 144(2) above require the publication of a prospectus, it shall not be lawful, before the time of publication of the prospectus, to offer the securities in question to the public in the United Kingdom.

(2) An authorised person who contravenes subsection (1) above shall be treated as contravening rules made under Chapter V of Part I of this Act or, in the case of a person who is an authorised person by virtue of his membership of a recognised self-regulating organisation or certification by a recognised professional body, the rules of that organisation or body.

(3) A person, other than an authorised person, who contravenes subsection (1) above shall be guilty of an offence and liable—

(a) on conviction on indictment, to imprisonment for a term not exceeding two years or to a fine or to both;

(b) on summary conviction, to imprisonment for a term not exceeding three months or a fine not exceeding level 5 on the standard scale.

(4) Without prejudice to any liability under section 150 above, a person shall not be regarded as contravening subsection (1) above by reason only of a prospectus not having fully complied with the requirements of listing rules as to its form or content.

(5) Any contravention of subsection (1) above shall be actionable at the suit of a person who suffers loss as a result of the contravention subject to the defences and other incidents applying to actions for breach of statutory duty.'

3. Subsection (3) of section 156B of the Act shall not apply to a European institution carrying on home-regulated investment business in the United Kingdom which contravenes subsection (1) of that section, but it shall be treated for all purposes—

(a) if it is not a member of a recognised self-regulating organisation, as having contravened rules made under Chapter V of Part I of the Act; or

(b) if it is a member of a recognised self-regulating organisation, as having contravened the rules of that organisation.

PART II

CONSEQUENTIAL AMENDMENTS AND REPEALS

4. Part V of the Act is hereby repealed.

5. The following provisions of the Act are hereby repealed—

    (a) in section 48(5), the words 'and rules under that paragraph shall have effect subject to the provisions of Part V of this Act.';

    (b) in section 58(1)(d)(ii), the words 'or by an approved exchange under Part V of this Act';

    (c) section 58(2);

    (d) section 192(3);

    (e) in Schedule 16, paragraph 16.

6. In section 58 of the Act—

    (a) in subsection (1)(d)(ii), after the words 'supplementary listing particulars' there shall be inserted ', a prospectus approved in accordance with listing rules made under section 144(2) or 156A(1) below, a supplementary prospectus approved in accordance with listing rules made for the purposes of section 147(1) below as applied by section 154A or 156A(3) below'; and

    (b) in subsection (6), for 'Subsections (1)(c) and (2) above do' there shall be substituted 'Subsection (1)(c) above does'.

7. In section 199(1) of the Act, for '133 or 171(2) or (3)' there shall be substituted 'or 133'.

8. In section 207(1) of the Act, in the definition of 'listing particulars', for '144(2)' there shall be substituted '144(2A)'.

9. Paragraph 8 of Schedule 15 to the Act is hereby repealed.

10. Sections 198 and 199 of the Companies Act 1989 are hereby repealed.

11. In regulation 3 of the Control of Misleading Advertisements Regulations 1988—

    (a) in paragraph (1)(b), the words from 'except where' to the end of the paragraph; and

    (b) in paragraph (2), the words '"approved exchange",';
        shall be deleted.

12. In Schedule 9 to the Banking Coordination (Second Council Directive) Regulations 1992, paragraph 38 is hereby revoked.

SCHEDULE 3   Schedule 2, paragraph 3(2)

OFFERS OF SECURITIES TO THE PUBLIC IN THE UNITED KINGDOM

The following is the Schedule to be inserted into the Act as Schedule 11A—

'SCHEDULE 11A

OFFERS OF SECURITIES TO THE PUBLIC IN THE UNITED KINGDOM

1. A person offers securities to the public in the United Kingdom if—

    (a) to the extent that the offer is made to persons in the United Kingdom, it is made to the public; and

    (b) paragraph 2 below does not apply in relation to the offer;

and, for this purpose, an offer which is made to any section of the public, whether selected as members or debenture holders of a body corporate, or as clients of the person making the offer, or in any other manner, is to be regarded as made to the public.

2. This paragraph applies in relation to an offer of securities where, to the extent that the offer is made to persons in the United Kingdom—

    (a) the condition specified in any one of the paragraphs of sub-paragraph (1) of paragraph 3 below is satisfied in relation to the offer; or

    (b) paragraph 4 below applies in relation to the offer.

3. (1) The following are the conditions specified in this sub-paragraph—

    (a) the securities are offered to persons—

        (i) whose ordinary activities involve them in acquiring, holding, managing or disposing of investments (as principal or agent) for the purposes of their businesses; or

       (ii) who it is reasonable to expect will acquire, hold, manage or dispose of investments (as principal or agent) for the purposes of their businesses;

      or are otherwise offered to persons in the context of their trades, professions or occupations;

    (b) the securities are offered to no more than fifty persons;

    (c) the securities are offered to the members of a club or association (whether or not incorporated) and the members can reasonably be regarded as having a common interest with each other and with the club or association in the affairs of the club or association and in what is to be done with the proceeds of the offer;

    (d) the securities are offered to a restricted circle of persons whom the offeror reasonably believes to be sufficiently knowledgeable to understand the risks involved in accepting the offer;

    (e) the securities are offered in connection with a bona fide invitation to enter into an underwriting agreement with respect to them;

    (f) the securities are offered to a government, local authority or public authority, as defined in paragraph 3 of Schedule 1 to this Act;

    (g) the total consideration payable for the securities cannot exceed ecu 40,000 (or an equivalent amount);

    (h) the minimum consideration which may be paid for securities acquired pursuant to the offer is at least ecu 40,000 (or an equivalent amount);

    (i) the securities are denominated in amounts of at least ecu 40,000 (or an equivalent amount);

    (j) the securities are offered in connection with a takeover offer;

    (k) the securities are offered in connection with a merger within the meaning of Council Directive No. 78/855/EEC;

    (l) the securities are shares and are offered free of charge to any or all of the holders of shares in the issuer;

(m) the securities are shares, or investments falling within paragraph 4 or 5 of Schedule 1 to this Act relating to shares, in a body corporate and are offered in exchange for shares in the same body corporate, and the offer cannot result in any increase in the issued share capital of the body corporate;

(n) the securities are issued by a body corporate and offered—

    (i) by the issuer;

    (ii) only to qualifying persons; and

    (iii) on terms that a contract to acquire any such securities may be entered into only by the qualifying person to whom they were offered or, if the terms of the offer so permit, any qualifying person;

(o) the securities result from the conversion of convertible securities and listing particulars or a prospectus relating to the convertible securities were or was published in the United Kingdom under or by virtue of Part IV of this Act, Part III of the Companies Act 1985 or the Public Offers of Securities Regulations 1995;

(p) the securities are issued by—

    (i) a charity within the meaning of section 96(1) of the Charities Act 1993;

    (ii) a housing association within the meaning of section 5(1) of the Housing Act 1985;

    (iii) an industrial or provident society registered in accordance with section 1(2)(b) of the Industrial and Provident Societies Act 1965; or

    (iv) a non-profit making association or body, recognised by the country or territory in which it is established, with objectives similar to those of a body falling within any of sub-paragraphs (i) to (iii) above;

and the proceeds of the offer will be used for the purposes of the issuer's objectives;

(q) the securities offered are shares which are issued by, or ownership of which entitles the holder to membership of or to obtain the benefit of services provided by,—

    (i) a building society incorporated under the law of, or of any part of, the United Kingdom;

    (ii) any body incorporated under the law of, or of any part of, the United Kingdom relating to industrial and provident societies or credit unions; or

    (iii) a body of a similar nature established in a member State;

(r) the securities offered are Euro-securities and are not the subject of advertising likely to come to the attention of persons who are not professionally experienced in matters relating to investment;

(s) the securities are of the same class, and were issued at the same time, as securities in respect of which a prospectus has been published under or by virtue of Part IV of this Act, Part III of the Companies Act 1985 or the Public Offers of Securities Regulations 1995;

(t) the securities are investments falling within paragraph 2 of Schedule 1 to this Act with a maturity of less than one year from their date of issue;

(u) the securities are investments falling within paragraph 3 of Schedule 1 to this Act;

(v) the securities are not transferable.

(2) For the purposes of this paragraph—

'convertible securities' means—

    (a) securities falling within paragraph 2 of Schedule 1 to this Act which can be converted into, or exchanged for, or which confer rights to acquire, securities; or

    (b) securities falling within paragraph 4 or 5 of that Schedule (as applied for the purposes of section 142(2) of this Act);

and 'conversion' in relation to convertible securities means their conversion into or exchange for, or the exercise of rights conferred by them to acquire, other securities; 'credit institution' means a credit institution as defined in Article 1 of Council Directive No. 77/780/EEC;
'ecu' means the European currency unit as defined in Article 1 of Council Regulation No. 3320/94/EC or any Council regulation replacing the same, in either case as amended from time to time;
'Euro-securities' means investments which—

(a) are to be underwritten and distributed by a syndicate at least two of the members of which have their registered offices in different countries or territories;

(b) are to be offered on a significant scale in one or more countries or territories other than the country or territory in which the issuer has its registered office; and

(c) may be acquired pursuant to the offer only through a credit institution or other financial institution;

'financial institution' means a financial institution as defined in Article 1 of Council Directive No. 89/646/EEC; and
'shares', except in relation to a takeover offer, means investments which are securities by virtue of falling within paragraph 1 of Schedule 1 to this Act (as applied for the purposes of section 142(3) of this Act).

(3) For the purposes of determining whether the condition specified in paragraph (b) or (g) of sub-paragraph (1) above is satisfied in relation to an offer, the offer shall be taken together with any other offer of the same securities which was—

(a) made by the same person;

(b) open at any time within the period of 12 months ending with the date on which the offer is first made; and

(c) not an offer to the public in the United Kingdom by virtue of that condition being satisfied.

(4) In determining for the purposes of paragraph (d) of sub-paragraph (1) above whether a person is sufficiently knowledgeable to understand the risks involved in accepting an offer of securities, any information supplied by the person making the offer shall be disregarded, apart from information about—

(a) the issuer of the securities; or

(b) if the securities confer the right to acquire other securities, the issuer of those other securities.

(5) For the purposes of determining whether the condition specified in paragraph (g), (h) or (i) of sub-paragraph (1) above is satisfied in relation to an offer, an amount, in relation to an amount denominated in ecu, is an 'equivalent amount' if it is an amount of equal value, calculated at the latest practicable date before (but in any event not more than 3 days before) the date on which the offer is first made, denominated wholly or partly in another currency or unit of account.

(6) For the purposes of paragraph (j) of sub-paragraph (1) above, 'takeover offer' means—

(a) an offer which is a takeover offer within the meaning of Part XIIIA of the Companies Act 1985 (or would be such an offer if that Part of that Act applied in relation to any body corporate); or

(b) an offer made to all the holders of shares, or of shares of a particular class, in a body corporate to acquire a specified proportion of those shares ('holders' and 'shares' being construed in accordance with that Part);

but in determining for the purposes of paragraph (b) above whether an offer is made to all the holders of shares, or of shares of any class, the offeror, any associate of his (within the meaning of section 430E of that Act) and any person whose shares the offeror or any such associate has contracted to acquire shall not be regarded as holders of the shares.

(7) For the purposes of paragraph (l) of sub-paragraph (1) above, 'holders of shares' means the persons who, at the close of business on a date specified in the offer and falling within the period of 28 days ending with the date on which the offer is first made, were the holders of such shares.

(8) For the purposes of paragraph (n) of sub-paragraph (1) above—

(a) a person is a 'qualifying person', in relation to an issuer, if he is a bona fide employee or former employee of the issuer or of another body corporate in the same group or the wife, husband, widow, widower or child or stepchild under the age of eighteen of such an employee or former employee; and
(b) the definition of 'issuer' in section 142(7) applies with the omission of the words from 'except that' to the end of the definition.

4. (1) This paragraph applies in relation to an offer where the condition specified in one relevant paragraph is satisfied in relation to part, but not the whole, of the offer and, in relation to each other part of the offer, the condition specified in a different relevant paragraph is satisfied.

(2) For the purposes of this paragraph, 'relevant paragraph' means any of paragraphs (a) to (f), (j) to (m), (o), (p) and (s) of paragraph 3(1) above.'

SCHEDULE 4   Regulation 20

MUTUAL RECOGNITION OF PROSPECTUSES AND LISTING PARTICULARS

PART I

RECOGNITION FOR THE PURPOSES OF PART IV OF THE FINANCIAL SERVICES ACT 1986 OF PROSPECTUSES AND LISTING PARTICULARS APPROVED IN OTHER MEMBER STATES

1. In this Part of this Schedule—

(a) the term 'competent authority' includes a body designated by a member State pursuant to Article 12 of Council Directive No. 89/298/EEC;
(b) 'the UK authority' means the competent authority for the purposes of Part IV of the Act.
(c) 'European document' means—
    (i) listing particulars which have been approved by the competent authority in another member State and which Article 24a of Council Directive No. 80/390/EEC requires or paragraph 5 of that article permits to be recognised as listing particulars;
    (ii) a prospectus which has been approved by the competent authority in another member State and which Article 24b of Council Directive No. 80/390/EEC requires or which paragraph 2 of that article, in referring to

paragraph 5 of Article 24a of that Directive, permits to be recognised as listing particulars; or

(iii) a prospectus which has been approved by the competent authority in another member State, which Article 21 of Council Directive No. 89/298/EEC requires or which paragraph 4 of that article permits to be recognised and which relates to securities which are the subject of an application for listing in the United Kingdom and which are to be offered in the United Kingdom prior to admission to listing in the United Kingdom by means of the prospectus;

including in each case any supplement to listing particulars or a prospectus which, before the completion of the preparation of the recognised document for submission to the UK authority pursuant to an application for listing, has been approved pursuant to Article 23 of Council Directive No. 80/390/EEC or Article 18 of Council Directive No. 89/298/EEC by the competent authorities which approved the listing particulars or prospectus.

Where the European document submitted to the UK authority is a translation into English of the document approved by the competent authorities in another member State then, unless the context otherwise requires, the document as translated shall be regarded as the European document rather than the document as approved.

2. In this Part of this Schedule, 'recognised European document' means a document consisting of a European document submitted to the UK authority pursuant to an application for listing under section 143 of the Act and, if information is required to be added to it in accordance with listing rules, including that information.

3. Subject to paragraph 4, Part IV of the Act shall apply to a recognised European document as it applies—

(a) in relation to listing particulars, within the meaning of section 144(2) of the Act (in a case where the securities to which it relates will not be offered in the United Kingdom prior to admission to listing in the United Kingdom); or

(b) in relation to a prospectus to which section 144 of the Act applies (in a case where the recognised European document is a prospectus and the securities to which it relates are to be offered in the United Kingdom prior to admission to listing in the United Kingdom).

4. Part IV of the Act shall apply to a recognised European document subject to the following modifications—

(a) nothing in Part IV shall require the approval by the UK authority of a recognised European document which has been approved as described in paragraph 1(c);

(b) in sections 146, 147(1)(a) and 150(2) of the Act, any reference to information specified or required by listing rules or required by the competent authority or to matter whose inclusion was required by listing rules or by the competent authority shall apply as if it were a reference to information required by or to matter whose inclusion was required by the legislation relating to the contents of prospectuses and listing particulars, or by the competent authorities, of the member State where the European document forming part of that recognised European document was approved;

(c) nothing in section 147 of the Act shall require the approval by the UK authority of supplementary listing particulars or a supplementary prospectus which is, or is a translation into English of, a supplement which has been approved pursuant to Article 23 of Council Directive No. 80/390/EEC or Article 18 of Council Directive No. 89/298/EEC by the competent authority which approved the listing particulars or prospectus to which the supplement relates.

5. Subject to paragraphs 1 and 3, references in Part IV of the Act to supplementary listing particulars shall be taken to include references to supplementary prospectuses.

6. This Part of this Schedule shall not apply to listing particulars or a prospectus approved in another member State prior to the coming into force of these Regulations.

PART II

RECOGNITION FOR THE PURPOSES OF PART II OF THESE REGULATIONS OF PROSPECTUSES APPROVED IN OTHER MEMBER STATES

7. In this Part of this Schedule 'recognised prospectus' means a prospectus which has been approved in accordance with Article 20 of Council Directive No. 89/298/EEC in another member State and satisfies the requirements of paragraphs (a) to (c) of paragraph 8(1); and where the prospectus has been translated into English, the English version shall be the recognised prospectus.

8. (1) Where a prospectus has been approved in accordance with Article 20 of Council Directive No. 89/298/EEC in another member State it shall, subject to sub-paragraph (2), be deemed for the purposes of regulation 4(1) to comply with regulations 8 and 9 of these Regulations provided that—

(a) where the prospectus as approved in the other member State was written in a language other than English, the prospectus has been translated into English and the translation has been certified to be a correct translation in the manner prescribed in regulation 6 of the Companies (Forms) Regulations 1985 or the corresponding Northern Ireland provision;
(b) the offer of securities to which the prospectus relates is made in the United Kingdom simultaneously with the making of the offer in the member State where the prospectus was approved or within 3 months after the making of that offer;
(c) there is added to the information contained in the prospectus as approved in the other member State such of the following information as is not included in the prospectus as so approved—
  (i) a summary of the tax treatment relevant to United Kingdom resident holders of the securities;
  (ii) the names and addresses of the paying agents for the securities in the United Kingdom (if any);
  (iii) a statement of how notice of meetings and other notices from the issuer of the securities will be given to United Kingdom resident holders of the securities; and
(d) where a partial exemption or partial derogation has been granted in the other member State pursuant to Council Directive No. 89/298/EEC—
  (i) the partial exemption or partial derogation in question is of a type for which a corresponding partial exemption or partial derogation is made in these Regulations; and
  (ii) the circumstances that justify the partial exemption or partial derogation also exist in the United Kingdom.

(2) Where, prior to the delivery for registration to the registrar of companies of a prospectus which has been approved in another member State, a supplement to the prospectus has been approved pursuant to Article 23 of Council Directive No. 80/390/EEC or Article 18 of Council Directive No. 89/298/EEC in the member State where the prospectus was approved, the references in sub-paragraph (1) and in paragraph 7 to a prospectus shall be taken to be references to the prospectus taken together with the supplement.

9. Subject to paragraph 8(2), Part II of these Regulations shall apply in relation to a recognised prospectus as it applies in relation to a prospectus to which the said Part II would apply apart from this paragraph except that in regulations 9(1), 10(1)(a) and 14(2) of these Regulations the references to information or any matter required to be included in a prospectus by these Regulations shall be taken to be references to information or any matter required to be included by virtue of the legislation relating to the contents of prospectuses of the member State where the recognised prospectus was approved and by virtue of paragraph 8(1)(c).

PART III

RECOGNITION FOR THE PURPOSES OF THE COMPANIES ACT 1985 OF PROSPECTUSES APPROVED IN OTHER MEMBER STATES

10. In this Part of this Schedule, 'recognised prospectus' has the same meaning as in Part II of this Schedule.

11. The provisions of the Companies Act 1985, other than—

    (a) section 83; and
    (b) in section 84, the words 'This is without prejudice to section 83.',

shall apply to a recognised prospectus.

12. A recognised prospectus shall be deemed to comply with sections 97(3) and 693(1)(a) and (d) of the Companies Act 1985.

SCHEDULE 5   Regulation 24

AMENDMENTS TO REGULATIONS MADE UNDER THE BANKING ACT 1987

1. (1) The Banking Act 1987 (Advertisements) Regulations 1988 shall be amended as follows.

(2) In regulation 2(4)(a), for the words 'to which section 56 of the Companies Act 1985 applies or would apply if not excluded by paragraph (a) or (b) of subsection (5) of that section' there shall be substituted—

   'a prospectus to which regulation 8 of the Public Offers of Securities Regulations 1995 applies, or would apply but for regulation 7 of those regulations where—
      (i) the prospectus is issued to existing members of debenture holders of a company; and
      (ii) the prospectus relates to shares in or debentures of the company,
   whether an applicant for shares or debentures will or will not have the right to renounce in favour of other persons'.

(3) In regulation 2(4)(b), for the words 'a prospectus to which section 72 of that Act applies or would apply if not excluded by paragraph (a) or (b) of subsection (6) of that section' there shall be substituted—

   'a prospectus to which regulation 8 of the Public Offers of Securities Regulations 1995 applies, or would apply but for regulation 7 of those regulations where—
      (i) the prospectus is issued to existing members or debenture holders of a company; and

   (ii) the prospectus relates to shares in or debentures of the company,
whether an applicant for shares or debentures will or will not have the right to
renounce in favour of other persons'.

(4) In regulation 2(4)(c), for the words from 'together with' to the end there shall be
substituted—

> 'together with a prospectus to which regulation 8 of the Public Offers of Securities
> Regulations 1995 applies, or would apply but for regulation 7 of those regulations
> where—
>> (i) the prospectus is issued to existing members or debenture holders of a
>> company; and
>> (ii) the prospectus relates to shares in or debentures of the company,
> whether an applicant for shares or debentures will or will not have the right to
> renounce in favour of other persons.'

2. In regulation 13(d)(iv) of the Banking Act 1987 (Exempt Transactions) Regulations
1988, for the words 'section 56 or 72 of the Companies Act 1985 or the corresponding
Northern Ireland legislation' there shall be substituted 'regulation 8 of the Public Offers
of Securities Regulations 1995'.

TRADED SECURITIES (DISCLOSURE) REGULATIONS 1994

(SI 1994/188)

1 Citation and commencement

(1) These Regulations may be cited as the Traded Securities (Disclosure) Regulations 1994.

(2) These Regulations shall come into force on 1st March 1994.

2 Interpretation

In these Regulations—

'the Official List' has the meaning given by section 142(7) of the Financial Services Act 1986;

'overseas investment exchange' and 'recognised investment exchange' have the meaning given by section 207(1) of the Financial Services Act 1986;

'regulated market' means any market in the United Kingdom on which securities are admitted to trading being a market which is regulated and supervised by a recognised investment exchange and which operates regularly and is accessible directly or indirectly to the public; and

'security' means any security which falls within any paragraph of the Schedule to these Regulations but does not include an investment which is admitted to the Official List in accordance with Part IV of the Financial Services Act 1986.

and the expressions 'admitting to trading' and 'company' and 'undertaking' have the same meaning as in the Council Directive of 13th November 1989 co-ordinating regulations on insider dealing (89/592/EEC)

3 Obligation to disclose information

(1) Subject to paragraph (2) below, a company or undertaking which is an issuer of a security admitted to trading on a regulated market (an 'issuer') shall inform the public as soon as possible of any major new developments in the issuer's sphere of activity which are not public knowledge and which may, by virtue of their effect on the issuer's assets and liabilities or financial position or on the general course of its business, lead to substantial movements in the price of that security.

(2) A recognised investment exchange which regulates and supervises a regulated market on which an issuer's securities are admitted to trading may exempt the issuer from the obligation imposed by paragraph (1) above if satisfied that the disclosure of the particular information would prejudice the legitimate interests of that issuer.

(3) The rules of a recognised investment exchange must, at least, enable the exchange, in the event of a failure by an issuer whose securities are admitted to trading on a

regulated market which the exchange regulates and supervises to comply with the obligation imposed by paragraph (1) above, to do any of the following, that is to say—

(a) discontinue the admission of the securities to trading;
(b) suspend trading in the securities;
(c) publish the fact that the issuer has failed to comply with the obligation; and
(d) itself make public any information which the issuer has failed to publish.

4 The Financial Services Act 1986 shall have effect as if the requirement set out in paragraph (3) of regulation 3 above was—

(a) in the case of a recognised investment exchange which is not an overseas investment exchange, among those specified in Schedule 4 to that Act (requirements for recognition of UK investment exchange); and
(b) in the case of an overseas investment exchange, among those mentioned in section 37(7)(a) of that Act (revocation of recognition order) and specified in section 740(2) of that Act (requirements for recognition of overseas investment exchange etc.).

SCHEDULE

Regulation 2

1. Shares and stock in the share capital of a company ('shares').

2. Any instrument creating or acknowledging indebtedness which is issued by a company or undertaking, including, in particular, debentures, debenture stock, loan stock, bonds and certificates of deposit ('debt securities').

3. Any right (whether conferred by warrant or otherwise) to subscribe for shares or debt securities ('warrants').

4. (1) The rights under any depositary receipt.

(2) For the purposes of sub-paragraph (1) above a 'depositary receipt' means a certificate or other record (whether or not in the form of a document)—

(a) which is issued by or on behalf of a person who holds any relevant securities of a particular issuer; and
(b) which acknowledges that another person is entitled to rights in relation to the relevant securities or relevant securities of the same kind.

(3) In sub-paragraph (2) above 'relevant securities' means shares, debt securities and warrants.

5. Any option to acquire or dispose of any security falling within any other paragraph of this Schedule.

6. Rights under a contract for the acquisition or disposal of relevant securities under which delivery is to be made at a future date and at a price agreed when the contract is made.

(2) In sub-paragraph (1) above—

(a) the references to a future date and to a price agreed when the contract is made include references to a date and a price determined in accordance with the terms of the contract; and
(b) 'relevant securities' means any security falling within any other paragraph of this Schedule.

7. (1) Rights under a contract which does not provide for the delivery of securities but whose purpose or pretended purpose is to secure a profit or avoid a loss by reference to fluctuations in—

(a) a share index or other similar factor connected with relevant securities; or

(b) the price of particular relevant securities.

(2) In sub-paragraph (1) above 'relevant securities' means any security falling within any other paragraph of this Schedule.

UNCERTIFICATED SECURITIES REGULATIONS 1995

(SI 1995/3272)

ARRANGEMENT OF THE REGULATIONS

PART I

CITATION, COMMENCEMENT AND INTERPRETATION

PART II

THE OPERATOR

Approval and compliance

Supervision

Miscellaneous

PART III

PARTICIPATING ISSUERS

Participation by issuers

PART IV

DEMATERIALISED INSTRUCTIONS ETC.

PART V

MISCELLANEOUS AND SUPPLEMENTAL

Miscellaneous

Appendix 1
STATUTORY MATERIALS

PART I

CITATION, COMMENCEMENT AND INTERPRETATION

1 Citation and commencement

These Regulations may be cited as the Uncertificated Securities Regulations 1995 and shall come into force the day after the day on which they are made.

2 Purposes and basic definitions

(1) These Regulations enable title to units of a security to be evidenced otherwise than by a certificate and transferred otherwise than by a written instrument, and make provision for certain supplementary and incidental matters; and in these Regulations 'relevant system' means a computer-based system, and procedures, which enable title to units of a security to be evidenced and transferred without a written instrument, and which facilitate supplementary and incidental matters.

(2) Where title to a unit of a security is evidenced otherwise than by a certificate by virtue of these Regulations, the transfer of title to such a unit of a security shall be subject to these Regulations.

(3) Part II of these Regulations has effect for the purpose of securing—

    (a) that the Operator of a relevant system is a person approved for the purpose by the Treasury; and

    (b) that a person is only approved if it appears to the Treasury that certain requirements are satisfied with respect to that person, the relevant system and his rules and practices.

(4) Part III of these Regulations has effect for the purpose—

    (a) of enabling companies and other persons to become participating issuers in relation to a relevant system, that is to say, persons who permit—

        (i) the holding of units of securities issued by them in uncertificated form; and

        (ii) the transfer by means of the system of title to units of such of the securities issued by them as are held in that form; and

    (b) of establishing the duties and obligations of participating issuers in relation to uncertificated units of a security with respect to the keeping of registers, the registration of transfers and other matters.

(5) Part IV of these Regulations has effect for the purpose of securing—

(a) in certain circumstances—
    (i) that the persons expressed to have sent instructions by means of a relevant system which are properly authenticated, and the persons on whose behalf those instructions are expressed to have been sent, are prevented from denying to the persons to whom those instructions are addressed that certain information relating to them is correct; and
    (ii) that the persons to whom the instructions referred to in subparagraph (a) (i) are addressed may accept that certain information relating to them is correct; and
(b) in certain circumstances that persons suffering loss are compensated by the person approved under Part II of these Regulations.

3 Interpretation

(1) In these Regulations—
  'the 1985 Act' means the Companies Act 1985;
  'the 1986 Act' means the Financial Services Act 1986;
  'certificate' means any certificate, instrument or other document of, or evidencing, title to units of a security;
  'company' means a company within the meaning of section 735(1) of the 1985 Act;
  'dematerialised instruction' means an instruction sent or received by means of a relevant system;
  'designated agency' has the meaning given by regulation 11(1);
  'enactment' includes an enactment comprised in any subordinate legislation within the meaning of the Interpretation Act 1978;
  'generate', in relation to an Operator-instruction, means to initiate the procedures by which an Operator-instruction comes to be sent;
  'guidance', in relation to an Operator, means guidance issued by him which is intended to have continuing effect and is issued in writing or other legible form, which if it were a rule, would come within the definition of a rule;
  'instruction' includes any instruction, election, acceptance or any other message of any kind;
  'interest in a security' means any legal or equitable interest or right in relation to a security, including—
    (a) an absolute or contingent right to acquire a security created, allotted or issued or to be created, allotted or issued; and
    (b) the interests or rights of a person for whom a security is held by a custodian or depositary;
  'issue', in relation to a new unit of a security, means to confer title to a new unit on a person;
  'issuer-instruction' means a properly authenticated dematerialised instruction attributable to a participating issuer;
  'officer', in relation to a participating issuer, includes—
    (a) where the participating issuer is a company, such persons as are mentioned in section 744 of the 1985 Act;
    (b) where the participating issuer is a partnership, a partner; or in the event that no partner is situated in the United Kingdom, a person in the United Kingdom who is acting on behalf of a partner; and
    (c) where the participating issuer is neither a company nor a partnership, any member of its governing body; or in the event that no member of its governing body is situated in the United Kingdom, a person in the United Kingdom who is acting on behalf of any member of its governing body;
  'Operator' means a person approved by the Treasury under these Regulations as Operator of a relevant system;

'Operator-instruction' means a properly authenticated dematerialised instruction attributable to an Operator;

'Operator-system' means those facilities and procedures which are part of the relevant system, which are maintained and operated by or for an Operator, by which he generates Operator-instructions and receives dematerialised instructions from system-participants and by which persons change the form in which units of a participating security are held;

'the 1986 Order' means the Companies (Northern Ireland) Order 1986;

'participating issuer' means a person who has issued a security which is a participating security;

'participating security' means a security title to units of which is permitted by an Operator to be transferred by means of a relevant system;

'register of members' means a register of members maintained by a company under section 352 of the 1985 Act;

'register of securities'—

  (a) in relation to shares, means a register of members; and
  (b) in relation to units of a security other than shares, means a register maintained by the issuer, whether by virtue of these Regulations or otherwise, of persons holding the units;

'relevant system' has the meaning given by regulation 2(1); and 'relevant system' includes an Operator-system;

'rules', in relation to an Operator, means rules made or conditions imposed by him with respect to the provision of the relevant system;

'securities' means shares, stock, debentures, debenture stock, loan stock, bonds, units of a collective investment scheme within the meaning of the 1986 Act, rights under a depositary receipt within the meaning of paragraph 4 of Schedule 2 to the Criminal Justice Act 1993, and other securities of any description, and interests in a security;

'settlement bank', in relation to a relevant system, means a person who has contracted to make payments in connection with transfers of title to uncertificated units of a security by means of that system;

'share' means share (or stock) in the share capital of a company;

'system-member', in relation to a relevant system, means a person who is permitted by an Operator to transfer by means of that system title to uncertificated units of a security held by him, and shall include, where relevant, two or more persons who are jointly so permitted;

'system-member instruction' means a properly authenticated dematerialised instruction attributable to a system-member;

'system-participant', in relation to a relevant system, means a person who is permitted by an Operator to send and receive properly authenticated dematerialised instructions; and 'sponsoring system-participant' means a system-participant who is permitted by an Operator to send properly authenticated dematerialised instructions attributable to another person and to receive properly authenticated dematerialised instructions on another person's behalf;

'system-user', in relation to a relevant system, means a person who as regards that system is a participating issuer, system-member, system-participant or settlement bank;

'uncertificated unit of a security' means a unit of a security title to which is recorded on the relevant register of securities as being held in uncertificated form, and title to which, by virtue of these Regulations, may be transferred by means of a relevant system; and 'certificated unit of a security' means a unit of a security which is not an uncertificated unit;

'unit of a security' means the smallest possible transferable unit of the security (for example a single share);

and other expressions have the meanings given to them by the 1985 Act.

(2) For the purposes of these Regulations—

(a) a dematerialised instruction is properly authenticated if it complies with the specifications referred to in paragraph 5(b) of Schedule 1 to these Regulations; and

(b) a dematerialised instruction is attributable to a person if it is expressed to have been sent by that person, or if it is expressed to have been sent on behalf of that person, in accordance with the specifications of the Operator referred to in paragraph 5(c) of Schedule 1 to these Regulations; and a dematerialised instruction may be attributable to more than one person.

(3) In these Regulations, except where otherwise indicated—

(a) a reference to a numbered regulation or Schedule is a reference to the regulation of or the Schedule to these Regulations so numbered;

(b) a reference in a regulation to a numbered paragraph is a reference to the paragraph of that regulation so numbered;

(c) a reference in a Schedule to a numbered paragraph is a reference to the paragraph of that Schedule so numbered; and

(d) a reference in a paragraph to a numbered subparagraph is a reference to the subparagraph of that paragraph so numbered.

PART II

THE OPERATOR

Approval and compliance

4 Applications for approval

(1) A person may apply to the Treasury for their approval of him as Operator of a relevant system.

(2) Any such application—

(a) shall be made in such a manner as the Treasury may direct; and

(b) shall be accompanied by such information as the Treasury may reasonably require for the purpose of determining the application.

(3) At any time after receiving an application and before determining it, the Treasury may require the applicant to furnish additional information.

(4) The directions and requirements given or imposed under paragraphs (2) and (3) may differ as between different applications.

(5) Any information to be furnished to the Treasury under this regulation shall, if they so require, be in such form or verified in such manner as they may specify.

(6) Every application shall be accompanied by a copy of any rules and guidance to be issued by the applicant.

5 Grant and refusal of approval

(1) If, on an application made under regulation 4, it appears to the Treasury that the requirements of Schedule 1 are satisfied with respect to the application, they may—

(a) subject to the payment of any fee charged by virtue of regulation 6(1); and

(b) subject to the provisions of Schedule 2,

approve the applicant as Operator of a relevant system.

(2) An approval under this regulation shall be by instrument in writing and shall state the date on which it takes effect.

(3) Schedule 1 (which imposes requirements which must appear to the Treasury to be satisfied with respect to an Operator, the relevant system and his rules and practices) shall have effect.

(4) Where the Treasury refuse an application for approval they shall give the applicant a written notice to that effect stating the reasons for the refusal.

6 Fees

(1) The Treasury may charge a fee to a person seeking approval as Operator of a relevant system.

(2) The Treasury may charge an Operator a periodical fee.

(3) Any fee chargeable by the Treasury under this regulation shall not exceed an amount which reasonably represents the amount of costs incurred—

(a) in the case of a fee charged to a person seeking approval, in determining whether approval ought to be granted; and

(b) in the case of a periodical fee, in satisfying themselves that the Operator and the relevant system in question continue to meet the requirements of Schedule 1 to these Regulations and that the Operator is complying with any obligations to which he is subject by virtue of them.

(4) For the purposes of paragraph (3), the costs incurred by the Treasury shall be determined on the basis that they include such proportion of the following matters as are properly attributable to the performance of the relevant function—

(a) expenditure on staff, equipment, premises, facilities, research and development;

(b) the allocation, over a period of years, whether before or after the coming into force of these Regulations, of any initial expenditure incurred wholly and exclusively to perform the function or to prepare for its performance;

(c) any notional interest incurred on any capital expended on or in connection with the performance of the function or in preparing for its performance and, in a case in which any function is exercisable by a designated agency, any actual interest payable on any sums borrowed which have been so expended; and

(d) any other matter which, in accordance with generally accepted accounting principles, may properly be taken account of in ascertaining the costs properly attributable to the performance of the function.

(5) For the purposes of paragraph (4)(c)—

(a) 'notional interest' means any interest which that person might reasonably have been expected to have been liable to pay had the sums expended been borrowed at arm's length; and

(b) 'actual interest' means the actual interest paid on sums borrowed in a transaction at arm's length and, where a sum has been borrowed otherwise than in such a transaction, means whichever is the lesser of the interest actually paid and the interest that might reasonably have been expected to be paid had the transaction been at arm's length.

(6) Any fee received by the Treasury under this regulation shall be paid into the Consolidated Fund.

(7) Any fee received by a designated agency under this regulation may be retained by it.

Supervision

7 Withdrawal of approval

(1) If at any time it appears to the Treasury that any requirement of Schedule 1 is not satisfied, or that an Operator has failed to comply with any obligation to which he is subject by virtue of these Regulations, they may, by written instrument, subject to paragraph (2), withdraw approval from that Operator.

(2) Subsections (2) to (9) of section 11 of the 1986 Act shall apply in relation to the withdrawal of approval from an Operator under paragraph (1) as they apply in relation to the revocation of a recognition order under subsection (1) of that section; and in those subsections as they so apply—

   (a) any reference to a recognised organisation shall be taken to be a reference to an Operator; and

   (b) any reference to members of a recognised organisation shall be taken to be a reference to system-users.

8 Compliance orders and directions

(1) If at any time it appears to the Treasury that any requirement of Schedule 1 is not satisfied, or that an Operator has failed to comply with any obligation to which he is subject by virtue of these Regulations, they may—

   (a) make an application to the court; or

   (b) subject to paragraph (3), give to the Operator such directions as they think fit for securing that the relevant requirement is satisfied or obligation complied with.

(2) If on any application by the Treasury under paragraph (1)(a) the court is satisfied that the requirement is not satisfied or, as the case may be, that the Operator has failed to comply with the obligation in question, it may order the Operator to take such steps as the court directs for securing that the requirement is satisfied or that the obligation is complied with.

(3) Before giving a direction under paragraph (1)(b) the Treasury shall—

   (a) if circumstances permit, consult the Operator and afford him an opportunity to make representations; and

   (b) so far as it is practicable to estimate it, have regard to the cost to the Operator of complying with any term of any direction and to the costs to other persons resulting from the Operator's compliance.

(4) The jurisdiction conferred by paragraph (2) shall be exercised by the High Court and the Court of Session.

9 Injunctions and restitution orders

(1) If on the application of the Treasury the court is satisfied that—

   (a) there is a reasonable likelihood that any person will contravene any provision of the rules of an Operator to which that person is subject and which regulate the carrying on by him of investment business within the meaning of the 1986 Act;

(b) any person has contravened any such rule, and that there is a reasonable likelihood that the contravention will continue or be repeated; or

(c) any person has contravened any such rule, and that there are steps that could be taken for remedying the contravention,

the court may grant an injunction restraining the contravention or, in Scotland, an interdict prohibiting the contravention or, as the case may be, make an order requiring that person and any other person who appears to the court to have been knowingly concerned in the contravention to take such steps as the court may direct to remedy it.

(2) Subsections (2) to (9) of section 61 of the 1986 Act shall apply in relation to the application of the Treasury for an injunction or, in Scotland, an interdict under paragraph (1) as they have effect in relation to the application of the Secretary of State for an injunction or, in Scotland, an interdict under subsection (1) of that section; and in those subsections as they so apply—

(a) the reference to a recognised clearing house shall be taken to be a reference to an Operator;

(b) the reference in subsection (2) to such rules as are mentioned in subsection (1)(a)(iv) shall be taken to be a reference to the rules mentioned in paragraph (1)(a);

(c) the reference to such steps as are mentioned in subsection (1) shall be taken to be a reference to such steps as are mentioned in paragraph (1);

(d) the reference in subsection (3)(a) to profits having accrued to any person as a result of his contravention of any provision or condition mentioned in subsection (1)(a) shall be taken to be a reference to profits having accrued to any person as a result of his contravention of any rule mentioned in paragraph (1)(a);

(e) the references to subsection (3) shall be taken to be references to that subsection as it so applies.

10 Provision of information by Operators

(1) The Treasury may, in writing, require an Operator to give them such information as they may specify.

(2) The Treasury may, in writing, require an Operator to furnish them at such times or in respect of such periods as they may specify with such information relating to that Operator as is so specified.

(3) Where an Operator amends, revokes or adds to his rules or guidance he shall within seven days give written notice to the Treasury of the amendment, revocation or addition.

(4) The notices and information required to be given or furnished under the foregoing provisions of this regulation shall be such as the Treasury reasonably require for the exercise of their functions under these Regulations.

(5) The Treasury may require information to be given by a specfied time, in a specified form and be verified in a specified manner.

Miscellaneous

11 Delegation of Treasury functions

(1) If it appears to the Treasury that there is a body corporate—

(a) to which functions have been transferred under section 114 of the 1986 Act; and

(b) which is able and willing to discharge all or any of the functions conferred by this Part of these Regulations,

they may, subject to paragraphs (2) and (3), by instrument in writing delegate all or any of those functions to that body; and a body to which functions are so delegated is referred to in these Regulations as a 'designated agency'.

(2) The functions conferred on the Treasury by regulation 12 may not be delegated.

(3) A designated agency shall send to the Treasury a copy of any guidance issued by virtue of these Regulations and any requirements imposed by it on the Operator by virtue of regulation 10, and give them written notice of any amendment or revocation of or addition to any such guidance or requirements.

(4) A designated agency shall—

(a) send to the Treasury a copy of any guidance issued by it which is intended to have continuing effect and is issued in writing or other legible form; and
(b) give them written notice of any amendment, revocation of or addition to guidance issued by it,

but notice need not be given of the revocation of guidance other than is mentioned in subparagraph (a) or of any amendment or addition which does not result in or consist of such guidance as is there mentioned.

(5) The Treasury shall not delegate any function to a designated agency unless they are satisfied that—

(a) any guidance issued by it in the exercise of its functions under these Regulations;
(b) requirements imposed by it on the Operator by virtue of regulation 10;
(c) any guidance proposed to be issued by it in the exercise of its functions under these Regulations; or
(d) any requirements it proposes to impose on the Operator by virtue of regulation 10,

do not have, and are not intended or likely to have, to any significant extent the effect of restricting, distorting or preventing competition, or if they have or are intended or likely to have that effect to any significant extent, that the effect is not greater than is necessary for the protection of investors.

(6) The powers conferred by paragraph (7) shall be exercisable by the Treasury if at any time it appears to them that—

(a) any guidance issued by the designated agency in the exercise of its functions under these Regulations;
(b) requirements imposed by the designated agency on the Operator by virtue of regulation 10; or
(c) any practices of a designated agency followed in the exercise of its functions under these Regulations,

have, or are intended or are likely to have, to any significant extent the effect of restricting, distorting or preventing competition and that the effect is greater than is necessary for the protection of investors.

(7) The powers exercisable under this paragraph are—

(a) to resume all or any of the functions delegated to the designated agency by the written instrument referred to in paragraph (1); or

   (b) to direct the designated agency to take specified steps for the purpose of securing that the guidance, requirements or practices in question do not have the effect mentioned in paragraph (6).

(8) The Treasury may by written instrument—

   (a) at the request or with the consent of a designated agency; or
   (b) if at any time it appears to them that a designated agency is unable or unwilling to discharge all or any of the functions delegated to it,

resume all or any of the functions delegated to the agency under paragraph (1).

(9) Section 187(3) of the 1986 Act shall apply in relation to anything done or omitted in the discharge or purported discharge of functions delegated under paragraph (1) as it applies in relation to anything done or omitted to be done in the discharge or purported discharge of functions exercisable by virtue of a delegation order made by virtue of section 114 of the 1986 Act.

(10) In this regulation—

   (a) any reference to guidance issued to an Operator by a designated agency is a reference to any guidance issued or any recommendation made by the designated agency in writing, or other legible form, which is intended to have continuing effect, and is issued or made to an Operator; and
   (b) references to the practices of the designated agency are references to the practices of the designated agency in its capacity as such.

12 International obligations

(1) If it appears to the Treasury—

   (a) that any action proposed to be taken by an Operator or designated agency would be incompatible with Community obligations or any other international obligations of the United Kingdom; or
   (b) that any action which an Operator or designated agency has power to take is required for the purpose of implementing any such obligation,

they may direct the Operator or designated agency not to take or, as the case may be, to take the action in question.

(2) A direction under this regulation may include such supplementary or incidental requirements as the Treasury think necessary or expedient.

(3) Where the function of granting under regulation 5, or withdrawing under regulation 7, an Operator's approval is exercisable by a designated agency, any direction under paragraph (1) in respect of that Operator shall be a direction requiring the agency to give the Operator such a direction as is specified in the direction by the Treasury.

(4) Any direction under this regulation is enforceable on application of the person who gave it, by injunction or, in Scotland, by an order under section 45 of the Court of Session Act 1988.

13 Prevention of restrictive practices

Schedule 2 (which reproduces, with necessary modifications, the provisions of sections 119, 120 and 122 to 126 and 128 of the 1986 Act) shall have effect.

Appendix 1

STATUTORY MATERIALS

PART III

PARTICIPATING ISSUERS

Participation by issuers

14 Participation in respect of shares

(1) Where an Operator permits a class of shares in relation to which regulation 15 applies, or in relation to which a directors' resolution passed in accordance with regulation 16 is effective, to be a participating security, title to shares of that class which are recorded on a register of members as being held in uncertificated form may be transferred by means of the relevant system to which the permission relates.

(2) In paragraph (1) the reference to a register of members shall not include an overseas branch register.

15 (1) This regulation applies to a class of shares if a company's articles of association in all respects are consistent with—

    (a) the holding of shares in that class in uncertificated form;

    (b) the transfer of title to shares in that class by means of a relevant system; and

    (c) these Regulations.

(2) A company may permit the holding of shares in a class to which this regulation applies in uncertificated form, and the transfer of title to any such shares by means of a relevant system.

16 (1) This regulation applies to a class of shares if a company's articles of association in any respect are inconsistent with—

    (a) the holding of shares in that class in uncertificated form;

    (b) the transfer of title to shares in that class by means of a relevant system; or

    (c) any provision of these Regulations.

(2) A company may resolve, subject to paragraph (6)(a), by resolution of its directors (in this Part referred to as a 'directors' resolution') that title to shares of a class issued or to be issued by it may be transferred by means of a relevant system.

(3) Upon a directors' resolution becoming effective in accordance with its terms, and for as long as it is in force, the articles of association in relation to the class of shares which were the subject of the directors' resolution shall not apply to any uncertificated shares of that class to the extent that they are inconsistent with—

    (a) the holding of shares of that class in uncertificated form;

    (b) the transfer of title to shares of that class by means of a relevant system; and

    (c) any provision of these Regulations.

(4) Unless a company has given notice to every member of the company in accordance with its articles of association of its intention to pass a directors' resolution before the passing of such a resolution, it shall give such notice within 60 days of the passing of the resolution.

(5) Notice given by the company before the coming into force of these Regulations of its intention to pass a directors' resolution which, if it had been given after the coming into force of these Regulations would have satisfied the requirements of paragraph (4), shall be taken to satisfy the requirements of that paragraph.

(6) In respect of a class of shares, the members of a company may by ordinary resolution—

(a) if a directors' resolution has not been passed, resolve that the directors of the company shall not pass a directors' resolution; or

(b) if a directors' resolution has been passed but not yet come into effect in accordance with its terms, resolve that it shall not come into effect; or

(c) if a directors' resolution has been passed and is effective in accordance with its terms but the class of shares has not yet been permitted by the Operator to be a participating security, resolve that the directors' resolution shall cease to have effect; or

(d) if a directors' resolution has been passed and is effective in accordance with its terms and the class of shares has been permitted by the Operator to be a participating security, resolve that the directors shall take the necessary steps to ensure that title to shares of the class that was the subject of the directors' resolution shall cease to be transferable by means of a relevant system and that the directors' resolution shall cease to have effect;

and the directors shall be bound by the terms of any such ordinary resolution.

(7) Such sanctions as apply to a company and its officers in the event of a default in complying with section 376 of the 1985 Act shall apply to a participating issuer and his officers in the event of a default in complying with paragraph (4).

(8) A company shall not permit the holding of shares in such a class as is referred to in paragraph (1) in uncertificated form, or the transfer of title to shares in such a class by means of a relevant system, unless in relation to that class of shares a directors' resolution is effective.

(9) This regulation shall not be taken to exclude the right of the members of a company to amend the articles of association of the company, in accordance with the articles, to allow the holding of any class of its shares in uncertificated form and the transfer of title to shares in such a class by means of a relevant system.

17 Interpretation of regulations 15 and 16

For the purposes of regulations 15 and 16 any shares with respect to which share warrants to bearer are issued under section 188 of the 1985 Act shall be regarded as forming a separate class of shares.

18 Participation in respect of securities other than shares

(1) Subject to paragraph (2), where an Operator permits a security other than a share to be a participating security, title to units of that security which are recorded in a register of securities as being held in uncertificated form may be transferred by means of a relevant system.

(2) In relation to any security (other than a share), if the law under which it is constituted is not a law of England and Wales, Northern Ireland or Scotland, or if a current term of its issue is in any respect inconsistent with—

(a) the holding of title to units of that security in uncertificated form;

(b) the transfer of title to units of that security by means of a relevant system; or

(c) these Regulations,

the issuer shall not permit the holding of units of that security in uncertificated form, or the transfer of title to units of that security by means of a relevant system.

(3) In this regulation the terms of issue of a security shall be taken to include the terms prescribed by the issuer on which units of the security are held and title to them is transferred.

Keeping of registers

19 Entries on registers

(1) A participating issuer which is a company shall enter on its register of members, in respect of any class of shares which is a participating security, how many shares each member holds in uncertificated form and certificated form respectively.

(2) Without prejudice to sections 190 and 191 of the 1985 Act, a participating issuer who, apart from this regulation, is required by or under an enactment or instrument to maintain in the United Kingdom a register of persons holding securities (other than shares) issued by him, shall enter on that register in respect of any class of security which is a participating security—

    (a) the names and addresses of the persons holding units of that security; and

    (b) how many units of that security each person holds in uncertificated form and certificated form respectively.

(3) A participating issuer who, apart from this regulation, is not required by or under an enactment or instrument to maintain in the United Kingdom in respect of a participating security issued by him a register of persons holding units of that participating security, shall maintain in the United Kingdom a register recording—

    (a) the names and addresses of the persons holding units of that security in uncertificated form; and

    (b) how many units of that security each person holds in that form.

(4) Such sanctions as apply to a company and its officers in the event of a default in complying with section 352 of the 1985 Act shall apply to a participating issuer and his officers in the event of a default in complying with paragraph (1), (2) or (3).

(5) Without prejudice to any lesser period of limitation and to any rule as to the prescription of rights, liability incurred by a participating issuer arising—

    (a) from the making or deletion of an entry in a register of securities pursuant to paragraph (1), (2) or (3); or

    (b) from a failure to make or delete any such entry,

shall not be enforceable more than 20 years after the date on which the entry was made or deleted or, in the case of a failure, the failure first occurred.

(6) For the purposes of paragraph (1)—

    (a) notwithstanding section 362 of, or paragraph 2(1) of Schedule 14 to, the 1985 Act, the reference to a company's register of members shall not be taken to include an overseas branch register;

    (b) those members who hold shares in uncertificated form may not be entered as holders of those shares on an overseas branch register; and

    (c) any shares with respect to which share warrants to bearer are issued under section 188 of the 1985 Act shall be regarded as forming a separate class of shares.

(7) No notice of any trust, expressed, implied or constructive, shall be entered on a register of securities which is maintained by virtue of paragraph (3) in relation to uncertificated units of a security, or be receivable by the registrar of such a register.

(8) Paragraph (7) shall not apply to a participating issuer constituted under the law of Scotland.

20 Effect of entries on registers

(1) Subject to regulation 23(7), an entry on such a register as is mentioned in regulation 19(1) or (2) which records a person as holding units of a security in uncertificated form shall be evidence of such title to the units as would be evidenced if the entry on the register related to units of that security held in certificated form.

(2) Subject to regulation 23(7), an entry on a register maintained by virtue of regulation 19(3) shall be prima facie evidence, and in Scotland sufficient evidence unless the contrary is shown, that the person to whom the entry relates has such title to the units of the security which he is recorded as holding in uncertificated form as he would have if he held the units in certificated form.

21 Rectification of and changes to registers of securities

(1) A participating issuer shall not rectify a register of securities in relation to uncertificated units of a security held by a system-member except—

    (a) with the consent of the Operator; or
    (b) by order of a court in the United Kingdom.

(2) A participating issuer who rectifies or otherwise changes an entry on a register of securities in relation to uncertificated units of a security (except in response to an Operator-instruction) shall immediately—

    (a) notify the Operator; and
    (b) inform the system-members concerned,

of the change to the entry.

22 Closing registers

Notwithstanding section 358 of the 1985 Act or any other enactment, a participating issuer shall not close a register of securities relating to a participating security without the consent of the Operator.

23 Registration of transfers of securities

(1) A participating issuer shall register a transfer of title to uncertificated units of a security on a register of securities in accordance with an Operator-instruction unless—

    (a) the transfer is prohibited—
        (i) by order of a court in the United Kingdom; or
        (ii) by or under an enactment; or
    (b) he has actual notice that the transfer is—
        (i) avoided by or under an enactment; or
        (ii) a transfer to a deceased person; or
        (iii) where the participating issuer is constituted under the law of Scotland, prohibited by or under an arrestment; or
    (c) the circumstances described in paragraph (2) apply; or
    (d) he is entitled by virtue of paragraph (3) to refuse to register the transfer.

(2) The circumstances referred to in paragraph (1)(c) are that the transfer is one of two or more transfers in respect of which the Operator has notified the participating issuer

in accordance with regulation 24(1), and that to those transfers regulation 24(2) does not apply by virtue of regulation 24(3).

(3) A participating issuer may refuse to register a transfer of title to uncertificated units of a security in accordance with an Operator-instruction if the instruction requires a transfer of units—

(a) to an entity which is not a natural or legal person;
(b) to a minor (which in relation to a participating issuer constituted under the law of Scotland, shall mean a person under 16 years of age);
(c) to be held jointly in the names of more persons than is permitted under the terms of the issue of the security; or
(d) where, in relation to the Operator-instruction, the participating issuer has actual notice from the Operator of any of the matters specified in regulation 29(5)(a)(i) to (iii).

(4) A participating issuer shall notify the Operator by issuer-instruction whether he has registered a transfer in response to an Operator-instruction to do so.

(5) A participating issuer shall not register a transfer of title to uncertificated units of a security on a register of securities unless he is required to do so by an Operator-instruction, an order of a court in the United Kingdom, by regulation 35(2), or by or under an enactment.

(6) Paragraph (5) shall not be taken to prevent a participating issuer from entering a person on a register of securities to whom title to uncertificated units of a security has been transmitted by operation of law.

(7) Any purported registration of a transfer of title to an uncertificated unit of a security other than in accordance with this regulation shall be of no effect.

(8) Subsection (5) of section 183 of the 1985 Act shall apply in relation to a refusal by a participating issuer to register a transfer of securities in any of the circumstances specified in paragraph (1), as it applies in relation to a refusal by a company to register a transfer of shares or debentures; and in that subsection as it so applies the reference to the date on which the transfer was lodged with the company shall be taken to be a reference to the date on which the Operator-instruction was received by the participating issuer.

(9) Such sanctions as apply to a company and its officers in the event of a default in complying with subsection (5) of that section shall apply to a participating issuer and his officers in the event of a default in complying with subsection (5) of that section as applied by paragraph (8).

24 Registration of linked transfers

(1) Where an Operator sends two or more Operator-instructions requiring a participating issuer to register two or more transfers of title to uncertificated units of a security, and it appears to the Operator—

(a) either—
(i) that there are fewer units of the security registered in the name of a person identified in any one of the Operator-instructions as a transferor than the number of units to be transferred from him; or
(ii) that any one of the transfers taken alone is one in relation to which it has not been established in accordance with paragraph 15(1)(c) of Schedule 1 that a settlement bank has agreed to make a payment; and

(b) that registration of all of the transfers would result in each of the persons identified in the Operator-instructions as a transferor having title to a number of units of a security equal to or greater than nil; and

(c) that the combined effect of all the transfers taken together would result in paragraph 15(1)(c) of Schedule I being satisfied,

the Operator may notify the participating issuer that the transfers are linked transfers.

(2) Except in the circumstances described in paragraph (3), notwithstanding that there may be fewer uncertificated units of the security registered in the name of a person identified in any one of the Operator-instructions as a transferor than the number of uncertificated units to be transferred from him, where an Operator notifies a participating issuer that transfers are linked transfers, the participating issuer may either—

(a) register the combined effect of all the transfers taken together; or

(b) register all the transfers simultaneously.

(3) Paragraph (2) does not apply in a case in which—

(a) registration of the combined effect of the linked transfers, or simultaneous registration of all the transfers (as the case may be), would not result in each of the persons identified in the Operator-instructions as a transferor having title to a number of uncertificated units of the security equal to or greater than nil; or

(b) one or more of the transfers constituting the linked transfers may not be registered by virtue of the circumstances specified in regulation 23(1)(a) or (b), or is to be refused registration by virtue of regulation 23(3).

25 Position of a transferee prior to entry on a register

(1) At the time an Operator-instruction is generated which will require a participating issuer to register on a register of securities a transfer of title to any uncertificated units of a security constituted under the law of England and Wales or Northern Ireland—

(a) the transferee shall acquire an equitable interest in the requisite number of uncertificated units of the security of the kind specified in the Operator-instruction in which the transferor has an equitable interest by virtue of this regulation, or in relation to which the transferor is recorded on the relevant register of securities as having title; and

(b) the equitable interest shall subsist until the time specified in paragraph (4).

(2) At the time an Operator-instruction is generated which will require a participating issuer to register on a register of securities a transfer of title to any uncertificated units of a security constituted under the law of Scotland—

(a) the transferor shall as from that time be deemed to hold the requisite number of uncertificated units of the security in which he has an interest by virtue of this regulation, or in relation to which he is recorded on the relevant register of securities as having title, on trust for the benefit of the transferee; and

(b) the trust shall subsist until the time specified in paragraph (4).

(3) For the purposes of paragraphs (1)(a) and (2)(a), it shall not be denied that the transferee has obtained the equitable interest referred to in paragraph (1)(a), or that the transferor holds the interest referred to in paragraph (2)(a) on trust for the benefit of the transferee, solely by reason of the fact that the transferor acquired his equitable interest by virtue of paragraph (1)(a) at the same time as the transferee's equitable interest arises in that interest, or that the transferor acquired his interest by virtue of

paragraph (2) (a) at the same time that he is deemed to hold that interest on trust for the transferee.

(4) Subject to any enactment or rule of law, an interest acquired under paragraph (1) or (2)—

(a) in a case other than one in which under regulation 24(2) (a) a participating issuer registers the combined effect of linked transfers, shall subsist until the time that the transferee is entered on the register of securities in respect of the transfer of units to him; and

(b) in a case in which under regulation 24(2) (a) a participating issuer registers the combined effect of linked transfers, shall subsist until the time that the combined effect of all the linked transfers is registered.

(5) The requisite number for the purposes of this regulation is whichever of the following is the lower at the time that the Operator-instruction is sent, namely—

(a) the number of units which are specified in the Operator-instruction; and

(b) the total of the number of uncertificated units in relation to which the transferor is recorded on the register of securities as having title and the number in which he has an interest by virtue of paragraph (1) or (2), less that number of units in which such interests subsist in favour of a third party by virtue of an earlier Operator-instruction requiring a participating issuer to register on a register of securities a transfer of title to those units.

(6) This regulation has effect notwithstanding that the units to which the Operator-instruction relates, or in which an interest arises by virtue of paragraph (1) or (2), or any of them, may be unascertained.

(7) In Scotland—

(a) this regulation has effect notwithstanding that the requirements relating to the creation of a trust under any enactment or rule of law have not been complied with; and

(b) as from the time the trust referred to in paragraph (2) arises, any holder, or any holder thereafter, of a floating charge over any part of the property of the transferor shall be deemed to have received notice of the trust's existence and of the property to which it relates.

(8) Subject to paragraphs (6) and (7), this regulation shall not be construed as conferring a proprietary interest (whether of the kind referred to in paragraphs (1) or (2), or any other kind) in units of a security if the conferring of such an interest at the time specified in these Regulations would otherwise be void by or under an enactment or rule of law.

(9) In this regulation—

(a) 'the transferee' means the person identified in the Operator-instruction as the transferee; and

(b) 'the transferor' means the person identified in the Operator-instruction as the transferor.

Conversions and new issues

26 Conversion of securities into certificated form

(1) A participating issuer shall not change a unit of a participating security from uncertificated to certificated form except—

(a) where permitted by the rules made and practices instituted by an Operator in order to comply with paragraphs 13, 19(b) or (c) of Schedule 1; or

(b) following receipt of an Operator-instruction requiring the conversion into certificated form of uncertificated units of a participating security registered in the name of a system-member; or

(c) subject to regulation 23, following receipt of an Operator-instruction requiring the registration of a transfer of title to uncertificated units of a security to a person who is not a system-member; or

(d) on the registration, in accordance with regulation 35(2), of an offeror who is not a system-member as holder of the units of the security referred to in that regulation.

(2) In the circumstances specified in paragraph (1)(b) to (d) a participating issuer shall—

(a) record on the register of securities that the units of the security are held in certificated form;

(b) where a certificate can be issued for the security, issue a certificate in respect of the units of the security to the relevant person; and

(c) notify the Operator that the units are no longer held in uncertificated form.

(3) Subsection (1)(b) of section 185 of the 1985 Act shall apply in the circumstances specified in paragraph (1)(b) to (d) in relation to the issue of a certificate by a participating issuer pursuant to paragraph (2)(b) as it applies in relation to the completion and having ready for delivery by a company of share certificates, debentures or certificates of debenture stock; and in that subsection as it so applies the reference to the date on which a transfer was lodged with the company shall be a reference to the date on which the participating issuer received the relevant Operator-instruction or, where relevant, the date on which the participating issuer registered the offeror as holding the units of the security referred to in regulation 35(2).

(4) Such sanctions as apply to a company and its officers in the event of a default in complying with that section shall apply to a participating issuer and his officers in the event of a default in complying with paragraph (2) in accordance with the requirements laid down in paragraph (3).

27 Conversion of securities into uncertificated form

(1) A participating issuer shall not change a unit of a participating security from certificated form to uncertificated form except in the circumstances specified in paragraph (2).

(2) The circumstances referred to in paragraph (1) are—

(a) where the unit of the participating security is held by a system-member, that the participating issuer has received—

(i) a request in writing in the form required by the rules made and practices instituted by an Operator in order to comply with paragraph 13 of Schedule 1 to register the system-member as holding the unit in uncertificated form; and

(ii) subject to paragraph (4), the certificate relating to the certificated unit which is to be converted into uncertificated form;

(b) where the unit of the participating security is to be registered on a register of securities in the name of a system-member following a transfer of the unit to him from a person other than the nominee of a recognised investment exchange, that the participating issuer—

(i) subject to paragraph (3), has received by means of the Operator-system a proper instrument of transfer in favour of the system-member relating to the unit to be transferred;

(ii) subject to paragraph (4), has received by means of the Operator-system the certificate relating to the certificated unit which is to be transferred and converted into uncertificated form; and

(iii) may accept by virtue of the rules made and practices instituted by an Operator in order to comply with paragraph 13 of Schedule 1 that the system-member to whom the unit is to be transferred wishes to hold it in uncertificated form; and

(c) where the unit of the participating security is to be registered on a register of securities in the name of a system-member following a transfer of the unit to him from a nominee of a recognised investment exchange, that the participating issuer—

(i) has received a proper instrument of transfer in favour of the system-member from the nominee relating to the unit to be transferred; and

(ii) may accept by virtue of the rules made and practices instituted by an Operator in order to comply with paragraph 13 of Schedule 1 that the system-member to whom the unit is to be transferred wishes to hold it in uncertificated form.

(3) The requirement in paragraph (2)(b)(i) that the participating issuer shall have received an instrument of transfer relating to the unit of the participating security shall not apply in a case where for a transfer of a unit of that security no instrument of transfer is required.

(4) The requirements in paragraphs (2)(a)(ii) and (2)(b)(ii) that the participating issuer shall have received a certificate relating to the unit of the participating security shall not apply in a case where the system-member or transferor (as the case may be) does not have a certificate in respect of the unit to be converted into uncertificated form because no certificate has yet been issued to him.

(5) In the circumstances specified in paragraph (2)(a), on receipt of the request referred to in paragraph (2)(a)(i) and (except where paragraph (4) applies) the certificate referred to in paragraph (2)(a)(ii), the participating issuer shall, within two months—

(a) enter on the register of securities that the system-member holds the unit in uncertificated form; and

(b) send the Operator an issuer-instruction informing him of the entry on the relevant register of securities.

(6) In the circumstances specified in paragraph (2)(b), on receipt of the instrument of transfer referred to in paragraph (2)(b)(i) (except where paragraph (3) applies) and the certificate referred to in paragraph (2)(b)(ii) (except where paragraph (4) applies), the participating issuer shall—

(a) upon recording that the system-member holds the unit, enter on the register of securities that he holds the unit in uncertificated form; and

(b) within 2 months thereafter, send the Operator an issuer-instruction informing him of the entry on the register of securities.

(7) In the circumstances specified in paragraph (2)(c), on receipt of the instrument of transfer referred to in paragraph (2)(c)(i), the participating issuer shall—

(a) upon recording that the system-member holds the unit, enter on the register of securities that he holds the unit in uncertificated form; and

(b) within 2 months thereafter, send the Operator an issuer-instruction informing him of the entry on the register of securities.

(8) Such sanctions as apply to a company in the event of a default by it in complying with subsection (5) of section 183 of the 1985 Act shall apply to a participating issuer in the event of a default by him in complying with paragraph (5), (6) or (7).

(9) In this regulation 'recognised investment exchange' has the same meaning as in the 1986 Act.

28 New issues in uncertificated form

(1) A participating issuer may issue units of a participating security in uncertificated form to a person if, and only if, that person is a system-member.

(2) For the purposes of calculating the number of new units to which a system-member is entitled a participating issuer may treat a system-member's holdings of certificated and uncertificated units of a security as if they were separate holdings.

(3) On the issue in uncertificated form of new units of a participating security, the participating issuer shall by issuer-instruction notify the Operator of the persons to whom the uncertificated units of a security have been issued and of the number of such units issued to each of those persons.

PART IV

DEMATERIALISED INSTRUCTIONS ETC.

29 Properly authenticated dematerialised instructions

(1) This regulation has effect for the purpose of determining the rights and obligations of persons to whom properly authenticated dematerialised instructions are attributable and of persons to whom properly authenticated dematerialised instructions are addressed, when such instructions relate to an uncertificated unit of a security, or relate to a right, benefit or privilege attaching to or arising from such a unit, or relate to the details of a holder of such a unit.

(2) Where a properly authenticated dematerialised instruction is expressed to have been sent on behalf of a person by a sponsoring system-participant or the Operator—
   (a) the person on whose behalf the instruction is expressed to have been sent shall not be able to deny to the addressee—
      (i) that the properly authenticated dematerialised instruction was sent with his authority; or
      (ii) that the information contained in the properly authenticated dematerialised instruction is correct; and
   (b) the sponsoring system-participant or the Operator (as the case may be) shall not be able to deny to the addressee—
      (i) that he has authority to send the properly authenticated dematerialised instruction; or
      (ii) that he has sent the properly authenticated dematerialised instruction.

(3) Where a properly authenticated dematerialised instruction is expressed to have been sent by a person, and the properly authenticated dematerialised instruction is not expressed to have been sent on behalf of another person, the person shall not be able to deny to the addressee—

(a) that the information contained in the properly authenticated dematerialised instruction is correct; or

(b) that he has sent the properly authenticated dematerialised instruction.

(4) An addressee who receives (whether directly, or by means of the facilities of a sponsoring system-participant acting on his behalf) a properly authenticated dematerialised instruction may, subject to paragraph (5), accept that at the time at which the properly authenticated dematerialised instruction was sent—

(a) the information contained in the instruction was correct;

(b) the system-participant or the Operator (as the case may be) identified in the instruction as having sent the instruction sent the instruction; and

(c) the instruction, where relevant, was sent with the authority of the person on whose behalf it is expressed to have been sent.

(5) Subject to paragraph (6), an addressee may not accept any of the matters specified in paragraph (4) if at the time he received the properly authenticated dematerialised instruction—

(a) he was a person other than a participating issuer or a sponsoring system-participant receiving properly authenticated dematerialised instructions on behalf of a participating issuer, and he had actual notice—

   (i) that any information contained in it was incorrect;

   (ii) that the system-participant or the Operator (as the case may be) expressed to have sent the instruction did not send the instruction; or

   (iii) where relevant, that the person on whose behalf it was expressed to have been sent had not given to the Operator or the sponsoring system-participant (as the case may be), identified in the properly authenticated dematerialised instruction as having sent it, his authority to send the properly authenticated dematerialised instruction on his behalf; or

(b) he was a participating issuer, or a sponsoring system-participant receiving properly authenticated dematerialised instructions on behalf of a participating issuer, and

   (i) he had actual notice from the Operator of any of the matters specified in subparagraph (a); or

   (ii) the instruction was an Operator-instruction requiring the registration of title in the circumstances specified in regulation 23(1)(a), (b) or (c); or

(c) he was an Operator and the instruction related to a transfer of units of a security which was in excess of any limit imposed by virtue of paragraph 12 of Schedule 1.

(6) Notwithstanding that an addressee has received in respect of a properly authenticated dematerialised instruction actual notice of the kind referred to in paragraph (5), the addressee may accept the matters specified in paragraph (4) if at the time that he received the actual notice it was not practicable for him to halt his processing of the instruction.

(7) Subject to paragraph (8), a person who is permitted by this regulation to accept any matter shall not be liable in damages or otherwise to any person by reason of his having relied on the matter that he was permitted to accept.

(8) The provisions of paragraph (7) do not affect—

(a) any liability of the Operator to pay compensation under regulation 30; or

(b) any liability of a participating issuer under regulation 37 arising by reason of a default in complying with, or contravention of, regulation 23(5).

(9) Subject to paragraph (7), this regulation has effect without prejudice to the liability of any person for causing or permitting a dematerialised instruction—

  (a) to be sent without authority; or
  (b) to contain information which is incorrect; or
  (c) to be expressed to have been sent by a person who did not send it.

(10) For the purposes of this regulation—

  (a) a properly authenticated dematerialised instruction is expressed to have been sent by a person or on behalf of a person if it is attributable to that person; and
  (b) an addressee is the person to whom a properly authenticated dematerialised instruction indicates it is addressed in accordance with the specifications of the Operator drawn up in order to satisfy paragraph 5(d) of Schedule 1.

30 Liability for forged dematerialised instructions and induced Operator-instructions

(1) For the purpose of this regulation—

  (a) a dematerialised instruction is a forged dematerialised instruction if—
    (i) it was not sent from the computers of a system-participant or the computers comprising an Operator-system; or
    (ii) it was not sent from the computers of the system-participant or the computers comprising an Operator-system (as the case may be) from which it is expressed to have been sent;
  (b) an act is a causative act if, not being a dematerialised instruction and not being an act which causes a dematerialised instruction to be sent from the computer of a system-participant, it unlawfully causes the Operator to send an Operator-instruction to a participating issuer; and
  (c) an Operator-instruction is an induced Operator-instruction if it is an Operator-instruction to a participating issuer which results from a causative act or a forged dematerialised instruction.

(2) If, as a result of either a forged dematerialised instruction (not being one which results in an induced Operator-instruction) or an induced Operator-instruction any one of the following events occurs—

  (a) the name of any person remains on, is entered on, or is removed or omitted from, a register of securities;
  (b) the number of units of a security in relation to which the name of any person is entered on a register of securities is increased, reduced, or remains unaltered;
  (c) the description of any units of a security in relation to which the name of any person is entered on a register of securities is changed or remains unaltered;

and that person suffers loss as a result, he may apply to the court for an order that the Operator compensate him for his loss.

(3) It is immaterial for the purposes of paragraph (2)(a) to (c) whether the event is permanent or temporary.

(4) The court shall not make an order under paragraph (2)—

  (a) if the Operator identifies a person as being responsible (whether alone or with others) for the forged dematerialised instruction (not being one which results in an induced Operator-instruction) or the causative act or forged dematerialised instruction resulting in the induced Operator-instruction (as the case may be) notwithstanding that it is impossible (for whatever reason) for the applicant to obtain satisfactory compensation from that person; or

(b) if the Operator shows that a participating issuer would be liable under regulation 37 to compensate the applicant for the loss in respect of which the application is made, by reason of the participating issuer's default in complying with, or contravention of, regulation 23(5).

(5) Subject to paragraph (6), the court may award to an applicant compensation for—

(a) each forged dematerialised instruction (not being one which results in an induced Operator-instruction); and

(b) each induced Operator-instruction,

resulting in an event mentioned in paragraph (2)(a) to (c); provided that the court shall not award to an applicant more than £50000 for each such forged dematerialised instruction or induced Operator-instruction.

(6) In respect of liability arising under this regulation the court shall—

(a) in awarding compensation only order the Operator to pay such amount of compensation as it appears to it to be just and equitable in all the circumstances having regard to the loss sustained by the applicant as a result of the forged dematerialised instruction or induced Operator-instruction;

(b) in ascertaining the loss, apply the same rules concerning the duty of a person to mitigate his loss as apply to damages recoverable under the common law of England and Wales, Northern Ireland, or Scotland, (as the case may be); and

(c) where it finds that the loss was to any extent caused or contributed to by any act or omission of the applicant, reduce the amount of the award by such proportion as it thinks just and equitable having regard to that finding.

(7) An application to a court for an order under paragraph (2) shall not prejudice any right of the Operator to recover from a third party any sum that he may be ordered to pay.

(8) This regulation does not affect any liability or right which any person may incur or have apart from this regulation.

(9) Where an application is made under paragraph (2), and the Operator receives from the applicant a request for information or documents relating to—

(a) a forged dematerialised instruction; or

(b) an induced Operator-instruction,

in respect of which the application is made, the Operator shall, in so far as he is able, and in so far as the request is reasonable, within one month furnish the applicant with the information and documents.

(10) The applicant shall, in so far as he is able, within one month furnish the Operator with such information or documents as the Operator reasonably requests in connection with an application under paragraph (2) with respect to—

(a) steps taken by the applicant to prevent the giving of any forged dematerialised instruction (whether of the kind referred to in paragraph (2) or any other kind); and

(b) steps taken by the applicant to mitigate loss suffered by him;

provided that the applicant need not furnish information or documents pursuant to this paragraph until the Operator has complied with any request made by virtue of paragraph (9).

(11) Neither the Operator nor the applicant shall be required to disclose any information by virtue of, respectively, paragraph (9) or (10) which would be privileged in the course of civil proceedings; and which in Scotland they would be entitled to refuse to disclose on grounds of confidentiality as between client and professional legal adviser in proceedings in the Court of Session.

(12) The jurisdiction conferred by this regulation shall be exercisable, in the case of a participating security constituted under the law of England and Wales, or Northern Ireland, by the High Court; and in the case of a participating security constituted under the law of Scotland by the Court of Session.

PART V

MISCELLANEOUS AND SUPPLEMENTAL

Miscellaneous

31 Construction of references to transfers etc.

References in any enactment or rule of law to a proper instrument of transfer or to a transfer with respect to securities, or any expression having like meaning, shall be taken to include a reference to an Operator-instruction to a participating issuer to register a transfer of title on the relevant register of securities in accordance with the Operator-instruction.

32 Certain formalities and requirements not to apply

(1) Any requirements in an enactment or rule of law which apply in respect of the transfer of securities otherwise than by means of a relevant system shall not prevent an Operator-instruction from requiring a participating issuer to register a transfer of title to uncertificated units of a security.

(2) Subject to regulation 26(2), notwithstanding any enactment, instrument or rule of law, a participating issuer shall not issue a certificate in relation to any uncertificated units of a participating security.

(3) A document issued by or on behalf of a participating issuer purportedly evidencing title to an uncertificated unit of a participating security shall not be evidence of title to the unit of the security; and in particular section 186 of the 1985 Act shall not apply to any document issued with respect to uncertificated shares.

(4) Any requirement in or under any enactment to endorse any statement or information on a certificate evidencing title to a unit of a security—

  (a) shall not prohibit the conversion into, or issue of, units of the security in uncertificated form; and

  (b) in relation to uncertificated units of the security, shall be taken to be a requirement to provide the holder of the units with the statement or information on request by him.

(5) Sections 53(1)(c) and 136 of the Law of Property Act 1925 (which impose requirements for certain dispositions and assignments to be in writing) shall not apply (if they would otherwise do so) to—

  (a) any transfer of title to uncertificated units of a security by means of a relevant system; and

    (b) any disposition or assignment of an interest in uncertificated units of a security title to which is held by a relevant nominee, or in which the relevant nominee has an interest by virtue of regulation 25(1) or (2).

(6) In paragraph (5) 'relevant nominee' means a subsidiary undertaking of an Operator designated by him as a relevant nominee in accordance with such rules and practices as are mentioned in paragraph 19(d) of Schedule 1 to these Regulations.

33 Trusts, trustees and personal representatives etc.

(1) Unless expressly prohibited from transferring units of a security by means of any computer-based system, a trustee or personal representative shall not be chargeable with a breach of trust or, as the case may be, with default in administering the estate by reason only of the fact that—

    (a) for the purpose of acquiring units of a security which he has the power to acquire in connection with the trust or estate, he has paid for the units under arrangements which provide for them to be transferred to him from a system-member but not to be so transferred until after the payment of the price;

    (b) for the purpose of disposing of units of a security which he has power to dispose of in connection with the trust or estate, he has transferred the units to a system-member under arrangements which provide that the price is not to be paid to him until after the transfer is made; or

    (c) for the purpose of holding units of a security belonging to the trust or estate in uncertificated form and for transferring title to them by means of a relevant system, he has become a system-member.

(2) Notwithstanding section 192 of the 1985 Act, a trustee of a trust deed for securing an issue of debentures shall not be chargeable with a breach of trust by reason only of the fact that he has assented to an amendment of the trust deed only for the purposes of—

    (a) allowing the holding of the debentures in uncertificated form;

    (b) allowing the exercise of rights attaching to the debentures by means of a relevant system; or

    (c) allowing the transfer of title to the debentures by means of a relevant system;

provided that he has given or caused to be given notice of the amendment in accordance with the trust deed not less than 30 days prior to its becoming effective to all persons registered as holding the debentures on a date not more than 21 days before the dispatch of the notice.

(3) The Operator shall not be bound by or compelled to recognise any express, implied or constructive trust or other interest in respect of uncertificated units of a security, even if he has actual or constructive notice of the said trust or interest.

(4) Paragraph (3) shall not prevent, in the case of a participating issuer constituted under the law of Scotland, the Operator giving notice of a trust to the participating issuer on behalf of the system-member.

34 Notices of meetings

(1) For the purposes of determining which persons are entitled to attend or vote at a meeting, and how many votes such persons may cast, the participating issuer may specify in the notice of the meeting a time, not more than 48 hours before the time fixed for the meeting, by which a person must be entered on the relevant register of securities in order to have the right to attend or vote at the meeting.

(2) Changes to entries on the relevant register of securities after the time specified by virtue of paragraph (1) shall be disregarded in determining the rights of any person to attend or vote at the meeting, notwithstanding any provisions in any enactment, articles of association or other instrument to the contrary.

(3) For the purposes of serving notices of meetings, whether under section 370(2) of the 1985 Act, any other enactment, a provision in the articles of association or any other instrument, a participating issuer may determine that persons entitled to receive such notices are those persons entered on the relevant register of securities at the close of business on a day determined by him.

(4) The day determined by a participating issuer under paragraph (3) may not be more than 21 days before the day that the notices of the meeting are sent.

35 Notices to minority shareholders

(1) This regulation shall apply in relation to any uncertificated units of a security to which a notice given pursuant to section 429 of the 1985 Act relates, in place of the provisions of section 430(6) of that Act.

(2) On receipt of a notice sent pursuant to section 430(5)(a) of the 1985 Act, a company which is a participating issuer shall be under the same obligation to enter the offeror on its register of securities as the holder of the uncertificated units of the security to which the notice relates, in place of the system-member who was immediately prior to such entry registered as the holder of such units, as it would be if it had received an Operator-instruction requiring it to amend its register of securities in such manner; and regulation 23(9) shall have effect accordingly.

(3) A company which amends its register of securities in accordance with paragraph (2) shall forthwith notify the Operator by issuer-instruction of the amendment.

(4) The reference in section 430D(5) of the 1985 Act to section 430(6) shall be taken to include a reference to the provisions of paragraph (2).

(5) In this regulation, 'offeror' has the meaning given by section 428(8) of the 1985 Act as construed in accordance with section 430D(5) of that Act.

36 Irrevocable powers of attorney

(1) This regulation applies where the terms of an offer for all or any uncertificated units of a participating security provide that a person accepting the offer creates an irrevocable power of attorney in favour of the offeror, or a person nominated by the offeror, in the terms set out in the offer.

(2) An acceptance communicated by properly authenticated dematerialised instruction in respect of uncertificated units of a security shall constitute a grant of an irrevocable power of attorney by the system-member accepting the offer in favour of the offeror, or person nominated by the offeror, in the terms set out in the offer.

(3) Where the contract constituted by such offer and acceptance referred to in paragraphs (1) and (2) respectively is governed by the law of England and Wales, section 4 of the Powers of Attorney Act 1971 shall apply to a power of attorney constituted in accordance with this regulation.

(4) A declaration in writing by the offeror stating the terms of a power of attorney and that it has been granted by virtue of this regulation and stating the name and address of

the grantor shall be prima facie evidence, and in Scotland sufficient evidence unless the contrary is shown, of the grant; and any requirement in any enactment, rule of law, or instrument to produce a copy of the power of attorney, or such a copy certified in a particular manner, shall be satisfied by the production of the declaration or a copy of the declaration certified in that manner.

(5) In the application of this regulation to an offer, acceptance or contract governed by the law of Scotland, any reference to an irrevocable power of attorney shall mean and include reference to an irrevocable mandate, however expressed.

Defaults and contraventions

37 Breaches of statutory duty

(1) A default in complying with, or a contravention of, regulation 16(8), 18(2), 21(1) or (2), 22, 23(4) or (5), 26(1), 26(2)(a) or (c), 27(1), 28(3) or 35(3) shall be actionable at the suit of a person who suffers loss as a result of the default or contravention, or who is otherwise adversely affected by it, subject to the defences and other incidents applying to actions for breach of statutory duty.

(2) Paragraph (1) shall not affect the liability which any person may incur, nor affect any right which any person may have, apart from paragraph (1).

38 Liability of officers for contraventions

In regulation 16(7), 19(4), 23(9), 26(4) or 27(8) an officer of a participating issuer shall be in default in complying with, or in contravention of, the provision mentioned in that regulation if, and only if, he knowingly and wilfully authorised or permitted the default or contravention.

Northern Ireland

39 Application to Northern Ireland

(1) In their application to Northern Ireland, these Regulations shall have effect with the following modifications.

(2) In regulation 32(5)—

(a) for the reference to section 53(1)(c) of the Law of Property Act 1925 there shall be substituted a reference to section 6 of the Statute of Frauds (Ireland) 1695; and

(b) for the reference to section 136 of the Law of Property Act 1925 there shall be substituted a reference to section 87 of the Judicature (Northern Ireland) Act 1978.

(3) In regulation 36(3) for the reference to section 4 of the Powers of Attorney Act 1971 there shall be substituted a reference to section 3 of the Powers of Attorney Act (Northern Ireland) 1971.

(4) For references to provisions of the 1985 Act there shall be substituted references to the equivalent provisions of the 1986 Order and, in particular, for the references to the 1985 Act listed in column 1 of Schedule 3 in the provisions of these Regulations listed in column 2 of that Schedule, there shall be substituted the references to the 1986 Order listed in column 3 of that Schedule.

Amendments and revocations

40 Minor and consequential amendments

(1) In subsection (1)(b) of section 182 of the 1985 Act after 'simplified process)' there shall be inserted 'and to regulations made under section 207 of the Companies Act 1989 (which enable title to securities to be evidenced and transferred without a written instrument).'.

(2) In section 183 of that Act—

(a) in subsection (1), after 'Stock Transfer Act 1982' there shall be inserted 'or is in accordance with regulations made under section 207 of the Companies Act 1989.'; and

(b) subsection (4) shall not apply in relation to the transfer of uncertificated units of a security by means of a relevant system.

(3) In subsection (4) of section 380 of the 1985 Act, after paragraph (k) the following paragraphs shall be added—

'(1) a resolution of the directors passed by virtue of regulation 16(2) of the Uncertificated Securities Regulations 1995 (which allow title to a company's shares to be evidenced and transferred without written instrument); and

(m) a resolution of a company passed by virtue of regulation 16(6) of the Uncertificated Securities Regulations 1995 (which prevents or reverses a resolution of the directors under regulation 16(2) of those Regulations).'.

(4) In subsection (1) of section 180 of the 1986 Act, after paragraph (n) there shall be added the following paragraph—

'(nn) to an Operator approved under the Uncertificated Securities Regulations 1995 if the information is necessary to ensure the proper functioning of a relevant system within the meaning of those Regulations in relation to defaults and potential defaults by market-participants;'.

41 Revocations

The Uncertificated Securities Regulations 1992 are hereby revoked.

SCHEDULE 1   Regulation 5(3)

REQUIREMENTS FOR APPROVAL OF A PERSON AS OPERATOR

Arrangements and resources

1. An Operator must have adequate arrangements and resources for the effective monitoring and enforcement of compliance with his rules or, as respects monitoring, arrangements providing for that function to be performed on his behalf (and without affecting his responsibility) by another body or person who is able and willing to perform it.

Financial resources

2. An Operator must have financial resources sufficient for the proper performance of his functions as an Operator.

Promotion and maintenance of standards

3. An Operator must be able and willing to promote and maintain high standards of integrity and fair dealing in the operation of the relevant system and to cooperate, by the sharing of information or otherwise, with the Treasury and any other authority, body or person having responsibility for the supervision or regulation of investment business or other financial services.

Operation of the relevant system

4. Where an Operator causes or permits a part of the relevant system which is not the Operator-system to be operated by another person (other than as his agent) the Operator—

(a) shall monitor compliance by the person and that part with the requirements of this Schedule; and

(b) shall have arrangements to ensure that the person provides him with such information and such assistance as he may require in order to meet his obligations under these Regulations.

System security

5. A relevant system must be constructed and operate in such a way—

(a) so as to minimise the possibility of unauthorised access to, or modification of, any program or data held in any computer forming part of the Operator-system;

(b) that each dematerialised instruction is properly authenticated in accordance with the specifications of the Operator, which shall provide that each dematerialised instruction—

　(i) is identifiable as being from the computers of a particular system-participant; and

　(ii) is designed to minimise fraud and forgery;

(c) that each dematerialised instruction, in accordance with the specifications of the Operator, expresses by whom it has been sent and, where relevant, on whose behalf it has been sent;

(d) that each dematerialised instruction, in accordance with the specifications of the Operator, indicates—

　(i) where it is sent to a system-participant or the Operator, that it is addressed to that system-participant or the Operator; and

　(ii) where it is sent to a person who is using the facilities of a sponsoring system-participant to receive dematerialised instructions, that it is addressed to that person and the sponsoring system-participant; and

　(iii) where it is sent to the Operator in order for him to send an Operator-instruction to a system-participant, that it is addressed to the Operator, to the system-participant and, if the system-participant is acting as a sponsoring system-participant, to the relevant person on whose behalf the sponsoring system-participant receives dematerialised instructions; and

(e) that the possibility for a system-participant to send a dematerialised instruction on behalf of a person from whom he has no authority is minimised.

System capabilities

6. A relevant system must ensure that the Operator-system can send and respond to properly authenticated dematerialised instructions in sufficient volume and speed.

7. Before an Operator-instruction to a participating issuer to register a transfer of uncertificated units of a security is generated, a relevant system must—

    (a) be able to establish that the transferor is likely to have title to or, by virtue of regulation 25(1) or (2), an interest in, such number of units of the security as is in aggregate at least equal to the number to be transferred; or

    (b) be able to notify the participating issuer in accordance with regulation 24(1) that the transfer is one of two or more transfers which may be registered in accordance with regulation 24(2).

8. A relevant system must maintain adequate records of all dematerialised instructions.

9. A relevant system must be able—

    (a) to permit each system-member to obtain a copy of any records relating to him as are maintained by the relevant system in order to comply with paragraph 7(a) or 8; and

    (b) to make correcting entries in such records as are maintained in order to comply with paragraph 7(a) which are inaccurate.

10. A relevant system must be able to establish, where there is a transfer of uncertificated units of a security to a system-member for value, that a settlement bank has agreed to make payment in respect of the transfer, whether alone or taken together with another transfer for value.

11. A relevant system must ensure that the Operator-system is able to generate Operator-instructions—

    (a) requiring participating issuers to amend the appropriate registers of securities kept by them; and

    (b) informing settlement banks of their payment obligations.

12. A relevant system must—

    (a) enable a system-member—
        (i) to grant authority to a sponsoring system-participant to send properly authenticated dematerialised instructions on his behalf; and
        (ii) to limit such authority by reference to the net value of the units of securities to be transferred in any one day; and

    (b) prevent the transfer of units in excess of that limit.

13. A relevant system must enable system-members—

    (a) to change the form in which they hold or are to hold units of a participating security; and

    (b) where appropriate, to require participating issuers to issue certificates relating to units of a participating security held or to be held by them.

Operating procedures

14. A relevant system must comprise procedures which provide that it responds only to properly authenticated dematerialised instructions which are attributable to a system-user or an Operator.

15. (1) Subject to subparagraph (2), a relevant system must comprise procedures which provide that an Operator-instruction requiring a participating issuer to register a transfer of uncertificated units of a security, or informing a settlement bank of its payment obligations in respect of such a transfer, is generated only if—

(a) it has—

    (i) received a system-member instruction from the transferor; or

    (ii) been required to do so by a court in the United Kingdom or by or under an enactment;

(b) it has—

    (i) established that the transferor is likely to have title to, or is likely to have by virtue of regulation 25(1) or (2) an interest in, such number of units as is in aggregate at least equal to the number to be transferred; or

    (ii) established that the transfer is one of two or more transfers which may be notified to the participating issuer in accordance with regulation 24(1);

(c) in the case of a transfer to a system-member for value, it has established that a settlement bank has agreed to make payment in respect of the transfer, whether alone or taken together with another transfer for value; and

(d) the transfer is not in excess of any limit which by virtue of paragraph 12(a)(ii) the transferor has set on an authority given by him to a sponsoring system-participant.

(2) A relevant system must comprise procedures which provide that an Operator-instruction requiring a participating issuer to register a transfer of uncertificated units of a security, or informing a settlement bank of its payment obligations in respect of such a transfer, may be generated if necessary to correct an error and if in accordance with the rules and practices of an Operator instituted in order to comply with this Schedule.

16. (1) Subject to subparagraph (2), a relevant system must comprise procedures which provide that an Operator-instruction to a participating issuer relating to a right, privilege or benefit attaching to or arising from an uncertificated unit of a security, is generated only if it has—

(a) received a properly authenticated dematerialised instruction attributable to the system-member having the right, privilege or benefit requiring the Operator to generate an Operator-instruction to the participating issuer; or

(b) been required to do so by a court in the United Kingdom or by or under an enactment.

(2) A relevant system must comprise procedures which provide that an Operator-instruction to a participating issuer relating to a right, privilege or benefit attaching to or arising from an uncertificated unit of a security, may be generated if necessary to correct an error and if in accordance with the rules and practices of an Operator instituted in order to comply with this Schedule.

17. A relevant system must comprise procedures which ensure that, where the relevant system maintains records in order to comply with paragraph 15(1)(b)(i), the records are regularly reconciled with the registers of securities maintained by participating issuers.

18. A relevant system must comprise procedures which—

(a) enable system-users to notify the Operator of an error in or relating to a dematerialised instruction; and

(b) ensure that, where the Operator becomes aware of an error in or relating to a dematerialised instruction, he takes appropriate corrective action.

Rules and practices

19. An Operator's rules and practices—

(a) must bind system-members and participating issuers—

     (i) so as to ensure the efficient processing of transfers of title to uncertificated units of a security in response to Operator-instructions; and

    (ii) as to the action to be taken where transfer of title in response to an Operator-instruction cannot be effected;

(b) must make provision for a participating issuer to cease to participate in respect of a participating security so as—

     (i) to minimise so far as practicable any disruption to system-members in respect of their ability to transfer the relevant security; and

    (ii) to provide the participating issuer with any relevant information held by the Operator relating to uncertificated units of the relevant security held by system-members;

(c) must make provision for the orderly termination of participation by system-members and system-participants whose participation is disruptive to other system-members or system-participants or to participating issuers; and

(d) if they make provision for the designation of a subsidiary undertaking as a relevant nominee, must require that the relevant nominee maintain adequate records of—

     (i) the names of the persons who have an interest in the securities it holds; and

    (ii) the nature and extent of their interests.

20. An Operator's rules and practices must require—

(a) that each system-participant is able to send and receive properly authenticated dematerialised instructions;

(b) that each system-member has arrangements—

     (i) for properly authenticated dematerialised instructions attributable to him to be sent;

    (ii) for properly authenticated dematerialised instructions to be received by or for him; and

   (iii) with a settlement bank for payments to be made, where appropriate, for units of a security transferred by means of the relevant system; and

(c) that each participating issuer is able to respond with sufficient speed to Operator-instructions.

21. An Operator must have rules which require system-users and former system-users to provide him with such information in their possession as he may require in order to meet his obligations under these Regulations.

SCHEDULE 2   Regulation 13

PREVENTION OF RESTRICTIVE PRACTICES

Examination of rules and practices

1. (1) The Treasury shall not approve a person as Operator of a relevant system unless they are satisfied that the rules and any guidance of which copies are furnished with the application for approval—

(a) do not have, and are not intended or likely to have, to any significant extent the effect of restricting, distorting or preventing competition; or

(b) if they have or are intended to have that effect to any significant extent, that the effect is not greater than is necessary for the protection of investors, or for compliance with Council Directive 89/646/EEC.

(2) The powers conferred by subparagraph (3) shall be exercisable by the Treasury if at any time it appears to them that—

(a) any rules made or guidance issued by an Operator;

(b) any practices of an Operator; or

(c) any practices of a system-user,

have, or are intended or likely to have, to a significant extent the effect of restricting, distorting or preventing competition and that the effect is greater than is necessary for the protection of investors or for compliance with Council Directive 89/646/EEC.

(3) The powers exercisable under this paragraph are—

(a) to withdraw approval from the Operator;

(b) to direct the Operator to take specified steps for the purpose of securing that the rules, guidance or practices in question do not have the effect mentioned in subparagraph (2); or

(c) to make alterations in the rules of the Operator for that purpose.

(4) Subsections (2) to (5), (7) and (9) of section 11 of the 1986 Act shall apply in relation to the withdrawal of approval under subparagraph (3) as they apply in relation to the revocation of an order under subsection (1) of that section; and in those subsections as they so apply—

(a) any reference to a recognised organisation shall be taken to be a reference to the Operator; and

(b) any reference to members of a recognised organisation shall be taken to be a reference to system-users.

(5) The practices referred to in subparagraph (2)(b) are practices of the Operator in his capacity as such.

(6) The practices referred to in subparagraph (2)(c) are practices in relation to business in respect of which system-users are subject to the rules of the Operator and which are required or contemplated by his rules or guidance or otherwise attributable to his conduct in his capacity as Operator.

Modification of paragraph 1 where delegation order is made

2. (1) This paragraph applies instead of paragraph 1 where the function of approving a person as Operator has been delegated to a designated agency by virtue of regulation 11.

(2) The designated agency—

(a) shall send to the Treasury a copy of the rules and any guidance copies of which are furnished with the application for approval together with any other information supplied with or in connection with the application; and

(b) shall not grant the approval without the leave of the Treasury,

and the Treasury shall not give leave in any case in which they would (apart from the delegation of functions to a designated agency) have been precluded by paragraph 1(1) from granting approval.

(3) A designated agency shall send to the Treasury a copy of any notice received by it from an Operator under regulation 10(3).

(4) If at any time it appears to the Treasury that there are circumstances such that (apart from a delegation order) they would have been able to exercise any of the powers conferred by paragraph 1(3) they may, notwithstanding the delegation order—

(a) themselves exercise the power conferred by paragraph 1(3)(a); or

(b) direct the designated agency to exercise the power conferred by paragraph 1(3)(b) or (c) in such manner as they may specify.

(5) In this paragraph 'delegation order' means an instrument in writing under regulation 11.

Reports by the Director General of Fair Trading

3. (1) The Treasury shall before deciding—

 (a) whether to refuse to grant an approval in pursuance of paragraph 1(1); or
 (b) whether to refuse leave for the granting of an approval in pursuance of paragraph 2(2),

send to the Director General of Fair Trading (in this Schedule referred to as 'the Director') a copy of the rules and of any guidance which the Treasury are required to consider in making that decision together with such other information as the Treasury consider will assist in discharging his functions under subparagraph (2).

(2) The Director shall report to the Treasury whether, in his opinion, the rules and guidance copies of which are sent to him under subparagraph (1) have, or are intended or likely to have, to any significant extent the effect of restricting, distorting or preventing competition and, if so, what that effect is likely to be; and in making any decision as is mentioned in subparagraph (1) the Treasury shall have regard to the Director's report.

(3) The Treasury shall send to the Director copies of any notice received by them under regulation 10(3) or paragraph 2(3) together with such other information as the Treasury consider will assist the Director in discharging his functions under subparagraphs (4) and (5).

(4) The Director shall keep under review—

 (a) the rules, guidance and practices mentioned in paragraph 1(2); and
 (b) the matters specified in the notices of which copies are sent to him under subparagraph(3),

and if at any time he is of the opinion that any such rules or guidance taken together with any such matters, have, or are intended or likely to have, to any significant extent the effect mentioned in subparagraph (2), he shall report his opinion to the Treasury stating what in his opinion that effect is or is likely to be.

(5) The Director may report to the Treasury his opinion that any such matter as is mentioned in subparagraph (4)(b) does not in his opinion have, and is not intended or likely to have, to any significant extent the effect mentioned in subparagraph (2).

(6) The Director may from time to time consider whether any such practices as are mentioned in paragraph 1(2) have, or are intended or likely to have, to any significant extent the effect mentioned in subparagraph (2) and, if so, what that effect is or is likely to be; and if he is of that opinion he shall make a report to the Treasury stating his opinion and what the effect is or is likely to be.

(7) The Treasury shall not exercise their powers under paragraph 1(3) or 2(4) except after receiving a report from the Director under subparagraph (4) or (6).

(8) The Director may, if he thinks fit, publish any report made by him under this paragraph but shall exclude from a published report, so far as practicable, any matter which relates to the affairs of a particular person (other than the person seeking approval as an Operator) the publication of which would or might in his opinion seriously and prejudicially affect the interests of that person.

Investigations by the Director General of Fair Trading

4. (1) For the purpose of investigating any matter with a view to his consideration under paragraph 3 the Director may by a notice in writing—

    (a) require any person to produce, at any time and place specified in the notice, to the Director or to any person appointed by him for the purpose, any documents which are specified or described in the notice and which are documents in his custody or under his control and relating to any matter relevant to the investigation; or

    (b) require any person carrying on business to furnish to the Director such information as may be specified or described in the notice, and specify the time within which, and the manner and form in which, any such information is to be furnished.

(2) A person shall not under this paragraph be required to produce any document or disclose any information which he would be entitled to refuse to produce or disclose on grounds of legal professional privilege in proceedings in the High Court or on grounds of confidentiality as between client and professional legal adviser in proceedings in the Court of Session.

(3) Subsections (6) to (8) of section 85 of the Fair Trading Act 1973 (enforcement provisions) shall apply in relation to a notice under this paragraph as they apply in relation to a notice under subsection (1) of that section but as if in subsection (7) of that section, for the words from 'any one' to 'the Commission' there were substituted 'the Director'.

Exemptions from the Fair Trading Act 1973

5. (1) For the purpose of determining whether a monopoly situation within the meaning of the Fair Trading Act 1973 exists by reason of the circumstances mentioned in section 7(1)(c) of that Act, no account shall be taken of—

    (a) the rules or guidance issued by an Operator or any conduct constituting such a practice as is mentioned in paragraph 1(2); or

    (b) any guidance issued by a designated agency in the exercise of its functions under these Regulations or any practices of a designated agency in the exercise of its functions under these Regulations.

(2) Where approval is withdrawn there shall be disregarded for the purpose mentioned in subparagraph (1) any such conduct as is mentioned in that subparagraph which occurred while the approval was in force.

(3) Where on a monopoly reference under section 50 or 51 of said Act of 1973 falling within section 49 of that Act the Monopolies and Mergers Commission find that a monopoly situation within the meaning of that Act exists and—

    (a) that the person (or, if more than one, any of the persons) in whose favour it exists is subject to the rules of an Operator or to the requirements imposed and guidance issued by a designated agency in the exercise of functions delegated to it under regulation 11(1); or

    (b) that any such person's conduct in carrying on any business to which those rules relate is the subject of guidance issued by an Operator or designated agency; or

    (c) that the person (or, if more than one, any of the persons) in whose favour the monopoly situation exists is an Operator or designated agency,

the Commission, in making their report on that reference, shall exclude from their consideration the question whether the rules, guidance or any acts or omissions of such an Operator or agency as is mentioned in subparagraph (c) in his or its capacity as such operate, or may be expected to operate, against the public interest; and section 54(3) of that Act shall apply subject to the provisions of this paragraph.

Exemptions from Restrictive Trade Practices Act 1976

6. (1) The Restrictive Trade Practices Act 1976 shall not apply to any agreement for the constitution of an Operator, including any term deemed to be contained in it by virtue of section 8(2) or 16(3) of that Act.

(2) The said Act of 1976 shall not apply to any agreement the parties to which consist of or include—

(a) an Operator; or
(b) a person who is subject to the rules of an Operator,

by reason of any term the inclusion of which in the agreement is required or contemplated by the rules or guidance of the Operator.

(3) Where approval is withdrawn from an Operator the foregoing provisions shall have effect as if the Operator had continued to have approval until the end of the period of six months beginning with the day on which the withdrawal takes effect.

(4) Where an agreement ceases by virtue of this paragraph to be subject to registration—

(a) the Director shall remove from the register maintained by him under the said Act of 1976 any particulars which are entered or filed in that register in respect of the agreement; and
(b) any proceedings in respect of the agreement which are pending before the Restrictive Practices Court shall be discontinued.

(5) Where an agreement which has been exempt from registration by virtue of this paragraph ceases to be exempt in consequence of a withdrawal of approval from an Operator, the time within which particulars of the agreement are to be furnished in accordance with section 24 of, and Schedule 2 to, the said Act of 1976 shall be the period of one month beginning with the day on which the agreement ceased to be exempt from registration.

(6) Where in the case of an agreement registered under the said Act of 1976 a term ceases to fall within subparagraph (2) in consequence of the withdrawal of approval from an Operator and particulars of that term have not previously been furnished to the Director under section 24 of that Act, those particulars shall be furnished to him within the period of one month beginning with the day on which the term ceased to fall within that subparagraph.

Exemptions from Competition Act 1980

7. (1) No course of conduct constituting any such practice as is mentioned in paragraph 1(2) shall constitute an anti-competitive practice for the purpose of the Competition Act 1980.

(2) Where approval is withdrawn from an Operator, there shall not be treated as an anti-competitive practice for the purposes of that Act any such course of conduct as is mentioned in subparagraph (1) which occurred while the approval was effective.

Supplementary provisions

8. (1) Before the Treasury exercise a power under paragraph 1(3)(b) or (c), or their power to refuse leave under paragraph 2(2), or their power to give a direction under paragraph 2(4), in respect of an Operator, they shall—

    (a) give written notice of their intention to do so to the Operator and take such steps (whether by publication or otherwise) as they think appropriate for bringing the notice to the attention of any other person who in their opinion is likely to be affected by the exercise of the power; and

    (b) have regard to any representation made within such time as they consider reasonable by the Operator or by any such other person.

(2) A notice under subparagraph (1) shall give particulars of the manner in which the Treasury propose to exercise the power in question and state the reasons for which they propose to act; and the statement of reasons may include matters contained in any report received by them under paragraph 3.

(3) Any direction given under this Schedule shall, on the application of the person by whom it was given, be enforceable by injunction or, in Scotland, by an order for specific performance under section 45 of the Court of Session Act 1988.

(4) The fact that any rules made by an Operator have been altered by or pursuant to a direction given by the Treasury under this Schedule shall not preclude their subsequent alteration or revocation by the Operator.

(5) In determining under this Schedule whether any guidance has, or is likely to have, any particular effect the Treasury and the Director may assume that the persons to whom it is addressed will act in conformity with it.

SCHEDULE 3 Regulation 39(4)

ADAPTATIONS IN RESPECT OF NORTHERN IRELAND

Column 1 Reference to the 1985 Act	Column 2 Provisions of these Regulations	Column 3 Reference to the 1986 Order
Section 182	Regulation 40(1)	Article 192
Section 183	Regulation 23(8)	Article 193
	Regulation 27(8)	
	Regulation 40(2)	
Section 185	Regulation 26(3)	Article 195
Section 186	Regulation 32(3)	Article 196
Section 188	Regulation 17	Article 198
	Regulation 19(6)	
Section 190	Regulation 19(2)	Article 199
Section 191	Regulation 19(2)	Article 200
Section 192	Regulation 33(2)	Article 201
Section 352	Regulation 3(1)	Article 360
	Regulation 19(4)	
Section 358	Regulation 22	Article 366
Section 362	Regulation 19(6)	Article 370
Section 370	Regulation 34(3)	Article 378
Section 376	Regulation 16(7)	Article 384
Section 380	Regulation 40(3)	Article 388
Section 428	Regulation 35(5)	Article 421
Section 429	Regulation 35(1)	Article 422
Section 430	Regulation 35(1)	Article 423
	Regulation 35(2)	
	Regulation 35(4)	
Section 430D	Regulation 35(4)	Article 423D
	Regulation 35(5)	
Section 735	Regulation 3(1)	Article 3
Section 744	Regulation 3(1)	Article 2
Paragraph (2) of Schedule 14	Regulation 19(6)	Paragraph (2) of Schedule 14

Appendix 2

AIM MATERIALS

The AIM rules and Chapter 17 of the Rules of the Stock Exchange are subject to regular amendment and therefore the following material may not be up to date. They should therefore be used for guidance purposes only. If you require a set of the AIM rules which are currently in operation, a copy, together with guidance notes, can be obtained direct from the Financial Services Authority.

AIM RULES

INTRODUCTION

The Alternative Investment Market ('AIM') opened on 19 June 1995. It is regulated by London Stock Exchange plc.

This booklet sets out the rules for AIM companies and their nominated advisers. Defined terms are in bold.

This booklet contains brief guidance notes. These guidance notes do not form part of the rules but are intended to assist in their interpretation.

Where an AIM company has concerns about the interpretation of these rules, it should consult its nominated adviser.

The rules for trading AIM securities are set out in 'Rules of the London Stock Exchange.'

ELIGIBILITY FOR AIM

Nominated adviser

1. An **applicant** must appoint a **nominated adviser**.

APPLICANTS FOR AIM

Ten day announcement

2. An **applicant** must provide the **Exchange**, at least ten **business days** before the expected date of **admission** to **AIM**, with the information specified by **schedule one**.

If there are any changes to such information prior to **admission**, the **applicant** must advise the **Exchange** immediately. Where, in the opinion of the **Exchange**, such changes result in the information being significantly different from that originally provided, the **Exchange** may delay the expected date of **admission** for a further ten **business days**.

The **Exchange** will **notify** the **Company Announcements Office** of information it receives under this rule.

Admission document

3. An **applicant** must produce an **admission document** disclosing the information specified by **schedule two**. This document must be available publicly, free of charge, for at least one month from the **admission** of the **applicant's** securities to **AIM**.

Omissions from admission documents

4. The **Exchange** may authorise the omission of information from an **admisson document** of an **applicant** where its **nominated adviser** confirms that:

- the information is of minor importance only and not likely to influence assessment of the **applicant's** assets and liabilities, financial position, profits and losses and prospects; or
- disclosure of that information would be seriously detrimental to the **applicant** and its omission would not be likely to mislead investors with regard to facts and circumstances necessary to form an informed assessment of the **applicant's** securities.

Application documents

5. At least three **business days** before the expected date of **admission**, an **applicant** must submit to the **Exchange** six copies of its **admission document**, a cheque for its first year's **AIM** fee and a completed **application form**. These must be accompanied by a **nominated adviser's declaration**.

Admission to AIM

6. **Admission** becomes effective only when the **Exchange** issues a **dealing notice** to that effect.

SPECIAL CONDITIONS FOR CERTAIN APPLICANTS

Lock-ins for new businesses

7. Where an **applicant's** main activity is a business which has not been independent and earning revenue for at least two years, it must ensure that all **related parties** and **applicable employees** as at the date of **admission** agree not to dispose of any interest in its securities for one year from the **admission** of its securities.

This rule will not apply in the event of an intervening court order, the death of a party who has been subject to this rule or in respect of an acceptance of a take-over offer for the **AIM company** which is open to all shareholders.

Other conditions

8. The **Exchange** may make the **admission** of an **applicant** subject to a special condition.

The **Exchange** may refuse **admission** to **AIM** if the **applicant** has not complied with any special condition which the **Exchange** considers appropriate and of which the **Exchange** has informed the **applicant** and its **nominated adviser**.

Where matters are brought to the attention of the **Exchange** which could affect an **applicant's** appropriateness for **AIM**, it may delay an **admission** for up to two **business days**. The **Exchange** will inform the **applicant** and its **nominated adviser** and will **notify** the **Company Announcements Office** that it has asked the **applicant** and its **nominated adviser** to undertake further due diligence.

PRINCIPLES OF DISCLOSURE

9. The information which is required by these rules must be **notified** by the **AIM company** to the **Company Announcements Office** no later than it is published elsewhere.

An **AIM company** must take reasonable care to ensure that any information it **notifies** is not misleading, false or deceptive and does not omit anything likely to affect the import of such information.

It will be presumed that information **notified** to the **Company Announcements Office** is required by these rules or other legal or regulatory requirement.

GENERAL DISCLOSURE OF PRICE SENSITIVE INFORMATION

10. An **AIM company** must **notify** the **Company Announcements Office** without delay of any new developments which are not public knowledge concerning a change in:

- its financial condition;
- its sphere of activity;
- the performance of its business; or
- its expectation of its performance,

which, if made public, would be likely to lead to a substantial movement in the price of its **AIM securities**.

DISCLOSURE OF CORPORATE TRANSACTIONS

Substantial transactions

11. A substantial transaction is one which exceeds 10% in any of the **class tests** which are set out in **schedule three**. It includes any transaction by a subsidiary of the **AIM company** but excludes any transactions of a revenue nature in the ordinary course of business and transactions to raise finance which do not involve a change in the fixed assets of the **AIM company** or its subsidiaries.

An **AIM company** must **notify** the **Company Announcements Office** without delay as soon as the terms of any substantial transaction are agreed disclosing the information specified by **schedule four**.

Related party transactions

12. This rule applies to any transaction whatsoever with a **related party** which exceeds 5% in any of the **class tests** which are set out in **schedule three**.

An **AIM company** must **notify** the **Company Announcements Office** without delay as soon as the terms of a transaction with a **related party** are agreed disclosing:

- the information specified by **schedule four**;
- the name of the **related party** concerned and the nature and extent of their interest in the transaction; and
- a statement that with the exception of any **director** who is involved in the transaction as a **related party**, its **directors** consider, having consulted with its **nominated adviser**, that the terms of the transaction are fair and reasonable insofar as the holders of its **AIM securities** are concerned.

Reverse take-overs

13. A reverse take-over is an acquisition or acquisitions in a 12 month period which for an **AIM company** would:

- exceed 100% in any of the **class tests** set out in **schedule three**;
- result in a fundamental change in its business, board or voting control; or
- in the case of an **investing company**, depart substantially from the investment strategy stated in its **admission document**.

Any agreement which would effect a reverse take-over must be:

- conditional on the consent of the holders of its **AIM securities** being given in general meeting;
- notified to the **Company Announcements Office** without delay disclosing the information specified by **schedule four** and insofar as it is with a **related party**, the additional information required by rule 12; and
- accompanied by the publication of an **admission document** in respect of the proposed enlarged entity and convening the general meeting.

Where shareholder approval is given for the reverse take-over, trading in the **AIM securities** of the **AIM company** will be cancelled. If the enlarged entity seeks **admission**, it must make an application in the same manner as any other **applicant** applying for **admission** of its securities for the first time.

Aggregation of transactions

14. Transactions completed during the twelve months prior to the date of the latest transaction must be aggregated with that transaction for the purpose of determining whether rules 11, 12, 13 and/or 17 apply where:

- they are entered into by the **AIM company** with the same **person** or **persons** or their **families**;
- they involve the acquisition or disposal of securities or an interest in one particlar business; or
- together they lead to a principal involvement in any business activity or activities which did not previously form a part of the **AIM company's** principal activities.

DISCLOSURE OF MISCELLANEOUS INFORMATION

15. An **AIM company** must **notify** the **Company Announcements Office** without delay of:

- any **deals** by **directors** disclosing, insofar as it has such information, the information specified by **schedule five**;
- any **relevant changes** to any **significant shareholders**, disclosing, insofar as it has such information, the information specified by **schedule five**;
- the resignation, dismissal or appointment of any **director**, giving the date of such occurrence and for an appointment, the information specified by **schedule two** paragraph (f);
- any change in its accounting reference date;
- any material change between its actual trading performance or financial condition and any profit forecast, estimate or projection included in the **admission document** or otherwise made public on its behalf;
- any decision to make any payment in respect of its **AIM securities** specifying the net amount payable per security, the payment date and the **record date**;
- the reason for the issue or cancellation of any **AIM securities**; and
- the resignation, dismissal or appointment of its **nominated adviser** or **broker**.

HALF-YEARLY REPORTS

16. An **AIM company** must prepare a half-yearly report in respect of the six month period from the end of the financial period for which financial information has been disclosed in its **admission document** and at least every subsequent six months thereafter

(apart from the final period of six months preceding its accounting reference date for its annual audited accounts). All such reports must be **notified** to the **Company Announcements Office** without delay and in any event not later than three months after the end of the relevant period.

ANNUAL ACCOUNTS

17. An **AIM company** must publish annual audited accounts prepared in accordance with United Kingdom or United States generally accepted accounting practice or International Accounting Standards. These accounts must be sent to the holders of its **AIM securities** without delay and in any event not later than six months after the end of the financial period to which they relate.

These accounts must disclose any transaction with a **related party**, whether or not previously disclosed under these rules, where any of the **class tests** which are set out in **schedule three** exceed 0.25% and must specify the identity of the **related party** and the consideration for the transaction.

PUBLICATION OF DOCUMENTS SENT TO SHAREHOLDERS

18. Any document provided by an **AIM company** to the holders of its **AIM securities**, must be made available to the public at the same time for at least one month, free of charge, at an address **notified** to the **Company Announcements Office**.

Three copies of all such documents must be sent to the **Exchange**.

RESTRICTIONS ON DEALS

19. An **AIM company** must ensure that its **directors** and **applicable employees** do not **deal** in any of its **AIM securities** during a **close period**.

This rule will not apply, however, where such individuals have entered into a binding commitment prior to the **AIM company** being in such a **close period** where it was not reasonably foreseeable at the time such commitment was made that a **close period** was likely and provided that the commitment was **notified** to the **Company Announcements Office** at the time it was made.

The **Exchange** may permit a **director** or **applicable employee** of an **AIM company** to sell its **AIM securities** during a **close period** to alleviate severe personal hardship.

PROVISION AND DISCLOSURE OF INFORMATION

20. The **Exchange** may require an **AIM company**:

- to provide it with such information in such form and within such time limit as it considers appropriate; and
- to publish such information.

21. The **Exchange** may disclose any information in its possession as follows:

- to co-operate with any **person** responsible for supervision or regulation or financial services or for law enforcement;
- to enable it to discharge its legal or regulatory functions, including instituting, carrying on or defending proceedings;
- for any other purpose where it has the consent of the **person** from whom the information was obtained and, if different, the **person** to whom it relates.

Appendix 2
AIM MATERIALS

FURTHER ISSUES OF SECURITIES FOLLOWING ADMISSION

Further admission documents

22. A further **admission document** will be required for an **AIM company** only when it is:

*   required to issue a prospectus under the **POS Regulations** for a further issue of **AIM securities**;
*   seeking **admission** for a new class of securities; or
*   treated as an **applicant** following a reverse take-over under rule 13.

Exemptions from further admission documents

23. Am **AIM company** is exempted from preparing a further **admission document** which would otherwise be required by rule 22 where less than 10% of a class of **AIM securities** are being offered and the **AIM company** has been complying with these rules.

In such circumstances, the **nominated adviser** to an **AIM company** must confirm to the **Exchange** in writing that equivalent information is available publicly by reason of the **AIM company's** compliance with these rules.

Omissions from further admission documents

24. The **Exchange** may authorise the omission of information from further **admission documents** in the same circumstances as for an **applicant** under rule 4.

In addition, an **AIM company** may omit **specified information** from any further **admission document** where further **AIM securities** are offered on a pre-emptive basis to some or all of the existing holders of such securities provided that the **AIM company** has been complying with the requirements of these rules.

In such circumstances, the **nominated adviser** to an **AIM company** must confirm to the **Exchange** in writing that equivalent information is available publicly by reason of the **AIM company's** compliance with these rules.

Applications for further issues

25. At least three **business days** before the expected date of **admission** of further **AIM securities** an **AIM company** must submit an **application form** and where required by rule 22, any further **admission document**.

LANGUAGE

26. All **admission documents**, any documents sent to holders of **AIM securities** and information **notified** to the **Company Announcements Office** must be in English.

DIRECTORS RESPONSIBILITY FOR COMPLIANCE

27. An **AIM company** must ensure that each of its **directors**:

*   accepts full responsibility, collectively and individually, for its compliance with these rules;
*   discloses without delay all information which it needs in order to comply with rule 15 insofar as that information is known to the **director** or could with reasonable diligence be ascertained by the **director**; and
*   seeks advice from its **nominated adviser** regarding its compliance with these rules whenever appropriate and takes that advice into account.

ONGOING ELIGIBILITY REQUIREMENTS

Transferability of shares

28. An **AIM company** must ensure that its **AIM securities** are freely transferable except where:

- in any jurisdiction, statute or regulation places restrictions upon transferability; or
- the **AIM company** is seeking to ensure that it does not become subject to statute or regulation if it has a particular number of shareholders domiciled in a particular country.

Securities to be admitted

29. Only securities which have been unconditionally allotted can be **admitted** as **AIM securities**.

An **AIM company** must ensure that application is made to admit all securities within a class of **AIM securities**.

Retention of nominated advisers

30. An **AIM company** must retain a **nominated adviser** at all times.

If an **AIM company** ceases to have a **nominated adviser** the **Exchange** will suspend trading in its **AIM securities**. If within one month the **AIM company** has failed to appoint a replacement **nominated adviser** the **admission** of its **AIM securities** will be cancelled.

Retention of a broker

31. An **AIM company** must retain a **broker** at all times.

Settlement

32. An **AIM company** must ensure that appropriate settlement arrangements are in place. In particular, save where the **Exchange** otherwise agrees, **AIM securities** must be eligible for electronic settlement.

Fees

33. An **AIM company** must pay the fees set by the **Exchange** from time to time.

NOMINATED ADVISERS

34. Only an adviser whose name appears on the **register** may act as a **nominated adviser**. The responsibilities which a **nominated adviser** owes solely to the **Exchange** are to:

- confirm to the **Exchange** in writing the information set out by **schedule six** in relation to any application for **admission** which requires the production of an **admission document**;
- comply with its obligations under these rules;
- be available at all times to advise and guide the **directors** for an **AIM company** for which it acts about their obligations to ensure compliance by the **AIM company** on an ongoing basis with these rules;
- submit a **nominated adviser's declaration** in respect of any **AIM company** for which it takes over the role of **nominated adviser**;

- provide the **Exchange** with any other information, in such form and within such time limits as the **Exchange** may reasonably require;
- liaise with the **Exchange** where requested so to do by the **Exchange** or an **AIM company** for which it acts;
- review reguarly an **AIM company's** actual trading performance and financial condition against any profit forecast, estimate or protection included in the **admission document** or otherwise made public on behalf of the **AIM company** in order to assist it in determining whether an announcement is necessary under rule 15;
- inform the **Exchange** when it ceases to be the **nominated adviser** to an **AIM company**; and
- abide by the **eligibility criteria** at all times.

MAINTENANCE OF ORDERLY MARKETS

Precautionary Suspension

35. The **Exchange** may suspend the trading of **AIM securities** where:

- trading in those securities is not being conducted in an orderly manner;
- it considers that an **AIM company** has failed to comply with these rules;
- the protection of investors so requires; or
- the integrity and reputation of the market has been or may be impaired by dealings in those securities.

Suspensions are effected by a **dealing notice**.

Cancellation for lack of trading

36. The **Exchange** will cancel the **admission** of **AIM securities** where these have been suspended from trading for six months.

Cancellations are effected by a **dealing notice**.

SANCTIONS AND APPEALS

Disciplinary action against an AIM company

37. If the **Exchange** considers that an **AIM company** has contravened these rules, it may take the following measures:

- fine it;
- censure it;
- publish the fact that it has been fined or censured; and/or
- cancel the **admission** of its **AIM securities**.

Disciplinary action against a nominated adviser

38. If the **Exchange** considers that a **nominated adviser** is either in breach of its responsibilities under rule 34, or has failed to act with due skill and care, or that the integrity and reputation of **AIM** has been or may be impaired as a result of its conduct or judgement, the **Exchange** may:

- censure the **nominated adviser**;
- remove it from the **register**; and/or
- publish the action it has taken and the reasons for that action.

DISCIPLINARY PROCESS

39. Where the **Exchange** proposes to take any of the steps described in rules 37 and 38, the **Exchange** will follow the procedures set out in the **Disciplinary Procedures and Appeals Handbook**.

Appeals

40. Any decision of the **Exchange** in relation to these rules may be appealed to an appeals committee in accordance with the procedures set out in the **Disciplinary Procedures and Appeals Handbook**.

Schedule One

Pursuant to rule 2, an **applicant** must provide the **Exchange** with the following information:

(a) its name;

(b) its country of incorporation;

(c) its address;

(d) a brief description of its business;

(e) the number and type of securities in rsepect of which it seeks **admission**;

(f) an indication of whether it will be raising capital on **admission**;

(g) the full names and functions of its **directors** and proposed **directors**;

(h) insofar as known to it, the name of any **person** who is interested directly or indirectly in 3% or more of its securities, together with the percentage, of each such **person's** interest;

(i) the names and addresses of any **persons** who will be disclosed in the **admission document** under **schedule two**, paragraph (g);

(j) its anticipated accounting reference date;

(k) the name and address of its **nominated adviser** and **broker**; and

(l) details of where its **admission document** will be available with a statement that this will contain full details about the **applicant** and the **admission** of its securities.

Schedule Two

A company which is required to produce an **admission document** must ensure that document discloses the following:

(a) information equivalent to that which would be required by the **POS Regulations** whether or not it is required to produce a document under those regulations;

(b) a statement by its **directors** that in their opinion having made due and careful enquiry, the working capital available to it and its group will be sufficient for its present requirements, that is for at least twelve months from the date of the **admission** of its securities;

(c) where it contains a profit forecast, estimate or projection (which includes any form of words which expressly or by implication states a minimum or maximum for the likely level of profits or losses for a period subsequent to that for which audited accounts have been published, or contains data from which a calculation of an approximate figure for future profits or losses may be made, even if no particular figure is mentioned and the words 'profit' or 'loss' are not used):

(i)   a statement by its **directors** that such forecast, estimate or projection has been made after due and careful enquiry;

(ii)   a statement of the principal assumptions for each factor which could have a material effect on the achievement of the forecast, estimate or projection. The assumptions must be readily understandable by investors and be specific and precise; and

(iii)   confirmation from the **nominated adviser** to the **applicant** that it has satisfied itself that the forecast, estimate or projection has been made after due and careful enquiry by the **directors** of the **applicant**;

(d)   on the first page, prominently and in bold the name of its **nominated adviser** and the following paragraphs:

'The Alternative Investment Market (AIM) is a market designed primarily for emerging or smaller companies to which a higher investment risk tends to be attached than to larger or more established companies. AIM securities are not Officially Listed.

A prospective investor should be aware of the risks of investing in such companies and should make the decision to invest only after careful consideration and if appropriate, consultation with an independent financial adviser.

London Stock Exchange plc has not itself examined or approved the contents of this document.';

(e)   where rule 7 applies, a statement that its **related parties** and **applicable employees** have agreed not to dispose of any interests in any of its **AIM securities** for a period of twelve months from the **admission** of its securities;

(f)   the following information relating to each **director** and each proposed **director**:

(i)   the **director's** full name, any previous names and age;

(ii)   the names of all companies and partnerships of which the **director** has been a **director** or partner at any time in the previous five years, indicating whether or not the **director** is still a **director** or partner;

(iii)   any unspent convictions in relation to indictable offences;

(iv)   details of any bankruptcies or individual voluntary arrangements of such **director**;

(v)   details of any receiverships, compulsory liquidations, creditors voluntary liquidations, administrations, company voluntary arrangements or any composition or arrangement with its creditors generally or any class of its creditors of any company where such **director** was a **director** at the time of or within the 12 months preceding such events;

(vi)   details of any compulsory liquidations, administrations or partnership voluntary arrangements of any partnerships where such **director** was a partner at the time of or within the 12 months preceding such events;

(vii)   details of receiverships of any asset of such **director** or of a partnership of which the **director** was a partner at the time of or within the 12 months preceding such events; and

(viii) details of any public criticisms of such **director** by statutory or regulatory authorities (incuding recognised professional bodies), and whether such **director** has ever been disqualified by a court from acting as a **director** of a company or from acting in the management or conduct of the affairs of any company.

(g) the name of any **person** (excluding professional advisers otherwise disclosed in the **admission document** and trade suppliers) who has:

  (i) received, directly or indirectly, from it within the 12 months preceding the application for **admission** to **AIM**; or

  (ii) entered into contractual arrangements (not otherwise disclosed in the **admission document**) to receive, directly or indirectly, from it on or after **admission** any of the following:

  - fees totalling £10,000 or more;
  - its securities where these have a value of £10,000 or more calculated by reference to the issue price or, in the case of an introduction, the expected opening price; or
  - any other benefit with a value of £10,000 or more at the date of **admission**;

  giving full details of the relationship of such **person** with the **applicant** and of the fees, securities or other benefit received or to be received;

(h) the name of any **person** who, insofar as known to its **directors**, is interested directly or indirectly in 3% or more of its capital, together with the amount, expressed as a percentage, of each such **person's** interest;

(i) where it is an **investing company**, details of its investment strategy; and

(j) any other factual information which it reasonably considers necessary to enable investors to form a fully understanding of the matters contained in the **admission document**.

Schedule Three

The **class tests** for determining the size of a transaction pursuant to rules 11, 12, 13 and 17 are as follows:

The Gross Assets test

$$\frac{\text{Gross assets the subject of the transaction}}{\text{Gross assets of the AIM company}} \times 100\%$$

Figures to use for the Gross assets test:

1. The 'gross assets' of the **AIM company** means the total of its fixed assets plus total current assets. These figures should be taken from the most recent of the following:

(a) the most recent consolidated balance sheet **notified** to the **Company Announcements Office**; or

(b) where an **admission document** has been produced for the purposes of **admission** following a reverse takeover, any pro forma net asset statement published in the **admission document** may be used, provided it is derived from information taken from the last published audited consolidated accounts and that any adjustments to this information are clearly shown and explained; or

Appendix 2
AIM MATERIALS

(c)   in a case where transactions are aggregated pursuant to rule 14, the most recent consolidated balance sheet (as at a date prior to the earliest aggregated transaction) **notified** to the **Company Announcements Office**.

2. The 'gross assets the subject of the transaction' means:

(a)   in the cases of an acquisition of an interest in an undertaking which will result in consolidation of the undertaking's net assets in the accounts of the **AIM company**, or a disposal of an interest in an undertaking which will result in the undertaking's net assets no longer being consolidated in the accounts of the **AIM company**, the assets the subject of the transaction means the value of 100% of the undertaking's assets, irrespective of what interest is acquired or disposed.

(b)   in the case of an acquisition or disposal which does not fall within paragraph 2(a), the assets the subject of the transaction means:

- for an acquisition, the consideration plus any liabilities assumed; and
- for a disposal, the book value of the assets attributed to that interest in the **AIM company's** last audited accounts.

(c)   in the case of an acquisition of assets other than an interest in an undertaking, the assets the subject of the transaction means the greater of the consideration or the book value of those assets.

(d)   In the case of a disposal of assets other than an interest in an undertaking, the assets the subject of the transaction means the book value of the assets.

The Profits test

$$\frac{\text{Profits attributable to the assets of the subject of a transaction}}{\text{Profits of the AIM company}} \times 100\%$$

Figures to use for the Profits test:

3. 'Profits of the **AIM company**' means profits before taxation and extraordinary items as stated in the following:

(a)   the last published annual consolidated accounts;

(b)   the last preliminary statement of annual results **notified** to the **Company Announcements Office**; or

(c)   in a case where transactions are aggregated pursuant to rule 14, the last such accounts or statement prior to the earliest transaction.

In a case of an acquisition or disposal of an interest in an undertaking of the type described within paragraph 2(a), the 'profits attributable to the assets the subject of the transaction' means 100% of the profits of the undertaking irrespective of what interest is acquired or disposed.

The Turnover test

$$\frac{\text{Turnover attributable to the assets of the subject of a transaction}}{\text{Turnover of the AIM company}} \times 100\%$$

Figures to use for the Turnover test:

4. The 'turnover of the **AIM company**' means the turnover figure as stated in the following:

(a)   the last published annual consolidated accounts;

(b)   the last preliminary statement of annual results **notified** to the **Company Announcements Office**; or

(c)   in a case where transactions are aggregated pursuant to rule 14, the last such accounts or statement prior to the earliest transaction.

In a case of an acquisition or disposal of an interest in an undertaking of the type described within paragraph 2(a), the 'turnover attributable to the assets the subject of the transaction' means 100% of the turnover of the undertaking irrespective of what interest is acquired or disposed.

The Consideration test

$$\frac{\text{Consideration}}{\text{Aggregate market value of all the ordinary shares of the AIM company}} \times 100\%$$

Figures to use for the Consideration test:

5. 'Consideration' means the amount paid to the vendors.

(a)   Where all or part of the consideration is in the form of securities to be **listed**, or traded on **AIM**, the consideration attributable to those securities means the aggregate market value of those securities.

(b)   If deferred consideration is, or may be payable or receivable by the **AIM company** in the future, the consideration means the maximum total consideration payable or receivable under the agreement.

6. 'Aggregate market value of all the ordinary shares of the **AIM company**' means the value of its enfranchised securities on the day prior to the announcement of the transaction.

The Gross capital test

This test should only be applied in the case of an acquisition of a company or business.

$$\frac{\text{Gross capital of the company or business being acquired}}{\text{Gross capital of the AIM company}} \times 100\%$$

Figures to use for the Gross capital test:

7. 'Gross capital of the company or business being acquired' means the aggregate of:

(a)   the consideration;

(b)   If a company, any of its shares and debt securities which are not being acquired;

(c)   all other liabilities (other than current liabilities), including for this purpose minority interests and deferred taxation; and

(d)   any excess of current liabilities over current assets.

8. 'Gross capital of the **AIM company**' means the aggregate of:

(a)   the aggregate market value of its securities;

(b)   all other liabilities (other than current liabilities), including minority interest and deferred taxation; and

(c)   any excess of current liabilities over current assets.

The figures to be used must be the aggregate market value of the enfranchised securities on the day prior to the announcement of the transaction.

Substitute tests

In circumstances where the above tests produce anomalous results or where the tests are inappropriate to the sphere of activity of the **AIM company**, the **Exchange** may (except in the case of a transaction with a **related party**), disregard the calculation and substitute other relevant indicators of size, including industry specific tests. Only the **Exchange** can decide to disregard one or more of the **class tests**, or substitute another test.

Schedule Four

In respect of transactions which require announcements pursuant to rules 11, 12 and 13 an **AIM company** must **notify** the **Company Announcements Office** of the following information:

(a)   particulars of the transaction, including the name of any company or business, where relevant;

(b)   a description of the business carried on by, or using, the assets which are the subject of the transaction;

(c)   the profits attributable to those assets;

(d)   the value of those assets;

(e)   the full consideration and how it is being satisfied;

(f)   the effect on the **AIM company**;

(g)   details of any service contracts of its proposed **directors**;

(h)   in the case of a disposal, the application of the sale proceeds;

(i)   in the case of a disposal, if shares or other securities are to form part of the consideration received, a statement whether such securities are to be sold or retained; and

(j)   any other information necessary to enable investors to evaluate the effect of the transaction upon the **AIM company**.

Schedule Five

Pursuant to rule 15, an **AIM company** must **notify** the **Company Announcements Office** of:

(i)   the identity of the **director** or **significant shareholder** concerned;

(ii)   the date on which the disclosure was made to it;

(iii)   the date on which the **deal** or **relevant change** to the **holding** was effected;

(iv)   the price, amount and class of the **AIM securities** concerned;

(v)   the nature of the transaction;

(vi)   the nature and extent of the **director's** or **significant shareholder's** interest in the transaction; and

(vii) where a **deal** takes place when it is in any **close period** under rule 19, the date upon which any previous binding commitment was **notified** to the **Company Announcements Office** or the date upon which the **Exchange** granted permission to **deal** in order to mitigate severe personal hardship.

Schedule Six

Pursuant to rule 34 a **nominated adviser** must confirm that:

(a) the **directors** of the **AIM company** have received satisfactory advice and guidance as to the nature of their obligations to ensure compliance by the **AIM company** with these rules;

(b) to the best of its knowledge and belief, having made due and careful enquiry, all relevant requirements of these rules (save for the **admission document's** compliance with Regulation 9 of the **POS Regulations**) have been complied with; and

(c) in its opinion, it is satisfied that the **applicant** and the securities which are the subject of the application are appropriate to be **admitted** to **AIM**.

STOCK EXCHANGE RULE BOOK

Chapter 17: AIM trading rules

Scope

17.1   The rules in this chapter apply to AIM.

Application for permission to effect transactions

17.2   (a)   A **member firm** may apply to the **Exchange** for permission to effect transactions in AIM securities, trading in which is for the time being suspended by the **Exchange**.

(b)   Permission under paragraph (a) must be obtained in respect of each proposed transaction.

Communication

17.3   Information and orders shall be input to or removed from **SEATS PLUS** by **member firms** and by such means as the **Exchange** shall specify from time to time. *(rule 17.3 last amended N18&N39/96 – effective 27 August 1996)*

Nominated brokers responsibilities

17.4   In relation to any **AIM security** a **member firm** which is the **nominated broker**:

(a)   shall input to **SEATS PLUS** such information about the issuer for display on **SEATS PLUS** as the **Exchange** may specify from time to time;

(b)   during the **mandatory quote period**, shall upon request use its best endeavours to find matching business in those securities in which there is no registered **market maker**; and

(c)   may nominate another **member firm** to fulfil its obligations under this rule as **agent** subject to the agreement of that **member firm** and the **Exchange**.

(rule 17.4 last amended N18&N39/96 – effective 27 August 1996)

Registration of market makers

17.5   (a)   Only a **member firm** registered as a **market maker** in the **AIM security** in question may display prices for that security on **SEATS PLUS**.

(b)   Every **market maker** shall install, maintain and use voice recording equipment with respect to its market making activities under this chapter and shall retain all recordings made for a minimum of one month.

(rule 17.5 last amended N18&N39/96 – effective 27 August 1996)

Input of orders

17.6   During the **mandatory quote period**, a **member firm** may input as **principal** or **agent** the following orders in an **AIM security** to **SEATS PLUS**:

(a)   in the case of a security with no registered **market maker** making a firm quote, **firm exposure orders** or **indicative exposure orders**;

(b)   in the case of a security with one or more registered **market maker**s making a firm quote, **firm exposure orders** only.

(rule 17.6 last amended N18&N39/96 – effective 27 August 1996)

Display of indicative orders

17.7   A **member firm** may display an **indicative exposure order** in respect of an **AIM security** only if it or the **person** on whose behalf it is dealing intends to deal at or near to the displayed price. *(rule 17.7 last amended N18&N39/96 – effective 27 August 1996)*

Indicative orders

17.8   Notwithstanding the displayed status of any order, an order in respect of an **AIM security** shall be deemed to be indicative:

(a)   outside the **mandatory quote period**;

(b)   when a fast market is declared pursuant to rule 17.9;

(c)   when **SEATS PLUS** is declared indicative;

(d)   where the market in the relevant security or group of securities is declared indicative;

(e)   for thirty minutes following the release of an announcement on the **Regulatory News Service** about the **AIM security** or its issuer; or

(f)   following an announcement that the **member firm** which input the order is unable to update orders or is experiencing difficulties in updating orders.

(rule 17.8 last amended N18&N39/96 – effective 27 August 1996)

Fast markets

17.9   The **Exchange** may declare a fast market in AIM securities where the frequency of submission of **trade reports** or changes to **market maker**s' quotations or **member firm**s' orders exceed that which **SEATS PLUS** or **member firm**s' systems can accommodate. Where a fast market is declared:

(a)   a **market maker** is not obliged to effect a transaction at its displayed price in an affected security;

(b)   a **market maker** shall quote a firm two-way price in at least the **minimum quote size** to an enquiring **member firm**, other than a **market maker** registered in the same security;

(c)   a **member firm** shall not enter **hit orders**;

(d)   a **member firm** may contact another **member firm** which is displaying an order to ascertain whether that **member firm** will deal at the price and size displayed. A **member firm** approached under this rule is under no obligation to deal.

(rule 17.9 last amended N18&N39/96 – effective 27 August 1996)

Indicative markets

17.10 (a)   The **Exchange** may declare an indicative market in an **AIM security** (or group of AIM securities) where:

(i)   it is not possible for **market makers** to display up-to-date prices;

(ii)   it is not possible for **member firms** to enter or delete orders.

(iii)   it is necessary in the interests of maintaining an orderly market in a security (or group of securities).

(b)   Where a security or group of securities is declared indicative, or a stand-by announcement concerning a company has been issued and the full related announcement has not yet been published,

(i)   a **market maker** is not obliged to effect transactions in an affected security at the price it is displaying;

(ii)   a **market maker** is not obliged to quote a price in an affected security in which it is registered to an enquiring **member firm** over the telephone but if it chooses to do so, that price must be firm;

(iii)   a **member firm** shall not enter **hit orders** in the affected security;

(iv)   a **member firm** may contact another **member firm** which is displaying an order in the affected security to ascertain whether that **member firm** will deal at the price and size displayed. A **member firm** approached under this rule is under no obligation to deal.

(rule 17.10 last amended N18&N39/96 – effective 27 August 1996)

Market making obligations during the mandatory quote period

17.11 During the **mandatory quote period**, a registered **market maker** in an **AIM security** shall:

(a)   display on **SEATS PLUS**:

(i)   firm continuous two-way prices;

(ii)   deleted with effect from 5 June 2000

(iii)   deleted with effect from 5 June 2000

in not less than the **minimum quote size** in each **AIM security** in which it is registered.

(b)   if displaying firm prices, deal with an enquiring **member firm** at the price and in up to the size displayed;

(c)   obtain the consent of the **Exchange** before withdrawing or re-entering its quotation;

(d)   deleted with effect from 5 June 2000

(e)   deleted with effect from 5 June 2000

(f)   be entitled, where it has effected a transaction in a security and received another enquiry to deal in the same security before having had a reasonable time to alter its price, to declare 'dealer in front' to the **person** making the enquiry and alter the price at which it is prepared to deal.

(rule 17.11 last amended N04&N14/00 – effective 5 June 2000)

17.12 Where the withdrawal of a quotation made pursuant to rule 17.11(c) was caused by the failure of a **market maker**'s computer system, the **market maker** shall re-enter its quotation as soon as it is able to do so. Where a **market maker** has informed the **Exchange** that its computer system has failed, thus preventing the updating of its prices, it shall not be obliged to deal at its displayed price until the system is operative again. *(last amended N18&N39/96 – effective 27 August 1996)*

17.13 A **market maker** shall not display a **firm exposure order** or an **indicative exposure order** in an **AIM security** in which it is registered as a **market maker**.

(rule 17.13 last amended N18&N39/96 – effective 27 August 1996)

17.14 Where a **market maker** is approached by another **market maker** (or a member of a group which includes a **market maker**) in the same security and the enquiring **member firm**:

(a) wishes to sell the security, and it (or the market making member of the group of which it is a member) is displaying on **SEATS PLUS** a lower **bid price** and a lower **offer price** than the **market maker** approached; or

(b) wishes to buy the security, and it (or the market making member of the group of which it is a member), is displaying on **SEATS PLUS** a higher **bid price** and a higher **offer price** than the **market maker** approached;

the **market maker** approached shall effect a transaction in that security with the enquiring **member firm** in up to the **minimum quote size** but shall not be obliged to do so in a larger size.

(rule 17.14 last amended N18&N39/96 – effective 27 August 1996)

Obligations of market makers outside the mandatory quote period

17.15 Where a **market maker** displays in an **AIM security**

(a) between the opening of the system and the commencement of the **mandatory quote period** the **market makers** prices are indicative;

(b) between the end of the **mandatory quote period** and the close of **SEATS PLUS**, a **market maker** which elects to remain open shall display two way prices in not less than the **minimum quote size**;

(c) and maintains the same quotation that it was making at the end of the **mandatory quote period**, that quotation is firm to another **market maker** which is also open in the security, to a **member firm** other than a **market maker** or to a **counterparty**;

(d) and changes its quotation after the end of the **mandatory quote period**, its obligations are as follows:

(i) where its **bid price** is improved, that price is firm to any other **member firm** or **counterparty**. The **offer price** is firm to a **counterparty** and any **member firm** other than a **market maker** which is also open in the security, to a **member firm** other than a **market maker** or to a **counterparty**;

(ii)   where its **offer price** is improved, that price is firm to any other **member firm** or **counterparty**. The **bid price** is firm to a **counterparty** and any **member firm** other than a **market maker** which is not open in the security;

(e)   and it has closed its quotation after the end of the **mandatory quote period**, it may re-open its quotations provided it maintains its quotations until the close of **SEATS PLUS**.

(rule 17.15 last amended N18&N39/96 – effective 27 August 1996)

Obligations of member firms before effecting transactions

17.16 (a)   Before effecting a transaction in an **AIM security** a **member firm** shall check whether there are any **firm exposure orders** displayed in that security on **SEATS PLUS** at a price which is the same as or more competitive than the price of its proposed transaction, even if the proposed transaction on the checking **member firm** is for non-**standard settlement**.

(b)   If there is a **firm exposure order** displayed and the checking firm is not a **market maker** in that security, it shall satisfy the displayed order to the extent that the size of its proposed transaction allows at the price displayed or, if its proposed transaction is for non **standard settlement**, contact the **member firm** displaying the order and offer to transact business for the proposed settlement date; unless

(i)   the displayed order is all or none and the size of its proposed transaction is less than the size of the displayed order; or

(ii)   its proposed transaction is of a larger size than the displayed order and completion of, or the price available for, the remainder of its proposed transaction through either a **market maker** or other displayed orders is prejudiced, either by the execution of the displayed order or the splitting of its proposed transaction.

(c)   If there is a **firm exposure order** displayed and the checking firm is a **market maker** in that security, it shall satisfy the displayed order, as far as possible given the extent of the size of its proposed transaction and any of its outstanding **limit orders** which are eligible for satisfaction, unless the displayed order is all or none and the aggregate size of its proposed transaction and eligible outstanding **limit orders** is less than the size of the displayed order.

(d)   Where more than one **firm exposure order** is eligible for execution under this rule the most competitively priced order shall be satisfied first. Where more than one **firm exposure order** at the same price is eligible for execution the earliest entered order shall be satisfied first.

(e)   Any transaction effected as a result of the provisions of this rule shall be trade reported with trade type indicator 'O'.

(rule 17.16 last amended N04&N14/00 – effective 5 June 2000)

Obligations of market makers before changing quotations

17.17 (a)   Before changing its quote in an **AIM security**, a **market maker** shall check whether there are any **firm exposure orders** in that security displayed on

SEATS PLUS at a price which is the same as or more competitive than the price to which it intends to change. Where there is such an order the **market maker** shall satisfy that order in full at the price at which it is displayed.

(b) Where more than one **firm exposure order** is eligible for execution under this rule the most competitively prices order shall be satisfied first. Where more than one **firm exposure order** at the same price is eligible for execution the earliest entered order shall be satisfied first.

(c) A **market maker** must enter a **hit order** to execute orders eligible for execution under this rule.

(rule 17.17 last amended N18&N39/96 – effective 27 August 1996)

Execution of orders

17.18 A **member firm** may not enter a **hit order** against an **indicative exposure order**, or an order deemed indicative pursuant to rule 17.8. *(rule 17.18 last amended N18&N39/96 – effective 27 August 1996)*

17.19 Rule deleted with effect from 27 August 1996. *(N18&N39/96)*

Exposure of business to market makers

17.20 (a) Where during the **mandatory quote period**, a **member firm** proposes to effect an **agency cross** or **riskless principal transaction** in an **AIM security** in which a **market maker** is displaying a price, it shall inform the **market maker** displaying the best price in the nearest size of:

(i) the total size;

(ii) the indicated price;

(iii) any other limits or instructions in the security given by the **client**; and

(iv) whether the initiating non-member is a **buyer** or a **seller**.

(b) A **market maker** contacted under paragraph (a) shall agree a price which is fair to the non-members having regard to their instructions and, where a price is agreed that **market maker**, if it is displaying a firm continuous two way quote in the security, shall participate in a stated amount of the business at the agreed dealing price in order to fulfil any **limit orders** and may participate to level a long or short position. The **market maker** shall not thereby prevent the execution by the **member firm** of the order of the initiating non-member.

(c) Paragraph (a) shall not apply where the **member firm**:

(i) is the broking arm of a group which includes a **market maker** registered in the security, in which case the particulars may be given to that **market maker**;

(ii) has recently effected a transaction in the security with another **market maker**, in which case the particulars may be given to that **market maker**; or

(iii) gives the particulars to the **market maker** which that **member firm** believes to be 'the market'.

Obligation when quoting prices larger than displayed

17.21 Where a **market maker** quotes a price on the telephone in a size larger than it is displaying on **SEATS PLUS** the **market maker** is obliged to deal at that quoted price and size. *(rule 17.21 last amended N18&N39/96 – effective 27 August 1996)*

Designated fund manager status

17.22 The **Exchange** may grant **designated fund manager** status to a **member firm** if the **Exchange** is satisfied that the fund manager is incorporated and managed separately from any market making or broker dealing **member firm** within the same group. A **designated fund manager** shall be treated as being a **member firm** unrelated to any **market maker** in the group for the purposes of the **market maker** obligations in this chapter in respect of being approached by another **market maker** or a firm related to another **market maker**.

Removal of orders from SEATS PLUS

17.23 The **member firm** on whose behalf an order in respect of an **AIM security** which is no longer current is displayed shall remove it from **SEATS PLUS**. *(rule 17.23 last amended N18&N39/96 – effective 27 August 1996)*

Dealing agents

17.24 (a) Where a **dealing agent** seeks to effect a transaction for another **member firm** and does not have a relationship with that firm as introducing broker and clearing firm, prior to asking for a price and prior to dealing, the **dealing agent** shall disclose to the firm it approaches:

(i) that it is acting for another **member firm** and shall on request disclose the identity of the firm for which it is acting; and

(ii) if appropriate, that it is acting for a competing **market maker** registered in the security of a **member firm** which is part of a group which includes such a **market maker**;

except where the **dealing agent** is acting at the request of a **designated fund manager** or is approaching a **designated fund manager** and seeking to deal.

(b) A **market maker** which is approached by a **dealing agent** acting for another **market maker** registered in the security in question or a **member firm** which is part of a group which includes a **market maker** in the **AIM security** in question is under no obligation to deal.

17.25 Rule deleted with effect from 27 August 1996. *(N18&N39/96)*

Orders left with member firms

17.26 (a) A **member firm** may accept an order with a **specified price** and size and, if it does so, it is obliged to use its best endeavours to execute that order at the earliest available opportunity. A **member firm** may improve on the original terms of a such an order.

(b) The **member firm** shall prioritise orders with a **specified price** and size by reference to price. Orders at the same price shall be prioritised by order of receipt for execution. An order with a **specified price** and size may be executed in part if the terms of the order so permit.

(c) Where a **member firm** leaves an order with a **specified price** and size with another **member firm** and subsequently wishes to complete any part of that order elsewhere, it shall first inform the other **member firm** that the order is withdrawn or to be re-negotiated and is obliged to fulfil any part of the order which that other **member firm** had already dealt.

(d) If a **market maker** moves its **bid price** on **SEATS PLUS** to or through the **limit** price for which it has a sell order with a **specified price** and size or its **offer price** on **SEATS PLUS** to or through the **limit** price for which it has a buy order with a **specified price** and size, it shall execute that order in full immediately following its change.

(e) Where a **member firm** buys as **principal** at a price lower than the **limit** price for which it has a buy order with a **specified price** and size or sells as **principal** at a higher price than the **limit** price for which it has a sell order with a **specified price** and size, it shall fulfil such orders to the extent that the purchase or sale permits.

(f) A **member firm** may execute a buy order with a **specified price** and size against a sell order with a **specified price** and size.

(rule 17.26 last amended N59&N66/97 – effective 20 October 1997)

Uncompleted business

17.27 (a) An order including a order with a **specified price** and size left by a non-member with a **member firm** during a **business day** shall be treated as being firm for the remainder of the **mandatory quote period** on that day, unless otherwise specifically agreed at or before the time the order was placed. Any unexecuted portion of the order may be cancelled by agreement of the non-member and the **member firm**. If an announcement is released by the **Regulatory News Service** concerning the security involved before the full order has been completed and confirmed to the non-member, the unexecuted portion of the order may be re-negotiated.

(b) If a **member firm**'s business to be dealt is part of an uncompleted or on-going order during the current **mandatory quote period**, it shall disclose that fact to a **market maker**.

(rule 17.27 last amended N59&N66/97 – effective 20 October 1997)

17.28 Rule deleted with effect from 27 August 1996. *(N18&N39/96)*

Settlement agents

17.29 (a) When a **member firm** employs a **settlement agent** as a Model A clearer, as permitted in rule 10.13, transactions shall be effected in the name of the firm transacting the business.

(b) When a **member firm** employs a **settlement agent** as a Model B clearer, as permitted in rule 10.13, transactions shall be effected in the name of the **settlement agent**.

(rule 17.29 last amended N23&N29/97 – effective 22 May 1997)

Appendix 2
AIM MATERIALS

Back and Choice prices

17.30 (a)   When a **market maker** creates a **choice price** or a **back** by opening or moving its quote on **SEATS PLUS** for the duration of the **choice price** or **back** that **market maker** shall effect a deal at its screen price and in a size up to its displayed size upon being approached by a competing **market maker** in the security.

(b)   A **member firm** has the right to effect a transaction on a **back** when it appears on **SEATS PLUS** unless the **Exchange** has declared a fast or an indicative market or the **market maker** has notified the **Exchange** of system problems.

(c)   If, after five minutes, the **choice price** or **back** remains or if a **choice price** or **back** is created before the start of the **mandatory quote period** by a **market maker** opening or changing its quote on **SEATS PLUS** and it is still in place five minutes after the start of the **mandatory quote period**, the **market maker** that created it shall:

(i)   contact the first competing **market maker** with the then best opposing **bid price** or **offer price** (as the case may be) and offer to effect a transaction in up to its own quoted size and at its own quoted price;

(ii)   if its business remains incomplete, contact subsequent **market makers** with the then best opposing **bid price** or **offer price** (as the case may be) on a similar basis; and

(iii)   change its price once its business is completed;

provided, that if the **market maker** that created the **choice price** or **back** has already been approached under paragraph (a), its obligations under sub-paragraphs (c)(i) to (iii) shall begin with **market maker**s with whom it had not already dealt.

(d)   A competing **market maker** contacted under sub-paragraphs (c)(i)–(iii) shall effect a transaction in accordance with rule 17.14 and if it deals in less than the smaller of either **market maker**s displayed size, immediately change its price.

(e)   Paragraphs (c) and (d) do not apply:

(i)   when the market or relevant security had been declared indicative;

(ii)   in a fast market;

(iii)   if either of the relevant **market makers** has notified the **Exchange** of systems problems.

(rule 17.30 last amended N18&N39/96 – effective 27 August 1996)

Tender offers

Procedure for making tender offers

17.31 (a)   In order to provide adequate transparency for **tender offer** arrangements, every **tender offer**, except those made under the **SARs**, must, unless otherwise agreed with the **Exchange**, be conducted in accordance with rules 17.31 to 17.34 inclusive.

(b)   The **Exchange** must be provided with a copy of the circular or advertisement for a **striking price tender** or **fixed price tender** at least five days before the **tender offer** is announced. For any other **tender offer**, a copy of the circular or advertisement must be submitted to the **Exchange** for approval at least five days before the **tender offer** is announced.

(c)   Paid advertisements conforming with the standards in the **SARs** must appear in two national newspapers on the day the **tender offer** is announced, unless a circular is sent to all shareholders in accordance with the requirements of the **Listing Rules**.

(d)   Every **tender offer** must remain open for a minimum of ten calendar days. This period shall begin on the day following the posting of the circular or the publication of the advertisement (as applicable) and shall include the day the **tender offer** closes.

(e)   The **member firm** must provide shareholders with a tender application form, either with the circular or in the advertisement (as applicable), which must include the following:

(i)   the date and time when the **tender offer** closes;

(ii)   the address to which completed tender applications must be returned; and

(iii)   full instructions for completion of tender applications by certificated and uncertificated holders.

(f)   Only applications submitted on valid tender application forms (including a clear photocopy) are to be accepted.

(g)   Separate tender applications must be completed for each shareholder. In the case of dematerialised holdings, the **CREST** participant must submit separate applications for each member account ID within **CREST**.

(h)   The circular or advertisement must contain a statement indicating whether the tender application is revocable or irrevocable once lodged. The conditions of revocable tenders must be approved by the **Exchange** in advance of the **tender offer** announcement referred to in rule 17.31(c).

(i)   In the case of a **net asset value tender**, the circular or advertisement must set out the basis on which the tender price will be calculated.

(rule 17.31 last amended N22/00 – effective 1 May 2000)

Determining the results of tender offers

17.32 (a)   In the case of a **striking price tender**, the **member firm** shall at its discretion set the **striking price**. The **member firm** conducting the offer shall apply the following rules:

(i)   unless sub-paragraph (a)(ii) or paragraph (c) applies, all tender applications offering the **striking price** or a price below the **striking price**, are to be fully accepted at the **striking price**;

(ii)   in the event that there is an over-subscription, tender applications offering the **striking price** are to be scaled down pro rata, unless the circular or advertisement provides that up to a minimum value or quantity of shares tendered at or below the **striking price** will be accepted in full prior to scaling down. Fractions of shares are to be treated equally when determining pro rata entitlements;

(iii) tender applications offering a price above the **striking price** are to be rejected;

(iv) if the circular or advertisement provides that a particular value of shares tendered at or below the **striking price** will be accepted in full prior to scaling down, it must set out the basis on which the value of the holding will be calculated;

(v) if the circular or advertisement sets a minimum price and provides that tender applications can be submitted without a price, then all such tender applications shall be accepted at the **striking price**.

(b) In the case of a **fixed price tender** and a **net asset value tender**:

(i) unless sub-paragraph (b)(ii) or paragraph (c) applies, all tender applications are to be fully accepted;

(ii) in the event that there is an over-subscription, all tender applications are to be scaled down pro rata, unless the circular or advertisement provides that a minimum value or quantity of shares will be accepted in full prior to scaling down. Fractions of shares are to be treated equally when determining pro rata entitlements.

(c) A **tender offer** is void if the total number of shares tendered by shareholders represents less than 1% of the issued share capital of the class of securities to which the offer relates. The **member firm** may stipulate a higher percentage below which the **tender offer** shall be void in the advertisement or circular referred to in rule 17.31(c). Any figure higher than 5% is not permitted unless approved by the **Exchange** in advance of the **tender offer** announcement.

(d) The results of the **tender offer** shall be determined by the **member firm** conducting the offer, and the decision of the **member firm** shall be final. The results must be announced prior to the opening of the **mandatory quote period** on the day following the close of the **tender offer**.

(e) The **member firm** conducting the **tender offer** must make available to the **Exchange**, on request, copies of tender application forms for all tender applications that have not been fully accepted (including invalidly submitted tender applications).

(rule 17.32 last amended N52&N73/99 – effective 9 December 1999)

Reporting of tender offers

17.33 All transactions resulting from a **tender offer** must be trade and **transaction reported** in accordance with the requirements in Chapter 8. *(rule 17.33 last amended N52&N73/99 – effective 9 December 1999)*

17.34 Member firms must separately provide the following information to the **Exchange** once the results of a **striking price tender** are known:

(a) the total number of shares tendered by shareholders and the corresponding percentage of the class of securities tendered for;

(b)   all prices at which the shares were tendered for and the aggregate number of shares tendered at each price;

(c)   the **striking price** applicable in the tender; and

(d)   the aggregate number of shares tendered at the **striking price**.

(rule 17.34 last amended N52&N73/99 – effective 9 December 1999)

17.35–17.39   Rules deleted with effect from 27 August 1996. *(N18&N39/96)*

Publication

17.40 (a)   deleted with effect from 27 August 1996.

(b)   transferred to 17.43(d) with effect from 27 August 1996. *(N18&N39/96)*

Contract notes

17.41 In addition to the requirements of rule 2.8, each contract note issued by a **member firm** in respect of transactions in AIM securities shall bear the following legend:

'This transaction is in respect of AIM securities. Such securities are not admitted to the Official List of the UK Listing Authority. AIM is a market for emerging or smaller companies'.

(rule 17.41 last amended N22/00 – effective 1 May 2000)

Settlement

17.42 (a)   Every transaction in an **AIM security** issued by an issuer in the British Isles shall be settled pursuant to Chapter 10.

(b)   In respect of AIM securities issued by **overseas** issuers, rules 3.24 to 3.32 shall apply to the settlement of transactions in those securities unless:

(i)   the parties agree that the transaction shall be settled in the British Isles; or

(ii)   a transaction is not thereafter duly settled as agreed

and in either case, the rules in Chapter 10 shall apply.

Notification of substantial shareholdings

17.43 (a)   Where a **market maker**'s interest in the nominal value of the relevant share capital of an **AIM security** moves through three per cent or any higher percentage point (whether upwards or downwards), it shall notify the **Exchange** within two days of the transaction or the event which occasioned the increase or decrease.

(b)   Section 208 of the Companies Act 1985 applies in determining whether a firm has a notifiable interest in shares.

(c)   The determination of whether notification is required pursuant to paragraph (a) shall take place at the end of the day on which the transaction or the event occurs.

(d)   The **Exchange** shall publish via the **Regulatory News Service**, in such manner and at such times in accordance with such criteria as it may from time to time specify, details of substantial shareholdings of **market makers** that have been notified to the **Exchange** in accordance with rule 17.43.

(rule 17.43 last amended N18&N39/96 – effective 27 August 1996)

AIM ADMISSION FORM

  London **STOCK EXCHANGE**

Application to be signed by the company

To: AIM, Company Services
     London Stock Exchange
     London EC2N 1HP

_____20___

Name of issuer of the securities:

('The issuer')

hereby applies for the securities detailed below to be admitted for trading on AIM subject to the Rules of the London Stock Exchange

Details of securities to be admitted to trading on AIM

Amounts and descriptions of securities for which application is now being made (e.g. 1,000,000 Ordinary Shares of 5p each):

Details of transaction (e.g. exercise of options, vendor consideration, placing for cash):

Are the securities for which application is now made

(a) identical in all respects?   Yes   No

If no, how do they differ and when will they become identical?

(b) identical in all respects with an existing class of security (further issues only)?   Yes   No

If no, how do they differ and when will they become identical?

Admission to AIM expected on: _____20___

Details of documents of title

Please give details of renounceable document (where applicable)

(a) type of document

(b) Proposed date of issue:

(c) Last day for splitting:
     (i)   Nil paid:
     (ii)   Partly paid:
     (iii)   Fully paid:

(d) Last day for renunciation:

Company's accounting year end:

Name(s) and position(s) of contact(s) of issuer regarding the application:

Contact address and telephone number:

Registered address (if different from above)

Declaration

(i)   The directors of the issuer have received advice and guidance (from the nominated adviser or other appropriate professional adviser) as to the nature of their responsibilities and obligations to ensure compliance by the issuer with the AIM Admission Rules in Chapter 16 of the Rules of the London Stock Exchange as amended from time to time and fully understand and accept these responsibilities and obligations

(ii)   the issuer has taken appropriate advice where necessary and has acted appropriately on any advice given

(iii) the admission document complies with the AIM Admission Rules and includes all such information as investors would reasonably require, and reasonably expect to find there, for the purposes of making an informed assessment of the assets and liabilities, financial position, profits and losses, and prospects of the issuer of the securities and the rights attaching to those securities

(iv)   in the opinion of the issuer, having made due and careful enquiry, the working capital available to the issuer and its group is sufficient for their present requirements

(v)   any profit forecast, estimate or projection in the admission document has been made after due and careful enquiry by the issuer; and

(vi)   procedures have been established which provide a reasonable basis for the directors to make proper judgements as to the financial position and prospects of the issuer and its group.

Undertaking

We undertake to:
i   comply with the AIM Admission Rules set out in Chapter 16 of the Rules of the London Stock Exchange as amended from time to time by the Exchange; and

ii   seek advice and guidance from the nominated adviser when appropriate and act appropriately on such advice.

Signed:

Director, secretary or other duly authorised officer for and on behalf of
Name of the issuer:

Note: paragraphs (iii) and (v) of the Declaration are applicable only if this application relates to an issue of securities requiring the publication of an admission document. Delete if appropriate.

Appendix 3

NOMINATED ADVISERS

Appendix 3
NOMINATED ADVISERS

EXAMPLE: UNDERTAKING IN NOMINATED ADVISER AGREEMENT

The Company and each of the Directors hereby acknowledges that *NOMAD* owes responsibilities to the London Stock Exchange as Nominated Adviser, and that the London Stock Exchange may review *NOMAD*'s registration as a Nominated Adviser and impose sanctions upon *NOMAD* with regard to the conduct of the Company and the Directors in relation to the AIM rules and, accordingly:

> The Company and each of the Directors hereby undertakes to comply (and insofar as he is able to do so, to procure such compliance by the Company) forthwith with all proper and reasonable directions given by *NOMAD* in relation to the AIM Rules; and
>
> The Company agrees to indemnify *NOMAD* and each of its Directors, Officers, Employees and Agents against all losses, liabilities, demands, claims, costs, charges and expenses (including proper and reasonable legal fees and expenses) which any of them may suffer or incur as a result of or arising out of or in connection with any breach of the AIM Rules by the Company or any Director and which does not arise as a result of the provision by *NOMAD* of material or incorrect advice in relation to the AIM Rules.
>
> Each of the Company and the Directors undertakes to inform *NOMAD* forthwith upon becoming aware of any breach by the Company and/or any Director of the AIM Rules and to request the advice and guidance of *NOMAD* in relation to all matters relevant to the Company's compliance with the AIM Rules.

The Company undertakes to *NOMAD* to comply on a timely basis with all obligations upon AIM companies in the form from time to time specified by the London Stock Exchange, the obligations at the date of this agreement being those referred to in Chapter 16 of the AIM Rules and each Director severally undertakes that for so long as he is a Director of the Company he will do everything reasonably within his power as such to procure that the Company complies with such continuing obligations.

EXAMPLE: DIRECTOR'S LETTER TO A NOMINATED ADVISER

Dear Sirs

I hereby confirm that, being a Director of . . . plc ('the Company') I have had explained to me by . . .[1] my responsibilities as a Director of a Company whose securities are traded on the Alternative Investment Market.

In consideration of your agreeing to be the Nominated Adviser to the Company, I hereby undertake:

(a) to comply forthwith with all proper and reasonable directions given by you in relation to compliance of the AIM Rules;

(b) to inform you forthwith upon becoming aware of any breach by the Company and/or any Director of the AIM Rules and to request your advice and guidance in relation to all matters relevant to the Company's compliance with the AIM Rules;

(c) to comply on a timely basis for so long as I am a Director of the Company and to do everything reasonably within my power as such to procure that the Company complies with all obligations upon AIM companies in the form from time to time specified by the London Stock Exchange, the obligations at the date of this letter being those referred to in the AIM Rules.

---

1   This may be the Nominated Adviser, the Company's lawyer or the Director's personal lawyer.

APPLICATION FORM NA1

**Nominated advisers
application form – NA1**

 London **STOCK EXCHANGE**

1. Name of applicant:

Trading name (if different):

Address:

Postcode:

Tel: | Fax: | STX:

2. Nature of entity (limited company, unlimited company, partnership):

If a body corporate, country of incorporation:

3. Name of contact:

4. Is the applicant:
 i Authorised under the Financial Services Act 1986? | Yes | No

Please indicate any self regulating organisation(s) or recognised professional body of which the applicant is a member:

If appropriate, state the applicant's lead regulator:

 ii A member of the London Stock Exchange | Yes | No

5. Has the applicant been operating in a principal corporate finance advisory role for at least the last three years? | Yes | No

ID. 2.1568

6. Describe completed initial public offers, demergers, or other issues of securities involving listing particulars, USM particulars, a Companies Act prospectus or equivalent EU documents or other appropriate major transactions involving listed or other public companies, in which the applicant has acted in a principal corporate finance advisory role within the last three years*:

Transaction:	Experience:	Date:

*Continue on a separate sheet where necessary

7. Name at least four suitably qualified and experienced executive staff, as defined in the Nominated Advisers Eligibility Criteria as published by the Exchange from time to time.

Title	First name	Surname

8. State the number of staff who will be involved in an executive capacity in nominated adviser activities:

9. What procedures and controls are in place to ensure that personnel do not act beyond their proper authority?

Note: Copies of procedures may be requested during the application process.

10. Is there any other information which you think may be relevant to the Exchange in considering this application? Yes No

If the answer is yes, give details on a separate sheet.

**Appendix 3
NOMINATED ADVISERS**

3

11. Nominated adviser's undertaking to the London Stock Exchange (to be signed by all applicants)

Name of nominated adviser

```
┌─────────────────────────────────────────────────────────────────────┐
│                                                                       │
└─────────────────────────────────────────────────────────────────────┘
```

hereby applies for approval as a nominated adviser for the purpose of the AIM Admission Rules and if you grant this application undertakes to:

i   discharge its responsibilities as a nominated adviser under the AIM Admission Rules from time to time
ii   advise you in writing without delay if:
    a   it ceases to be an authorised person as required by Rule 16.28 of the AIM Admission Rules
    b   it is the subject of an intervention order or any disciplinary proceedings or similar action by any regulator under the Financial Services Act 1986 or under any comparable legislation in any member state outside the United Kingdom
iii advise you without delay of any change to the staff who are involved in an executive capacity in nominated adviser activities, including details of the qualifications and experience of any new staff to be involved in an executive capacity in nominated adviser activities
iv   advise you in writing without delay of its resignation or dismissal, giving details of any relevant facts or circumstances
v   perform the role of nominated adviser only for any organisation from which it is independent as defined in the eligibility criteria as published by the Exchange from time to time
vi   continue to comply with the eligibility criteria

and acknowledges that:

vii you may censure it and/or remove its name from the register of nominated advisers maintained by you if:
    a   you consider that it is in breach of its responsibilities
    b   you consider that the integrity and reputation of the market may have been impaired as a result of its conduct or judgement; or
    c   the number of suitably qualified and experienced executive staff in its employ falls below four

and that you may publicise the fact that you have done so and the reasons for your action

viii appeals to the AIM Appeals Committee will be dealt with in accordance with the AIM Appeals Procedures as published from time to time.

We declare that the information supplied is complete and correct and agree to comply with the additional notification requirements.

We have read the Nominated Advisers Eligibility Criteria and framework for making applications and believe that this application conforms to the criteria (except as specifically notified to you with this application).

This undertaking must be signed by two directors, partners or duly authorised officers of the nominated adviser.

Signed:	Date:
Name of signatory in block capitals:	
Partner, director or duly authorised officer, for and on behalf of (name of nominated adviser):	

Signed:	Date:
Name of signatory in block capitals:	
Partner/director or duly authorised officer, for and on behalf of (name of nominated adviser):	

Please return this form to:
AIM
London Stock Exchange
London EC2N 1HP

Appendix to nominated advisers form NA1

1. Name of applicant:

2. Give details of executive staff who will be involved in nominated adviser activities*.

In the examination column enter the appropriate number as follows:

i   the individual has passed, been exempted or grandfathered from the SFA's Corporate Finance Representative Examination or General/Securities Representative Examination

ii the individual is applying for a waiver from the nominated adviser examination requirements. **Form NA3 must be attached in such cases.**

iii the individual has already been granted a waiver from the nominated adviser examination requirements

All Form NA2s must be submitted at the time of application or as soon as possible thereafter. Delay in sending the forms will lead to delay in the handling of the application.

If any of the executive staff involved in nominated adviser activities are seeking to have the examination requirement waived, attach Form NA3 in addition to Form NA2.

Title:	First name(s):	Surname:	Examination:	Form NA2 attached:	
				Yes	No
				Yes	No
				Yes	No
				Yes	No
				Yes	No
				Yes	No
				Yes	No
				Yes	No
				Yes	No
				Yes	No
				Yes	No
				Yes	No
				Yes	No
				Yes	No
				Yes	No

*Continue on a separate sheet where necessary

Appendix 3 NOMINATED ADVISERS

APPLICATION FORM NA2

Nominated adviser
employee form – NA2

  London **STOCK EXCHANGE**

This form is to be completed when:

A   An initial application is submitted by a nominated adviser applicant

B   An executive staff member who has not previously been involved in nominated adviser activities joins an existing nominated adviser; or

C   An executive staff member is to be named by a nominated adviser as being suitably qualified and experienced, as defined in the Nominated Advisers Eligibility Criteria as published by the London Stock Exchange from time to time.

1. Personal details:

Name of nominated adviser applicant:

2. Executive staff member's full name:

Title: First name(s):

Surname: Date of birth:

3. Private address:

Postcode:

4. Qualifications:
Provide details of any professional or business qualifications and/or memberships of any professional bodies, exchanges or trade associations obtained or applied for.*

5. Have you passed, been grandfathered into, exempted or received a waiver from the SFA RP5 or General/Securities Representatives Examination?   Yes No

If yes, which?

If no, are you applying for a waiver from the examination requirements for executive staff involved in nominated adviser activities?   Yes No

If yes, attach completed form NA3 and fee if appropriate.

*Continue answers on a separate sheet where necessary

ID: 2.1568

6. Employment History

Provide details of your employment history (last 10 years, most recent first)*:

Dates from/to:	Name and address of organisation:	Position held/responsibilities:

7. Transaction history

Describe completed initial public offers, demergers, or other issues of securities involving listing particulars, USM particulars, a Companies Act prospectus or equivalent EU documents or other appropriate major transactions involving listed or other public companies in which the nominated adviser applicant has acted in a principal corporate finance advisory role within the last three years and in which you have had direct experience. If this includes equivalent experience gained whilst working for a previous employer, this fact must be indicated*.

Transaction:	Experience:	Date:

8. Declaration

I declare that the information supplied is complete and correct.

Signature:	Date:
Name of signatory in block capitals:	

*Continue answers on a separate sheet where necessary

Please return this form to:
AIM
London Stock Exchange
London EC2N 1HP

Appendix 3
NOMINATED ADVISERS

EXAMINATION WAIVER APPLICATION FORM NA3

Nominated advisers
Examination waiver
application form – NA3

 London STOCK EXCHANGE

Application for waiver of examination requirements

Name:

Date of birth:

Name of applicant:

Category of waiver applied for:

Notes

There are three categories of waiver:

Category A applies where an individual has reasonably continuous relevant corporate finance experience since 1 January 1986. To demonstrate 'relevant experience' an individual must have been involved in an executive capacity in giving corporate finance advice, including having direct contact with client companies and/or the London Stock Exchange.

Category A applicants must complete questions 1 and 2 and the declaration.

Category B applies where an individual has had three years' recent and reasonably continuous experience in giving relevant corporate finance advice and holds one of the following:

i   qualifications of a barrister, advocate or solicitor who has been called or admitted in any part of the UK

ii   qualifications for appointment as an auditor, accountant or public company secretary in the UK

iii   membership of the Securities Institute.

Category B applicants must complete questions 1 and 2 and the declaration.

Category C applies where other individuals seek a waiver by virtue of the breadth of their experience in giving corporate finance advice. Very few applications are expected to be granted under category C.

Category C applicants must complete questions 1 and 3 and the declaration.

ID: 2.1568

1. (All applicants)

Describe your corporate finance experience since 1 January 1986. State in the direct contact column if you had direct contact with client companies and/or the Exchange.

Date: (month and year)	Employer:	Job title and major responsibilities	Direct contact:

2. (Category A and B applicants)

Do you have one of the following:

i   qualifications of a barrister, advocate or solicitor who has been called or admitted in any part of the UK?   Yes   No

ii   qualifications of an auditor, accountant or public company secretary in the UK?   Yes   No

iii membership of the Securities Institute?   Yes   No

If yes, **provide documentary evidence.** If you have answered yes to more than one, you need only provide documentary evidence for one of the above.

3. (Category C applicants only)

Describe your corporate finance experience and your justification for seeking an exceptional waiver*:

*Continue on a separate sheet if necessary

Declaration (All applicants)

I declare that the information supplied is complete and correct.

I understand that the information may be verified in such manner as the Exchange may decide.

I attach (**Category B** applicants only) documentary evidence of qualifications/Securities Institute membership ☐

(tick if appropriate)

Signature: Date:

Please return this form to:
AIM
London Stock Exchange
London EC2N 1HP

UNDERTAKING IN NOMINATED ADVISER AGREEMENT

 London **STOCK EXCHANGE**

Declaration by the nominated adviser

To: AIM, Company Services
London Stock Exchange
London EC2N 1HP

_____20____

Full name of nominated adviser

Full name of issuer and details of the securities to which this declaration applies (e.g. company name, 1,000,000 Ordinary Shares of 5p each):

Type of issue for which application for admission to trading on AIM is being made (indicate if not appropriate):

Method of settlement:

1. _____ , a partner/director of the above nominated adviser, or an officer duly authorised to give this declaration, hereby confirm

a that, in relation to the application for admission:

   i the directors of the issuer have received advice and guidance (from this firm or other appropriate professional advisers) as to the nature of their responsibilities and obligations to ensure compliance by the issuer with the AIM Admission Rules in Chapter 16 of the Rules of the London Stock Exchange as amended from time to time;

   ii to the best of my knowledge and belief, having made due and careful enquiry, all relevant requirements of the AIM Admission Rules (save for the admission document's compliance with Regulation 9 of the Public Offers of Securities Regulations 1995) have been complied with; and

   iii we are satisfied that, in our opinion, the issue and its securities are appropriate to be admitted to AIM.

(The statements in paragraph a are applicable only if this application relates to an issue of securities requiring the publication of an admission document. Delete if inappropriate).

b that this firm will be available at all times to advise and guide the directors of the issuer as to their responsibilities and obligations to ensure compliance by the issuer on an ongoing basis with the AIM Admission Rules;

c that this firm will comply with the AIM Admission Rules applicable to it in its role as nominated adviser; and

d that this firm will confirm to the Exchange in writing when it ceases to be the issuer's nominated adviser.

Signed:

Partner/director or duly authorised officer, for and on behalf of
Name of nominated adviser:

Admission to AIM expected on: _____20_____

Name(s) of contact(s) at nominated adviser regarding the application:

Appendix 3
NOMINATED ADVISERS

Telephone/STX number.

AIM REGISTER OF NOMINATED ADVISERS (1 June 2001)

	Contact	*Telephone/website*
AIB Corporate Finance Limited		
85 Pembroke Road	Jarlath Quinn	00 353 1 667 0233
Ballsbridge, Dublin 4		
Ireland		
Altium Capital Limited		
15 Portland Place	Stephen Georgiadis	020 7872 6300
London W1N 3AA		
5 Ralli Court	Mark Dickenson	0161 831 9133
West Riverside		www.apax.co.uk
Manchester M3 5FT		
ARM Corporate Finance Limited		
12 Pepper Street	Ian Fenn	020 7512 0191
London E14 9RP	Jim McGeever	www.armcf.com
Arthur Andersen		
1 Surrey Street	Jonathan Hinton	020 7438 3000
London WC2R 2PS		
1 Victoria Square	Christopher Hawkley	0121 233 2101
Birmingham B1 1BD		
1 City Square	Philip Evans	0113 207 7000
Leeds LS1 2AL		www.arthurandersen.com
Beaumont Cornish		
Georgian House	Roland Cornish	020 7628 3396
63 Coleman Street		www.beaumontcornish.co.uk
London EC2R 5BB		
Beeson Gregory Limited		
The Registry	Chris Callaway	020 7488 4040
Royal Mint Court	Julia Henderson	www.beeson-gregory.co.uk
London EC3N 4EY	Nicholas Rodgers	
Brewin Dolphin Securities Limited		
48 Vincent Street	Elizabeth Kennedy	0141 221 7733
Glasgow G2 5TS		
PO Box 512	Mark Brady	0161 839 4222
National House		www.brewindolphin.co.uk
36 St Annes Street		
Manchester M60 2EP		

Bridgewell Corporate Finance Limited
6 Oxford Street   Doug Manuel   0115 941 9721
Nottingham
NG7 5BH

21 New Street   Mike Sutton   020 7623 3000
Bishopsgate   www.bridgewell.co.uk
London EC2M 4HR

British Linen Advisers Limited
12 Melville Street   William Macdonald   0131 243 8534
Edinburgh EH3 7NS

Brown, Shipley & Co. Limited
Founders Court   Andrew Smith   020 7606 9833
Lothbury   www.brownshipley.com
London EC2R 7HE

Cazenove & Co.
12 Tokenhouse Yard   Zofia Kwiatek   020 7588 2828
London EC2R 7AN   www.cazenove.com

Charles Stanley & Company Limited
25 Luke Street   Robin Dunham   020 7739 8200
London EC2A 4AR   www.charlesstanley.co.uk

Close Brothers Corporate Finance Limited
10 Crown Place   James Oliver   020 7655 3100
Clifton Street   www.cbcf.com
London EC2A 4FT

Collins Stewart Limited
21 New Street   Doug Manuel   020 7283 1133
Bishopsgate   www.collinsstewart.com
London EC2M 4HR

Corporate Synergy plc
Piercy House   Lindsay Mair   020 7256 2576
7/9 Copthall Avenue   www.corporate.uk
London EC2R 7NJ

Broadwalk House   Simon Bennett   020 7588 4000
5 Appold Street   www.creditlyonnais.com
London EC2A 2DA

Credit Suisse First Boston (Europe) Limited
One Cabot Square   Mark Seligman   020 7888 8888
London E14 4QR   www.csfb.com

Dawnay, Day Corporate Finance Limited
8–10 Grosvenor Gardens   David Floyd   020 7509 4570
London SW1W 0DH

Deloitte & Touche

Columbia Centre	Lionel Young	01344 454 445
Market Street		
Bracknell		
Berkshire RG12 1PA		

Leda House	Ann Kennedy	01223 460 222
Station Road		
Cambridge CB1 2RN		

Stonecutter Court	Lionel Young	020 7936 3000
1 Stonecutter Street		www.deloitte.co.uk
London EC4A 4TR		

Deutsche Bank AG London

Winchester House	Anthony MacWinnie	020 7545 8000
1 Great Winchester Street		www.db.com
London EC2N 2DB		

Ermgassen & Co. Ltd

24 Lombard Street	Christopher Stainforth	020 7929 2000
London EC3V 9AD		www.ermgassen.com

Ernst & Young

Becket House	Paul Smith	020 7928 2000
1 Lambeth Palace Road		www.eyuk.com
London SE1 7EU		

Goodbody Corporate Finance Limited

122 Pembroke Road	Carole Corby	00 353 1 667 0420
Ballsbridge Park		www.goodbody.ie
Ballsbridge		
Dublin 4		

Grant Thornton

Grant Thornton House	Ian Smart	020 7383 5100
Melton Street	Gerald Beaney	www.grantthornton.co.uk
Euston Square		
London NW1 2EP		

Granville Baird Limited

Mint House	Andrew Perkins	020 7488 1212
77 Mansell Street		www.granville-plc.com
London E1 8AF		

Hawkpoint Partners Limited

4 Great St Helens	Jeremy Moczarski	020 7665 4500
London EC3A 6HA		www.hawkpoint.com

Hoare Govett Limited

250 Bishopsgate	Carol Raymond	020 7678 8000
London EC2M 4AA		www.abnamro.com

Appendix 3
NOMINATED ADVISERS

HSBC Investment Bank plc
Vintner's Place   Anthony Stewart-Jones   020 7336 9000
68 Upper Thames Street   www.hsbc.com
London EC4V 3BJ

IBI Corporate Finance Limited
26 Fitzwilliam Place   Gerard Heffernan   00 353 1 661 6633
Dublin 2
Ireland

ING Barings Limited
60 London Wall   Ian Douglas   020 7767 1000
London EC2M 5TQ   www.ingbarings.com

Insinger English Trust
44 Worship Street   Alexandra Cornforth   020 7377 6161
London EC2A 2JT   e-mail
                                                            infocorpfin@insinger.com
                                                            www.insinger.com

Investec Bank (UK) Limited trading as Investec Henderson Crosthwaite
2 Gresham Street   Simon Grafftey-Smith   020 7597 5970
London EC2V 7QP   www.investec.co.uk

J & E Davy
Davy House   Tom Byrne   00 353 1 679 6363
49 Dawson Street   www.davy.ie
Dublin 2
Republic of Ireland

John East & Partners Limited
Crystal Gate   John East   020 7628 2200
28–30 Worship Street   www.johneastpartners.com
London EC2A 2AH

Kennedy Gee Corporate Finance Ltd
19 Cavendish Square   Keith Lassman   020 7636 1616
London W1A 2AW   www.hk.law.co.uk

Kleinwort Benson Limited trading as Dresdner Kleinwort Benson
20 Fenchurch Street   Robert Murdin   020 7623 8000
London EC3P 3DB   www.dresdnerkb.com

KPMG Corporate Finance
8 Salisbury Square   Susan Hodge   020 7311 1000
London EC4Y 8BB

Saltire Court   David McCorquodale   0131 222 2000
20 Castle Terrace
Edinburgh EH1 2EH

2 Cornwall Street   Stephen Halbert   0121 2333 1666
Birmingham B3 2DL

1 Forest Gate   Nick Standen   01293 652 000
Brighton Road   www.kpmg.com
Crawley RH11 9PT

Marshall Securities Limited
Crusader House   John Webb   020 7490 3788
145–157 St John Street
London EC1V 4QJ

Matrix Corporate Finance
9–10 Savile Row   Stephen Mischler   020 7439 6050
London W1X 1AF   www.matrixgroup.co.uk

Nabarro Wells & Co. Limited
Saddlers House   John Robertson   020 7710 7400
Gutter Lane   www.nabarro-wells.co.uk
Cheapside
London EC2V 6BR

NCB Stockbrokers Limited
3 George's Dock   Diane Hodgson   00 3531 611 5611
International Financial   www.ncb.ie
Services Centre
Dublin 1

NM Rothschild & Sons Limited
82 King Street   Peter Bates   0161 827 3800
Manchester M2 4WQ   www.nmrothschild.com

Noble & Company Limited
4th Floor   020 7367 5600
1 Frederick's Place
London EC2R 8AB

76 George Street
Edinburgh EH2 3BU   Henry Chaplin   0131 225 9677

Nomura International plc
Nomura House   Catherine McLoughlin 020 7521 2000
1 St Martin's-le-Grand   www.nomura.co.uk
London EC1A 4NP

Numis Securities Limited
Cheapside House   Henry Jenkins   020 7776 1500
138 Cheapside   www.numiscorp.com
London EC2V 6LH

Old Mutual Securities
30 Lombard Street   John Folliott Vaughan 020 7002 4600
London EC3V 9EN

Temple Court   John Folliott Vaughan 0121 200 2244
35 Bull Street
Birmingham B4 6ES

1 St James Square   Kevin Wilson   0161 827 7000
Manchester M2 6DN   www.omsecurities.co.uk

Peel, Hunt & Company Limited
62 Threadneedle Street   Christopher   020 7418 8900
London EC2R 8HP   Holdsworth-Hunt   www.peelhunt.com
                          Adam Hart

PricewaterhouseCoopers
1 London Bridge   Peter Clokey   020 7939 3000
London SE1 9QL

Plumtree Court   William Morgan   020 7582 5000
London EC4A 4HT   Mark Speller   www.pwcglobal.com

Rathbone Neilson Cobbold Limited
Port of Liverpool Building Mike Sawbridge   0151 236 6666
Pier Head   www.rathbones.com
Liverpool L3 1NW

Robert Fleming & Co. Limited
25 Copthall Avenue   Jeremy Kean   020 7638 5858
London EC2R 7DR   www.flemings.com

Rowan Dartington & Co. Limited
7th Floor   John Wakefield   0117 933 0020
The Colson Centre   www.rowan-dartington.co.uk
Bristol BS1 4XE

Salomon Brothers UK Equity Limited
111 Buckingham Palace Road
London SW1W 0SB   James Anderson   020 7721 2000

Seymour Pierce Limited
2nd Floor, 29/30 Cornhill   Richard Feigen   020 7648 8700
London EC3V 3NF   www.seymourpierce.com

SG Securities (London) Limited
Exchange House   David Mordaunt   020 7638 9000
Primrose Street   www.socgen.com
London EC2A 2DD

Shore Capital & Corporate Limited
Bond Street House   Graham Shore   020 7734 7293
14 Clifford Street   www.shorecap.co.uk
London W1X 1RE

Smith & Williamson
No 1 Riding House Street   Dr A. Basirov   020 7637 5377
London W1A 3AS   www.smith.williamson.co.uk

Société Générale trading as SG Hambros

SG House	Roger Bawcutt	020 7676 6000
41 Tower Hill		www.socgen.co.uk
London EC3N 4SG		

Solomon Hare Corporate Finance

Oakfield House	Stephen Toole	0117 933 3344
Oakfield Grove		www.solomonhare.co.uk
Clifton		
Bristol BS8 2BN		

Strand Partners Limited

110 Park Street	Richard Fenhalls	020 7409 3494
London W1Y 3RB		

Teather & Greenwood Limited

Beaufort House	Jeremy Delmar-Morgan	020 7426 9000
15 St Botolph Street		www.teathers.com
London EC3A 7QR		

UBS Warburg

1 Finsbury Avenue	Michael Lacey-Solymar	020 7567 8000
London EC2M 2PP		www.wdr.com

WestLB Panmure Limited

New Broad Street House	Richard Potts	020 7638 4010
35 New Broad Street		www.westlbpanmure.com
London EC2M 1SQ		

Williams de Broë Plc

PO Box 515	Tim Worlledge	020 7588 7511
6 Broadgate		
London EC2M 2RP		
1 Waterloo Street	Ian R. Stanway	0121 609 0050
Birmingham B2 5PG		
4 Park Place		
Leeds LS1 2RU	Joanne Lake	0113 243 1619

Appendix 3
NOMINATED ADVISERS

SAMPLE TIMETABLE OF A PROPOSED ADMISSION TO THE STOCK EXCHANGE

Date	Event	Responsibility
D–40	Instruct all parties	Company
D–35	Engagement letters signed	Company/all parties
D–30	Initial draft document	NOMAD
D–36	Comments on initial draft	All parties
D–32	Discussion meeting	NOMAD/broker/company
D–27	First draft document	NOMAD/company/solicitors
D–22	Comments on first draft	All parties
D–20	Second draft	NOMAD/company/solicitors
	Draft accountant's report	Reporting accountants
	Draft statutory accounts	Company/auditors
D–15	Comments on second draft	All parties
	Draft verification notes	Solicitors
D–13	Final draft	NOMAD/company/solicitors
D–12	Verification	All parties
D–11	Completion	All parties
	Placing commences	Broker
D–10	10-day documents	NOMAD
D–6	Placing completed	Broker
D–4	Application to AIM	NOMAD/company
D Day	Admission	

The above timetable assumes that the company is established and has unqualified audited accounts for previous years available, and that there is no necessity for any independent reports on technology, patents etc. The preparation of any accounts or reports will extend the timetable.

Prospectus meetings and discussion meetings will take place within the above timetable as necessary.

Appendix 4

CORPORATE GOVERNANCE

THE COMBINED CODE
PRINCIPLES OF GOOD GOVERNANCE AND CODE OF BEST PRACTICE

Derived by the Committee on Corporate Governance from the Committee's Final Report and from the Cadbury and Greenbury Reports.[1]

Preamble

1. In the Committee's final report we said that, in response to many requests, we intended to produce a set of principles and code which embraced Cadbury, Greenbury and the committee's own work. This Combined Code fulfils that undertaking.

2. The Combined Code is now issued in final form, and includes a number of changes made by The London Stock Exchange, with the Committee's agreement, following the consultation undertaken by the Exchange on the committee's original draft.

3. The Combined Code contains both principles and detailed Code provisions. We understand that it is the intention of The London Stock Exchange to introduce a requirement on listed companies to make a disclosure statement in two parts.

4. In the first part of the statement, the company will be required to report on how it applies the principles in the Combined Code. We make clear in our report that we do not prescribe the form or content of this part of the statement, the intention being that companies should have a free hand to explain their governance policies in the light of the principles, including any special circumstances applying to them which have led to a particular approach. It must be for shareholders and others to evaluate this part of the company's statement.

5. In the second part of the statement the company will be required either to confirm that it complies with the Code provisions or – where it does not – provide an explanation. Again, it must be for shareholders and others to evaluate such explanations.

6. In our report we make clear that companies should be ready to explain their governance policies, including any circumstances justifying departure from best practice; and that those concerned with the evaluation of governance should do so with common sense, and with due regard to companies' individual circumstances.

7. We also make clear in our report that it is still too soon to assess definitively the results of the Cadbury and more especially the Greenbury codes. We see this Combined Code as a consolidation of the work of the three committees, not as a new departure. We have therefore retained the substance of the two earlier codes except

Appendix 4
CORPORATE GOVERNANCE

---

1   The Combined Code has been reproduced by kind permission of The Financial Services Authority.

in those few cases where we take a different view from our predecessors. We should in particular like to make clear, in relation to the detailed provisions in the Listing Rules on directors' remuneration, that we envisage no change except where we take a different view from the Greenbury committee. With two exceptions, relating to the status of the remuneration committee, and the compensation payable to an executive director on loss of office, these changes are minor.

8. Section 1 of the Combined Code contains the corporate governance principles and code provisions applicable to all listed companies incorporated in the United Kingdom. These would be covered by the statement referred to in paragraphs 3–5 above, which will be required by the Listing Rules. Section 2 contains principles and code provisions applicable to institutional shareholders with regard to their voting, dialogue with companies and evaluation of a company's governance arrangements. These are not matters which are appropriate for the Listing Rules to include within the disclosure requirement. Nevertheless we regard Section 2 of this Combined Code as an integral part of our recommendations; we commend it to the organisations representing institutional shareholders and we hope that at least the major institutions will voluntarily disclose to their clients and the public the extent to which they are able to give effect to these provisions.

9. We have not included in the Combined Code principle D.IV in Chapter 2 of our final report, which reads as follows:

    'External Auditors. The external auditors should independently report to shareholders in accordance with statutory and professional requirements and independently assure the board on the discharge of its responsibilities under D.I and D.II above in accordance with professional guidance.'

    We say in paragraph 6.7 of the report that we recommend neither any additional prescribed requirements nor the removal of any existing requirements for auditors in relation to governance or publicly reported information, some of which derive from the Listing Rules. This recommendation is accepted by The London Stock Exchange. But the existing requirements for auditors will be kept under review, as a matter of course, by the responsible organisations.

Committee on Corporate Governance

June 1998

Part 1: Principles of Good Governance

Section 1 Companies

A. Directors

The Board

1. Every listed company should be headed by an effective board which should lead and control the company.

Chairman and CEO

2. There are two key tasks at the top of every public company – the running of the board and the executive responsibility of the company's business. There should be a

clear division of responsibilities at the head of the company which will ensure a balance of power and authority, such that no one individual has unfettered powers of decision.

Board Balance

3. The board should include a balance of executive and non-executive directors (including independent non-executives) such that no individual or small group of individuals can dominate the board's decision taking.

Supply of Information

4. The board should be supplied in a timely manner with information in a form and of a quality appropriate to enable it to discharge its duties.

Appointments to the Board

5. There should be a formal and transparent procedure for the appointment of new directors to the board.

Re-election

6. All directors should be required to submit themselves for re-election at regular intervals and at least every three years.

B. Directors' Remuneration

The Level and Make-up of Remuneration

1. Levels of remuneration should be sufficient to attract and retain the directors needed to run the company successfully, but companies should avoid paying more than is necessary for this purpose. A proportion of executive directors' remuneration should be structured so as to link rewards to corporate and individual performance.

Procedure

2. Companies should establish a formal and transparent procedure for developing policy on executive remuneration and for fixing the remuneration packages of individual directors. No director should be involved in deciding his or her own remuneration.

Disclosure

3. The company's annual report should contain a statement of remuneration policy and details of the remuneration of each director.

C. Relations with Shareholders

Dialogue with Institutional Shareholders

1. Companies should be ready, where practicable, to enter into a dialogue with institutional shareholders based on the mutual understanding of objectives.

Appendix 4
CORPORATE GOVERNANCE

Constructive Use of the AGM

2. Boards should use the AGM to communicate with private investors and encourage their participation.

D. Accountability and Audit

Financial Reporting

1. The board should present a balanced and understandable assessment of the company's position and prospects.

Internal Control

2. The board should maintain a sound system of internal control to safeguard shareholders' investment and the company's assets.

Audit Committee and Auditors

3. The board should establish formal and transparent arrangements for considering how they should apply the financial reporting and internal control principles and for maintaining an appropriate relationship with the company's auditors.

Section 2 Institutional Shareholders

E. Institutional Investors

Shareholder Voting

1. Institutional shareholders have a responsibility to make considered use of their votes.

Dialogue with Companies

2. Institutional shareholders should be ready where practicable, to enter into a dialogue with companies based on the mutual understanding of objectives.

Evaluation of Governance Disclosures

3. When evaluating companies' governance arrangements, particularly those relating to board structure and composition, institutional investors should give due weight to all relevant factors drawn to their attention.

Part 2: Code of Best Practice

Section 1 Companies

A. Directors

A.1 *The Board*

Principle **Every listed company should be headed by an effective board which should lead and control the company.**

Code Provisions

A.1.1 The board should meet regularly.

A.1.2 The board should have a formal schedule of matters specifically reserved to it for decision.

A.1.3 There should be a procedure agreed by the board for directors in the furtherance of their duties to take independent professional advice if necessary, at the company's expense.

A.1.4 All directors should have access to the advice and services of the company secretary, who is responsible to the board for ensuring that board procedures are followed and that applicable rules and regulations are complied with. Any question of the removal of the company secretary should be a matter for the board as a whole.

A.1.5 All directors should bring an independent judgement to bear on issues of strategy, performance, resources, including key appointments, and standards of conduct.

A.1.6 Every director should receive appropriate training on the first occasion that he or she is appointed to the board of a listed company, and subsequently as necessary.

A.2 Chairman and CEO

Principle **There are two key tasks at the top of every public company – the running of the board and the executive responsibility for the running of the company's business. There should be a clear division of responsibilities at the head of the company which will ensure a balance of power and authority, such that no one individual has unfettered powers of decision.**

Code Provision

A.2.1 A decision to combine the posts of chairman and chief executive officer in one person should be publicly justified. Whether the posts are held by different people or by the same person, there should be a strong and independent non-executive element on the board, with a recognised senior member other than the chairman to whom concerns can be conveyed. The chairman, chief executive and senior independent director should be identified in the annual report.

A.3 Board Balance

Principle **The board should include a balance of executive and non-executive directors (including independent non-executives) such that no individual or small group of individuals can dominate the board's decision taking.**

Code Provisions

A.3.1 The board should include non-executive directors of sufficient calibre and number for their views to carry significant weight in the board's decisions. Non-executive directors should comprise not less than one third of the board.

A.3.2 The majority of non-executive directors should be independent of management and free from any business or other relationship which could materially interfere with the exercise of their independent judgement.

Non-executive directors considered by the board to be independent in this sense should be identified in the annual report.

A.4 *Supply of information*

Principle **The board should be supplied in a timely manner with information in a form and of a quality appropriate to enable it to discharge its duties.**

Code Provision

A.4.1   Management has an obligation to provide the board with appropriate and timely information, but information volunteered by management is unlikely to be enough in all circumstances and directors should make further enquiries where necessary. The chairman should ensure that all directors are properly briefed on issues arising at board meetings.

A.5 *Appointments to the Board*

Principle **There should be a formal and transparent procedure for the appointment of new directors to the board.**

Code Provision

A.5.1   Unless the board is small, a nomination committee should be established to make recommendations to the board on all new board appointments. A majority of the members of this committee should be non-executive directors, and the chairman should be either the chairman of the board or a non-executive director. The chairman and members of the nomination committee should be identified in the annual report.

A.6 *Re-election*

Principle **All directors should be required to submit themselves for re-election at regular intervals and at least every three years.**

Code Provisions

A.6.1   Non-executive directors should be appointed for specified terms subject to re-election and to Companies Act provisions relating to the removal of a director, and reappointment should not be automatic.

A.6.2   All directors should be subject to election by shareholders at the first opportunity after their appointment, and to re-election thereafter at intervals of no more than three years. The names of directors submitted for election or re-election should be accompanied by sufficient biographical details to enable shareholders to take an informed decision on their election.

B. Directors' Remuneration

B.1 *The Level and Make-up of Remuneration*

Principle **Levels of remuneration should be sufficient to attract and retain the directors needed to run the company successfully, but companies should avoid paying more than is necessary for this purpose. A proportion of executive directors' remuneration should be structured so as to link rewards to corporate and individual performance.**

Code Provisions

Remuneration policy

B.1.1   The remuneration committee should provide the packages needed to attract, retain and motivate executive directors of the quality required but should avoid paying more than is necessary for this purpose.

B.1.2   Remuneration committees should judge where to position their company relative to other companies. They should be aware what comparable companies are paying and should take account of relative performance. But they should use such comparisons with caution, in view of the risk that they can result in an upward ratchet of remuneration levels with no corresponding improvement in performance.

B.1.3   Remuneration committees should be sensitive to the wider scene, including pay and employment conditions elsewhere in the group, especially when determining annual salary increases.

B.1.4   The performance-related elements of remuneration should form a significant proportion of the total remuneration package of executive directors and should be designed to align their interests with those of shareholders and to give these directors keen incentives to perform at the highest levels.

B.1.5   Executive share options should not be offered at a discount save as permitted by paragraphs 13.30 and 13.31 of the Listing Rules.

B.1.6   In designing schemes of performance related remuneration, remuneration committees should follow the provisions in Schedule A to this code.

Service Contracts and Compensation

B.1.7   There is a strong case for setting notice or contract periods at, or reducing them to, one year or less. Boards should set this as an objective; but they should recognise that it may not be possible to achieve it immediately.

B.1.8   If it is necessary to offer longer notice or contract periods to new directors recruited from outside, such periods should reduce after the initial period.

B.1.9   Remuneration committees should consider what compensation commitments (including pension contributions) their directors' contracts of service, if any, would entail in the event of early termination. They should in particular consider the advantages of providing explicitly in the initial contract for such compensation commitments except in the case of removal for misconduct.

B.1.10   Where the initial contract does not explicitly provide for compensation commitments, remuneration committees should, within legal constraints, tailor their approach in individual early termination cases to the wide variety of circumstances. The broad aim should be to avoid rewarding poor performance while dealing fairly with cases where departure is not due to poor performance and to take a robust line on reducing compensation to reflect departing directors' obligations to mitigate loss.

B.2   *Procedure*

Principle   **Companies should establish a formal and transparent procedure for developing policy on executive remuneration and for fixing the remuneration packages**

Appendix 4 CORPORATE GOVERNANCE

of individual directors. No director should be involved in deciding his or her own remuneration.

Code Provisions

B.2.1   To avoid potential conflicts of interest, boards of directors should set up remuneration committees of independent non-executive directors to make recommendations to the board, within agreed terms of reference, on the company's framework of executive remuneration and its cost; and to determine on their behalf specific remuneration packages for each of the executive directors, including pension rights and any compensation payments.

B.2.2   Remuneration committees should consist exclusively of non-executive directors who are independent of management and free from any business or other relationship which could materially interfere with the exercise of their independent judgement.

B.2.3   The members of the remuneration committee should be listed each year in the board's remuneration report to shareholders (B.3.1 below).

B.2.4   The board itself or, where required by the Articles of Association, the shareholders should determine the remuneration of the non-executive directors, including members of the remuneration committee, within the limits set in the Articles of Association. Where permitted by the Articles, the board may however delegate this responsibility to a small subcommittee, which might include the chief executive officer.

B.2.5   Remuneration committees should consult the chairman and/or chief executive officer about their proposals relating to the remuneration of other executive directors and have access to professional advice inside and outside the company.

B.2.6   The chairman of the board should ensure that the company maintains contact as required with its principal shareholders about remuneration in the same way as for other matters.

B.3   *Disclosure*

Principle   **The company's annual report should contain a statement of remuneration policy and details of the remuneration of each director.**

Code Provisions

B.3.1   The board should report to the shareholders each year on remuneration. The report should form part of, or be annexed to, the company's annual report and accounts. It should be the main vehicle through which the company reports to shareholders on directors' remuneration.

B.3.2   The report should set out the company's policy on executive directors' remuneration. It should draw attention to factors specific to the company.

B.3.3   In preparing the remuneration report, the board should follow the provisions in Schedule B to this code.

B.3.4   Shareholders should be invited specifically to approve all new long term incentive schemes (as defined in the Listing Rules) save in the circumstances permitted by paragraph 13.13A of the Listing Rules.

B.3.5   The board's annual remuneration report to shareholders need not be a standard item of agenda for AGMs. But the board should consider each year whether the circumstances are such that the AGM should be invited to approve the policy set out in the report and should minute their conclusions.

C.   Relations with Shareholders

C.1   *Dialogue with Institutional Shareholders*

Principle   **Companies should be ready, where practicable, to enter into a dialogue with institutional shareholders based on the mutual understanding of objectives.**

C.2   *Constructive Use of the AGM*

Principle   **Boards should use the AGM to communicate with private investors and encourage their participation.**

Code Provisions

C.2.1   Companies should count all proxy votes and, except where a poll is called, should indicate the level of proxies lodged on each resolution, and the balance for and against the resolution, after it has been dealt with on a show of hands.

C.2.2   Companies should propose a separate resolution at the AGM on each substantially separate issue, and should in particular propose a resolution at the AGM relating to the report and accounts.

C.2.3   The chairman of the board should arrange for the chairmen of the audit, remuneration and nomination committees to be available to answer questions at the AGM.

C.2.4   Companies should arrange for the Notice of the AGM and related papers to be sent to shareholders at least 20 working days before the meeting.

D.   Accountability and Audit

D.1   *Financial Reporting*

Principle   **The board should present a balanced and understandable assessment of the company's position and prospects.**

Code Provisions

D.1.1   The directors should explain their responsibility for preparing the accounts, and there should be a statement by the auditors about the reporting responsibilities.

D.1.2   The board's responsibility to present a balanced and understandable assessment extends to interim and other price-sensitive public reports and reports to regulators as well as to information required to be presented by statutory requirements.

D.1.3   The directors should report that the business is a going concern, with supporting assumptions or qualifications as necessary.

D.2   *Internal Control*

Principle   **The board should maintain a sound system of internal control to safeguard shareholders' investment and the company's assets.**

Code Provisions

D.2.1   The directors should, at least annually, conduct a review of the effectiveness of the group's system of internal control and should report to shareholders that they have done so. The review should cover all controls, including financial, operational and compliance controls and risk management.

D.2.2   Companies which do not have an internal audit function should from time to time review the need for one.

D.3   *Audit Committee and Auditors*

Principle **The board should establish formal and transparent arrangements for considering how they should apply the financial reporting and internal control principles and for maintaining an appropriate relationship with the company's auditors.**

Code Provisions

D.3.1   The board should establish an audit committee of at least three directors, all non-executive, with written terms of reference which deal clearly with its authority and duties. The members of the committee, a majority of whom should be independent non-executive directors, should be named in the report and accounts.

D.3.2   The duties of the audit committee should include keeping under review the scope and results of the audit and its cost effectiveness and the independence and objectivity of the auditors. Where the auditors also supply a substantial volume of non-audit services to the company, the committee should keep the nature and extent of such services under review, seeking to balance the maintenance of objectivity and value for money.

Section 2 Institutional Shareholders

E.   Institutional Investors

E.1   *Shareholder Voting*

Principle **Institutional shareholders have a responsibility to make considered use of their votes.**

Code Provisions

E.1.1   Institutional shareholders should endeavour to eliminate unnecessary variations in the criteria which each applies to the corporate governance arrangements and performance of the companies in which they invest.

E.1.2   Institutional shareholders should, on request, make available to their clients information on the proportion of resolutions on which votes were cast and non-discretionary proxies lodged.

E.1.3   Institutional shareholders should take steps to ensure that their voting intentions are being translated into practice.

E.2   *Dialogue with Companies*

Principle **Institutional shareholders should be ready, where practicable, to enter into a dialogue with companies based on the mutual understanding of objectives.**

E.3 *Evaluation of Governance Disclosures*

Principle **When evaluating companies' governance arrangements, particularly those relating to board structure and composition, institutional investors should give due weight to all relevant factors drawn to their attention.**

Schedule A: Provisions on the Design of Performance Related Remuneration

1. Remuneration committees should consider whether the directors should be eligible for annual bonuses. If so, performance conditions should be relevant, stretching and designed to enhance the business. Upper limits should always be considered. There may be a case for part payment in shares to be held for a significant period.

2. Remuneration committees should consider whether the directors should be eligible for benefits under long-term incentive schemes. Traditional share option schemes should be weighed against other kinds of long-term incentive scheme. In normal circumstances, shares granted or other forms of deferred remuneration should not vest, and options should not be exercisable, in under three years. Directors should be encouraged to hold their shares for a further period after vesting or exercise, subject to the need to finance any costs of acquisition and associated tax liability.

3. Any new long-term incentive schemes which are proposed should be approved by shareholders and should preferably replace existing schemes or at least form part of a well considered overall plan, incorporating existing schemes. The total rewards potentially available should not be excessive.

4. Payouts or grants under all incentive schemes, including new grants under existing share option schemes, should be subject to challenging performance criteria reflecting the company's objectives. Consideration should be given to criteria which reflect the company's performance relative to a group of comparator companies in some key variables such as total shareholder return.

5. Grants under executive share option and other long-term incentive schemes should normally be phased rather than awarded in one large block.

6. Remuneration committees should consider the pension consequences and associated costs to the company of basic salary increases and other changes in remuneration, especially for directors close to retirement.

7. In general, neither annual bonuses nor benefits in kind should be pensionable.

Schedule B: Provisions on what should be Included in the Remuneration Report

1. The report should include full details of all elements in the remuneration package of each individual director by name, such as basic salary, benefits in kind, annual bonuses and long term incentive schemes including share options.

2. Information on share options, including SAYE options, should be given for each director in accordance with the recommendations of the Accounting Standards Board's Urgent Issues Task Force Abstract 10 and its successors.

3. If grants under executive share option or other long-term incentive schemes are awarded in one large block rather than phased, the report should explain and justify.

4. Also included in the report should be pension entitlements earned by each individual director during the year, disclosed on one of the alternative bases recommended by the Faculty of Actuaries and the Institute of Actuaries and included in the Stock Exchange Listing Rules. Companies may wish to make clear that the transfer value represents a liability of the company, not a sum paid or due to the individual.

5. If annual bonuses or benefits in kind are pensionable the report should explain and justify.

6. The amounts received by, and commitments made to, each director under 1, 2 and 4 above should be subject to audit.

7. Any service contracts which provide for, or imply, notice periods in excess of one year (or any provisions for predetermined compensation on termination which exceed one year's salary and benefits) should be disclosed and the reasons for the longer notice periods explained.

INTERNAL CONTROL

Guidance for Directors on the Combined Code

(The Institue of Chartered Accountants in England and Wales)

FOREWORD

from the London Stock Exchange

The London Stock Exchange welcomes the publication of *Internal Control: Guidance for Directors on the Combined Code,* published by the Internal Control Working Party of the Institute of Chartered Accountants in England & Wales. The work involved in preparing this guidance for directors of UK incorporated listed companies in respect of Principle D.2 of the Combined Code, and its associated Provisions D.2.1 and D.2.2, is greatly appreciated.

The Working Party's guidance is consistent with both the requirements of the Combined Code and of the related Listing Rule disclosure requirements, and clarifies to boards of directors of listed companies what is expected of them. We consider that compliance with the guidance will constitute compliance with Combined Code provisions D.2.1 and D.2.2 and provide appropriate narrative disclosure of how Code principle D.2 has been applied.

Once the guidance has been adopted in full by a company the guidance on Internal Control and Financial Reporting (the Rutteman guidance) will have been superseded and full compliance with the Combined Code and Listing Rule requirements is possible.

Paul Geradine
Head of Listing
London Stock Exchange

September 1999

CONTENTS

Appendix 4   **CORPORATE GOVERNANCE**

INTRODUCTION

Internal control requirements of the Combined Code

1. When the Combined Code of the Committee on Corporate Governance (the Code) was published, the Institute of Chartered Accountants in England & Wales agreed with the London Stock Exchange that it would provide guidance to assist listed companies to implement the requirements in the Code relating to internal control.

2. **Principle D.2** of the Code states that 'The board should maintain a sound system of internal control to safeguard shareholders' investment and the company's assets'.

3. **Provision D.2.1** states that 'The directors should, at least annually, conduct a review of the effectiveness of the group's system of internal control and should report to shareholders that they have done so. The review should cover all controls, including financial, operational and compliance controls and risk management'.

4. **Provision D.2.2** states that 'Companies which do not have an internal audit function should from time to time review the need for one'.

5. Paragraph 12.43A of the London Stock Exchange Listing Rules states that 'in the case of a company incorporated in the United Kingdom, the following additional items must be included in its annual report and accounts:

    (a)   a narrative statement of how it has applied the principles set out in Section 1 of the Combined Code, providing explanation which enables its shareholders to evaluate how the principles have been applied;

    (b)   a statement as to whether or not it has complied throughout the accounting period with the Code provisions set out in Section 1 of the Combined Code. A company that has not complied with the Code provisions, or complied with only some of the Code provisions or (in the case of provisions whose requirements are of a continuing nature) complied for only part of an accounting period, must specify the Code provisions with which it has not complied, and (where relevant) for what part of the period such non-compliance continued, and give reasons for any non-compliance'.

6.   The Preamble to the Code, which is appended to the Listing Rules, makes it clear that there is no prescribed form or content for the statement setting out how the various principles in the Code have been applied. The intention is that companies should have a free hand to explain their governance policies in the light of the principles, including any special circumstances which have led to them adopting a particular approach.

7.   The guidance in this document should be followed by boards of listed companies in:

   •   assessing how the company has applied Code principle D.2;

   •   implementing the requirements of Code provisions D.2.1 and D.2.2; and

   •   reporting on these matters to shareholders in the annual report and accounts.

Objectives of the guidance

8.   This guidance is intended to:

   •   reflect sound business practice whereby internal control is embedded in the business processes by which a company pursues its objectives;

   •   remain relevant over time in the continually evolving business environment; and

   •   enable each company to apply it in a manner which takes account of its particular circumstances.

   The guidance requires directors to exercise judgement in reviewing how the company has implemented the requirements of the Code relating to internal control and reporting to shareholders thereon.

9.   The guidance is based on the adoption by a company's board of a risk-based approach to establishing a sound system of internal control and reviewing its effectiveness. This should be incorporated by the company within its normal management and governance processes. It should not be treated as a separate exercise undertaken to meet regulatory requirements.

The importance of internal control and risk management

10.   A company's system of internal control has a key role in the management of risks that are significant to the fulfilment of its business objectives. A sound system of internal control contributes to safeguarding the shareholders' investment and the company's assets.

11.   Internal control (as referred to in paragraph 20) facilitates the effectiveness and efficiency of operations, helps ensure the reliability of internal and external reporting and assists compliance with laws and regulations.

12.   Effective financial controls, including the maintenance of proper accounting records, are an important element of internal control. They help ensure that the company is not unnecessarily exposed to avoidable financial risks and that financial information used within the business and for publication is reliable. They also contribute to the safeguarding of assets, including the prevention and detection of fraud.

Appendix 4
CORPORATE GOVERNANCE

13.   A company's objectives, its internal organisation and the environment in which it operates are continually evolving and, as a result, the risks it faces are continually changing. A sound system of internal control therefore depends on a thorough and regular evaluation of the nature and extent of the risks to which the company is exposed. Since profits are, in part, the reward for successful risk-taking in business, the purpose of internal control is to help manage and control risk appropriately rather than to eliminate it.

Groups of companies

14.   Throughout this guidance, where reference is made to 'company' it should be taken, where applicable, as referring to the group of which the reporting company is the parent company. For groups of companies, the review of effectiveness of internal control and the report to the shareholders should be from the perspective of the group as a whole.

The Appendix

15.   The Appendix to this document contains questions which boards may wish to consider in applying this guidance.

MAINTAINING A SOUND SYSTEM OF INTERNAL CONTROL

Responsibilities

16.   The board of directors is responsible for the company's system of internal control. It should set appropriate policies on internal control and seek regular assurance that will enable it to satisfy itself that the system is functioning effectively. The board must further ensure that the system of internal control is effective in managing risks in the manner which it has approved.

17.   In determining its policies with regard to internal control, and thereby assessing what constitutes a sound system of internal control in the particular circumstances of the company, the board's deliberations should include consideration of the following factors:

●   the nature and extent of the risks facing the company;

●   the extent and categories of risk which it regards as acceptable for the company to bear;

●   the likelihood of the risks concerned materialising;

●   the company's ability to reduce the incidence and impact on the business of risks that do materialise; and

●   the costs of operating particular controls relative to the benefit thereby obtained in managing the related risks.

18.   It is the role of management to implement board policies on risk and control. In fulfilling its responsibilities, management should identify and evaluate the risks faced by the company for consideration by the board and design, operate and monitor a suitable system of internal control which implements the policies adopted by the board.

19.   All employees have some responsibility for internal control as part of their accountability for achieving objectives. They, collectively, should have the necessary knowledge, skills, information and authority to establish, operate and

monitor the system of internal control. This will require an understanding of the company, its objectives, the industries and markets in which it operates, and the risks it faces.

Elements of a sound system of internal control

20. An internal control system encompasses the policies, processes, tasks, behaviours and other aspects of a company that, taken together:

- facilitate its effective and efficient operation by enabling it to respond appropriately to significant business, operational, financial, compliance and other risks to achieving the company's objectives. This includes the safeguarding of assets from inappropriate use or from loss and fraud, and ensuring that liabilities are identified and managed;

- help ensure the quality of internal and external reporting. This requires the maintenance of proper records and processes that generate a flow of timely, relevant and reliable information from within and outside the organisation;

- help ensure compliance with applicable laws and regulations, and also with internal policies with respect to the conduct of business.

21. A company's system of internal control will reflect its control environment which encompasses its organisational structure. The system will include:

- control activities;

- information and communications processes; and

- processes for monitoring the continuing effectiveness of the system of internal control.

22. The system of internal control should:

- be embedded in the operations of the company and form part of its culture;

- be capable of responding quickly to evolving risks to the business arising from factors within the company and to changes in the business environment; and

- include procedures for reporting immediately to appropriate levels of management any significant control failings or weaknesses that are identified together with details of corrective action being undertaken.

23. A sound system of internal control reduces, but cannot eliminate, the possibility of poor judgement in decision-making; human error; control processes being deliberately circumvented by employees and others; management overriding controls; and the occurrence of unforeseeable circumstances.

24. A sound system of internal control therefore provides reasonable, but not absolute, assurance that a company will not be hindered in achieving its business objectives, or in the orderly and legitimate conduct of its business, by circumstances which may reasonably be foreseen. A system of internal control cannot, however, provide protection with certainty against a company failing to meet its business objectives or all material errors, losses, fraud, or breaches of laws or regulations.

REVIEWING THE EFFECTIVENESS OF INTERNAL CONTROL

Responsibilities

25. Reviewing the effectiveness of internal control is an essential part of the board's responsibilities. The board will need to form its own view on effectiveness after due and careful enquiry based on the information and assurances provided to it. Management is accountable to the board for monitoring the system of internal control and for providing assurance to the board that it has done so.

26. The role of board committees in the review process, including that of the audit committee, is for the board to decide and will depend upon factors such as the size and composition of the board; the scale, diversity and complexity of the company's operations; and the nature of the significant risks that the company faces. To the extent that designated board committees carry out, on behalf of the board, tasks that are attributed in this guidance document to the board, the results of the relevant committees' work should be reported to, and considered by, the board. The board takes responsibility for the disclosures on internal control in the annual report and accounts.

The process for reviewing effectiveness

27. Effective monitoring on a continuous basis is an essential component of a sound system of internal control. The board cannot, however, rely solely on the embedded monitoring processes within the company to discharge its responsibilities. It should regularly receive and review reports on internal control. In addition, the board should undertake an annual assessment for the purposes of making its public statement on internal control to ensure that it has considered all significant aspects of internal control for the company for the year under review and up to the date of approval of the annual report and accounts.

28. The reference to 'all controls' in Code Provision D.2.1 should not be taken to mean that the effectiveness of every internal control (including controls designed to manage immaterial risks) should be subject to review by the board. Rather it means that, for the purposes of this guidance, internal controls considered by the board should include all types of controls including those of an operational and compliance nature, as well as internal financial controls.

29. The board should define the process to be adopted for its review of the effectiveness of internal control. This should encompass both the scope and frequency of the reports it receives and reviews during the year, and also the process for its annual assessment, such that it will be provided with sound, appropriately documented, support for its statement on internal control in the company's annual report and accounts.

30. The reports from management to the board should, in relation to the areas covered by them, provide a balanced assessment of the significant risks and the effectiveness of the system of internal control in managing those risks. Any significant control failings or weaknesses identified should be discussed in the reports, including the impact that they have had, could have had, or may have, on the company and the actions being taken to rectify them. It is essential that there be openness of communication by management with the board on matters relating to risk and control.

31. When reviewing reports during the year, the board should:

- consider what are the significant risks and assess how they have been identified, evaluated and managed;

- assess the effectiveness of the related system of internal control in managing the significant risks, having regard, in particular, to any significant failings or weaknesses in internal control that have been reported;

- consider whether necessary actions are being taken promptly to remedy any significant failings or weaknesses; and

- consider whether the findings indicate a need for more extensive monitoring of the system of internal control.

32. Additionally, the board should undertake an annual assessment for the purpose of making its public statement on internal control. The assessment should consider issues dealt with in reports reviewed by it during the year together with any additional information necessary to ensure that the board has taken account of all significant aspects of internal control for the company for the year under review and up to the date of approval of the annual report and accounts.

33. The board's annual assessment should, in particular, consider:

- the changes since the last annual assessment in the nature and extent of significant risks, and the company's ability to respond to changes in its business and the external environment;

- the scope and quality of management's ongoing monitoring of risks and of the system of internal control, and, where applicable, the work of its internal audit function and other providers of assurance;

- the extent and frequency of the communication of the results of the monitoring to the board (or board committee(s)) which enable it to build up a cumulative assessment of the state of control in the company and the effectiveness with which risk is being managed;

- the incidence of significant control failings or weaknesses that have been identified at any time during the period and the extent to which they have resulted in unforeseen outcomes or contingencies that have had, could have had, or may in the future have, a material impact on the company's financial performance or condition; and

- the effectiveness of the company's public reporting processes.

34. Should the board become aware at any time of a significant failing or weakness in internal control, it should determine how the failing or weakness arose and re-assess the effectiveness of management's ongoing processes for designing, operating and monitoring the system of internal control.

THE BOARD'S STATEMENT ON INTERNAL CONTROL

35. In its narrative statement of how the company has applied Code principle D.2, the board should, as a minimum, disclose that there is an ongoing process for identifying, evaluating and managing the significant risks faced by the company, that it has been in place for the year under review and up to the date of approval of the annual report and accounts, that it is regularly reviewed by the board and accords with the guidance in this document.

Appendix 4
CORPORATE GOVERNANCE

36.   The board may wish to provide additional information in the annual report and accounts to assist understanding of the company's risk management processes and system of internal control.

37.   The disclosures relating to the application of principle D.2 should include an acknowledgement by the board that it is responsible for the company's system of internal control and for reviewing its effectiveness. It should also explain that such a system is designed to manage rather than eliminate the risk of failure to achieve business objectives, and can only provide reasonable and not absolute assurance against material misstatement or loss.

38.   In relation to Code provision D.2.1, the board should summarise the process it (where applicable, through its committees) has applied in reviewing the effectiveness of the system of internal control. It should also disclose the process it has applied to deal with material internal control aspects of any significant problems disclosed in the annual report and accounts.

39.   Where a board cannot make one or more of the disclosures in paragraphs 35 and 38, it should state this fact and provide an explanation. The Listing Rules require the board to disclose if it has failed to conduct a review of the effectiveness of the company's system of internal control.

40.   The board should ensure that its disclosures provide meaningful, high-level information and do not give a misleading impression.

41.   Where material joint ventures and associates have not been dealt with as part of the group for the purposes of applying this guidance, this should be disclosed.

INTERNAL AUDIT

42.   Provision D.2.2 of the Code states that companies which do not have an internal audit function should from time to time review the need for one.

43.   The need for an internal audit function will vary depending on company-specific factors including the scale, diversity and complexity of the company's activities and the number of employees, as well as cost/benefit considerations. Senior management and the board may desire objective assurance and advice on risk and control. An adequately resourced internal audit function (or its equivalent where, for example, a third party is contracted to perform some or all of the work concerned) may provide such assurance and advice. There may be other functions within the company that also provide assurance and advice covering specialist areas such as health and safety, regulatory and legal compliance and environmental issues.

44.   In the absence of an internal audit function, management needs to apply other monitoring processes in order to assure itself and the board that the system of internal control is functioning as intended. In these circumstances, the board will need to assess whether such processes provide sufficient and objective assurance.

45.   When undertaking its assessment of the need for an internal audit function, the board should also consider whether there are any trends or current factors relevant to the company's activities, markets or other aspects of its external environment, that have increased, or are expected to increase, the risks faced by the company. Such an increase in risk may also arise from internal factors such as organisational restructuring or from changes in reporting processes or underlying information systems. Other matters to be taken into account may

include adverse trends evident from the monitoring of internal control systems or an increased incidence of unexpected occurrences.

46.   The board of a company that does not have an internal audit function should assess the need for such a function annually having regard to the factors referred to in paragraphs 43 and 45 above. Where there is an internal audit function, the board should annually review its scope of work, authority and resources, again having regard to those factors.

47.   If the company does not have an internal audit function and the board has not reviewed the need for one, the Listing Rules require the board to disclose these facts.

APPENDIX

Assessing the effectiveness of the company's risk and control processes

Some questions which the board may wish to consider and discuss with management when regularly reviewing reports on internal control and carrying out its annual assessment are set out below. The questions are not intended to be exhaustive and will need to be tailored to the particular circumstances of the company.

This Appendix should be read in conjunction with the guidance set out in this document.

1.   *Risk assessment*

   - Does the company have clear objectives and have they been communicated so as to provide effective direction to employees on risk assessment and control issues? For example, do objectives and related plans include measurable performance targets and indicators?

   - Are the significant internal and external operational, financial, compliance and other risks identified and assessed on an ongoing basis? (Significant risks may, for example, include those related to market, credit, liquidity, technological, legal, health, safety and environmental, reputation, and business probity issues.)

   - Is there a clear understanding by management and others within the company of what risks are acceptable to the board?

2.   *Control environment and control activities*

   - Does the board have clear strategies for dealing with the significant risks that have been identified? Is there a policy on how to manage these risks?

   - Do the company's culture, code of conduct, human resource policies and performance reward systems support the business objectives and risk management and internal control system?

   - Does senior management demonstrate, through its actions as well as its policies, the necessary commitment to competence, integrity and fostering a climate of trust within the company?

   - Are authority, responsibility and accountability defined clearly such that decisions are made and actions taken by the appropriate people? Are the decisions and actions of different parts of the company appropriately co-ordinated?

- Does the company communicate to its employees what is expected of them and the scope of their freedom to act? This may apply to areas such as customer relations; service levels for both internal and outsourced activities; health, safety and environmental protection; security of tangible and intangible assets; business continuity issues; expenditure matters; accounting; and financial and other reporting.

- Do people in the company (and in its providers of outsourced services) have the knowledge, skills and tools to support the achievement of the company's objectives and to manage effectively risks to their achievement?

- How are processes/controls adjusted to reflect new or changing risks, or operational deficiencies?

3.   *Information and communication*

- Do management and the board receive timely, relevant and reliable reports on progress against business objectives and the related risks that provide them with the information, from inside and outside the company, needed for decision-making and management review purposes? This could include performance reports and indicators of change, together with qualitative information such as on customer satisfaction, employee attitudes etc.

- Are information needs and related information systems reassessed as objectives and related risks change or as reporting deficiencies are identified?

- Are periodic reporting procedures, including half-yearly and annual reporting, effective in communicating a balanced and understandable account of the company's position and prospects?

- Are there established channels of communication for individuals to report suspected breaches of laws or regulations or other improprieties?

4.   *Monitoring*

- Are there ongoing processes embedded within the company's overall business operations, and addressed by senior management, which monitor the effective appliation of the policies, processes and activities related to internal control and risk management? (Such processes may include control self-assessment, confirmation by personnel of compliance with policies and codes of conduct, internal audit reviews or other management reviews).

- Do these processes monitor the company's ability to re-evaluate risks and adjust controls effectively in response to changes in its objectives, its business, and its external environment?

- Are there effective follow-up procedures to ensure that appropriate change or action occurs in response to changes in risk and control assessments?

- Is there appropriate communication to the board (or board committees) on the effectiveness of the ongoing monitoring processes on risk and control matters? This should include reporting any significant failings or weaknesses on a timely basis.

- Are there specific arrangements for management monitoring and reporting to the board on risk and control matters of particular importance? These could include, for example, actual or suspected fraud and other illegal or irregular acts, or matters that could adversely affect the company's reputation or financial position?

MEMBERSHIP OF THE INTERNAL CONTROL WORKING PARTY

Nigel Turnbull (Chairman)	*Executive Director* *Rank Group Plc*
Roger Davis (Deputy Chairman)	*Head of Professional Affairs* *PricewaterhouseCoopers*
Douglas Flint	*Group Finance Director* *HSBC Holdings plc*
Huw Jones	*Director of Corporate Finance* *Prudential Portfolio Managers*
David Lindsell	*Partner* *Ernst & Young*
Tim Rowbury	*Internal Audit Consultant*
Jonathan Southern	*Director of Accounting and Reporting* *Diageo plc*
David Wilson	*Company Secretary and General Counsel* *Debenhams plc*

Staff

Anthony Carey	*Project Director, ICAEW*
Jonathan Hunt	*Project Manager, ICAEW*

Appendix 4
CORPORATE GOVERNANCE

Appendix 5

GUIDELINE PUBLICATIONS OF THE ASSOCIATION OF BRITISH INSURERS

LIST OF GUIDELINE PUBLICATIONS OF THE ABI

ABI GUIDELINES & GUIDANCE NOTES

1	Share Option Schemes	17 February 1995
2	ABI/NAPF Joint Statement	15 July 1993
3	S. 80 and S. 95 Resolutions	10 September 1992
4	Own Share Purchase	27 August 1993
5	Scrip Dividends	24 July 1992
6	Role and Duties of Directors (A Discussion Paper)	12 June 1990
7	The Responsibilities of Institutional Shareholders (A Discussion Paper)	14 March 1991
8	(i) Long Term Remuneration for Senior Executives	25 May 1994
	(ii) Long Term Remuneration for Senior Executives plus Addendum – Note of Emerging Good Practice	2 May 1996

PRE-EMPTION GROUP GUIDELINES & REPORTS

9	The Pre-Emption Group – Shareholders' Pre-Emptive Rights	20 October 1987
10	ABI Pre-Emption/Vendor Placings	August 1993
11	Pre-Emption Guidelines	
12	The Pre-Emption Group Reports:	

Chairman's letter
- 21 March 1991   –   February 1994
- January 1993   –   March 1995

OTHER PUBLICATIONS

13	Property Mortgage Debenture Stocks – A Comment on Recent Developments	January 1994 (reprinted) June 1994
14	Report of the ABI Working Party on the Landlord and Tenant (Covenants) Act 1995	January 1996

Appendix 5
GUIDELINE
PUBLICATIONS OF ABI

ISC DOCUMENTS

15 The Role and Duties of Directors – A Statement of
   Best Practice (first editon)   18 April 1991
   (second edition)   August 1993

16 The Responsibilities of Institutional Shareholders in the UK   December 1991

17 Suggested Disclosure of Research & Development Expenditure   April 1992

18 Management Buy-outs   December 1989

Appendix 6

USEFUL NAMES AND ADDRESSES

LIST OF USEFUL NAMES AND ADDRESSES

Markets

London Stock Exchange plc
London EC2N 1HP
Tel 020 7797 1000

www.londonstockexchange.com

NASDAQ Europe
Exchange Tower
Old Broad Street
London EC2N 1HP
Tel 020 7786 6400
Fax 020 7786 6401

www.nasdaqeurope.com

NASDAQ Stock Market
Durrant House
8/13 Chiswell Street
London EC1Y 4XY
Tel 020 7374 6969
Fax 020 7374 4488

www.nasdaq.com

OFEX
J P Jenkins Ltd
Lloyds Court
1 Goodman's Yard
Tower Hill
London E1 8AT
Tel 020 7488 3993
Fax 020 7488 2427

Corporate Governance

Association of British Insurers
51 Gresham Street
London EC2 7HQ
Tel 020 7216 7670/1
Fax 020 7696 8979

Contact Peter Montagnon

www.abi.org.uk
www.computasost.com (for guidelines)

National Association of Pension Funds
4 Victoria Street
London SW1 0NX
Tel 020 7808 1300

www.napf.co.uk

Contact John Rogers (e-mail john.rogers@napf.co.uk)

INDEX

References are to paragraph numbers and appendix numbers.